the
ECOPOETRY
anthology

EDITED BY

Ann Fisher-Wirth and
Laura-Gray Street

Introduction by Robert Hass

TRINITY UNIVERSITY PRESS
San Antonio, Texas

Published by Trinity University Press
San Antonio, Texas 78212

Cover design by Nicole Hayward
Book design by BookMatters, Berkeley
Jacket illustration: *Sea road,* by Piotr Krol (Bax), 2011, http://bax.wroclaw.pl/

Trinity University Press strives to produce its books using methods and
materials in an environmentally sensitive manner. We favor working with
manufacturers that practice sustainable management of all natural resources,
produce paper using recycled stock, and manage forests with the best possible
practices for people, biodiversity, and sustainability. The press is a member of
the Green Press Initiative, a nonprofit program dedicated to supporting pub-
lishers in their efforts to reduce their impacts on endangered forests, climate
change, and forest-dependent communities.

The paper used in this publication meets the minimum requirements of the
American National Standard for Information Sciences—Permanence of Paper
for Printed Library Materials, ANSI 39.48–1992.

Library of Congress Cataloging-in-Publication Data

The Ecopoetry Anthology / Edited by Ann Fisher-Wirth and Laura-Gray
Street ; Introduction by Rober Hass.
      p.   cm.
Summary: "An anthology of American poetry about nature and the environ-
ment, divided into a historical section with poetry written from roughly the
mid-nineteenth to the mid-twentieth century and a contemporary section
with over 300 poems written since 1960 by a diverse group of more than
170 poets. Introduction by Robert Hass"—Provided by pubisher. Includes
bibliographical references.
ISBN 978-1-59534-146-4 (pbk. : alk. paper)
ISBN 978-1-59534-145-7 (e-book)
   1. American poetry. 2. Nature in literature. 3.Ecology in literature.
I. Fisher-Wirth, Ann W., editor of compilation. II. Street, Laura-Gray,
editor of compilation.
   PS595.N22E27   2013
   811.008'036—dc23   2012040477

17   16   15   14   5   4   3   2

Praise for *The Ecopoetry Anthology*

"*The Ecopoetry Anthology* is a necessary book, a radical intervention, a daring collection of human calls and cries which respond to our endangered and disappearing world."
—EDWARD HIRSCH

" 'An ethics occurs at the edge / of what we know,' writes Brenda Hillman, and you can consider this plump volume an encyclopedia of things worth knowing: places, species, but also passions, ideas, rays of light and barrels of poison. For by 'environment' we mean the world of tangible things and a way of thinking systematically: this book deepens your relationship to both those things and is a pleasure besides."
—REBECCA SOLNIT

"Cutting a broad swathe from 'the natural history of tears' to 'surreal / popcorn, surrounded by the reborn,' with unerring ears and curatorial finesse the editors have assembled a genuine constellation of feisty, testy, funny, worried, disconcerted, perplexed, grieving, and roaring poems."
—JED RASULA

"This varied and generous anthology is a crash course in anglophone, North American ecopoetry, ideal as a textbook, even better as a springboard for reflection. The critic and translator John Felstiner has asked, 'Can poetry save the Earth?' While reading *The Ecopoetry Anthology*, one begins to think it possible."
—SCOTT SLOVIC

"We surely need anthologies of nature poetry, so this new one featuring a historical section is doubly heartening. Whitman and Dickinson, Frost and Williams, Jeffers and Moore and Bishop seldom find that position these days. Then a uniquely generous contemporary section, fully covering the country—and alphabet, except for X-Y-Z. Acquire this book, absorb what you like, read it to friends and family!"
—JOHN FELSTINER

Trinity University Press gratefully acknowledges the support of
THE CHARLES AND ROBERTA KATZ FAMILY FOUNDATION,
THE EDOUARD FOUNDATION,
and
THE SARAH E. HARTE AND JOHN S. GUTZLER FUND
OF THE SAN ANTONIO AREA FOUNDATION
in the publication of this book

For my grandchildren
Sylvie   Benjamin   Eve   Dylan   Rowan
And for all the children

They step into the world we have made

A. F. W.

For Kyle and Sydna

L. G. S.

CONTENTS

Editors' Preface · xxvii
A Scattering, a Shining, by Ann Fisher-Wirth · xxxiii
The Roots of It, by Laura-Gray Street · xxxvii
American Ecopoetry: An Introduction, by Robert Hass · xli

HISTORICAL

Walt Whitman
from Song of Myself · *3*
Out of the Cradle Endlessly Rocking · *4*
Crossing Brooklyn Ferry · *10*

Emily Dickinson
#116/328 · *16*
#126/348 · *16*
#184/465 · *17*
#209/520 · *18*
#498/1400 · *19*
#537/1593 · *19*

Robert Frost
An Old Man's Winter Night · *21*
The Need of Being Versed in Country Things · *22*

Stopping by Woods on a Snowy Evening · 23
Spring Pools · 23
Design · 24
The Most of It · 24
Directive · 25

Wallace Stevens
Sunday Morning · 27
Anecdote of the Jar · 31
The Snow Man · 31
The River of Rivers in Connecticut · 32

William Carlos Williams
Spring and All · 33
The Sea-Elephant · 34
Between Walls · 36
Raleigh Was Right · 36
The High Bridge above the Tagus River at Toledo · 37

Ezra Pound
The Tree · 38
Salutation · 38
Ancient Music · 39
from Canto LXXXI · 39

H.D.
Oread · 40
Sea Iris · 40
The Pool · 41

Robinson Jeffers
Shine, Perishing Republic · 42
Hurt Hawks · 43
The Purse-Seine · 44
Carmel Point · 45
The Deer Lay Down Their Bones · 46

Marianne Moore
   The Fish · *48*
   A Grave · *49*
   The Paper Nautilus · *50*

T. S. Eliot
   from The Waste Land
      I. The Burial of the Dead · *52*
      III. The Fire Sermon · *54*

e. e. cummings
   Me up at does · *58*

Jean Toomer
   Reapers · *59*
   November Cotton Flower · *59*

Stephen Vincent Benét
   Metropolitan Nightmare · *60*

Hart Crane
   Repose of Rivers · *63*
   from The Bridge
      To Brooklyn Bridge · *64*
      The River · *65*

Sterling A. Brown
   Riverbank Blues · *70*

Langston Hughes
   The Negro Speaks of Rivers · *72*
   Daybreak in Alabama · *72*

Lorine Niedecker
   (untitled) · *74*
   from Paean to Place · *74*

Kenneth Rexroth
   Toward an Organic Philosophy · *78*
   Lute Music · *81*

    Lyell's Hypothesis Again · *82*
    Andrée Rexroth · *84*

Theodore Roethke
  from North American Sequence
    Meditation at Oyster River · *85*

George Oppen
  Eclogue · *88*
  California · *88*
  Psalm · *89*
  The Occurrences · *90*

Charles Olson
  The Kingfishers · *91*
  West Gloucester · *97*

Elizabeth Bishop
  At the Fishhouses · *99*
  The Moose · *101*

William Everson
  San Joaquin · *107*
  Clouds · *107*

Robert Hayden
  The Night-Blooming Cereus · *109*

Muriel Rukeyser
  from The Book of the Dead
    Alloy · *112*
    The Dam · *113*

William Stafford
  Traveling through the Dark · *117*
  At the Bomb Testing Site · *117*

Robert Duncan
  Often I Am Permitted to Return to a Meadow · *119*

Poetry, a Natural Thing · *120*
A Little Language · *121*

Barbara Guest
Santa Fe Trail · *123*

James Dickey
The Heaven of Animals · *124*

Denise Levertov
O Taste and See · *126*
Souvenir d'amitié · *126*
The Past III · *127*

James Schuyler
Haze · *129*

CONTEMPORARY

A. R. Ammons
Corsons Inlet · *133*
Gravelly Run · *136*
from Garbage · *137*

Karen Leona Anderson
Snowshoe Hare · *141*

Christopher Arigo
Gone feral: minor gestures · *143*

Rae Armantrout
Thing · *145*
Natural History · *145*
Dusk · *147*

John Ashbery
Into the Dusk-Charged Air · *148*
For John Clare · *152*

Alcove · *153*

River of the Canoefish · *153*

Jimmy Santiago Baca

As Children Know · *154*

Juliana Baggott

The Place Poem: Sparrow's Point · *156*

Living Where They Raised Me · *156*

Ellen Bass

Birdsong from My Patio · *158*

The Big Picture · *159*

Dan Beachy-Quick

Arcadian · *161*

Lois Beardslee

Wawaskwanmiinan · *163*

Sandra Beasley

Unit of Measure · *164*

Marvin Bell

The Book of the Dead Man (Fungi) · *166*

Dan Bellm

Aspens · *168*

Margo Berdeshevsky

After the End After the Beginning · *172*

Wendell Berry

Horses · *174*

Water · *176*

The Hidden Singer · *176*

The Peace of Wild Things · *177*

To the Unseeable Animal · *178*

Mei-mei Berssenbrugge
    The Star Field · *179*
    from A Context of a Wave · *180*

Linda Bierds
    April · *183*

Ralph Black
    21st Century Lecture · *185*

Robert Bly
    The Dead Seal · *188*

Marianne Boruch
    Birdsong, face it, some male machine · *190*
    It includes the butterfly and the rat, the shit · *190*

Annie Boutelle
    The Rapture of Bees · *192*

Elizabeth Bradfield
    Multi-Use Area · *193*
    Legacy · *194*

Laynie Browne
    from Mermaid's Purse · *196*

Derick Burleson
    Outside Fairbanks · *198*

Cyrus Cassells
    Down from the Houses of Magic · *200*

Grace Cavalieri
    A Field of Finches without Sight Still Singing · *205*

Lorna Dee Cervantes
    Freeway 280 · *206*
    Emplumada · *207*

Jennifer Chang
    Genealogy · *208*

Patricia Clark
    Out with the Monarch, the Vole, and the Toad · *209*

Lucille Clifton
    the earth is a living thing · *210*
    the beginning of the end of the world · *210*
    grief · *211*
    defending my tongue · *212*
    the killing of the trees · *213*

Henri Cole
    Green Shade · *215*

Jack Collom
    Ruddy Duck · *216*
    Ecology · *217*

Julia Connor
    m(other) tongue · *218*
    from Canto for the Birds · *219*

Matthew Cooperman
    Still: Environment · *222*

Stephen Cushman
    The Rain in Maine · *224*

Kwame Dawes
    Genocide, Again · *225*

Alison Hawthorne Deming
    Specimens Collected at the Clear Cut · *226*

Deborah Digges
    Damascus · *228*

Elizabeth Dodd
    House Sparrow at Skara Brae · *229*

Sharon Dolin
    For I Will Consider the Overlooked Dragonfly · *230*

Camille T. Dungy
    On the rocks · *232*
    The Blue · *232*

Rachel Blau DuPlessis
    Pastoral and Gigue · *235*
    Praxilla's Silliness · *236*

Tim Earley
    I Like Green Things · *240*

Larry Eigner
    September 21   65 · *241*
    June 17   68 · *241*
    May 3   71 · *241*
    [trees green   the quiet sun] · *242*

Louise Erdrich
    The Strange People · *243*
    The Red Sleep of Beasts · *244*

B. H. Fairchild
    Maize · *246*
    West Texas · *247*

Patricia Fargnoli
    Should the Fox Come Again to My Cabin in the Snow · *248*
    Then · *248*

Annie Finch
    Watching the Oregon Whale · *249*

Jessica Fisher
    Elegy · *250*

Ann Fisher-Wirth
    from Dream Cabinet · *252*

Lisa Fishman
  Out of the Field · 257

Kathleen Flenniken
  Plume · 258
  Green Run · 260

Carolyn Forché
  The Museum of Stones · 261
  Morning on the Island · 262

Carol Frost
  The St. Louis Zoo · 263

Juan Carlos Galeano
  Árbol · 265
  Historia · 266

Brendan Galvin
  An Intermission · 267

James Galvin
  Three Sonnets · 268
  They Haven't Heard the West Is Over · 268
  Cartography · 269

Forrest Gander
  Field Guide to Southern Virginia · 270
  from Of Sum · 272

C. S. Giscombe
  from Giscome Road · 273

Peter Gizzi
  Human Memory Is Organic · 278

Louise Glück
  Scilla · 279
  Witchgrass · 279

Ray Gonzalez
  Rattlesnakes Hammered on the Wall · 281

Charles Goodrich
  Millennial Spring · 282

Jorie Graham
  Evolution · 286
  Sea Change · 289

Michael Gregory
  The Cranes · 292

Tami Haaland
  Goldeye, Vole · 293

John Haines
  If the Owl Calls Again · 294

Donald Hall
  Digging · 295

Joy Harjo
  from She Had Some Horses · 296
  My House Is the Red Earth · 297
  Eagle Poem · 298

Lola Haskins
  The Sandhill Cranes · 299
  Prayer for the Everglades · 299

Robert Hass
  Palo Alto: The Marshes · 301
  Ezra Pound's Proposition · 304
  Exit, Pursued by a Sierra Meadow · 305
  State of the Planet · 306

Brooks Haxton
  Submersible · 313

Chris Hayes
   After My Daughter's Birth, a Late Night Self-Portrait with
      a Running Mare · 314

Allison Hedge Coke
   Dust: Dad's Days · 315

William Heyen
   The Swamp · 318
   Blackbird Spring · 319

Brenda Hillman
   Practical Water · 320
   Request to the Berkeley City Council Concerning
      Strawberry Creek · 322
   A Violet in the Crucible · 324
   To Spirits of Fire after Harvest · 325

Jane Hirshfield
   The Supple Deer · 327
   Three Foxes by the Edge of the Field at Twilight · 327
   Articulation: An Assay · 328
   Optimism · 329
   Inflection Finally Ungraspable by Grammar · 329
   Speed and Perfection · 329
   For the *Lobaria, Usnea,* Witches' Hair, Map Lichen, Beard Lichen,
      Ground Lichen, Shield Lichen · 330

H. L. Hix
   The Last Crows Whose Cries Are Audible Here · 331

Tony Hoagland
   Romantic Moment · 332
   Wild · 333

Richard Hoffman
   Cove · 335

Linda Hogan
  Turtle Watchers · *336*
  Moving the Woodpile · *337*

Cynthia Hogue
  Fluff · *339*

Richard Hugo
  Skykomish River Running · *341*

Luisa A. Igloria
  Ziggurats there aren't here, my Sweethearts— · *342*

Ronald Johnson
  [earthearthearth] · *343*
  from Spring
    4 Emanations · *343*
    5 April 13th · *344*
  from Summer
    What the Earth Told Me · *345*
    'Unless the Humming of a Gnat Is as the Music of the Spheres · *346*

Rodney Jones
  The Assault on the Fields · *347*

Judy Jordan
  Long Drop to Black Water · *350*
  from Dream of the End · *351*

Brigit Pegeen Kelly
  The Leaving · *353*
  Blessed Is the Field · *354*
  Windfall · *355*

Galway Kinnell
  The Bear · *357*
  Daybreak · *360*
  Burning the Brush Pile · *361*

Yusef Komunyakaa
  The Millpond · 363
  Blackberries · 365
  Dream Animal · 366
  Blessing the Animals · 366

Ted Kooser
  Flying at Night · 368
  Grasshoppers · 368

Maxine Kumin
  The Whole Hog · 369

Stanley Kunitz
  The Wellfleet Whale · 371

Dorianne Laux
  The Orgasms of Organisms · 375
  Life Is Beautiful · 375

Patrick Lawler
  Hummingbird · 377

Jay Leeming
  Law Office · 380

Shara Lessley
  Tooth of the Lion · 381

Philip Levine
  They Feed They Lion · 382
  Our Valley · 383

Larry Levis
  The Oldest Living Thing in L.A. · 384
  Anastasia & Sandman · 385

Audre Lorde
  What My Child Learns of the Sea · 389

Anne Marie Macari
   Migration South · *390*

Kelly Madigan
   Offering · *392*

Davis McCombs
   from Tobacco Mosaic
      Stripping Room · *394*
      Lexicon · *394*
      Drought · *395*
      The Sharecroppers · *395*

Jane Mead
   The Origin · *397*

Sandra Meek
   Biogeography · *398*
   Event One · *399*

W. S. Merwin
   For a Coming Extinction · *401*
   Vixen · *402*
   Nocturne · *403*
   Recognitions · *403*
   The Laughing Thrush · *404*

Deborah Miranda
   Eating a Mountain · *405*

Thorpe Moeckel
   Bartram's Trail · *407*

Patricia Monaghan
   Connemara Autumn · *408*

Richard O. Moore
   Driving to Fort Bragg · *409*

Lori Anderson Moseman
   Grate | Table Grace · *410*

Harryette Mullen
   from Muse and Drudge · *411*

Naomi Shihab Nye
   Negotiations with a Volcano · *412*
   The Turtle Shrine near Chittagong · *413*

dg nanouk okpik
   She Sang to Me Once at a Place for Hunting Owls: *Utkiavik* · *415*
   Tulunigraq: Something Like a Raven · *415*

Mary Oliver
   Alligator Poem · *417*
   Wild Geese · *418*
   The Lilies Break Open Over the Dark Water · *419*

Alicia Suskin Ostriker
   Love III · *420*

Michael Palmer
   Dearest Reader · *421*
   Notes for Echo Lake 6 · *421*
   Notes for Echo Lake 9 · *422*

G. E. Patterson
   The Natural World · *423*

Lucia Perillo
   Bulletin from Somewhere up the Creek · *424*
   The Crows Start Demanding Royalties · *425*
   Shrike Tree · *425*

Jim Peterson
   No Bite · *427*

D. A. Powell
   republic · *428*

John Pursley III
   Hand Over Fist · *430*

Bernard Quetchenbach
Dark Night of the Hermit · *431*

Janisse Ray
Justice · *432*

Srikanth Reddy
Monsoon Eclogue · *433*

Carter Revard
Aesculapius Unbound · *435*

Donald Revell
Election Year · *437*
My Mojave · *437*
"Birds small enough . . ." · *438*

Adrienne Rich
from Twenty-One Love Poems · *440*
Power · *440*
from The Spirit of Place · *441*
What Kind of Times Are These · *442*

Alberto Ríos
Beetles and Frogs · *443*
Uncovered Ants · *444*

Ed Roberson
be careful · *446*
Wave · *446*
To See the Earth before the End of the World · *447*
City Eclogue: Words for It · *448*
The Distant Stars as Paparazzi · *449*

Pattiann Rogers
Geocentric · *451*
Rolling Naked in the Morning Dew · *452*

William Pitt Root
  Dear Jeffers · 454
  Song of Returnings · 455

Michael Rothenberg
  The Bromeliad · 456

Ira Sadoff
  Nature · 458
  I've Always Despised the Wetlands · 459

Benjamin Alire Sáenz
  To the Desert · 460

Craig Santos Perez
  from all with ocean views · 461
  ginen aerial roots · 462
  from preterrain · 463
  from tidelands · 463

Tim Seibles
  Ambition: Cow & Microphone · 464
  First Verse · 465

Anthony Seidman
  Runoff · 467
  A Dog's Poetry · 467

Martha Serpas
  Fais Do-Do · 469

Eric Paul Shaffer
  The Open Secret of the Sea · 470

Derek Sheffield
  A Good Fish · 472
  Darwin's Eyes · 473

Reginald Shepherd
  Some Kind of Osiris · 474

Evie Shockley
    notes for the early journey · 476
    atlantis made easy · 476

Gary Short
    Near the Bravo 20 Bombing Range · 478

Kevin Simmonds
    Sighted · 479

giovanni singleton
    caged bird · 480

Jonathan Skinner
    Birds of the Holy Lands · 481
    Carnegia Gigantea (remixed) · 482

Charlie Smith
    Monadnock · 486

Patricia Smith
    5 P.M., Tuesday, August 23, 2005 · 487
    Man on the TV Say · 488
    Won't Be But a Minute · 488
    8 A.M., Sunday, August 28, 2005 · 489
    Looking for Bodies · 490

Gary Snyder
    from Hunting
        This Poem Is for Bear · 491
    from Burning
        The Text · 492
        The Myth · 493
    Piute Creek · 494
    Milton by Firelight · 495
    Riprap · 496
    For Nothing · 497
    Burning the Small Dead · 497

Wave · *498*
For the Children · *499*

Juliana Spahr
from Gentle Now, Don't Add to Heartache · *500*

Gerald Stern
Cow Worship · *503*
One Animal's Life · *503*

Susan Stewart
Four Questions Regarding the Dreams of Animals · *505*
The Forest · *507*

Sheryl St. Germain
Midnight Oil · *509*

Laura-Gray Street
An Entangled Bank · *514*
First Lessons in Beekeeping · *516*

Arthur Sze
The Angle of Reflection Equals the Angle of Incidence · *519*

Nathaniel Tarn
from Ins and Outs of the Forest Rivers · *523*

Susan Terris
No Golden Fish Were Harmed in the Making of This Poem · *531*

Jeffrey Thomson
from Celestial Emporium of Benevolent Knowledge · *532*

Melissa Tuckey
Refrain · *535*

Chase Twichell
City Animals · *536*

Pamela Uschuk
Snow Goose Migration at Tule Lake · *538*

Jean Valentine
The Badlands Said · *540*
The River at Wolf · *540*
Rain · *541*

Ellen Bryant Voigt
Chameleon · *542*
Cow · *542*

Gyorgyi Voros
Forest Orison · *544*

Frank X. Walker
Canning Memories · *546*

Emily Warn
Ox Herding Lesson · *548*

Rosanna Warren
Man in Stream · *550*

Eliot Weinberger
The Stars · *551*

Joel Weishaus
Bamboo · *556*

Lesley Wheeler
The Petroglyphs at Puakō · *557*

C. K. Williams
Tar · *558*
Blackbird · *560*
Canal · *561*
Not Soul · *561*

Susan Settlemyre Williams
Johnny Appleseed Contemplates Heaven · *563*

C. D. Wright
    Song of the Gourd · *565*
    from Deepstep Come Shining · *566*
    from One Big Self · *567*

Charles Wright
    Hardin County · *568*
    Rural Route · *569*
    Snow · *570*
    After Reading Tu Fu, I Go Outside to the Dwarf Orchard · *570*

William Wright
    from Chernobyl Eclogue · *571*

Robert Wrigley
    Ravens at Deer Creek · *573*
    Anything the River Gives · *574*
    Why Do the Crickets Sing? · *575*

Contributors' Notes · *577*
Acknowledgments and Credits · *607*

EDITORS' PREFACE

Some lines from William Carlos Williams's beautiful late poem "Asphodel, That Greeny Flower" have become practically a mantra for those who would affirm the centrality, the urgency, of poetry to contemporary life:

> Look at
> what passes for the new.
> You will not find it there but in
> despised poems.
> It is difficult
> to get the news from poems
> yet men die miserably every day
> for lack
> of what is found there.

Attentiveness, precision, tenderness toward existence—these are some of the qualities Williams is invoking, and his lines grow more prescient as the world hurtles toward environmental disaster. During the past few years, as we have been coediting *The Ecopoetry Anthology*, we've become ever more convinced that the environmental crisis is made possible by a profound failure of the imagination. What we humans disregard, what we fail to know and grasp, is easy to destroy: a mountaintop, a coral reef, a forest, a human community. Yet poetry returns us in countless ways to the world of our senses. It can act, in Franz Kafka's phrase, as "an ice axe to break the frozen sea inside us," awakening our dulled perceptions and feelings. This is the power of all poetry. With regard to the environment, it is particularly the power of ecopoetry.

Nature poetry has existed as long as poetry has existed. Around 1960, however, public attention increasingly turned to the burgeoning environmental crisis, and nature poetry began to reflect this concern. In recent decades, the term "ecopoetry" has come into use to designate poetry that in some way is shaped by and responds specifically to that crisis. The term has no precise definition and rather fluid boundaries, but some things can usefully be said about it. Generally, this poetry addresses contemporary problems and issues in ways that are ecocentric and that respect the integrity of the other-than-human world. It challenges the belief that we are meant to have dominion over nature and is skeptical of a hyperrationality that would separate mind from body—and earth and its creatures from human beings—and that would give preeminence to fantasies of control. Some of it is based in the conviction that poetry can help us find our way back to an awareness that we are at one with the more-than-human world. As J. Scott Bryson points out in *Ecopoetry: A Critical Introduction*, "eco-poets offer a vision of the world that values the interaction between two interdependent . . . desires, both of which are attempts to respond to the modern divorce between humanity and the rest of nature." Ecopoets work to "create place, making a conscious and concerted effort to know the more-than-human world," and they "value space, recognizing the extent to which that very world is ultimately unknowable."

In terms of poetry written since the rise of environmentalism in the 1960s, we have come to envision contemporary American ecopoetry as falling loosely into three main groupings. The first is nature poetry. In Wendell Berry's words, this is poetry that "considers nature as subject matter and inspiration." As shaped by romanticism and American transcendentalism, it often meditates on an encounter between the human subject and something in the other-than-human world that reveals an aspect of the meaning of life. But not all nature poetry is environmental or ecological poetry, and not all nature poetry evinces the accurate and unsentimental awareness of the natural world that is a sine qua non of ecopoetry. Think of Joyce Kilmer's "Trees," lifting their "leafy arms to pray," for an egregious example of anthropocentrism. Thus, according to this formulation, ecopoetry is neither a subset of nature poetry, as Bryson suggests, nor a term encompassing all nature poetry. Though some believe that traditional nature poetry can no longer be written, many ecopoets continue to write it very well, as this anthology reveals.

Juliana Spahr writes in "Things of Each Possible Relation" that nature poetry tends "to show the beautiful bird but not so often the bulldozer off to the side that [is] about to destroy the bird's habitat." Environmental poetry, our second grouping, emerges historically and philosophically out of nature poetry. This is poetry propelled by and directly engaged with active and politicized environmentalism. It is greatly influenced by social and environmental justice movements and is committed to questions of human injustice, as well as to issues of damage and degradation to the other-than-human world. If activist poetry sacrifices art and complexity for propaganda, it is, of course, simply agitprop. But powerful activist poems continue to be written—and are included here—even though the deconstruction of concepts such as "wilderness," "nature," and "environment" distinctly complicates the straightforward activist urgency of much environmental poetry. Also, postcolonialism and environmental justice issues continue fruitfully to blur the already shifting boundaries between human and ecological perspectives and concerns.

The third grouping, ecological poetry, is more elusive than the first two because it engages questions of form most directly, not only poetic form but also a form historically taken for granted—that of the singular, coherent self. The term "ecopoetry" is often used to refer to this kind of work, but we argue for a more inclusive sense of ecopoetry and therefore distinguish this subset as ecological poetry. This poetry can look strange and wild on the page; it is often described as experimental; and it tends to think in self-reflexive ways about how poems can be ecological or somehow enact ecology. Of the three groupings, ecological poetry is the most willing to engage with, even play with, postmodern and poststructuralist theories associated with L=A=N=G=U=A=G=E poetry and the avant garde. The poet Forrest Gander argues that it thematically and formally investigates "the relationship between nature and culture, language and perception." If the weakness of some nature poetry is sentimentalized anthropomorphism and the danger of some environmental poetry is that it becomes agenda-driven propaganda, the risks for ecological poetry include hyperintellectualism and emotional distance or detachment. But as the poems in this anthology demonstrate, there is great power in poetry informed by a biocentric perspective and by ecological interrelatedness and entanglement.

Each of these groupings is helpful as a starting point. Taken together, they are some of the many planes that meet at various angles to create the larger whole that is ecopoetry. The thinking about ecopoetry has continued to change since the term entered the conversation in the 1990s. We prefer to see that change not as teleological but as a shifting landscape in which all forms of poetry have bearing and legitimacy, their presences and purposes ebbing and flowing in different communities and contexts. We acknowledge some conflicts between the categories we describe, but we see good reason for allowing them to interact. For example, to dismiss the complex traditions of British romanticism and American transcendentalism, to dismiss traditional nature poetry, is too easy. The concept of self that romanticism espouses is problematic, but day to day we still have selves. This is not a flaw or a moral failing but something we can observe and ponder. Our vision and hearing and sense of smell are limited when compared to that of insects or bats or dogs, but our neocortex gives us—the animal that is *Homo sapiens sapiens*—a compound eye–like capacity for simultaneous multiple perspectives. As poets and poetry readers, we can engage in and slide between contemplation, activism, and self-reflexivity. We believe any definition of ecopoetry should allow for this capacity.

While the definitions of ecopoetry are fairly clear cut, the poems themselves are less easily categorized. Like ecological entities—species, watersheds, habitats, and so on—the categories that ecopoems fall into are overlapping, various, discontinuous, and permeable. A single poem may participate in multiple categories. Shifts in understanding as fundamental and mind-boggling as Copernicus's heliocentric universe, Darwin's theory of evolution, and Aldo Leopold's land ethic—which all move human beings from center stage and adjust our lens from an anthropocentric to an ecocentric view—contribute to the new sensibility that informs this poetry.

The poet Ed Roberson sums up ecopoetry beautifully: "[It] occurs when an individual's sense of the larger Earth enters into the world of human knowledge. The main understanding that results from this encounter is *the* Ecopoetic: that the world's desires do *not* run the Earth, but the Earth *does* run the world." Ecopoetry enacts through language the manifold relationship between the human and the other-than-human world.

When *The Ecopoetry Anthology* was in development, Robert Hass suggested we begin the book with a historical section, designed to give readers a sense of American poetry that predates the 1960s environmental movement but that presents the relations between humans and natural or built environments in striking and memorable ways. "Just thirty pages," he said. "Put together a selection of a few great poems beginning with Walt Whitman that could easily be detached for classroom use." As we dived into this section, so splendid were the choices that it grew, and grew, and grew. It is now well over 100 pages long, with thirty-one poets included. Some—Robinson Jeffers, Lorine Niedecker, Kenneth Rexroth—are often rightfully discussed as precursors of American ecopoetry. Others—especially, perhaps, Wallace Stevens, Ezra Pound, T. S. Eliot, Stephen Vincent Benét, Hart Crane, and Langston Hughes—are not usually considered in this context, but to do so is refreshing and revealing. The historical section of the anthology is arranged chronologically by the poets' years of birth, from Whitman to James Schuyler.

The contemporary section includes 176 poets, arranged alphabetically from A. R. Ammons to Robert Wrigley. It happens to begin with one of the seminal works of American ecopoetry, Ammons's great poem "Corsons Inlet." (That the eloquent colloquy of "Corsons Inlet" echoes Whitman's "Out of the Cradle Endlessly Rocking" in the historical section—both sea-drenched poems, the latter quintessentially romantic, the former quintessentially postmodern—is also serendipitous. These are the coincidences that keep editors in love with their work.)

Every step of the way, *The Ecopoetry Anthology* has been a genuine collaboration between us, its two coeditors, and also between us and the poet Barbara Ras, who is the director of Trinity University Press. When we began this project we had no idea how many hundreds of poets were addressing the environmental crisis in their work and writing about the complex interrelations between human and other-than-human worlds. Each reader will probably say at some point, "Why isn't so-and-so included?" The more we found, the more was left to find, and poets have inevitably been left out. This abundance of material is heartening, but it has made the selection process arduous.

There is a lot of variety in *The Ecopoetry Anthology*. Nature poems, environmental poems, ecological poems—in every case, our primary criterion was the excellence of the work as poetry. We believe you will find much to love here. In William Carlos Williams's sense, we believe you will find the "news."

A SCATTERING, A SHINING

Ann Fisher-Wirth

I don't remember when I first read "Spring Pools," by Robert Frost. But I do remember the feeling I got—something between a twinge of pain and a punch in the gut—when I reached the lines

> The trees that have it in their pent-up buds
> To darken nature and be summer woods—
> Let them think twice before they use their powers
> To blot out and drink up and sweep away
> These flowery waters and these watery flowers
> From snow that melted only yesterday.

Come on, I said to myself, trees can't think. Of course, Frost knew that. Still, the line is the crux of the poem for me. I can't help feeling grief and a kind of panic for the thoughtless trees even while I acknowledge Frost's irony. Though he is only (overtly) remarking the passage from spring to summer, he evokes the power that pushes all things toward death, toward dissolution. This power—call it time, nature—is inexorable. Humans know that; trees do not. To realize that gap, that otherness, was, for me, one beginning of ecological consciousness.

Other poems were equally important in awakening my awareness of the natural world. I am so enthusiastic about the poems collected in the contemporary section of *The Ecopoetry Anthology* that I don't want to single out any for special mention, except to urge readers to find and read the complete versions of poems we've had to excerpt. I will make one exception for Gary Snyder's "Piute Creek," because it so dramatically corrects our anthropocentric vision with its line "that / Which sees is truly seen."

Referring overtly to "Cougar or Coyote" that watch the poet "rise and go," the line expands to become a provocative reminder that everything in the world returns our gaze.

By and large, my own formative influences are poems I first read in college in the 1960s, and most of what I mention here is included in the book's historical section. I think, for instance, of Theodore Roethke's beautiful, hypnotic "Meditation at Oyster River," its long sinuous rhythms building to the quiet ecstasy of "In the first of the moon, / All's a scattering, / A shining." Or Elizabeth Bishop's "At the Fishhouses," its great repeated line describing the North Atlantic waters off Nova Scotia, "Cold dark deep and absolutely clear." Or Wallace Stevens's "Sunday Morning," evoking a sense of plenitude whether we humans are there or not, where "Sweet berries ripen in the wilderness."

I think, too, of Emily Dickinson's "certain slant of light," her "bird came down the walk," her sea and snake and spider. I think of the tender address to the grass in Walt Whitman's "Song of Myself" and of his "Out of the Cradle Endlessly Rocking," the wild, death-haunted ode that tells of the birth of the poet and of a "thousand songs . . . A thousand warbling echoes" inspired in a listening boy, one night as he walked along the beach, by a mockingbird's desolate "aria" for a lost mate and the seething, maternal roar of the ocean.

I think of Ezra Pound's stern and beautiful injunction,

Pull down thy vanity, it is not man
Made courage, or made order, or made grace,
    Pull down thy vanity, I say pull down.
Learn of the green world what can be thy place
In scaled invention or true artistry,
Pull down thy vanity

And I think of William Carlos Williams's "By the road to the contagious hospital," its praise for a muddy March day and for the "stark dignity of entrance," whether that entrance refers to plants that "grip down and begin to awaken" after their winter dormancy or, by extension, to every conception and every baby born.

My desire to take on the five-year project that has become *The Ecopoetry Anthology* had other sources as well. Traditional Japanese screen and scroll painting, which I first experienced as a child when my Army father was stationed at Camp Zama near Tokyo, taught me to love art in which humans took their place as small travelers or celebrants in a world of mountains and rivers without end. Growing up in Berkeley, California, in a house overlooking the San Francisco Bay, taught me to love the fog and the ever-changing ocean. Two decades later, living on a farm outside Charlottesville, Virginia, and spending thousands of hours walking in the fields and woods, canning fruit, and growing a garden, I discovered what I'd suspected was true since I first read *Walden*—I hungered for a life immersed in the natural world.

Now I live in Mississippi, a place of both great beauty and severe environmental damage. I've become especially aware of environmental justice issues, of how certain human communities—those without much economic or political power—tend to suffer disproportionately from environmental burdens. For twenty years I have been professionally involved with the Association for the Study of Literature and Environment. I teach poetry and direct the environmental studies minor at the University of Mississippi. And I write mostly poetry. All these aspects of my life have helped to form my interest in this project.

Coediting *The Ecopoetry Anthology* has been a labor of love against despair. As I write these words, Arctic ice levels are at a record low. Global climate disruption continues to wreak havoc in the form of droughts, storms, record-breaking temperatures, and runaway wildfires. The gap between rich and poor continues to widen catastrophically, and billions of people worldwide, victims of environmental injustice, lead lives of quiet or clamorous desperation. And this is only the short list of what's going on. We are living out a colossal failure of heart, will, and imagination.

I do not know what power *The Ecopoetry Anthology*—or indeed poetry altogether—may have against environmental disaster. But I have an abiding hope. William Carlos Williams writes in *Spring and All*, "Poetry does not tamper with the world, but moves it." The poems in *The Ecopoetry Anthology* are praise songs, incantations, narratives, meditations, lists, elegies, rhapsodies, jeremiads. Each of them, in their very different ways, has the power to move the world—to break through our dulled disregard, our carelessness, our despair, reawakening our sense of the vitality and beauty of nature. With that awareness, let us pledge to take actions that will preserve it.

THE ROOTS OF IT

Laura-Gray Street

> In the small beauty of the forest
> The wild deer are bedding down—
> That they are there!
> —George Oppen, "Psalm"

"Psalm" and bird song were my paths in.

"Psalm," George Oppen's lyric of awe and wonder (p. 89), shows the paradox of a world that is on the one hand near and that we are kin to, and that on the other hand is forever "alien" and "strange." The poem accepts, even embraces and shows the beauty of, that paradox. But it's the jump to language in the last stanza that gets me still, every time I read it: "The small nouns / crying faith / In this in which the wild deer / Startle, and stare out." With that leap, the poem becomes more than a poem about the natural world and our relationship to it. It embodies what I intuitively feel is true: language—the Word—is not something that separates us from and elevates us above the rest of this planet. Rather, language is an integral part of our biological selves. The "roots of it / Dangle from [our] mouths." We are language-making creatures in the same way that spiders are web-making creatures.

In "Psalm," the deer are linguistic structures, the "small nouns" are animate, and all are tangled together. The words of the poem are the small nouns, the things the words reference are the small nouns, the poet and we the readers are the small nouns (in fact "we" are pronouns, which are small nouns). Oppen's poem gave me a shape for a felt truth: meaning, including language, comes from things, a reversal of the usual thinking that things have meaning because we give it to them. Oppen suggests this reading with the poem's epigraph, "Veritas sequitur . . . ," which is taken from Saint Thomas Aquinas. *Veritas sequitur esse rerum*—truth follows the existence of things. Truth follows from following things the way Oppen followed the deer in the woods.

My thinking about this in terms of language and poetry was further complicated when I read that many songbirds learn language (song) as fledglings by listening to and mimicking adults the way we do as children. And birds often speak in dialects. Black-capped chickadees on Martha's Vineyard sing differently from black-capped chickadees on the mainland, Donald Kroodsma found, and the common yellowthroat develops a southern drawl in the South. What I've managed to learn simply reinforces my sense of how little we understand about the way other organisms communicate and how truly mundane—of this world—our own use of language is. For me, that insight is the way in to ecopoetry.

In a sense, poetry has always been ecopoetry, in that the origins of poetry are embedded in the natural world and poetry has traditionally foregrounded nature in a way that drama and fiction have not. But in our contemporary sense of it, ecopoetry isn't just any poetry garnished with birds or trees; it is a kind of paradigm shift. It is the apprehension of real biological selves (as opposed to fantasy selves) inhabiting this planet along with us, a mix of negative capability and empathy expressed with the cadence, imagery, and wit to make it visceral, so that it lodges in our neural systems and cultivates the environmental imagination that is analogue to the crucial biodiversity of the rainforests and our intestines.

In working on the anthology, I have come to think of ecopoetry not as a particular form or subject or style or school but as a way of thinking within and through all of these. Of a way of thinking ecocentrically rather than anthropocentrically. Of seeing the same things we've always seen, stuck on the same preoccupations, humming the same tunes off key, but with humankind as a contingent part of a much larger whole rather than the be-all and end-all of everything.

Ecopoetry is George Oppen's "small nouns / Crying faith," and e. e. cummings's poisoned mouse asking "What / have i done that / You wouldn't have," and Lucille Clifton's roaches "bold with they bad selves / marching up out of the drains."

It is Wendell Berry's celebratory plowing of fields with a pair of mares— "sorrels, with white / tails and manes, beautiful!"—and it is Larry Levis's melancholy rendering of a withered and stony field where a "horse named Sandman & a horse named Anastasia / Used to stand at the fence & watch the traffic pass."

It is Juan Carlos Galeano's whimsical marriage of ecology and magic realism and Jeffrey Thompson's Borges-inspired "Celestial Emporium of Benevolent Knowledge." It is Ira Sadoff's syntactical weediness, the "I" releasing multiple/fragmented selves like thistle seed, and the stream of voice-iness of Marianne Boruch, Luisa Igloria, Tim Seibles, and Anthony Seidman.

It is the unexpected sarcasm in Maxine Kumin's "The Whole Hog" and Tony Hoagland's "Romantic Moment," and the lyrical eroticism in Dorianne Laux's "The Orgasms of Organisms" and Patrick Lawler's "Hummingbird."

It is giovanni singleton's emphatically caged bird, and Ronald Johnson's concrete "earthearthearth." It is Jonathan Skinner's and Mei-mei Berssenbrugge's grafting of deconstruction and L=A=N=G=U=A=G=E and the avant garde onto lyric rootstock. It is the stark "nothing that is not there and the nothing that is" of Wallace Stevens's "The Snowman" and Marianne Moore's sea that "has nothing to give but a well excavated grave." It is tender eulogy for Robinson Jeffers's hurt hawk and Robert Bly's dead seal and Stanley Kunitz's Wellfleet whale.

It is the Nabokov-like "passion of the scientist and precision of the poet" in the poems of Alison Hawthorne Deming, Pattiann Rogers, and Elizabeth Bradfield. It is the documenting of environmental injustice in Muriel Rukeyser's "Book of the Dead" and Charles Goodrich's "Millennial Spring" and Brenda Hillman's "Request to the Berkeley City Council Concerning Strawberry Creek."

It is the emotionally complex environmental history of Allison Hedge Coke's "Dust: Dad's Days" and Davis McCombs's "Tobacco Mosaic." It is the chronic illnesses of D. A. Powell's "monochromatic and mechanized" republic and C. K. Williams's "leftover carats of tar in the gutter" in the shadow of Three Mile Island.

It is the incantation of loss and runoff of Julianna Spahr's "Gentle Now Don't Add to Heartache," and Sheryl St. Germain's complaint for the Gulf spill—oiled birds and waters and beaches: "Let's ask those responsible . . . // to walk deep out into the waters . . . // and then, / when they are thick and covered/ with the stuff . . . // then / let them try to swim back // then / let them try to explain."

It is Linda Bierds's breathtakingly minute "moon-skin of a microbe."

It is Eliot Weinberger's catalog of stars and our conceptions of stars that accumulates into a portrait of humanity as movingly encompassing as the "Blue Marble," Apollo 17's first full-view photographs of Earth.

It is the way every poet and every poem in this anthology complicates our assumptions about ecopoetry. It is a way we see and learn.

Maybe one day we won't need a term like ecopoetry because all poetry will be inherently ecological. And maybe we won't need environmental science departments or sustainability studies because all curricula and projects will have an understanding of the complexity and value of natural systems at their core. Maybe one day we won't need to prefix every aspect of our lives with "green," creating an algal bloom of subcategories like green technology, green building, green chic, green parenting, because every category will be infused with all hues and shades in the spirit of Tim Earley's "I Like Green Things." But in the meantime we will continue to need green lenses like *The Ecopoetry Anthology*. We will need to keep following green things—all things strange and wild and small—listening to and learning their songs/psalms, and singing back our own.

AMERICAN ECOPOETRY: AN INTRODUCTION

Robert Hass

Geology, Biology, Astronomy, and a Poem

Here is Gary Snyder in the western mountains in the 1950s:

> burning the small dead
> > branches
> broke from beneath
> > thick spreading
> > > whitebark pine
>
> > > a hundred summers
> snowmelt   rock   and air
>
> hiss in a twisted bough.
>
> > sierra granite;
> > > mt. Ritter—
> > > black rock twice as old.
>
> Deneb, Altair
>
> windy fire

A couple of facts about the poem. Whitebark pines grow in the highest elevations of the Sierra Nevada, just below timberline, so in this poem we must be at least 10,000 feet above sea level, high up there in the American sublime. The pines are very tough plants to survive ice and snow; their branches are often low-growing and contorted, and they flourish in their habitat, being perfectly adapted to it since at least the last ice age. So Snyder's description of them—"thick spreading," "twisted"—is apt and accurate. According to foresters the tree has a life span of about 120 years, so that next line is about right too. The branches might very well be 100 years old, and they are made of snowmelt, rock, and air, and the fine high mountain soils begot by snowmelt, light, and air. Pines, like other conifers, stop supplying water and minerals to their lower branches as the new growth of the higher branches does the work of photosynthesis. The shutdown lower branches die, and they are the ones broken off and burned in the poem. In the dancelike movement of Snyder's accentual verse, when you come to the verb "hiss" you can almost hear the sound of the branches in the campfire giving off the oxygen that nourished them.

The Sierra Nevada, geologists now think, began to form into a single massive block about 80 million years ago, began to rise 10 million years ago, and was carved into massive peaks and canyons by glaciers even as it continued to rise, about 2.5 million years ago. Looking at the rock, looking at the fire, the speaker in the poem finds himself thinking about time. And from that elevation in the central Sierra, the distant glimpse of Mount Ritter and the Minarets is a familiar sight. Geologists tell us that the almost chocolate-colored rock of Ritter is very old, volcanic, and ancestral to the gray granite of most of the Sierra Nevada. Any time you get that high up, you see it, and it's a striking sight. It takes the mind far back into the geological history of the Earth. Another thing you see in summer in the Sierra Nevada with a special brilliance as dark comes on—when you might be starting a fire—are the three stars of the summer triangle, Deneb, Altair, and Vega. They are, of course, also fire, and that leads the mind of the thinker in the poem to leap from the small campfire to the fires that fashioned Sierra granite over millions of years to the windy fire of the stars and to the origin of the universe.

Snyder was, in those years, a student of classical Chinese and Japanese poetry and a beginning student of Buddhism. It seems likely that he took the cool self-effacement of his speaker in this poem, and also the lightness of touch, from Chinese poets like Han-shan, whom he'd translated in graduate school. If we are in the territory of the American sublime, it is sublimity with a difference. There's no evidence here of a transcendent realm to which the particulars of the poem refer and very little ego in the speaker. What we get is fire, fire and vast stretches of time and space, and wonder. And perhaps we are to hear an echo of the Buddha's Fire Sermon: "Bhikkus," he is supposed to have said, "everything is burning."

It's interesting, in trying to find a way to talk about the body of American nature poetry, to think about other facts that make this location of Snyder's poem possible. One could start, I suppose, in 1607, the year of the first permanent English colony on the American shore. Two years later Galileo, in Venice, heard of the invention of the telescope and had the thought of using it to look at heavenly bodies. This marks, if the thesis of Copernicus doesn't, the beginning of modern astronomy. Scholars like to quote well-known lines from John Donne's "An Anatomy of the World" to describe what effect Copernicus and Galileo had on the European imagination:

And new philosophy calls all in doubt,
The element of fire is quite put out,
The sun is lost, and th' earth, and no man's wit
Can well direct him where to look for it.
And freely men confess that this world's spent,
When in the planets and the firmament
They seek so many new; they see that this
Is crumbled out again to his atomies.
'Tis all in pieces, all coherence gone,
All just supply, and all relation;
Prince, subject, father, son, are things forgot,
For every man alone thinks he hath got
To be a phoenix, and that then can be
None of that kind, of which he is, but he.
This is the world's condition now

Between Donne and Snyder came that extraordinary history in which, through observation, technical invention, and inference, men discovered not just that the earth, now a planet among other planets, revolved around a sun, but also that our sun was one star in a galaxy, the one shepherds and poets had called the Milky Way; that this galaxy contained 200 billion stars like the sun; that the galaxy was rotating in what was calculated to be a 200-million-year cycle; that it was one among more than 150 billion such galaxies in the observable universe. And that the universe itself is about 15 billion years old, born apparently of a violent and explosive event that produced time, space, and matter in an instant, and it has been expanding ever since at what is—measured the way things on earth are measured—incredible speed. Windy fire, indeed. Most of this information was developed in the twentieth century, and it is a lot to expect the human imagination to assimilate in so short a time. The physicist who coined the term "Big Bang" did so in a radio interview in 1949 (radio had been invented! sound transmitted invisibly through the living air!), only a few years before Gary Snyder wrote this poem.

The other news that informs "Burning the Small Dead" is geological. Modern geology also has its initiating moment. Charles Lyell published the first volume of his *Principles of Geology* in 1830, a few years before Ralph Waldo Emerson gave a start to the American tradition of nature writing when he anonymously published the essay "Nature." Lyell's *Principles* famously argued that the earth was far older than theologians, the keepers of the story of creation, reckoned; that it came into existence and received its shape over vast stretches of time through natural forces that had operated in the past and were still observable in the present. This proposal gave people new eyes to see the earth with and touched off the excitement about understanding that sent John Muir a couple of decades later into the Sierra Nevada to piece together how the glaciers had forged the natural cathedral of the Yosemite. It also gave young Charles Darwin the time he needed to make probable his ideas about the origin of species, the immense stretches of time and slow change needed to produce, by natural selection, the shapes of orchids and hawk beaks and the human eye.

This seems like one place to begin to think about American nature poetry—with how the human imagination in the twentieth and twenty-first centuries has been absorbing the many possible meanings of what astronomy has to tell us about the universe, what geology has to tell us about the earth, and what evolutionary biology has to tell us about life. Students of the history of ideas have documented some of the impact, like Alfred, Lord Tennyson's dismay at a "Nature, red in tooth and claw." The larger impact, slower to take in, has been the development of an imagination of a world in which the hypothesis of a purposeful creation and a divine creator or a benign providence no longer seemed necessary. That loss was the terrifying negative. (It still is. A member of the U.S. House of Representatives Committee on Science, Space, and Technology, a congressman from Georgia, said in 2012 that he believes the earth is 9,000 years old. He also said evolution and the Big Bang theory are "lies straight from the pit of Hell.") The positive outcome was a new world to look at, founded on change—not the quick chemical change of fire perhaps, but a powerful, directionless, hungry, theatrical, terrifying, beautiful, and incessant play of the energies of transformation.

American poets responded to this quite early. Walt Whitman, writing before he read *The Origin of Species*, came to his sense of what the world was and of the poet's task within it from the German philosophers and scientists, from Hegel and the Humboldt brothers. "Urge and urge and urge," he would write in the 1855 version of "Song of Myself":

Always the procreant urge of the world.

Out of dimness opposite equals advance, always substance and increase,
    always sex,
Always a knit of identity, always distinction, always a breed of life.

Here is Ezra Pound fifty years later in "Blandula, Tenella, Vagula," a phrase describing the soul he borrowed from a Roman emperor. In this poem he is recalling Lake Como to his artist-fiancée Dorothy Shakespear, with whom he had spent some time there. It also helps to know that though Pound was raised a Presbyterian, in this period he had taken to calling Christianity a cult.

    If at Sirmio,
My soul, I meet thee, when this life's outrun,
Will we not find some headland consecrated
By aery apostles of terrene delight,
Will not our cult be founded on the waves,
Clear sapphire, cobalt, cyanine,
On triune azures, the impalpable
Mirrors unstill of the eternal change?

This is 1911, and art-for-art's-sake Pound is borrowing from Walter Pater and the aesthetic movement a response to an idea of a physical world constituted simply by change. He had snatched from it a new Trinitarian worship based on the changing blues of an alpine lake. Soon he would find the idea of beauty as a response to the new world and the new nature problematic, and the problem would set him on the project of *The Cantos*.

And here is Wallace Stevens four years later in "Sunday Morning":

We live in an old chaos of the sun,
Or old dependency of day and night,
Or island solitude, unsponsored, free,
Of that wide water, inescapable.

The "wide water" seems to be the quiet spaces across which, in contemplative moments, the meanings of our lives come to us, and in those spaces, no longer underwritten by a divine keeper, we are "unsponsored, free." What returns to Stevens across the water is the small ritual the poem begins with, consisting of coffee, oranges, and "the green freedom of a cockatoo upon a rug." This image might be one entry to the intricacies of the idea of an ecopoetics. "Deer walk upon our mountains," Stevens writes later in the poem, "and the quail / Whistle about us their spontaneous cries." That's an evocation of unmediated nature, but our experience of it in poetry is only to be had through the transformations of art. It is a made thing, and it is under our feet—a green cockatoo upon a rug. Seemingly not satisfied with "Sunday Morning" as a statement of the problematic relationship between the imagination and the new world, Stevens continued to meditate on this subject throughout the rest of his life.

We tend to think of the modernist generation, with the prominent exception of Robinson Jeffers, as turning from the romantic tradition and the notion of nature poetry to a poetry more urban in its rhythms and concerns. To some degree, this is true. But with the perspective of time, the young modernists seem much more clearly inheritors of the new worlds that nineteenth-century science and culture handed them. One of the virtues of this generous anthology is that it suggests these continuities.

Modernism and Ecology

Modernism in poetry developed in the early years of the twentieth century. So did the discipline of ecology. German biologist Ernst Haeckel coined the term in 1866 from the Greek word *oikos*, which means "household." Haeckel was interested in the morphology of sea creatures, and in reading Darwin he came to see that the bodily forms of animals and their evolution were best studied in relation to their interactions with their surroundings. Thus, *ökologie*. This concept was one sign of the intellectual recalibration taking place in response to the power of Darwin's remarkable observations on the origin and processes of life. A dramatic way to think about the difference between Linnaean and Darwinian nature is to visualize the cabinets of Sir Joseph Banks, president of the British Royal Society in the last years of the eighteenth century. Banks collected beetles, and his shelves contained specimens from every continent and hundreds of islands, copper and black and green and vermillion and spotted and tiger-striped and brilliantly iridescent several-colored beetles. In display they were a tribute to the orderly mind of Carl Linnaeus and the profligate grandeur of a deity who created so many unique animals in such plenty.

Darwin changed that. The cabinet of wonders had suddenly come alive, had become a complex family history, dynamic rather than static, a verb rather than a series of scintillant nouns. And in order to make sense of a large tiger-striped Malaysian beetle or a small bronze one from the American plains, one had to understand how they interacted with their environment. Hence, a science of natural households. By 1892 the *Boston Globe* was referring, for the first time in the United States, to "the new science of ecology." Darwin had given biology an enormous gift—thousands of questions to ask.

This was also the year of Walt Whitman's death and of the final edition of his *Leaves of Grass*, a book of poems full of questions about the natural world and how to know it—most famously in the sixth section of "Song of Myself":

A child said, What is the grass? Fetching it to me with full hands;
How could I answer the child? I do not know what it is any more than he.

Whitman goes on to give, by my count, twelve answers, as if to mimic the abundance and diversity of the grasses.

American poetry came into its force in the wake of English and German romantic poetry, which came to Whitman and Dickinson partly through Emerson's essays and gave them a benign nature as a place to touch the pulse of life in their poems. Dickinson, as a nature poet, is most powerfully a poet of the seasons and their aching transitions. "There's a certain Slant of light," she writes,

Winter Afternoons—
That oppresses, like the Heft
Of Cathedral Tunes—

And

As imperceptibly as Grief
The Summer lapsed away—

Here she is, famously, on the giddiness of the New England spring:

Inebriate of Air—am I—
And Debauchee of Dew—

And here are insects in the grasses in the August heat:

Further in Summer than the Birds
Pathetic from the Grass
A minor Nation celebrates
Its unobtrusive Mass.

No Ordinance be seen
So gradual the Grace
A pensive Custom it becomes
Enlarging Loneliness.

It's not exactly that Dickinson is an ecologist of the human relation to the season, but nearly so, because the relation between the speakers in her poems and the turning world is so intensely transitive, so specific to their moment and alive. For Whitman, at least in 1855, that intensity was a kind of answer:

Have you reckoned a thousand acres much? Have you reckoned the earth
    much?
Have you practiced so long to learn to read?
Have you felt so proud to get at the meaning of poems?

Stop this day and night with me and you shall possess the origin of all
    poems,
You shall possess the good of earth and sun—there are millions of suns left.

"You shall not look through my eyes," he writes. "You shall listen to all sides and filter them from yourself." Whitman liked the vocabulary of nineteenth-century science; the word "filter" must have had the up-to-date feel of a Victorian laboratory. He borrows it here to describe how our interaction with the world is both individual and intensely social.

In this way Whitman anticipated what was coming. Around the time of his death the discipline of ecology was beginning to develop. Botany, particularly the botany of fairly well defined places like ponds and dunes, was especially congenial to early ecologists, who began to map and classify all the kinds of transitive relationships and energy exchange among plants and animals in a specific geology and weather. In a botanical paper published in 1899, Frederic Clements, an American ecologist working in the Indiana Dunes on the southern end of Lake Michigan, took the notion of these interactions a step further, proposing that a community of plants is in some sense "an organic entity."

In the early years of the twentieth century, Clements did some of the work of legitimating ecology as a science. In *Plant Succession* (1916) he introduced what would become one of its central concepts—that a given ecosystem, having evolved in a particular place, tends toward a state of equilibrium, a set of relationships in the community of animals and plants to which, if it is disturbed by fire or flood, it will tend to return. Succession led to these mature "climax communities." Clements proposed ecology as the study of a deep order in nature—often disturbed, always in motion, yet still an order. But this view was contested. In "The Individualistic Concept of the Plant Association" (1926), botanist Henry Gleason argued that a group of plants is a community by metaphorical convenience only, that it is more usefully described as an "association," and that "an association is not an organism." It is a series of individual organisms competing for resources. Nature, he wrote, isn't circular and stable; it is, as Darwin said, dynamic and linear.

It isn't difficult to see familiar American themes here. Clements in the Progressive era proposes a natural world full of cooperative communities that developed in ways that make its members useful to each other. Gleason in the boom years of Coolidge and Hoover describes a competitive marketplace in which each individual plant takes its chances. It is not a stretch to notice an exploration of the nature of nature playing out in the century's young poets. Their time of growing up, from the 1890s to the 1920s, were the decades in which the U.S. conservation movement had become part of the national agenda. Conservation was at first both a practical and a cultural intervention. The cultural ground was a mix of the romantic spiritualization of nature and the identification of wide American spaces and places of exceptional natural beauty with a notion of patriotism. At the turn of the century, Frederick Jackson Turner had argued, the frontier was closed by the last Indian wars and the exploration of the last unmapped canyons of the Colorado. Now, conservationists argued, was the time to save the temples that had formed the American character. The national government owned immense stretches of land, the forests were not healthy, wildlife was disappearing, and the management of natural resources needed to be undertaken by the federal government in a rational and professional way.

It was the impulse of most modernist American poets to throw out both the comfortable beliefs of the past and the comforting and ordering habits of regular meter and rhyme, and to embark on a new search for order in a new art. That mostly involved a more urban art, a turning away from the conventions of romantic nineteenth-century art. It is fascinating to revisit their poems, as this anthology does, with the new science and the conservation movement in mind—Frost's inclination to a Darwinian darkness, Wallace Stevens's interrogation of the wilderness in "Anecdote of a Jar" and of meaning in the natural world in "The Snow Man," Marianne Moore's spectacular interrogation of Mount Rainier and its glacier in "An

Octopus" (too long a poem to be included in this anthology). It makes one realize that the project of Ezra Pound's *Cantos* to return the altar to the forest, to resurrect in the modern world the energies of the European pagan past, was in its way a conservation agenda. It also makes one realize that Hilda Doolittle—whose father was an astronomer and whose grandfather was a minister and distinguished naturalist who took his granddaughter on collecting trips around Pennsylvania—used her botanical lore to think about female identity and, in the war years in London, the meanings of the regeneration of a disturbed community.

And it makes one realize that the most influential American poems, Whitman's "Song of Myself" and Eliot's "The Waste Land," are both rooted in vegetation myth. Whitman's poem is a celebration of an endlessly renewable, deeply democratic power in the natural world, and Eliot's a portrait of the failure of nature in an urban world of spiritual drought and sexuality gone wrong. It is a world in which connection has failed and the renewing powers of the earth are a source of dread or melancholy regret. "April is the cruelest month," the poem begins, mocking, it seems, the opening of the *Canterbury Tales*. Critics and readers have been arguing for several generations about whether Eliot's poem, borrowing its theme of natural renewal from Jessie Weston's study of the agricultural roots of the Grail myth, should be read as a search for natural renewal or a rejection of it. It's not clear if Eliot himself knew. Passages like the one in which the young man turns to a woman whose arms are full of hyacinths have been read and reread to try to understand his intent:

> —Yet when we came back, late, from the Hyacinth garden,
> Your arms full, and your hair wet, I could not
> Speak, and my eyes failed, I was neither
> Living nor dead, and I knew nothing,
> Looking into the heart of light, the silence.

This passage has been placed against others, the nightmare scene in the last section of the poem when the images of fertility turn to horror:

> A woman drew her long black hair out tight
> And fiddled whisper music on those strings
> And bats with baby faces in the violet light
> Whistled, and beat their wings
> And crawled head downward down a blackened wall.

However one reads these passages, it's clear that the poem, which riveted a generation, is about the sense of a deep injury to the powers of natural and human renewal. "On Margate Sands," says one of the speakers, a young woman imagined to be a Thames suicide, "I can connect / Nothing with nothing."

During the years when the young Eliot was forging his art in London, another midwesterner, Aldo Leopold, was finding his way in the Forest Service and beginning to write about the desiccated forests and rangelands of the American Southwest, which had been overlogged and overgrazed for several generations. Leopold would later write *A Sand County Almanac*, perhaps the most influential volume of nature writing since Thoreau's *Walden* and John Muir's *The Mountains of California*, and the book credited with transforming the conservation movement by grounding it in ecology. *Sand County* was published in 1949, just about the time Eliot published the final version of his *Four Quartets*, his search for a spring beyond spring, so it is interesting to notice that while Eliot was describing a spiritual wasteland in London, Leopold was documenting a historical one in the American West. He had begun as a young hunter, enthusiastic about using his post in the Forest Service to restore wildlife and improve hunting grounds as part of the work of managing forests, and in the process he taught himself ecology—the ecology of Frederic Clements—and transformed the conservation movement from a hunting and fishing lobby into a movement for land conservation and preservation. *A Sand County Almanac*, the story of Leopold's education, moved ecology onto the literary agenda just as ecology was entering the popular consciousness as a deceptively simple proposition: everything is connected to everything else.

In the years after *Sand County* and *Four Quartets*, the consequences of our enormous industrial and agricultural production and the speed and efficiency of our transportation systems began to exact their costs in very visible ways. Rachel Carson told the story of another wasteland in *Silent Spring* (1962), her best-selling account of the ways pesticides and other forms of pollution produced by our chemical industry were poisoning the land. If the country needed yet another symbol of the trouble, it got one in August 1969 when the Cuyahoga River burst into flame as it flowed into Lake Erie near Cleveland. It made the lines in "The Dry Salvages," the third poem in *Four Quartets*, seem prescient:

> I do not know much about gods; but I think that the river
> Is a strong brown god—sullen, untamed and intractable,
> Patient to some degree, at first recognized as a frontier;
> Then only a problem confronting the builder of bridges.
> The problem once solved, the brown god is almost forgotten

By the dwellers in cities—ever, however, implacable,
Keeping his seasons and rages, destroyer, reminder
Of what men choose to forget. Unhonored, unpropitiated
By worshippers of the machine, but waiting, watching and waiting.

The literary readers of these lines over the years—or these lines from
the last poem in the series "Little Gidding"—did not necessarily have an
ecological perspective to think about them from.

> Water and fire succeed
> The town, the pasture and the weed.
> Water and fire deride
> The sacrifice that we denied.
> Water and fire shall rot
> The marred foundation we forgot,
> Of sanctuary and choir.
> This is the death of water and fire.

It is a little as if the priest and moralist in Eliot were welcoming the end
as he tried to imagine a world beyond change and the ravages of time.
Leopold, meanwhile, was articulating an ethic of renewal, his well-known
and influential land ethic: "A thing is right when it tends to preserve the
integrity, stability, and beauty of the biotic community." This proposition
was complicated by the ways this formulation of an earthly stability and
integrity was based on Clements's conceptual framing of ecology. In these
years the statistical study of ecosystems by plant ecologists was calling
into question the notion of stable climax communities, which makes the
tensions within modernist poetry and ecological science look similar. They
were each in different ways trying to understand what survives change.

There were other incentives to think ecologically. In 1972 Apollo 17 sent
back the first images of the earth seen from space. What people remarked
on first was its beauty—a blue marble in the circumambient dark—and
second that it looked so vulnerable.

Toward the Notion of an Ecopoetry

Then there is the North American continent, the physical geography of the
land as it emerged from the last ice age 12,000 or so years ago.

Here is John Muir at the turn of the nineteenth century on the processes that shaped this moment: "To prepare the ground, it was rolled and sifted in seas with infinite loving deliberation and forethought, lifted into the light, submerged and warmed over and over again, pressed and crumpled into folds and ridges, mountains and hills, subsoiled with heaving volcanic fires, ploughed and ground and sculptured into scenery and soil with glaciers and rivers . . ." And here he is on the outcome of this long geological drama that was pieced together by nineteenth-century science:

> In the fullness of time it was planted in groves, and belts, and broad, exuberant mantling forests, with the largest, most varied, most fruitful, and most beautiful trees in the world. Bright seas made its border with wave embroidery and icebergs; gray deserts were outspread in the middle of it, mossy tundras on the north, savannas on the south, and blooming prairies and plains; while lakes and rivers shone through all the vast forests and openings, and happy birds and beasts gave delightful animation.

If the North American continent is an ecosystem, then all the ways we have imagined it, all the conceptions of it—maps, geographies, metaphors, mentalities, technologies, infrastructures, peoples, languages, institutions, battlefields, creature life, seasons and the holidays that made ritual of them—are its cultural equivalent. And so are religions, farm implements, architectures, the lapels of coats and the hems of dresses, massacres and factories and statues in parks. So are the 10,000 years of Native American experience with the land and their expulsion from it by a combination of European diseases and wars. So are the flood of immigrants who swept across the continent, those early settlers who looked into the forests on the Eastern Seaboard and saw demonic darkness, who, where they did not see wheat fields, saw Satan; and the settlers who looked into the forests and saw fortunes to be made in the shipbuilding business; and the ones who saw ahead the incredible labor of girdling trees and uprooting them to prepare the land for a European agricultural regimen. And so is the extraordinary story of slavery, of the millions of Africans whose labor transformed the entire Southeast and the mid-Atlantic states, and the ways their struggle for freedom and equality shaped American culture as their labor shaped the land.

The poets of the second half of the twentieth century, when they inherited that first glimpse of the earth from space, also inherited this history of languages, of ways of seeing the land and what happened on it. And when the interstate highway system was creating a vast network of freeways from Bangor to San Diego, they inherited a certain tension that was already in the culture. A shorthand might describe it as a tension between the symbolic and the literal, between the capacity of human consciousness to read itself into nature and the capacity to see, or try to see, what's there on its own terms, between a literary and a scientific tradition. Emerson's essays and Thoreau's *Walden* and, quite gloriously, Melville's *Moby-Dick* are among the founding documents of that tension. It would later get tracked in the academic discipline of American studies in books like Leo Marx's *The Machine in the Garden: Technology and the Pastoral Ideal in America* (1964). It is no accident that this book appeared two years after *Silent Spring*. Rachel Carson's account of how American industry and industrial agriculture were poisoning people and the land proved transformative because the country sensed the truth of what it had to say before they read it or heard about it. The conflict between the machine and the garden, the boundless faith in technology and progress and the national identity created from the sense of a vibrant and majestic natural world, had come home to roost.

The remarkable thing about those years is that the country responded. In the span of a decade Congress passed a set of laws that amounted to an environmental bill of rights. (One result of Carson's work was that people began referring to the world conservationists were concerned with as "the environment." We were not talking anymore about nature apart from technology and its consequences.) Consider the legislative record: the 1964 Wilderness Act; the 1968 Wild and Scenic Rivers Act; the Clean Air Act and creation of the Environmental Protection Agency in 1970; the Clean Water Act and the Marine Protection, Research, and Sanctuaries Act, which limited chemical dumping in the oceans, both in 1972; and the Endangered Species Act and the EPA's banning of DDT—the target of *Silent Spring*—in 1973. The first efforts to require auto manufacturers to increase fuel efficiencies in the massive automobile engines Americans felt entitled to as they rocketed through the gardens of the continent and idled on its freeways came in the form of the Energy Policy and Conservation Act in 1975. When scientists reported that the chlorofluorocarbons used in the world's refrigerators were burning a hole in the atmosphere, chlorofluorocarbons were phased out by legislation and administrative action in 1978. In the tumultuous years of the Civil Rights Movement and protests against the Vietnam War, there was, in the conversation between the machine and the garden, every evidence of a functioning and responsive government.

The post–World War II years saw an enormous explosion of new American poets and poetries. In the 1950s, the era of Eisenhower's expansion of the freeway system, important additions to the American nature poetry tradition included Kenneth Rexroth's mountain poems, Charles Olson's Gloucester poems, Lorine Niedecker's watery poems of the Wisconsin lake country, and Theodore Roethke's North American sequence. Quietly these poets of the so-called middle generation were making a poetry of the neighborhoods they lived in and pointing the way to one notion of ecopoetry. By the mid-1950s and early 1960s a younger generation announced itself—poets who gave the innovative energies of nineteenth-century romanticism and early twentieth-century modernism a new push. Their work refracted the ways technology, ecology, and the condition of the natural world had come to seem intricately connected.

That refraction could be seen most directly, perhaps, in the work of Gary Snyder. His early books, *Riprap* and *Myths and Texts*, were published at the end of the 1950s. *The Back Country* appeared (in the wake of *Silent Spring*) in 1967, followed in 1969 by a book of essays and journals, which Snyder titled *Earth House Hold* to signal its roots in ecological thought. As an environmentalist and conservationist manifesto, it passed from hand to hand among the young, along with his poems. Snyder had achieved unusual visibility as a member of the Beat Generation and as the hero of Jack Kerouac's novel *The Dharma Bums*, which imagines a new generation of high mountain hoboes and spiritual seekers. In the meantime he had returned from Asia and moved with his family to the Sierra foothills, where he cleared land in the forest, built a house and a Zen meditation center from wood on the property, and began an experiment in living off the grid.

At about the same time another young American writer, Wendell Berry, was homing to Kentucky, where his grandfather had been a tobacco farmer and his father, in some allegory of generational transitions, had been an attorney and a farmer, and where Berry set about becoming a writer, professor, and farmer. Berry, who had studied with the novelist Wallace Stegner at Stanford University when Stegner was crafting the "Wilderness Letter" that became the manifesto of the movement to create the Wilderness Act, was disposed to be a conservationist. But he did not embark on preserving the remnant Kentucky wilderness and its rivers. He farmed— first, like Gary Snyder, building a house, then beginning to heal an abused piece of farmland, then in poems, novels, and stories, thinking through the agrarian tradition he had inherited as a southern writer and the challenges of farming in an industrial economy. The young who traced Snyder's development in this decade were also tracing Berry's. His first collection, *The Broken Ground* (1964), contained Emersonian poems, one could say, in an idiom that owed something to William Carlos Williams and something to contemporaries like Denise Levertov and Hayden Carruth. The poems in *Findings* (1968) and *Openings* (1969) more nearly focus Berry's project as an imaginative version of ecological restoration, a poetics of husbandry. *The Long-Legged House* (1969) recounts his efforts to resettle the land and teach himself its creature life. *The Unsettling of America: Culture and Agriculture* (1977), the book of essays that made him one of his generation's most influential environmental thinkers, lays out a series of arguments: the conservation movement has been about how not to use the land, and the country needs a culture that tells us how to use it; ecology has taught Berry's generation that nature's existence is always local and specific, and the use of it—what he calls "the kindly" use of it—depends on traditions of local knowledge; and the cultivation of the kinds of local knowledge and local *technes* that heal land and preserve it from one generation to the next come from communities. So, he writes, the ecological crisis is an agricultural one, and the agricultural crisis is one of culture brought on by large-scale, chemically dependent, monocrop agriculture geared to mass production at the expense of land health and local knowledge. It was a Jeffersonian assault, in short, on big agriculture and the legends of the so-called green revolution. Twenty years after *The Unsettling of America* was published, the food movement discovered Berry's arguments about agriculture. By then he and Gary Snyder, who also continued to produce poems and essays, were elder statesmen of the environmental movement and of what some critics were beginning to call "ecopoetry."

Most Americans in the second half of the twentieth century weren't living in rural communities. The country had been predominantly rural at the turn of the nineteenth century. Sixty percent of Americans lived in small towns and villages when the modernists were young. By 1990 almost 80 percent of Americans lived in cities and their suburbs, and it was increasingly clear that the lives of city and suburbs, city and wilderness, and city and farm country were intimately connected.

At about the same time the new American poetry was appearing and environmental legislation was moving through Congress, Jane Jacobs's *The Death and Life of Great American Cities* (1961) asked Americans to rethink their cities. The book was, among other things, a polemic with the 1950s city planning and urban renewal policies in the way that *The Unsettling of America* was a polemic with corporate agriculture, and it became another part of an emergent ecological literature. Jacobs began with the argument that theorists of cities and city planners in the early part of the century didn't like cities and tried to invent them top down with an antiurban prejudice that they should be more like gardens. Her example was social critic Lewis Mumford, whose *The City in History: Its Origins, Its Transformations, and Its Prospects* (1961) argued for "organic cities." Jacobs countered that to conceive of cities as gardens was to misunderstand them as a human invention; in her view, they were naturally occurring structures.

The argument is interesting for American poetry because two of its initiating poems, "Song of Myself" and "The Waste Land," are urban ones. Whitman's is a celebration of the abundance, diversity, fascination, and surprise of living in a city. Eliot's is a vision of the city as a kind of hell where fertility has failed. So it is interesting to watch a writer try to construct a notion of the vitality of cities. Jacobs argues that cities are good at inventing themselves; that they came into existence because humans love to watch each other and trade with each other and exchange ideas and techniques; that they have been economically and artistically terrific multipliers of human creativity; and that the study of cities ought to explore how to foster their fundamental liveliness and promote the safety that comes from neighborhoods full of many different kinds of people, familiar to each other but not intimate, who, by going about their business, provide the street with interest and with eyes. It is an argument for the city, when it is functioning properly, as a very rich ecosystem.

The new poets, not surprisingly, reflected the culture's pro- and anti-urban prejudices. In Allen Ginsberg's "Howl," the city where "Mohammedan angels [stagger] on tenement roofs illuminated" is both a visionary and a demonic space. In "The Day Lady Died" and Frank O'Hara's other early poems, it is an idyll of bookstores with new French and Irish plays and lunch-hour shopping in well-stocked liquor stores that carry handsome European liqueurs, of muggy streets and shoeshine stands and late afternoon trains to dinner parties near the ocean. And at the center of it—figured in the death of the singer Billie Holiday—heart-stopping beauty that is here and gone. O'Hara's cosmopolitanism, his celebration of the great, ravenous, constructive, and destructive energies of a great city, is something like Jacobs's. And the poems of Frank O'Hara shopping in Manhattan in the summer heat and of Wendell Berry sowing a meadow for silage amid the violence of the Vietnam War and of Gary Snyder in the Sierra staring up at the summer stars become figures for an ability of poetry to show us where we are, or to show us wondering where we are.

John Ashbery was also in those years a poet for the reinvention of a cosmopolitan imagination. After college he went to Paris and got a job as an art critic, which gave him a chance to soak up the art movements that had washed across the worlds of literature and painting in that city—the symbolist movement and Dada and surrealism and the experiments of a new set of formalist writers who called themselves Oulipo and whose relation to nature poetry was based on the idea that, if the universe is a matter of pure chance, numbers falling through numbers to make and dissolve what looks to us in our brevity like an order in things, maybe art should be made that way too. At the same time Ashbery had an eye on the history of modern painting, with its impressionisms and expressionisms and fauvisms, its cubisms and constructivism and, recently, excitingly, abstract expressionism. He returned to New York with the poems he had written in that spirit. He would in the next few years move toward an American idiom that mixed chance with metaphorical surprise and a kind of generous mimicking of the idea of a cosmopolitan imagination, a bit like a city, a place full of oddnesses and surprises and strangenesses and veerings. If an ecological accounting is in order, Ashbery's poems—and the poems of other writers of urban sensibility in those years—seemed to argue, poetry will have to account for the sheer variousness and voluminousness of the human imagination and the oddness of language in the way it gets embodied—something less like a mutualistic ecosystem, with jay and squirrel and bear and white pine, and more like an immense and liquid solution, full of all sorts of things, precipitating out something new every time something new is dropped into it.

It was another form of the tension between the symbolic and the literal, an attitude, a way of thinking about poetry that stretched the idea of poetry and the notion of an ecopoetics in the last decades of the twentieth century by attending to the wobbliness in language of the relation between word and thing. Here is a bit of one of Ashbery's poems in this anthology, a descriptive list of the world's rivers:

> The plain banks of the Neva are
> Gray. The dark Saône flows silently.
> And the Volga is long and wide
> As it flows across the brownish land. The Ebro
> Is blue, and slow. The Shannon flows
> Swiftly between its banks. The Mississippi
> Is one of the world's longest rivers, like the Amazon.
> It has the Missouri for a tributary.

The poem is partly about rivers and the abundance of the world. It is partly (because it goes nowhere in particular; it's a list) a send-up of the notion of knowledge—"the Mississippi / Is one of the world's longest rivers"—or a commentary on the sheer weirdness of the thingness of the world, the nouns and adjectives and verbs that make things into this and that for the human imagination.

This stands, if not in contrast to, then in tension with, the impulse of the writers one thinks of as literalists of the imagination, to use Marianne Moore's apt phrase. In *Tape for the Turn of the Year* (1965) A. R. Ammons was finding a language for his sense—often described as neo-Emersonian—of the way the order of the poem mimes the order of the world:

> *Ecology* is my word: tag
>   me with that: come
>   in there:
>   you will find yourself
> in a firmless country:
>   centers and peripheries
>   in motion,
>   organic,
>   interrelations!

And here is Ed Roberson, in "City Eclogue," coming from a mix of the realism of William Carlos Williams and the aesthetic of the Black Arts movement, looking at the planting of an urban tree and the city workers shoveling manure off the back of a truck:

> City of words we're not supposed to use
> Where everyone is lying when it's said these words
> are not accurate, that this shit is not the flowering

All of these impulses put under new and interesting pressures the basic procedures of a lyric poem. The other powerful pressure came from the emergence of a self-consciously feminist poetry in the 1970s and 1980s. Looking at the history of women's writing, at Emily Dickinson and Gertrude Stein, Marianne Moore and H.D., Lorine Niedecker and Muriel Rukeyser and Elizabeth Bishop, readers began to see a brilliantly skeptical and inquiring poetry that examined the natural world the female body had been asked to represent. The explosion of that writing came in the next generation—in Sylvia Plath's brief ferocious life and writing, in Denise Levertov and Adrienne Rich, Lucille Clifton and Audre Lorde—and some of that work sent readers back through American women's poetry with new eyes.

A Livable World

In 1988 James Hansen, a professor of environmental science at Columbia University and director of the NASA Goddard Institute on Space Studies, was invited to testify before a congressional committee about the warming of the earth's atmosphere. He had published his first essay on the subject in 1981. By 1988 the planet had experienced four of its hottest years on record, and Hansen was going to explain to the committee what scientists had come to think were the consequences and causes of this phenomena. It was also the year a Harvard entomologist, Edward O. Wilson, published *Biodiversity*, a collection of articles that brought attention to the rapid and accelerating loss of plant and animal species across the earth, mostly from the ecosystem fragmentation caused by the pressures of human population growth and economic development. Other changes were in the offing. A large part of the American manufacturing base that the environmental legislation was intended to regulate was moving overseas into developing countries with cheaper labor pools and weaker regulations. As the economy and the environmental problems it creates became global, so did electronic communication. The world was getting smaller in more ways than one, and in 1989 environmental journalist Bill McKibben argued in *The End of Nature* that, insofar as "nature" meant those parts of the world not essentially affected by human activity, nature was over.

The assimilation of these events fell to the next generation of poets, those coming of age in the 1970s and 1980s, and to the generation after that, and it will fall to the young readers and writers who find themselves holding this book in their hands. It is one of the reasons *The Ecopoetry Anthology* is a singularly rich and timely intervention in a conversation— not always explicitly recognized—that has been going on in American poetry for a long time, really since its beginning. The anthology gives us a look at the evolution of American poetry and the ways poets have imagined their lives on this continent, and their relationship to the changing notions of what nature is and what meanings our relationship to it has given to us. In certain fundamental ways, of course, poetry has always been about nature, because we are organic beings and part of the cycle of birth, flourishing, and death that renews all organic life. Trying to get into right relationship to these cycles is probably the oldest impulse of the kinds of utterance that come down to us as poetry. It is probably the reason, in one way or another, that elegy and ode, the poem that wards off destructive powers in us and outside us, and the poem that sings praise to the creative forces in us and outside us, are the oldest and most persistent forms of poetry. And the reason all poetry is in this sense nature poetry.

Still, it is not hyperbole, I think, to say that what human intelligence discovered about the processes of nature in the nineteenth and twentieth centuries required poets to rethink or feel their way into new understandings of those powers, or to open themselves to new imaginings of it. One can speak of poets "assimilating" the end of nature, and yet it's not at all clear that humans have assimilated the fact that the sun isn't really rising, that it's merely our way of experiencing the earth's revolution around an immobile star—well, immobile in relation to us on earth—or the fact that the starlight we see strewn across the skies comes to us from such vast distances that some of that glittering is the light from balls of gas that burned themselves to extinction a million years ago. One of the pivotal poems of the early twentieth century in English is Stevens's "Thirteen Ways of Looking at a Blackbird." It was written around 1915, and from here, thinking back across what we've come to know about the interior of the atoms that constitute matter, the maps in the tiny brains of migrating birds, the long history of sexual selection that produced the sumptuous plumage of the cockatoo that appears woven into a rug in that other Stevens poem, all the notes played on the expressive organ of the circular staircase of DNA, thirteen hardly seems like the beginning of a set of instances of how we might imagine the world.

Nor is it hyperbole, or merely the ancient human habit of imagining apocalypse, to say that some time at the end of the twentieth or beginning of the twenty-first century—because of climate change, growing population, a rising tide of extinctions among plant and animal species, the shrinking of the last wild places that harbored them, the acidification of the ocean, and the rapid spread of industrial technologies around the world—a new level of crisis was approaching or had already been reached. Poets have certainly sensed this urgency and tried to imagine its meanings. Galway Kinnell, in the later 1980s, could write these lines in a poem that begins as a meditation on the bomb at Hiroshima:

> To de-animalize human mentality, to purge it of obsolete
> evolutionary characteristics, in particular of death,
> which foreknowledge terrorizes the contents of skulls with,
> is the fundamental project of technology . . .

And in the first decade of the twenty-first century D. A. Powell, a poet of a younger generation, could make this account of the American land in a poem titled "republic":

soon, industry and agriculture converged
      and the combustion engine
sowed the dirtclod truck farms green
         with onion tops and chicory

mowed the hay, fed the swine and mutton
    through belts and chutes

cleared the blue oak and the chaparral
      chipping the wood for mulch

backfilled the marshes
    replacing buckbean with dent corn

removed the unsavory foliage of quag
      made the land into a production
made it *produce,* pistoned and oiled
    and forged against its own nature

This kind of poem was called, in the days of the Roman Empire, a geor-
gic. Its theme was agricultural advice. Virgil's poems about beekeeping,
one example, were translated into English by schoolboys for centuries. The
georgic's implicit theme was that the world, intelligently cultivated by peo-
ple kept sane by modesty of appetite, is a garden put into human keeping.
McKibben's proposal—that we have come to the end of nature—is a way
of saying the same thing. The wild as some electric alternative to the city,
or as some imagined freedom from constraint outside our civilized lives,
is over. And the other wild—the earth's actual evolutionary contexts—has
been put into our keeping, just as the weather patterns created by our
relentless use of carbon have made the garden unmanageable.

The young poets who inherited this imagination of our relation to
nature and to ecology as the science of earth housekeeping were—and
are—mostly children of the city and the suburbs. They also inherited a
rich, vital, constantly changing set of traditions in American poetry, which
they proceeded to explore and extend. It is interesting to think of T. S.
Eliot remarking in 1911 that when he got to college there were no models
for how to go about becoming a poet, no handle in the form of a vigorous
and supple style to proceed from. Walt Whitman wasn't available to the
advanced young men and women of his generation. Whitman looked, to
them, like the tiresome, oratorical Victorian who heard America singing.
And Emily Dickinson's poems, which had hardly come into print, carried

with them the legend of a reclusive spinster. In contrast, young poets setting out in the twenty-first century look back at many pathways—the one John Ashbery found out of Wallace Stevens and French poetry, the one Sylvia Plath found out of the greenhouse poems of Theodore Roethke, lineages out of Robert Frost and Hilda Doolittle and William Carlos Williams. Latino and Native American poets and poetries in English had begun to appear and flourish in the 1970s and 1980s. African Americans since the Harlem Renaissance had been developing several crossbred traditions, populist and traditional and avant-garde.

Throughout the twentieth century there was in American poetry a creative tension between traditionalists and avant-gardists, with a populist middle ground that learned and borrowed from both. The traditionalist-populist vein tended to make an expressive poetry that came to its power exploring emotional and psychological states. The avant-gardists tended to be more interested in new techniques, and in perception rather than emotion. By the 1980s this tension came to be described as one between the lyric and the language-based poem. If the confessional poet said, "I feel this," the experimentalist said, "What do you mean by 'I'?" If the nature poet said, "Look at that tree," the avant-gardist said, "Let's deconstruct what we mean in language by 'looking at a tree.'" A poem in this anthology, William Stafford's "Traveling through the Dark," figured in this argument. The San Francisco poet Bob Perelman wrote an essay addressing the romantic-modernist lyric's limitation by analyzing Stafford's poem, an account of an archetypal American experience—the machine-in-the-garden experience of coming upon a deer killed by an automobile.

Traveling through the dark, I found a deer
dead on the edge of the Wilson Creek road.
It is usually best to roll them into the canyon:
the road is narrow; to swerve might make more dead.

The wry understatement of this poem, of a phrase like "usually best" as the policy for driving a car across an already dead animal, the casual conjuring of a known place in naming "the Wilson Creek road," the quiet symbolism of "traveling through the dark," of a "narrow" road, of the impulse "to swerve" are all parts of a way we know to read a masterly poem in this American idiom. Perelman tracks it admiringly and says that this kind of poem—narrating an experience from a first-person point of view, in conscientiously unadorned and unadventurous language, leading to a seamlessly expressed insight or emotion—was used up and probably contributed to our sleepwalking accession to everything in civilization that preserves the status quo. Poets should have, he argued, a more recalcitrant and inventive relation to the language of the poem. I think I have got his argument accurately. It was a point of view that touched off lively arguments among poets in those years when the young scientists across campus were saying that our relation to the earth was in trouble.

The poets of all these lineages mostly found themselves employed by colleges and universities as creative writing programs spread across the country. In this way they shared their generation's common experience of occupational mobility. Most worked in the same institutional settings where geneticists were decoding the human genome and wildlife biologists were holding conferences with titles like "What Species Can Still Be Saved." It's also been an institutional habit of American higher education that poets and humanists and engineers and ecologist don't interact much, though poets are inveterate poachers in the fields of learning.

Most American writers are born in one place, educated in another, and take their adult jobs in another, or several others. These circumstances have made some version of a cosmopolitan style, some postmodernist stance of fragmentation, seem particularly apt to the circumstances of American life even as the need for some kind of engaged citizenship and community has created the conflicting pressure to make a local idiom. One result of these various pressures and possibilities has been the "greening of the humanities," the development of an environmental or ecological literary criticism (ecocriticism) and an environmental literary theory (ecopoetics) in the academy. Another result is the many possible forms of trying to make an art in the present and for the future out of this historical experience: an American ecopoetry.

Such an ecopoetry is in many ways already upon us. Last year two gifted poets in the middle of their careers, the American Forrest Gander and the Australian John Kinsella, collaborated on the book *Redstart: An Ecological Poetics*. Gander, writing an account of the project, has this to say:

> As globalization draws us together and industrialization and human population pressures take their toll on natural habitats, as species and plants flicker and are snuffed from the earth, it may be worthwhile to ask whether an ethnocentric view of human beings as a species independent from others underpins our exploitation of natural resources and sets in motion dire consequences. What we've perpetrated on our environment has certainly affected a poet's means and materials. But can poetry be ecological?

He heads where a poet is apt to head: "Aside from issues of theme and reference, how might syntax, line break, or the shape of the poem on the page express an ecological ethics?" Gander was educated in geology, and one of his poems in this anthology, "Field Guide to Southern Virginia," can stand for the development of a postmodern idiom:

> Snap-on
> tools glinting from magenta
> loosestrife, the air sultry
> with creosote and cicadas.
> You made me to lie down in a peri-Gondwanan back-arc basin.
> Roses of wave ripples and gutter casts.
> Your sex hidden by goat's beard.
> Laminations in the sediment. All
> Preserved as internal molds
> In a soft lilac shale.

The reader can't tell at first whether she is reading about a geological dig or a sexual encounter and probably then decides it's both—and comes to whatever conclusion about nature this thicket of evocative language invites.

It is probably not possible to construct a narrative of all the voices and traditions that have animated American poetry in the last twenty or fifty years. What does seem possible, what Ann Fisher-Wirth and Laura-Gray Street have given us, is their reading, sweeping across 150 years, of the ways American nature poetry developed toward an ecopoetics, toward the necessity of imagining a livable earth.

HISTORICAL

Walt Whitman
(1819–1892)

from Song of Myself

6

A child said *What is the grass?* fetching it to me with full hands;
How could I answer the child? I do not know what it is any more than he.

I guess it must be the flag of my disposition, out of hopeful green stuff
   woven.

Or I guess it is the handkerchief of the Lord,
A scented gift and remembrancer designedly dropt,
Bearing the owner's name someway in the corners, that we may see and
   remark, and say *Whose?*

Or I guess the grass is itself a child, the produced babe of the vegetation.

Or I guess it is a uniform hieroglyphic,
And it means, Sprouting alike in broad zones and narrow zones,
Growing among black folks as among white,
Kanuck, Tuckahoe, Congressman, Cuff, I give them the same, I receive
   them the same.

And now it seems to me the beautiful uncut hair of graves.

Tenderly will I use you curling grass,
It may be you transpire from the breasts of young men,
It may be if I had known them I would have loved them,
It may be you are from old people, or from offspring taken soon out of
   their mothers' laps,
And here you are the mothers' laps.

This grass is very dark to be from the white heads of old mothers,
Darker than the colorless beards of old men,
Dark to come from under the faint red roofs of mouths.

O I perceive after all so many uttering tongues,
And I perceive they do not come from the roofs of mouths for nothing.

I wish I could translate the hints about the dead young men and women,
And the hints about old men and mothers, and the offspring taken soon
    out of their laps.

What do you think has become of the young and old men?
And what do you think has become of the women and children?

They are alive and well somewhere,
The smallest sprout shows there is really no death,
And if ever there was it led forward life, and does not wait at the end to
    arrest it,
And ceas'd the moment life appear'd.

All goes onward and outward, nothing collapses,
And to die is different from what any one supposed, and luckier.

Out of the Cradle Endlessly Rocking

Out of the cradle endlessly rocking,
Out of the mocking-bird's throat, the musical shuttle,
Out of the Ninth-month midnight,
Over the sterile sands and the fields beyond, where the child leaving his
    bed wander'd alone, bareheaded, barefoot,
Down from the shower'd halo,
Up from the mystic play of shadows twining and twisting as if they were
    alive,
Out from the patches of briers and blackberries,
From the memories of the bird that chanted to me,
From your memories sad brother, from the fitful risings and fallings I
    heard,
From under that yellow half-moon late-risen and swollen as if with tears,
From those beginning notes of yearning and love there in the mist,
From the thousand responses of my heart never to cease,
From the myriad thence-arous'd words,
From the word stronger and more delicious than any,
From such as now they start the scene revisiting,
As a flock, twittering, rising, or overhead passing,
Borne hither, ere all eludes me, hurriedly,
A man, yet by these tears a little boy again,

Throwing myself on the sand, confronting the waves,
I, chanter of pains and joys, uniter of here and hereafter,
Taking all hints to use them, but swiftly leaping beyond them,
A reminiscence sing.

Once Paumanok,
When the lilac-scent was in the air and Fifth-month grass was growing,
Up this sea-shore in some briers,
Two feather'd guests from Alabama, two together,
And their nest, and four light-green eggs spotted with brown,
And every day the he-bird to and fro near at hand,
And every day the she-bird crouch'd on her nest, silent, with bright eyes,
And every day I, a curious boy, never too close, never disturbing them,
Cautiously peering, absorbing, translating.

Shine! shine! shine!
Pour down your warmth, great sun!
While we bask, we two together.

Two together!
Winds blow south, or winds blow north,
Day come white, or night come black,
Home, or rivers and mountains from home,
Singing all time, minding no time,
While we two keep together.

Till of a sudden,
May-be kill'd, unknown to her mate,
One forenoon the she-bird crouch'd not on the nest,
Nor return'd that afternoon, nor the next,
Nor ever appear'd again.

And thenceforward all summer in the sound of the sea,
And at night under the full of the moon in calmer weather,
Over the hoarse surging of the sea,
Or flitting from brier to brier by day,
I saw, I heard at intervals the remaining one, the he-bird,
The solitary guest from Alabama.

Blow! blow! blow!
Blow up sea-winds along Paumanok's shore;
I wait and I wait till you blow my mate to me.

Yes, when the stars glisten'd,
All night long on the prong of a moss-scallop'd stake,
Down almost amid the slapping waves,
Sat the lone singer wonderful causing tears.

He call'd on his mate,
He pour'd forth the meanings which I of all men know.

Yes my brother I know,
The rest might not, but I have treasur'd every note,
For more than once dimly down to the beach gliding,
Silent, avoiding the moonbeams, blending myself with the shadows,
Recalling now the obscure shapes, the echoes, the sounds and sights after
    their sorts,
The white arms out in the breakers tirelessly tossing,
I, with bare feet, a child, the wind wafting my hair,
Listen'd long and long.

Listen'd to keep, to sing, now translating the notes,
Following you my brother.

Soothe! soothe! soothe!
Close on its wave soothes the wave behind,
And again another behind embracing and lapping, every one close,
But my love soothes not me, not me.

Low hangs the moon, it rose late,
It is lagging—O I think it is heavy with love, with love.

O madly the sea pushes upon the land,
With love, with love.

O night! do I not see my love fluttering out among the breakers?
What is that little black thing I see there in the white?

Loud! loud! loud!
Loud I call to you, my love!

High and clear I shoot my voice over the waves,
Surely you must know who is here, is here,
You must know who I am, my love.

Low-hanging moon!
What is that dusky spot in your brown yellow?
O it is the shape, the shape of my mate!
O moon do not keep her from me any longer.

Land! land! O land!
Whichever way I turn, O I think you could give me my mate back again if
    you only would,
For I am almost sure I see her dimly whichever way I look.

O rising stars!
Perhaps the one I want so much will rise, will rise with some of you.

O throat! O trembling throat!
Sound clearer through the atmosphere!
Pierce the woods, the earth,
Somewhere listening to catch you must be the one I want.

Shake out carols!
Solitary here, the night's carols!
Carols of lonesome love! death's carols!
Carols under that lagging, yellow, waning moon!
O under that moon where she droops almost down into the sea!
O reckless despairing carols.

But soft! sink low!
Soft! let me just murmur,
And do you wait a moment you husky-nois'd sea,
For somewhere I believe I heard my mate responding to me,
So faint, I must be still, be still to listen,
But not altogether still, for then she might not come immediately to me.

Hither my love!
Here I am! here!
With this just-sustain'd note I announce myself to you,
This gentle call is for you my love, for you.

Do not be decoy'd elsewhere,
That is the whistle of the wind, it is not my voice,
That is the fluttering, the fluttering of the spray,
Those are the shadows of leaves.

O darkness! O in vain!
O I am very sick and sorrowful.

O brown halo in the sky near the moon, drooping upon the sea!
O troubled reflection in the sea!
O throat! O throbbing heart!
And I singing uselessly, uselessly all the night.

O past! O happy life! O songs of joy!
In the air, in the woods, over fields,
Loved! loved! loved! loved! loved!
But my mate no more, no more with me!
We two together no more.

The aria sinking,
All else continuing, the stars shining,
The winds blowing, the notes of the bird continuous echoing,
With angry moans the fierce old mother incessantly moaning,
On the sands of Paumanok's shore gray and rustling,
The yellow half-moon enlarged, sagging down, drooping, the face of the
    sea almost touching,
The boy ecstatic, with his bare feet the waves, with his hair the
    atmosphere dallying,
The love in the heart long pent, now loose, now at last tumultuously
    bursting,
The aria's meaning, the ears, the soul, swiftly depositing,
The strange tears down the cheeks coursing,
The colloquy there, the trio, each uttering,
The undertone, the savage old mother incessantly crying,
To the boy's soul's questions sullenly timing, some drown'd secret hissing,
To the outsetting bard.

Demon or bird! (said the boy's soul,)
Is it indeed toward your mate you sing? or is it really to me?
For I, that was a child, my tongue's use sleeping, now I have heard you,
Now in a moment I know what I am for, I awake,
And already a thousand singers, a thousand songs, clearer, louder and
    more sorrowful than yours,
A thousand warbling echoes have started to life within me, never to die.

O you singer solitary, singing by yourself, projecting me,
O solitary me listening, never more shall I cease perpetuating you,
Never more shall I escape, never more the reverberations,
Never more the cries of unsatisfied love be absent from me,
Never again leave me to be the peaceful child I was before what there in
    the night,
By the sea under the yellow and sagging moon,
The messenger there arous'd, the fire, the sweet hell within,
The unknown want, the destiny of me.

O give me the clew! (it lurks in the night here somewhere,)
O if I am to have so much, let me have more!

A word then, (for I will conquer it,)
The word final, superior to all,
Subtle, sent up—what is it?—I listen;
Are you whispering it, and have been all the time, you sea-waves?
Is that it from your liquid rims and wet sands?

Whereto answering, the sea,
Delaying not, hurrying not,
Whisper'd me through the night, and very plainly before daybreak,
Lisp'd to me the low and delicious word death,
And again death, death, death, death,
Hissing melodious, neither like the bird nor like my arous'd child's heart,
But edging near as privately for me rustling at my feet,
Creeping thence steadily up to my ears and laving me softly all over,
Death, death, death, death, death.
Which I do not forget,
But fuse the song of my dusky demon and brother,
That he sang to me in the moonlight on Paumanok's gray beach,
With the thousand responsive songs at random,
My own songs awaked from that hour,
And with them the key, the word up from the waves,
The word of the sweetest song and all songs,
That strong and delicious word which, creeping to my feet,
(Or like some old crone rocking the cradle, swathed in sweet garments,
    bending aside,)
The sea whisper'd me.

Crossing Brooklyn Ferry

1

Flood-tide below me! I see you face to face!
Clouds of the west—sun there half an hour high—I see you also face to
  face.

Crowds of men and women attired in the usual costumes, how curious
  you are to me!
On the ferry-boats the hundreds and hundreds that cross, returning
  home, are more curious to me than you suppose,
And you that shall cross from shore to shore years hence are more to me,
  and more in my meditations, than you might suppose.

2

The impalpable sustenance of me from all things at all hours of the day,
The simple, compact, well-join'd scheme, myself disintegrated, every one
  disintegrated yet part of the scheme,
The similitudes of the past and those of the future,
The glories strung like beads on my smallest sights and hearings, on the
  walk in the street and the passage over the river,
The current rushing so swiftly and swimming with me far away,
The others that are to follow me, the ties between me and them,
The certainty of others, the life, love, sight, hearing of others.

Others will enter the gates of the ferry and cross from shore to shore,
Others will watch the run of the flood-tide,
Others will see the shipping of Manhattan north and west, and the
  heights of Brooklyn to the south and east,
Others will see the islands large and small;
Fifty years hence, others will see them as they cross, the sun half an hour
  high,
A hundred years hence, or ever so many hundred years hence, others will
  see them,
Will enjoy the sunset, the pouring-in of the flood-tide, the falling-back to
  the sea of the ebb-tide.

3

It avails not, time nor place—distance avails not,
I am with you, you men and women of a generation, or ever so many
  generations hence,
Just as you feel when you look on the river and sky, so I felt,
Just as any of you is one of a living crowd, I was one of a crowd,
Just as you are refresh'd by the gladness of the river and the bright flow, I
  was refresh'd,
Just as you stand and lean on the rail, yet hurry with the swift current, I
  stood yet was hurried,
Just as you look on the numberless masts of ships and the thick-stemm'd
  pipes of steamboats, I look'd.

I too many and many a time cross'd the river of old,
Watched the Twelfth-month sea-gulls, saw them high in the air floating
  with motionless wings, oscillating their bodies,
Saw how the glistening yellow lit up parts of their bodies and left the rest
  in strong shadow,
Saw the slow-wheeling circles and the gradual edging toward the south,
Saw the reflection of the summer sky in the water,
Had my eyes dazzled by the shimmering track of beams,
Look'd at the fine centrifugal spokes of light round the shape of my head
  in the sunlit water,
Look'd on the haze on the hills southward and south-westward,
Look'd on the vapor as it flew in fleeces tinged with violet,
Look'd toward the lower bay to notice the vessels arriving,
Saw their approach, saw aboard those that were near me,
Saw the white sails of schooners and sloops, saw the ships at anchor,
The sailors at work in the rigging or out astride the spars,
The round masts, the swinging motion of the hulls, the slender
  serpentine pennants,
The large and small steamers in motion, the pilots in their pilot-houses,
The white wake left by the passage, the quick tremulous whirl of the
  wheels,
The flags of all nations, the falling of them at sunset,
The scallop-edged waves in the twilight, the ladled cups, the frolicsome
  crests and glistening,
The stretch afar growing dimmer and dimmer, the gray walls of the
  granite storehouses by the docks,

On the river the shadowy group, the big steam-tug closely flank'd on each
  side by the barges, the hay-boat, the belated lighter,
On the neighboring shore the fires from the foundry chimneys burning
  high and glaringly into the night,
Casting their flicker of black contrasted with wild red and yellow light
  over the tops of houses, and down into the clefts of streets.

4

These and all else were to me the same as they are to you,
I loved well those cities, loved well the stately and rapid river,
The men and women I saw were all near to me,
Others the same—others who look back on me because I look'd forward
  to them,
(The time will come, though I stop here to-day and to-night.)

5

What is it then between us?
What is the count of the scores or hundreds of years between us?

Whatever it is, it avails not—distance avails not, and place avails not,
I too lived, Brooklyn of ample hills was mine,
I too walk'd the streets of Manhattan island, and bathed in the waters
  around it,
I too felt the curious abrupt questionings stir within me,
In the day among crowds of people sometimes they came upon me,
In my walks home late at night or as I lay in my bed they came upon me,
I too had been struck from the float forever held in solution,
I too had receiv'd identity by my body,
That I was I knew was of my body, and what I should be I knew I should
  be of my body.

6

It is not upon you alone the dark patches fall,
The dark threw its patches down upon me also,
The best I had done seem'd to me blank and suspicious,
My great thoughts as I supposed them, were they not in reality meagre?
Nor is it you alone who know what it is to be evil,
I am he who knew what it was to be evil,
I too knitted the old knot of contrariety,

Blabb'd, blush'd, resented, lied, stole, grudg'd,
Had guile, anger, lust, hot wishes I dared not speak,
Was wayward, vain, greedy, shallow, sly, cowardly, malignant,
The wolf, the snake, the hog, not wanting in me,
The cheating look, the frivolous word, the adulterous wish, not wanting,
Refusals, hates, postponements, meanness, laziness, none of these
    wanting,
Was one with the rest, the days and haps of the rest,
Was call'd by my nighest name by clear loud voices of young men as they
    saw me approaching or passing,
Felt their arms on my neck as I stood, or the negligent leaning of their
    flesh against me as I sat,
Saw many I loved in the street or ferry-boat or public assembly, yet never
    told them a word,
Lived the same life with the rest, the same old laughing, gnawing,
    sleeping,
Play'd the part that still looks back on the actor or actress,
The same old role, the role that is what we make it, as great as we like,
Or as small as we like, or both great and small.

7

Closer yet I approach you,
What thought you have of me now, I had as much of you—I laid in my
    stores in advance,
I consider'd long and seriously of you before you were born.

Who was to know what should come home to me?
Who knows but I am enjoying this?
Who knows, for all the distance, but I am as good as looking at you now,
    for all you cannot see me?

8

Ah, what can ever be more stately and admirable to me than mast-
    hemm'd Manhattan?
River and sunset and scallop-edg'd waves of flood-tide?
The sea-gulls oscillating their bodies, the hay-boat in the twilight, and
    the belated lighter?
What gods can exceed these that clasp me by the hand, and with voices I
    love call me promptly and loudly by my nighest name as I approach?

What is more subtle than this which ties me to the woman or man that
    looks in my face?
Which fuses me into you now, and pours my meaning into you?

We understand then do we not?
What I promis'd without mentioning it, have you not accepted?
What the study could not teach—what the preaching could not
    accomplish is accomplish'd, is it not?

    9

Flow on, river! flow with the flood-tide, and ebb with the ebb-tide!
Frolic on, crested and scallop-edg'd waves!
Gorgeous clouds of the sunset! drench with your splendor me, or the
    men and women generations after me!
Cross from shore to shore, countless crowds of passengers!
Stand up, tall masts of Mannahatta! stand up, beautiful hills of Brooklyn!
Throb, baffled and curious brain! throw out questions and answers!
Suspend here and everywhere, eternal float of solution!
Gaze, loving and thirsting eyes, in the house or street or public assembly!
Sound out, voices of young men! loudly and musically call me by my
    nighest name!
Live, old life! play the part that looks back on the actor or actress!
Play the old role, the role that is great or small according as one makes it!
Consider, you who peruse me, whether I may not in unknown ways be
    looking upon you;
Be firm, rail over the river, to support those who lean idly, yet haste with
    the hasting current!
Fly on, sea-birds! fly sideways, or wheel in large circles high in the air;
Receive the summer sky, you water, and faithfully hold it till all downcast
    eyes have time to take it from you!
Diverge, fine spokes of light, from the shape of my head, or any one's
    head, in the sunlit water!
Come on, ships from the lower bay! pass up or down, white-sail'd
    schooners, sloops, lighters!
Flaunt away, flags of all nations! be duly lower'd at sunset!
Burn high your fires, foundry chimneys! cast black shadows at nightfall!
    cast red and yellow light over the tops of the houses!
Appearances, now or henceforth, indicate what you are,
You necessary film, continue to envelop the soul,

About my body for me, and your body for you, be hung our divinest aromas,
Thrive, cities—bring your freight, bring your shows, ample and sufficient rivers,
Expand, being than which none else is perhaps more spiritual,
Keep your places, objects than which none else is more lasting.

You have waited, you always wait, you dumb, beautiful ministers,
We receive you with free sense at last, and are insatiate henceforward,
Not you any more shall be able to foil us, or withhold yourselves from us,
We use you, and do not cast you aside—we plant you permanently within us,
We fathom you not—we love you—there is perfection in you also,
You furnish your parts toward eternity,
Great or small, you furnish your parts toward the soul.

Emily Dickinson

(1830–1886)

#116/328

A Bird came down the Walk—
He did not know I saw—
He bit an Angleworm in halves
And ate the fellow, raw,

And then he drank a Dew
From a convenient Grass—
And then hopped sidewise to the Wall
To let a Beetle pass—

He glanced with rapid eyes
That hurried all around—
They looked like frightened Beads, I thought—
He stirred his Velvet Head

Like one in danger, Cautious,
I offered him a Crumb
And he unrolled his feathers
And rowed him softer home—

Than Oars divide the Ocean,
Too silver for a seam—
Or Butterflies, off Banks of Noon,
Leap, plashless as they swim.

#126/348

I dreaded that first Robin, so,
But He is mastered, now,
I'm some accustomed to Him grown,
He hurts a little, though—

I thought if I could only live
Till that first Shout got by—
Not all Pianos in the Woods
Had power to mangle me—

I dared not meet the Daffodils—
For fear their Yellow Gown
Would pierce me with a fashion
So foreign to my own—

I wished the Grass would hurry—
So—when 'twas time to see—
He'd be too tall, the tallest one
Could stretch—to look at me—

I could not bear the Bees should come,
I wished they'd stay away
In those dim countries where they go,
What word had they, for me?

They're here, though; not a creature failed—
No Blossom stayed away
In gentle deference to me—
The Queen of Calvary—

Each one salutes me, as he goes,
And I, my childish Plumes,
Lift, in bereaved acknowledgment
Of their unthinking Drums—

#184/465

I heard a Fly buzz—when I died—
The Stillness in the Room
Was like the Stillness in the Air—
Between the Heaves of Storm—

The Eyes around—had wrung them dry—
And Breaths were gathering firm
For that last Onset—when the King
Be witnessed—in the Room—

I willed my Keepsakes—Signed away
What portion of me be
Assignable—and then it was
There interposed a Fly—

With Blue—uncertain stumbling Buzz—
Between the light—and me—
And then the Windows failed—and then
I could not see to see—

#209/520

I started Early—Took my Dog—
And visited the Sea—
The Mermaids in the Basement
Came out to look at me—

And Frigates—in the Upper Floor
Extended Hempen Hands—
Presuming Me to be a Mouse—
Aground—upon the Sands—

But no Man moved Me—till the Tide
Went past my simple Shoe—
And past my Apron—and my Belt
And past my Bodice—too—

And made as He would eat me up—
As wholly as a Dew
Upon a Dandelion's Sleeve—
And then—I started—too—

And He—He followed—close behind—
I felt His Silver Heel
Upon my Ankle—Then my Shoes
Would overflow with Pearl—

Until We met the Solid Town—
No One He seemed to know—
And bowing—with a Mighty look—
At me—The Sea withdrew—

#498/1400

What mystery pervades a well!
That water lives so far—
A neighbor from another world
Residing in a jar

Whose limit none have ever seen,
But just his lid of glass—
Like looking every time you please
In an abyss's face!

The grass does not appear afraid,
I often wonder he
Can stand so close and look so bold
To what is awe to me.

Related somehow they may be,
The sedge stands next the sea—
Where he is floorless
And does no timidity betray

But nature is a stranger yet;
The ones that cite her most
Have never passed her haunted house,
Nor simplified her ghost.

To pity those that know her not
Is helped by the regret
That those who know her, know her less
The nearer her they get.

#537/1593

There came a Wind like a Bugle—
It quivered through the Grass
And a Green Chill upon the Heat
So ominous did pass
We barred the Windows and the Doors
As from an Emerald Ghost—

The Doom's electric Moccasin
That very instant passed—
On a strange Mob of panting Trees
And Fences fled away
And Rivers where the Houses ran
Those looked that lived—that Day—
The Bell within the steeple wild
The flying tidings told—
How much can come
And much can go,
And yet abide the World!

Robert Frost

(1874–1963)

An Old Man's Winter Night

All out-of-doors looked darkly in at him
Through the thin frost, almost in separate stars,
That gathers on the pane in empty rooms.
What kept his eyes from giving back the gaze
Was the lamp tilted near them in his hand.
What kept him from remembering what it was
That brought him to that creaking room was age.
He stood with barrels round him—at a loss.
And having scared the cellar under him
In clomping here, he scared it once again
In clomping off—and scared the outer night,
Which has its sounds, familiar, like the roar
Of trees and crack of branches, common things,
But nothing so like beating on a box.
A light he was to no one but himself
Where now he sat, concerned with he knew what,
A quiet light, and then not even that.
He consigned to the moon—such as she was,
So late-arising—to the broken moon,
As better than the sun in any case
For such a charge, his snow upon the roof,
His icicles along the wall to keep;
And slept. The log that shifted with a jolt
Once in the stove, disturbed him and he shifted,
And eased his heavy breathing, but still slept.
One aged man—one man—can't keep a house,
A farm, a countryside, or if he can,
It's thus he does it of a winter night.

The Need of Being Versed in Country Things

The house had gone to bring again
To the midnight sky a sunset glow.
Now the chimney was all of the house that stood,
Like a pistil after the petals go.

The barn opposed across the way,
That would have joined the house in flame
Had it been the will of the wind, was left
To bear forsaken the place's name.

No more it opened with all one end
For teams that came by the stony road
To drum on the floor with scurrying hoofs
And brush the mow with the summer load.

The birds that came to it through the air
At broken windows flew out and in,
Their murmur more like the sigh we sigh
From too much dwelling on what has been.

Yet for them the lilac renewed its leaf,
And the aged elm, though touched with fire;
And the dry pump flung up an awkward arm;
And the fence post carried a strand of wire.

For them there was really nothing sad.
But though they rejoiced in the nest they kept,
One had to be versed in country things
Not to believe the phoebes wept.

Stopping by Woods on a Snowy Evening

Whose woods these are I think I know.
His house is in the village, though;
He will not see me stopping here
To watch his woods fill up with snow.

My little horse must think it queer
To stop without a farmhouse near
Between the woods and frozen lake
The darkest evening of the year.

He gives his harness bells a shake
To ask if there is some mistake.
The only other sound's the sweep
Of easy wind and downy flake.

The woods are lovely, dark and deep,
But I have promises to keep,
And miles to go before I sleep,
And miles to go before I sleep.

Spring Pools

These pools that, though in forests, still reflect
The total sky almost without defect,
And like the flowers beside them, chill and shiver,
Will like the flowers beside them soon be gone,
And yet not out by any brook or river,
But up by roots to bring dark foliage on.

The trees that have it in their pent-up buds
To darken nature and be summer woods—
Let them think twice before they use their powers
To blot out and drink up and sweep away
These flowery waters and these watery flowers
From snow that melted only yesterday.

Design

I found a dimpled spider, fat and white,
On a white heal-all, holding up a moth
Like a white piece of rigid satin cloth—
Assorted characters of death and blight
Mixed ready to begin the morning right,
Like the ingredients of a witches' broth—
A snow-drop spider, a flower like a froth,
And dead wings carried like a paper kite.

What had that flower to do with being white,
The wayside blue and innocent heal-all?
What brought the kindred spider to that height,
Then steered the white moth thither in the night?
What but design of darkness to appall?—
If design govern in a thing so small.

The Most of It

He thought he kept the universe alone;
For all the voice in answer he could wake
Was but the mocking echo of his own
From some tree-hidden cliff across the lake.
Some morning from the boulder-broken beach
He would cry out on life, that what it wants
Is not its own love back in copy speech,
But counter-love, original response.
And nothing ever came of what he cried
Unless it was the embodiment that crashed
In the cliff's talus on the other side,
And then in the far-distant water splashed,
But after a time allowed for it to swim,
Instead of proving human when it neared
And someone else additional to him,
As a great buck it powerfully appeared,

Pushing the crumpled water up ahead,
And landed pouring like a waterfall,
And stumbled through the rocks with horny tread,
And forced the underbrush—and that was all.

Directive

Back out of all this now too much for us,
Back in a time made simple by the loss
Of detail, burned, dissolved, and broken off
Like graveyard marble sculpture in the weather,
There is a house that is no more a house
Upon a farm that is no more a farm
And in a town that is no more a town.
The road there, if you'll let a guide direct you
Who only has at heart your getting lost,
May seem as if it should have been a quarry—
Great monolithic knees the former town
Long since gave up pretense of keeping covered.
And there's a story in a book about it:
Besides the wear of iron wagon wheels
The ledges show lines ruled southeast-northwest,
The chisel work of an enormous Glacier
That braced his feet against the Arctic Pole.
You must not mind a certain coolness from him
Still said to haunt this side of Panther Mountain.
Nor need you mind the serial ordeal
Of being watched from forty cellar holes
As if by eye pairs out of forty firkins.
As for the woods' excitement over you
That sends light rustle rushes to their leaves,
Charge that to upstart inexperience.
Where were they all not twenty years ago?
They think too much of having shaded out
A few old pecker-fretted apple trees.
Make yourself up a cheering song of how

Someone's road home from work this once was,
Who may be just ahead of you on foot
Or creaking with a buggy load of grain.
The height of the adventure is the height
Of country where two village cultures faded
Into each other. Both of them are lost.
And if you're lost enough to find yourself
By now, pull in your ladder road behind you
And put a sign up CLOSED to all but me.
Then make yourself at home. The only field
Now left's no bigger than a harness gall.
First there's the children's house of make-believe,
Some shattered dishes underneath a pine,
The playthings in the playhouse of the children.
Weep for what little things could make them glad.
Then for the house that is no more a house,
But only a belilaced cellar hole,
Now slowly closing like a dent in dough.
This was no playhouse but a house in earnest.
Your destination and your destiny's
A brook that was the water of the house,
Cold as a spring as yet so near its source,
Too lofty and original to rage.
(We know the valley streams that when aroused
Will leave their tatters hung on barb and thorn.)
I have kept hidden in the instep arch
Of an old cedar at the waterside
A broken drinking goblet like the Grail
Under a spell so the wrong ones can't find it,
So can't get saved, as Saint Mark says they mustn't.
(I stole the goblet from the children's playhouse.)
Here are your waters and your watering place.
Drink and be whole again beyond confusion.

Wallace Stevens
(1879–1955)

Sunday Morning

I

Complacencies of the peignoir, and late
Coffee and oranges in a sunny chair,
And the green freedom of a cockatoo
Upon a rug mingle to dissipate
The holy hush of ancient sacrifice.
She dreams a little, and she feels the dark
Encroachment of that old catastrophe,
As a calm darkens among water-lights.
The pungent oranges and bright, green wings
Seem things in some procession of the dead,
Winding across wide water, without sound.
The day is like wide water, without sound,
Stilled for the passing of her dreaming feet
Over the seas, to silent Palestine,
Dominion of the blood and sepulchre.

II

Why should she give her bounty to the dead?
What is divinity if it can come
Only in silent shadows and in dreams?
Shall she not find in comforts of the sun,
In pungent fruit and bright, green wings, or else
In any balm or beauty of the earth,
Things to be cherished like the thought of heaven?
Divinity must live within herself:
Passions of rain, or moods in falling snow;
Grievings in loneliness, or unsubdued
Elations when the forest blooms; gusty
Emotions on wet roads on autumn nights;
All pleasures and all pains, remembering

The bough of summer and the winter branch.
These are the measures destined for her soul.

III

Jove in the clouds had his inhuman birth.
No mother suckled him, no sweet land gave
Large-mannered motions to his mythy mind.
He moved among us, as a muttering king,
Magnificent, would move among his hinds,
Until our blood, commingling, virginal,
With heaven, brought such requital to desire
The very hinds discerned it, in a star.
Shall our blood fail? Or shall it come to be
The blood of paradise? And shall the earth
Seem all of paradise that we shall know?
The sky will be much friendlier then than now,
A part of labor and a part of pain,
And next in glory to enduring love,
Not this dividing and indifferent blue.

IV

She says, "I am content when wakened birds,
Before they fly, test the reality
Of misty fields, by their sweet questionings;
But when the birds are gone, and their warm fields
Return no more, where, then, is paradise?"
There is not any haunt of prophecy,
Nor any old chimera of the grave,
Neither the golden underground, nor isle
Melodious, where spirits gat them home,
Nor visionary south, nor cloudy palm
Remote on heaven's hill, that has endured
As April's green endures; or will endure
Like her remembrance of awakened birds,
Or her desire for June and evening, tipped
By the consummation of the swallow's wings.

V

She says, "But in contentment I still feel
The need of some imperishable bliss."
Death is the mother of beauty; hence from her,
Alone, shall come fulfilment to our dreams
And our desires. Although she strews the leaves
Of sure obliteration on our paths,
The path sick sorrow took, the many paths
Where triumph rang its brassy phrase, or love
Whispered a little out of tenderness,
She makes the willow shiver in the sun
For maidens who were wont to sit and gaze
Upon the grass, relinquished to their feet.
She causes boys to pile new plums and pears
On disregarded plate. The maidens taste
And stray impassioned in the littering leaves.

VI

Is there no change of death in paradise?
Does ripe fruit never fall? Or do the boughs
Hang always heavy in that perfect sky,
Unchanging, yet so like our perishing earth,
With rivers like our own that seek for seas
They never find, the same receding shores
That never touch with inarticulate pang?
Why set the pear upon those river-banks
Or spice the shores with odors of the plum?
Alas, that they should wear our colors there,
The silken weavings of our afternoons,
And pick the strings of our insipid lutes!
Death is the mother of beauty, mystical,
Within whose burning bosom we devise
Our earthly mothers waiting, sleeplessly.

VII

Supple and turbulent, a ring of men
Shall chant in orgy on a summer morn
Their boisterous devotion to the sun,
Not as a god, but as a god might be,
Naked among them, like a savage source.
Their chant shall be a chant of paradise,
Out of their blood, returning to the sky;
And in their chant shall enter, voice by voice,
The windy lake wherein their lord delights,
The trees, like serafin, and echoing hills,
That choir among themselves long afterward.
They shall know well the heavenly fellowship
Of men that perish and of summer morn.
And whence they came and whither they shall go
The dew upon their feet shall manifest.

VIII

She hears, upon that water without sound,
A voice that cries, "The tomb in Palestine
Is not the porch of spirits lingering.
It is the grave of Jesus, where he lay."
We live in an old chaos of the sun,
Or old dependency of day and night,
Or island solitude, unsponsored, free,
Of that wide water, inescapable.
Deer walk upon our mountains, and the quail
Whistle about us their spontaneous cries;
Sweet berries ripen in the wilderness;
And, in the isolation of the sky,
At evening, casual flocks of pigeons make
Ambiguous undulations as they sink,
Downward to darkness, on extended wings.

Anecdote of the Jar

I placed a jar in Tennessee,
And round it was, upon a hill.
It made the slovenly wilderness
Surround that hill.

The wilderness rose up to it,
And sprawled around, no longer wild.
The jar was round upon the ground
And tall and of a port in air.

It took dominion everywhere.
The jar was gray and bare.
It did not give of bird or bush,
Like nothing else in Tennessee.

The Snow Man

One must have a mind of winter
To regard the frost and the boughs
Of the pine-trees crusted with snow;

And have been cold a long time
To behold the junipers shagged with ice,
The spruces rough in the distant glitter

Of the January sun; and not to think
Of any misery in the sound of the wind,
In the sound of a few leaves,

Which is the sound of the land
Full of the same wind
That is blowing in the same bare place

For the listener, who listens in the snow,
And, nothing himself, beholds
Nothing that is not there and the nothing that is.

The River of Rivers in Connecticut

There is a great river this side of Stygia,
Before one comes to the first black cataracts
And trees that lack the intelligence of trees.

In that river, far this side of Stygia,
The mere flowing of the water is a gayety,
Flashing and flashing in the sun. On its banks,

No shadow walks. The river is fateful,
Like the last one. But there is no ferryman.
He could not bend against its propelling force.

It is not to be seen beneath the appearances
That tell of it. The steeple at Farmington
Stands glistening and Haddam shines and sways.

It is the third commonness with light and air,
A curriculum, a vigor, a local abstraction...
Call it, once more, a river, an unnamed flowing,

Space-filled, reflecting the seasons, the folk-lore
Of each of the senses; call it, again and again,
The river that flows nowhere, like a sea.

William Carlos Williams
(1883–1963)

Spring and All

By the road to the contagious hospital
under the surge of the blue
mottled clouds driven from the
northeast—a cold wind. Beyond, the
waste of broad, muddy fields
brown with dried weeds, standing and fallen

patches of standing water
the scattering of tall trees

All along the road the reddish
purplish, forked, upstanding, twiggy
stuff of bushes and small trees
with dead, brown leaves under them
leafless vines—

Lifeless in appearance, sluggish
dazed spring approaches—

They enter the new world naked,
cold, uncertain of all
save that they enter. All about them
the cold, familiar wind—

Now the grass, tomorrow
the stiff curl of wildcarrot leaf

One by one objects are defined—
It quickens: clarity, outline of leaf

But now the stark dignity of
entrance—Still, the profound change
has come upon them: rooted, they
grip down and begin to awaken

The Sea-Elephant

Trundled from
the strangeness of the sea—
a kind of
heaven—

Ladies and Gentlemen!
the greatest
sea-monster ever exhibited
alive

the gigantic
sea-elephant! O wallow
of flesh where
are

there fish enough for
that
appetite stupidity
cannot lessen?

Sick
of April's smallness
the little
leaves—

Flesh has lief of you
enormous sea—
Speak!
Blouaugh! (feed

me) my
flesh is riven—
fish after fish into his maw
unswallowing

to let them glide down
gulching back
half spittle half
brine

the
troubled eyes—torn
from the sea.
(In

a practical voice) They
ought
to put it back where
it came from.

Gape.
Strange head—
told by old sailors—
rising

bearded
to the surface—and
the only
sense out of them

is that woman's
Yes
it's wonderful but they
ought to

put it
back into the sea where
it came from.
Blouaugh!

Swing—ride
walk
on wires—toss balls
stoop and

contort yourselves—
But I
am love. I am
from the sea—

Blouaugh!
there is no crime save
the too-heavy
body

the sea
held playfully—comes
to the surface
the water

boiling
about the head the cows
scattering
fish dripping from

the bounty
of . . . and Spring
they say
Spring is icummen in—

Between Walls

the back wings
of the

hospital where
nothing

will grow lie
cinders

in which shine
the broken

pieces of a green
bottle

Raleigh Was Right

We cannot go to the country
for the country will bring us no peace
What can the small violets tell us
that grow on furry stems in
the long grass among lance shaped leaves?

Though you praise us
and call to mind the poets
who sung of our loveliness
it was long ago!
long ago! when country people
would plow and sow with
flowering minds and pockets at ease—
if ever this were true.

Not now. Love itself a flower
with roots in a parched ground.
Empty pockets make empty heads.
Cure it if you can but
do not believe that we can live
today in the country
for the country will bring us no peace.

The High Bridge above the Tagus River at Toledo

A young man, alone, on the high bridge over the Tagus which was too
    narrow to allow the sheep driven by the lean, enormous dogs whose
    hind legs worked slowly on cogs
to pass easily . . .
    (he didn't speak the language)

Pressed against the parapet either side by the crowding sheep, the
    relentless pressure of the dogs communicated itself to him also
above the waters in the gorge below.
They were hounds to him rather than sheep dogs because of their size
    and savage appearance, dog tired from the day's work.
The stiff jerking movement of the hind legs, the hanging heads at the
    shepherd's heels, slowly followed the excited and crowding sheep.

The whole flock, the shepherd and the dogs, were covered with dust as if
    they had been all day long on the road. The pace of the sheep, slow in
    the mass,
governed the man and the dogs. They were approaching the city at
    nightfall, the long journey completed.

In old age they walk in the old man's dreams and still walk in his dreams,
    peacefully continuing in his verse forever.

Ezra Pound
(1885–1972)

The Tree

I stood still and was a tree amid the wood,
Knowing the truth of things unseen before;
Of Daphne and the laurel bough
And that god-feasting couple old
That grew elm-oak amid the wold.
'Twas not until the gods had been
Kindly entreated, and been brought within
Unto the hearth of their heart's home
That they might do this wonder thing;
Nathless I have been a tree amid the wood
And many a new thing understood
That was rank folly to my head before.

Salutation

O generation of the thoroughly smug
    and thoroughly uncomfortable,
I have seen fishermen picnicking in the sun,
I have seen them with untidy families,
I have seen their smiles full of teeth
    and heard ungainly laughter.
And I am happier than you are,
And they were happier than I am;
And the fish swim in the lake
    and do not even own clothing.

Ancient Music

Winter is icummen in,
Lhude sing Goddamm,
Raineth drop and staineth slop,
And how the wind doth ramm!
                    Sing: Goddamm.
Skiddeth bus and sloppeth us,
An ague hath my ham.
Freezeth river, turneth liver,
                    Damn you, sing: Goddamm.
Goddamm, Goddamm, 'tis why I am, Goddamm,
                    So 'gainst the winter's balm.
Sing goddamm, damm, sing Goddamm.
Sing goddamm, sing goddamm, DAMM.

from Canto LXXXI

What thou lovest well remains,
                    the rest is dross
What thou lov'st well shall not be reft from thee
What thou lov'st well is thy true heritage
Whose world, or mine or theirs
                    or is it of none?
First came the seen, then thus the palpable
    Elysium, though it were in the halls of hell,
What thou lovest well is thy true heritage

The ant's a centaur in his dragon world.
Pull down thy vanity, it is not man
Made courage, or made order, or made grace,
    Pull down thy vanity, I say pull down.
Learn of the green world what can be thy place
In scaled invention or true artistry,
Pull down thy vanity,
                    Paquin pull down!
The green casque has outdone your elegance.

H.D.

(1886–1961)

Oread

Whirl up, sea—
Whirl your pointed pines,
Splash your great pines
On our rocks,
Hurl your green over us,
Cover us with your pools of fir.

Sea Iris

I

Weed, moss-weed,
root tangled in sand,
sea-iris, brittle flower,
one petal like a shell
is broken,
and you print a shadow
like a thin twig.

Fortunate one,
scented and stinging,
rigid myrrh-bud,
camphor-flower,
sweet and salt—you are wind
in our nostrils.

II

Do the murex-fishers
drench you as they pass?
Do your roots drag up colour
from the sand?
Have they slipped gold under you—
rivets of gold?

Band of iris-flowers
above the waves,
you are painted blue,
painted like a fresh prow
stained among the salt weeds.

The Pool

Are you alive?
I touch you.
You quiver like a sea-fish.
I cover you with my net.
What are you—banded one?

Robinson Jeffers
(1887–1962)

Shine, Perishing Republic

While this America settles in the mould of its vulgarity, heavily
 thickening to empire,
And protest, only a bubble in the molten mass, pops and sighs out, and
 the mass hardens,

I sadly smiling remember that the flower fades to make fruit, the fruit
 rots to make earth.
Out of the mother; and through the spring exultances, ripeness and
 decadence; and home to the mother.

You making haste haste on decay: not blameworthy; life is good, be it
 stubbornly long or suddenly
A mortal splendor: meteors are not needed less than mountains: shine,
 perishing republic.

But for my children, I would have them keep their distance from the
 thickening center; corruption
Never has been compulsory, when the cities lie at the monster's feet there
 are left the mountains.

And boys, be in nothing so moderate as in love of man, a clever servant,
 insufferable master.
There is the trap that catches noblest spirits, that caught—they say—God,
 when he walked on earth.

Hurt Hawks

I

The broken pillar of the wing jags from the clotted shoulder,
The wing trails like a banner in defeat,
No more to use the sky forever but live with famine
And pain a few days: cat nor coyote
Will shorten the week of waiting for death, there is game without talons.
He stands under the oak-bush and waits
The lame feet of salvation; at night he remembers freedom
And flies in a dream, the dawns ruin it.
He is strong and pain is worse to the strong, incapacity is worse.
The curs of the day come and torment him
At distance, no one but death the redeemer will humble that head,
The intrepid readiness, the terrible eyes.
The wild God of the world is sometimes merciful to those
That ask mercy, not often to the arrogant.
You do not know him, you communal people, or you have forgotten him;
Intemperate and savage, the hawk remembers him;
Beautiful and wild, the hawks, and men that are dying, remember him.

II

I'd sooner, except the penalties, kill a man than a hawk; but the great
    redtail
Had nothing left but unable misery
From the bone too shattered for mending, the wing that trailed under his
    talons when he moved.
We had fed him six weeks, I gave him freedom,
He wandered over the foreland hill and returned in the evening, asking
    for death,
Not like a beggar, still eyed with the old
Implacable arrogance. I gave him the lead gift in the twilight. What fell
    was relaxed,
Owl-downy, soft feminine feathers; but what
Soared: the fierce rush: the night-herons by the flooded river cried fear at
    its rising
Before it was quite unsheathed from reality.

The Purse-Seine

Our sardine fishermen work at night in the dark of the moon; daylight or
    moonlight
They could not tell where to spread the net, unable to see the
    phosphorescence of the shoals of fish.
They work northward from Monterey, coasting Santa Cruz; off New
    Year's Point or off Pigeon Point
The look-out man will see some lakes of milk-color light on the sea's
    night-purple; he points, and the helmsman
Turns the dark prow, the motorboat circles the gleaming shoal and drifts
    out her seine-net. They close the circle
And purse the bottom of the net, then with great labor haul it in.

                                                I cannot
    tell you
How beautiful the scene is, and a little terrible, then, when the crowded
    fish
Know they are caught, and wildly beat from one wall to the other of their
    closing destiny the phosphorescent
Water to a pool of flame, each beautiful slender body sheeted with flame,
    like a live rocket
A comet's tail wake of clear yellow flame; while outside the narrowing
Floats and cordage of the net great sea-lions come up to watch, sighing in
    the dark; the vast walls of night
Stand erect to the stars.

                            Lately I was looking from a night mountain-top
On a wide city, the colored splendor, galaxies of light: how could I help
    but recall the seine-net
Gathering the luminous fish? I cannot tell you how beautiful the city
    appeared, and a little terrible.
I thought, We have geared the machines and locked all together into
    interdependence; we have built the great cities; now
There is no escape. We have gathered vast populations incapable of free
    survival, insulated
From the strong earth, each person in himself helpless, on all dependent.
    The circle is closed, and the net
Is being hauled in. They hardly feel the cords drawing, yet they shine
    already. The inevitable mass-disasters

Will not come in our time nor in our children's, but we and our children
Must watch the net draw narrower, government take all powers—or
    revolution, and the new government
Take more than all, add to kept bodies kept souls—or anarchy, the
    mass-disasters.

                    These things are Progress;
Do you marvel our verse is troubled or frowning, while it keeps its
    reason? Or it lets go, lets the mood flow
In the manner of the recent young men into mere hysteria, splintered
    gleams, crackled laughter. But they are quite wrong.
There is no reason for amazement: surely one always knew that cultures
    decay, and life's end is death.

Carmel Point

The extraordinary patience of things!
This beautiful place defaced with a crop of surburban houses—
How beautiful when we first beheld it,
Unbroken field of poppy and lupin walled with clean cliffs;
No intrusion but two or three horses pasturing,
Or a few milch cows rubbing their flanks on the outcrop rockheads—
Now the spoiler has come: does it care?
Not faintly. It has all time. It knows the people are a tide
That swells and in time will ebb, and all
Their works dissolve. Meanwhile the image of the pristine beauty
Lives in the very grain of the granite,
Safe as the endless ocean that climbs our cliff. —As for us:
We must uncenter our minds from ourselves;
We must unhumanize our views a little, and become confident
As the rock and ocean that we were made from.

The Deer Lay Down Their Bones

I followed the narrow cliffside trail half way up the mountain
Above the deep river-canyon. There was a little cataract crossed the path,
    flinging itself
Over tree roots and rocks, shaking the jeweled fern-fronds, bright
    bubbling water
Pure from the mountain, but a bad smell came up. Wondering at it I
    clambered down the steep stream
Some forty feet, and found in the midst of bush-oak and laurel,
Hung like a bird's nest on the precipice brink a small hidden clearing,
Grass and a shallow pool. But all about there were bones lying in the
    grass, clean bones and stinking bones,
Antlers and bones: I understood that the place was a refuge for wounded
    deer; there are so many
Hurt ones escape the hunters and limp away to lie hidden; here they have
    water for the awful thirst
And peace to die in; dense green laurel and grim cliff
Make sanctuary, and a sweet wind blows upward from the deep gorge.—
    I wish my bones were with theirs.
But that's a foolish thing to confess, and a little cowardly. We know that
    life
Is on the whole quite equally good and bad, mostly gray neutral, and can
    be endured
To the dim end, no matter what magic of grass, water and precipice, and
    pain of wounds,
Makes death look dear. We have been given life and have used it—not a
    great gift perhaps—but in honesty
Should use it all. Mine's empty since my love died—Empty? The flame-
    haired grandchild with great blue eyes
That look like hers? —What can I do for the child? I gaze at her and
    wonder what sort of man
In the fall of the world . . . I am growing old, that is the trouble. My
    children and little grandchildren
Will find their way, and why should I wait ten years yet, having lived
    sixty-seven, ten years more or less,
Before I crawl out on a ledge of rock and die snapping, like a wolf

Who has lost his mate? —I am bound by my own thirty-year-decision:
    who drinks the wine
Should take the dregs; even in the bitter lees and sediment
New discovery may lie. The deer in that beautiful place lay down their
    bones: I must wear mine.

Marianne Moore

(1887–1972)

The Fish

wade
through black jade.
   Of the crow-blue mussel-shells, one keeps
   adjusting the ash-heaps;
      opening and shutting itself like

an
injured fan.
   The barnacles which encrust the side
   of the wave, cannot hide
      there for the submerged shafts of the

sun,
split like spun
   glass, move themselves with spotlight swiftness
   into the crevices—
      in and out, illuminating

the
turquoise sea
   of bodies. The water drives a wedge
   of iron through the iron edge
      of the cliff; whereupon the stars,

pink
rice-grains, ink-
   bespattered jelly-fish, crabs like green
   lilies, and submarine
      toadstools, slide each on the other.

All
external
   marks of abuse are present on this
   defiant edifice—
      all the physical features of

ac-
cident—lack
   of cornice, dynamite grooves, burns, and
   hatchet strokes, these things stand
     out on it; the chasm-side is

dead.
Repeated
   evidence has proved that it can live
   on what can not revive
     its youth. The sea grows old in it.

A Grave

Man looking into the sea,
taking the view from those who have as much right to it as you have to it
                                      yourself,
it is human nature to stand in the middle of a thing,
but you cannot stand in the middle of this;
the sea has nothing to give but a well excavated grave.
The firs stand in procession, each with an emerald turkey-foot at the top,
reserved as their contours, saying nothing;
repression, however, is not the most obvious characteristic of the sea;
the sea is a collector, quick to return a rapacious look.
There are others besides you who have worn that look—
whose expression is no longer a protest; the fish no longer investigate
                                         them
for their bones have not lasted:
men lower nets, unconscious of the fact that they are desecrating a grave,
and row quickly away—the blades of the oars
moving together like the feet of water-spiders as if there were no such
                                  thing as death.
The wrinkles progress among themselves in a phalanx—beautiful under
                              networks of foam,
and fade breathlessly while the sea rustles in and out of the seaweed;
the birds swim through the air at top speed, emitting cat-calls as
                              heretofore—
the tortoise-shell scourges about the feet of the cliffs, in motion beneath
                              them;

and the ocean, under the pulsation of lighthouses and noise of bell-buoys,
advances as usual, looking as if it were not that ocean in which dropped
                                            things are bound to sink—
in which if they turn and twist, it is neither with volition nor
                                            consciousness.

The Paper Nautilus

    For authorities whose hopes
are shaped by mercenaries?
    Writers entrapped by
    teatime fame and by
commuters' comforts? Not for these
    the paper nautilus
    constructs her thin glass shell.

    Giving her perishable
souvenir of hope, a dull
    white outside and smooth-
    edged inner surface
glossy as the sea, the watchful
    maker of it guards it
    day and night; she scarcely

    eats until the eggs are hatched.
Buried eight-fold in her eight
    arms, for she is in
    a sense a devil-
fish, her glass ram'shorn-cradled freight
    is hid but is not crushed;
    as Hercules, bitten

    by a crab loyal to the hydra,
was hindered to succeed,
    the intensively
    watched eggs coming from
the shell free it when they are freed,—
    leaving its wasp-nest flaws
    of white on white, and close-

laid Ionic chiton-folds
like the lines in the mane of
    a Parthenon horse,
    round which the arms had
wound themselves as if they knew love
    is the only fortress
    strong enough to trust to.

T. S. Eliot
(1888–1965)

from The Waste Land

I. THE BURIAL OF THE DEAD

April is the cruelest month, breeding
Lilacs out of the dead land, mixing
Memory and desire, stirring
Dull roots with spring rain.
Winter kept us warm, covering
Earth in forgetful snow, feeding
A little life with dried tubers.
Summer surprised us, coming over the Starnbergersee
With a shower of rain; we stopped in the colonnade,
And went on in sunlight, into the Hofgarten,
And drank coffee, and talked for an hour.
Bin gar keine Russin, stamm' aus Litauen, echt deutsch.
And when we were children, staying at the archduke's,
My cousin's, he took me out on a sled,
And I was frightened. He said, Marie,
Marie, hold on tight. And down we went.
In the mountains, there you feel free.
I read, much of the night, and go south in the winter.

What are the roots that clutch, what branches grow
Out of this stony rubbish? Son of man,
You cannot say, or guess, for you know only
A heap of broken images, where the sun beats,
And the dead tree gives no shelter, the cricket no relief,
And the dry stone no sound of water. Only
There is shadow under this red rock,
(Come in under the shadow of this red rock),
And I will show you something different from either
Your shadow at morning striding behind you
Or your shadow at evening rising to meet you;
I will show you fear in a handful of dust.

Frisch weht der Wind
Der Heimat zu
Mein Irisch Kind,
Wo weilest du?
"You gave me hyacinths first a year ago;
"They called me the hyacinth girl."
—Yet when we came back, late, from the Hyacinth garden,
Your arms full, and your hair wet, I could not
Speak, and my eyes failed, I was neither
Living nor dead, and I knew nothing,
Looking into the heart of light, the silence.
Oed' und leer das Meer.

Madame Sosostris, famous clairvoyante,
Had a bad cold, nevertheless
Is known to be the wisest woman in Europe,
With a wicked pack of cards. Here, said she,
Is your card, the drowned Phoenician Sailor,
(Those are pearls that were his eyes. Look!)
Here is Belladonna, the Lady of the Rocks,
The lady of situations.
Here is the man with three staves, and here the Wheel,
And here is the one-eyed merchant, and this card,
Which is blank, is something he carries on his back,
Which I am forbidden to see. I do not find
The Hanged Man. Fear death by water.
I see crowds of people, walking round in a ring.
Thank you. If you see dear Mrs. Equitone,
Tell her I bring the horoscope myself:
One must be so careful these days.

Unreal City,
Under the brown fog of a winter dawn,
A crowd flowed over London Bridge, so many,
I had not thought death had undone so many.
Sighs, short and infrequent, were exhaled,
And each man fixed his eyes before his feet.
Flowed up the hill and down King William Street,
To where Saint Mary Woolnoth kept the hours
With a dead sound on the final stroke of nine.
There I saw one I knew, and stopped him, crying: "Stetson!

"You who were with me in the ships at Mylae!
"That corpse you planted last year in your garden,
"Has it begun to sprout? Will it bloom this year?
"Or has the sudden frost disturbed its bed?
"Oh keep the Dog far hence, that's friend to men,
"Or with his nails he'll dig it up again!
"You! hypocrite lecteur!—mon semblable,—mon frère!"

.

III. THE FIRE SERMON

The river's tent is broken: the last fingers of leaf
Clutch and sink into the wet bank. The wind
Crosses the brown land, unheard. The nymphs are departed.
Sweet Thames, run softly, till I end my song.
The river bears no empty bottles, sandwich papers,
Silk handkerchiefs, cardboard boxes, cigarette ends
Or other testimony of summer nights. The nymphs are departed.
And their friends, the loitering heirs of city directors;
Departed, have left no addresses.
By the waters of Leman I sat down and wept . . .
Sweet Thames, run softly till I end my song,
Sweet Thames, run softly, for I speak not loud or long.
But at my back in a cold blast I hear
The rattle of the bones, and chuckle spread from ear to ear.
A rat crept softly through the vegetation
Dragging its slimy belly on the bank
While I was fishing in the dull canal
On a winter evening round behind the gashouse
Musing upon the king my brother's wreck
And on the king my father's death before him.
White bodies naked on the low damp ground
And bones cast in a little low dry garret,
Rattled by the rat's foot only, year to year.
But at my back from time to time I hear
The sound of horns and motors, which shall bring
Sweeney to Mrs. Porter in the spring.
O the moon shone bright on Mrs. Porter
And on her daughter
They wash their feet in soda water
Et O ces voix d'enfants, chantant dans la coupole!

        Twit twit twit
Jug jug jug jug jug jug
So rudely forc'd.
Tereu

        Unreal City
Under the brown fog of a winter noon
Mr. Eugenides, the Smyrna merchant
Unshaven, with a pocket full of currants
C.i.f. London: documents at sight,
Asked me in demotic French
To luncheon at the Cannon Street Hotel
Followed by a weekend at the Metropole.

        At the violet hour, when the eyes and back
Turn upward from the desk, when the human engine waits
Like a taxi throbbing waiting,
I Tiresias, though blind, throbbing between two lives,
Old man with wrinkled female breasts, can see
At the violet hour, the evening hour that strives
Homeward, and brings the sailor home from sea,
The typist home at teatime, clears her breakfast, lights
Her stove, and lays out food in tins.
Out of the window perilously spread
Her drying combinations touched by the sun's last rays,
On the divan are piled (at night her bed)
Stockings, slippers, camisoles, and stays.
I Tiresias, old man with wrinkled dugs
Perceived the scene, and foretold the rest—
I too awaited the expected guest.
He, the young man carbuncular, arrives,
A small house agent's clerk, with one bold stare,
One of the low on whom assurance sits
As a silk hat on a Bradford millionaire.
The time is now propitious, as he guesses,
The meal is ended, she is bored and tired,
Endeavors to engage her in caresses
Which still are unreproved, if undesired.
Flushed and decided, he assaults at once;
Exploring hands encounter no defence;
His vanity requires no response,

And makes a welcome of indifference.
(And I Tiresias have foresuffered all
Enacted on this same divan or bed;
I who have sat by Thebes below the wall
And walked among the lowest of the dead.)
Bestows one final patronising kiss,
And gropes his way, finding the stairs unlit . . .

    She turns and looks a moment in the glass,
Hardly aware of her departed lover;
Her brain allows one half-formed thought to pass:
"Well now that's done: and I'm glad it's over."
When lovely woman stoops to folly and
Paces about her room again, alone,
She smoothes her hair with automatic hand,
And puts a record on the gramophone.

    "This music crept by me upon the waters"
And along the Strand, up Queen Victoria Street.
O City city, I can sometimes hear
Beside a public bar in Lower Thames Street,
The pleasant whining of a mandoline
And a clatter and a chatter from within
Where fishmen lounge at noon: where the walls
Of Magnus Martyr hold
Inexplicable splendour of Ionian white and gold.

          The river sweats
        Oil and tar
        The barges drift
        With the turning tide
        Red sails
        Wide
        To leeward, swing on the heavy spar.
        The barges wash
        Drifting logs
        Down Greenwich reach
        Past the Isle of Dogs.
                    Weialala leia
                    Wallala leialala

    Elizabeth and Leicester
Beating oars
The stern was formed
A gilded shell
Red and gold
The brisk swell
Rippled both shores
Southwest wind
Carried down stream
The peal of bells
White towers
            Weialala leia
            Wallala leialala

   "Trams and dusty trees.
Highbury bore me. Richmond and Kew
Undid me. By Richmond I raised my knees
Supine on the floor of a narrow canoe."

   "My feet are at Moorgate, and my heart
Under my feet. After the event
He wept. He promised 'a new start.'
I made no comment. What should I resent?"

   "On Margate Sands.
I can connect
Nothing with nothing.
The broken fingernails of dirty hands.
My people humble people who expect
Nothing."
            la la

   To Carthage then I came

   Burning burning burning burning
O Lord Thou pluckest me out
O Lord Thou pluckest

burning

e. e. cummings
(1894–1962)

Me up at does

out of the floor
quietly Stare

a poisoned mouse

still who alive

is asking What
have i done that

You wouldn't have

Jean Toomer
(1894–1967)

Reapers

Black reapers with the sound of steel on stones
Are sharpening scythes. I see them place the hones
In their hip-pockets as a thing that's done,
And start their silent swinging, one by one.
Black horses drive a mower through the weeds,
And there, a field rat, startled, squealing bleeds,
His belly close to ground. I see the blade,
Blood-stained, continue cutting weeds and shade.

November Cotton Flower

Boll-weevil's coming, and the winter's cold,
Made cotton-stalks look rusty, seasons old,
And cotton, scarce as any southern snow,
Was vanishing; the branch, so pinched and slow,
Failed in its function as the autumn rake;
Drouth fighting soil had caused the soil to take
All water from the streams; dead birds were found
In wells a hundred feet below the ground—
Such was the season when the flower bloomed.
Old folks were startled, and it soon assumed
Significance. Superstition saw
Something it had never seen before:
Brown eyes that loved without a trace of fear,
Beauty so sudden for that time of year.

Stephen Vincent Benét

(1898–1943)

Metropolitan Nightmare

It rained quite a lot, that spring. You woke in the morning
And saw the sky still clouded, the streets still wet,
But nobody noticed so much, except the taxis
And the people who parade. You don't, in a city.
The parks got very green. All the trees were green
Far into July and August, heavy with leaf,
Heavy with leaf and the long roots boring and spreading,
But nobody noticed that but the city gardeners
And they don't talk.
                          Oh, on Sundays, perhaps, you'd notice:
Walking through certain blocks, by the shut, proud houses
With the windows boarded, the people gone away,
You'd suddenly see the queerest small shoots of green
Poking through cracks and crevices in the stone
And a bird-sown flower, red on a balcony,
But then you made jokes about grass growing in the streets
And politics and grass-roots—and there were songs
And gags and a musical show called "Hot and Wet."
It all made a good box for the papers. When the flamingo
Flew into a meeting of the Board of Estimate,
The new Mayor acted at once and called the photographers.
When the first green creeper crawled upon Brooklyn Bridge,
They thought it was ornamental. They let it stay.

That was the year the termites came to New York
And they don't do well in cold climates—but listen, Joe,
They're only ants and ants are nothing but insects.
It was funny and yet rather wistful in a way
(As Heywood Broun pointed out in the *World-Telegram*)
To think of them looking for wood in a steel city.
It made you feel about life. It was too divine.
There were funny pictures by all the smart, funny artists

And Macy's ran a terribly clever ad:
"The Widow's Termite" or something.
                                    There was no
Disturbance. Even the Communists didn't protest
And say they were Morgan hirelings. It was too hot,
Too hot to protest, too hot to get excited,
An even, African heat, lush, fertile and steamy,
That soaked into bone and mind and never once broke.
The warm rain fell in fierce showers and ceased and fell.
Pretty soon you got used to its always being that way.

You got used to the changed rhythm, the altered beat,
To people walking slower, to the whole bright
Fierce pulse of the city slowing, to men in shorts,
To the new sun-helmets from Best's and the cops' white uniforms,
And the long noon-rest in the offices, everywhere.
It wasn't a plan or anything. It just happened.
The fingers tapped slower, the office boys
Dozed on their benches, the bookkeeper yawned at his desk.
The A.T.& T. was the first to change the shifts
And establish an official siesta-room,
But they were always efficient. Mostly it just
Happened like sleep itself, like a tropic sleep,
Till even the Thirties were deserted at noon
Except for a few tourists and one damp cop.
They ran boats to see the big lilies on the North River
But it was only the tourists who really noticed
The flocks of rose-and-green parrots and parakeets
Nesting in the stone crannies of the Cathedral.
The rest of us had forgotten when they first came.

There wasn't any real change, it was just a heat spell,
A rain spell, a funny summer, a weather-man's joke,
In spite of the geraniums three feet high
In the tin-can gardens of Hester and Desbrosses.
New York was New York. It couldn't turn inside out.
When they got the news from Woods Hole about the Gulf Stream,
The *Times* ran an adequate story.
But nobody reads those stories but science-cranks.

Until, one day, a somnolent city-editor
Gave a new cub the termite yarn to break his teeth on.
The cub was just down from Vermont, so he took the time.
He was serious about it. He went around.
He read all about termites in the Public Library
And it made him sore when they fired him.

So, one evening,
Talking with an old watchman, beside the first
Raw girders of the new Planetopolis Building
(Ten thousand brine-cooled offices, each with shower)
He saw a dark line creeping across the rubble
And turned a flashlight on it.

"Say, buddy," he said,
"You better look out for those ants. They eat wood, you know,
They'll have your shack down in no time."

The watchman spat.
"Oh, they've quit eating wood," he said, in a casual voice,
"I thought everybody knew that."

—and reaching down,
He pried from the insect jaws the bright crumb of steel.

Hart Crane
(1899–1932)

Repose of Rivers

The willows carried a slow sound,
A sarabande the wind mowed on the mead.
I could never remember
That seething, steady leveling of the marshes
Till age had brought me to the sea.

Flags, weeds. And remembrance of steep alcoves
Where cypresses shared the noon's
Tyranny; they drew me into hades almost.
And mammoth turtles climbing sulphur dreams
Yielded, while sun-silt rippled them
Asunder . . .

How much I would have bartered! the black gorge
And all the singular nestings in the hills
Where beavers learn stitch and tooth.
The pond I entered once and quickly fled—
I remember now its singing willow rim.

And finally, in that memory all things nurse;
After the city that I finally passed
With scalding unguents spread and smoking darts
The monsoon cut across the delta
At gulf gates . . . There, beyond the dykes

I heard wind flaking sapphire, like this summer,
And willows could not hold more steady sound.

from The Bridge

How many dawns, chill from his rippling rest
The seagull's wings shall dip and pivot him,
Shedding white rings of tumult, building high
Over the chained bay waters Liberty—

Then, with inviolate curve, forsake our eyes
As apparitional as sails that cross
Some page of figures to be filed away;
—Till elevators drop us from our day . . .

I think of cinemas, panoramic sleights
With multitudes bent toward some flashing scene
Never disclosed, but hastened to again,
Foretold to other eyes on the same screen;

And Thee, across the harbor, silver-paced
As though the sun took step of thee, yet left
Some motion ever unspent in thy stride,—
Implicitly thy freedom staying thee!

Out of some subway scuttle, cell or loft
A bedlamite speeds to thy parapets,
Tilting there momently, shrill shirt ballooning,
A jest falls from the speechless caravan.

Down Wall, from girder into street noon leaks,
A rip-tooth of the sky's acetylene;
All afternoon the cloud-flown derricks turn . . .
Thy cables breathe the North Atlantic still.

And obscure as that heaven of the Jews,
Thy guerdon . . . Accolade thou dost bestow
Of anonymity time cannot raise:
Vibrant reprieve and pardon thou dost show.

O harp and altar, of the fury fused,
(How could mere toil align thy choiring strings!)
Terrific threshold of the prophet's pledge,
Prayer of pariah, and the lover's cry,—

Again the traffic lights that skim thy swift
Unfractioned idiom, immaculate sigh of stars,
Beading thy path—condense eternity:
And we have seen night lifted in thine arms.

Under thy shadow by the piers I waited;
Only in darkness is thy shadow clear.
The City's fiery parcels all undone,
Already snow submerges an iron year . . .

O Sleepless as the river under thee,
Vaulting the sea, the prairies' dreaming sod,
Unto us lowliest sometime sweep, descend
And of the curveship lend a myth to God.

THE RIVER

Stick your patent name on a signboard
brother—all over—going west—young man
Tintex—Japalac—Certain-teed Overall ads
and lands sakes! under the new playbill ripped
in the guaranteed corner—see Bert Williams what?
Minstrels when you steal a chicken just
save me the wing for if it isn't
Erie it ain't for miles around a
Mazda—and the telegraphic night coming on Thomas

*. . . and past
the din and
slogans of
the year—*

a Ediford—and whistling down the tracks
a headlight rushing with the sound—can you
imagine—while an EXPRESS makes time like
SCIENCE—COMMERCE and the HOLYGHOST
RADIO ROARS IN EVERY HOME WE HAVE THE NORTHPOLE
WALLSTREET AND VIRGINBIRTH WITHOUT STONES OR
WIRES OR EVEN RUNning brooks connecting ears
and no more sermons windows flashing roar
breathtaking—as you like it . . . eh?

.

So the 20th Century—so
whizzed the Limited—roared by and left
three men, still hungry on the tracks, ploddingly
watching the tail lights wizen and converge, slip-
ping gimleted and neatly out of sight.

· · · · · · · · · · · · · · · · ·

The last bear, shot drinking in the Dakotas
Loped under wires that span the mountain stream.
Keen instruments, strung to a vast precision
Bind town to town and dream to ticking dream.
But some men take their liquor slow—and count   *to those*
—Though they'll confess no rosary nor clue—   *whose*
The river's minute by the far brook's year.   *addresses*
Under a world of whistles, wires and steam   *are never near*
Caboose-like they go ruminating through
Ohio, Indiana—blind baggage—
To Cheyenne tagging . . . Maybe Kalamazoo.

Time's rendings, time's blendings they construe
As final reckonings of fire and snow;
Strange bird-wit, like the elemental gist
Of unwalled winds they offer, singing low
My Old Kentucky Home and *Casey Jones,*
Some Sunny Day. I heard a road-gang chanting so.
And afterwards, who had a colt's eyes—one said,
"Jesus! Oh I remember watermelon days!" And sped
High in a cloud of merriment, recalled
"—And when my Aunt Sally Simpson smiled," he drawled—
"It was almost Louisiana, long ago."
"There's no place like Booneville though, Buddy,"
One said, excising a last burr from his vest,
"—For early trouting." Then peering in the can,
"—But I kept on the tracks." Possessed, resigned,
He trod the fire down pensively and grinned,
Spreading dry shingles of a beard. . . .

                              Behind
My father's cannery works I used to see
Rail-squatters ranged in nomad raillery,
The ancient men—wifeless or runaway

Hobo-trekkers that forever search
An empire wilderness of freight and rails.
Each seemed a child, like me, on a loose perch,
Holding to childhood like some termless play.
John, Jake or Charley, hopping the slow freight
—Memphis to Tallahassee—riding the rods,
Blind fists of nothing, humpty-dumpty clods.

Yet they touch something like a key perhaps.
From pole to pole across the hills, the states
—They know a body under the wide rain;   *but who have*
Youngsters with eyes like fjords, old reprobates   *touched her,*
With racetrack jargon,—dotting immensity   *knowing her*
They lurk across her, knowing her yonder breast   *without name*
Snow-silvered, sumac-stained or smoky blue—
Is past the valley-sleepers, south or west.
—As I have trod the rumorous midnights, too,

And past the circuit of the lamp's thin flame
(O Nights that brought me to her body bare!)
Have dreamed beyond the print that bound her name.
Trains sounding the long blizzards out—I heard
Wail into distances I knew were hers.
Papooses crying on the wind's long mane
Screamed redskin dynasties that fled the brain,
—Dead echoes! But I knew her body there,
Time like a serpent down her shoulder, dark,
And space, an eaglet's wing, laid on her hair.

Under the Ozarks, domed by Iron Mountain,
The old gods of the rain lie wrapped in pools
Where eyeless fish curvet a sunken fountain   *nor the*
And re-descend with corn from querulous crows.   *myths of her*
Such pilferings make up their timeless eatage,   *fathers . . .*
Propitiate them for their timber torn
By iron, iron—always the iron dealt cleavage!
They doze now, below axe and powder horn.
And Pullman breakfasters glide glistening steel
From tunnel into field—iron strides the dew—
Straddles the hill, a dance of wheel on wheel.
You have a half-hour's wait at Siskiyou,

Or stay the night and take the next train through.
Southward, near Cairo passing, you can see
The Ohio merging,—borne down Tennessee;
And if it's summer and the sun's in dusk
Maybe the breeze will lift the River's musk
—As though the waters breathed that you might know
Memphis Johnny, Steamboat Bill, Missouri Joe.
Oh, lean from the window, if the train slows down,
As though you touched hands with some ancient clown,
—A little while gaze absently below
And hum Deep River with them while they go.

Yes, turn again and sniff once more—look see,
O Sheriff, Brakeman and Authority—
Hitch up your pants and crunch another quid,
For you, too, feed the River timelessly.
And few evade full measure of their fate;
Always they smile out eerily what they seem.
I could believe he joked at heaven's gate—
Dan Midland—jolted from the cold brake-beam.

Down, down—born pioneers in time's despite,
Grimed tributaries to an ancient flow—
They win no frontier by their wayward plight,
But drift in stillness, as from Jordan's brow.

You will not hear it as the sea; even stone
Is not more hushed by gravity . . . But slow,
As loth to take more tribute—sliding prone
Like one whose eyes were buried long ago

The River, spreading, flows—and spends your dream.
What are you, lost within this tideless spell?
You are your father's father, and the stream—
A liquid theme that floating niggers swell.

Damp tonnage and alluvial march of days—
Nights turbid, vascular with silted shale
And roots surrendered down of moraine clays:
The Mississippi drinks the farthest dale.

O quarrying passion, undertowed sunlight!
The basalt surface drags a jungle grace
Ochreous and lynx-barred in lengthening might;
Patience! and you shall reach the biding place!

Over De Soto's bones the freighted floors
Throb past the City stories of three thrones.
Down two more turns the Mississippi pours
(Anon tall ironsides up from salt lagoons)

And flows within itself, heaps itself free.
All fades but one thin skyline 'round . . . Ahead
No embrace opens but the stinging sea;
The River lifts itself from its long bed,

Poised wholly on its dream, a mustard glow
Tortured with history, its one will—flow!
—The Passion spreads in wide tongues, choked and slow,
Meeting the Gulf, hosannas silently below.

Sterling A. Brown

(1901–1989)

Riverbank Blues

A man git his feet set in a sticky mudbank,
A man git dis yellow water in his blood,
No need for hopin', no need for doin',
Muddy streams keep him fixed for good.

Little Muddy, Big Muddy, Moreau and Osage,
Little Mary's, Big Mary's, Cedar Creek,
Flood deir muddy water roundabout a man's roots,
Keep him soaked and stranded and git him weak.

Lazy sun shinin' on a little cabin,
Lazy moon glistenin' over river trees;
Ole river whisperin', lappin' 'gainst de long roots:
"Plenty of rest and peace in these . . . "

Big mules, black loam, apple and peach trees,
But seems lak de river washes us down
Past de rich farms, away from de fat lands,
Dumps us in some ornery riverbank town.

Went down to the river, sot me down an' listened,
Heard de water talkin' quiet, quiet lak an' slow:
"Ain' no need fo' hurry, take yo' time, take yo' time . . . "
Heard it sayin'—*"Baby, hyeahs de way life go . . . "*

Dat is what it tole me as I watched it slowly rollin',
But somp'n way inside me rared up an' say,
"Better be movin' . . . better be travelin' . . .
Riverbank'll git you ef you stay . . . "

Towns are sinkin' deeper, deeper in de riverbank,
Takin' on de ways of deir sulky Ole Man—

Takin' on his creepy ways, takin' on his evil ways,
"Bes' git way, a long way . . . whiles you can.

"Man got his sea too lak de Mississippi
Ain't got so long for a whole lot longer way,
Man better move some, better not git rooted
Muddy water fool you, ef you stay . . . "

Langston Hughes

(1902–1967)

The Negro Speaks of Rivers

I've known rivers:
I've known rivers ancient as the world and older than the
    flow of human blood in human veins.

My soul has grown deep like the rivers.

I bathed in the Euphrates when dawns were young.
I built my hut near the Congo and it lulled me to sleep.
I looked upon the Nile and raised the pyramids above it.
I heard the singing of the Mississippi when Abe Lincoln
    went down to New Orleans, and I've seen its muddy
    bosom turn all golden in the sunset.

I've known rivers:
Ancient, dusky rivers.

My soul has grown deep like the rivers.

Daybreak in Alabama

When I get to be a composer
I'm gonna write me some music about
Daybreak in Alabama
And I'm gonna put the purtiest songs in it
Rising out of the ground like a swamp mist
And falling out of heaven like soft dew.
I'm gonna put some tall tall trees in it
And the scent of pine needles
And the smell of red clay after rain
And long red necks
And poppy colored faces
And big brown arms

And the field daisy eyes
Of black and white black white black people
And I'm gonna put white hands
And black hands and brown and yellow hands
And red clay earth hands in it
Touching everybody with kind fingers
And touching each other natural as dew
In that dawn of music when I
Get to be a composer
And write about daybreak
In Alabama.

Lorine Niedecker

(1903–1970)

Black Hawk held: In reason
land cannot be sold,
only things to be carried away,
and I am old.

Young Lincoln's general moved,
pawpaw in bloom,
and to this day, Black Hawk,
reason has small room.

from Paean to Place

      And the place
      was water

Fish
    fowl
        flood
   Water lily mud
My life

in the leaves and on water
My mother and I
         born
in swale and swamp and sworn
to water

My father
thru marsh fog
   sculled down
      from high ground
saw her face

at the organ
bore the weight of lake water
        and the cold—
he seined for carp to be sold
that their daughter

might go high
on land
        to learn
Saw his wife turn
deaf

and away
She
        who knew boats
                and ropes
no longer played

She helped him string out nets
for tarring
        And she could shoot
                He was cool
to the man

who stole his minnows
by night and next day offered
        to sell them back
                He brought in a sack
of dandelion greens

if no flood
No oranges—none at hand
        No marsh marigold
                where the water rose
He kept us afloat

I mourn her not hearing canvasbacks
their blast-off rise
        from the water
                Not hearing sora
rails's sweet

spoon-tapped waterglass-
descending scale-
    tear-drop-tittle
        Did she giggle
as a girl?

His skiff skimmed
the coiled celery now gone
    from these streams
        due to carp
He knew duckweed

fall-migrates
toward Mud Lake bottom
    Knew what lay
        under leaf decay
and on pickerel weeds

before summer hum
To be counted on:
    new leaves
        new dead
leaves

He could not
—like water bugs—
    stride surface tension
        He netted
loneliness

As to his bright new car
my mother—her house
    next his—averred:
        A hummingbird
can't haul

Anchored here
in the rise and sink
    of life—
        middle years' nights
he sat

beside his shoes
rocking his chair
    Roped not "looped
        in the loop
of her hair"

I grew in green
slide and slant
    of shore and shade
        Child-time—wade
thru weeds

Maples to swing from
Pewee-glissando
    sublime
        slime-
song

Grew riding the river
Books
    at home-pier
        Shelley could steer
as he read

I was the solitary plover
a pencil
    for a wing-bone
From the secret notes
I must tilt

upon the pressure
execute and adjust
    In us sea-air rhythm
"We live by the urgent wave
of the verse"

Kenneth Rexroth

(1905–1982)

Toward an Organic Philosophy

SPRING, COAST RANGE

The glow of my campfire is dark red and flameless,
The circle of white ash widens around it.
I get up and walk off in the moonlight and each time
I look back the red is deeper and the light smaller.
Scorpio rises late with Mars caught in his claw;
The moon has come before them, the light
Like a choir of children in the young laurel trees.
It is April; the shad, the hot headed fish,
Climbs the rivers; there is trillium in the damp canyons;
The foetid adder's tongue lolls by the waterfall.
There was a farm at this campsite once, it is almost gone now.
There were sheep here after the farm, and fire
Long ago burned the redwoods out of the gulch,
The Douglas fir off the ridge; today the soil
Is stony and incoherent, the small stones lie flat
And plate the surface like scales.
Twenty years ago the spreading gully
Toppled the big oak over onto the house.
Now there is nothing left but the foundations
Hidden in poison oak, and above on the ridge,
Six lonely, ominous fenceposts;
The redwood beams of the barn make a footbridge
Over the deep waterless creek bed;
The hills are covered with wild oats
Dry and white by midsummer.
I walk in the random survivals of the orchard.
In a patch of moonlight a mole
Shakes his tunnel like an angry vein;
Orion walks waist deep in the fog coming in from the ocean;
Leo crouches under the zenith.

There are tiny hard fruits already on the plum trees.
The purity of the apple blossoms is incredible.
As the wind dies down their fragrance
Clusters around them like thick smoke.
All the day they roared with bees, in the moonlight
They are silent and immaculate.

SPRING, SIERRA NEVADA

Once more golden Scorpio glows over the col
Above Deadman Canyon, orderly and brilliant,
Like an inspiration in the brain of Archimedes.
I have seen its light over the warm sea,
Over the coconut beaches, phosphorescent and pulsing;
And the living light in the water
Shivering away from the swimming hand,
Creeping against the lips, filling the floating hair.
Here where the glaciers have been and the snow stays late,
The stone is clean as light, the light steady as stone.
The relationship of stone, ice and stars is systematic and enduring:
Novelty emerges after centuries, a rock spalls from the cliffs,
The glacier contracts and turns grayer,
The stream cuts new sinuosities in the meadow,
The sun moves through space and the earth with it,
The stars change places.
                              The snow has lasted longer this year,
Than anyone can remember. The lowest meadow is a lake,
The next two are snowfields, the pass is covered with snow,
Only the steepest rocks are bare. Between the pass
And the last meadow the snowfield gapes for a hundred feet,
In a narrow blue chasm through which a waterfall drops,
Spangled with sunset at the top, black and muscular
Where it disappears again in the snow.
The world is filled with hidden running water
That pounds in the ears like ether;
The granite needles rise from the snow, pale as steel;
Above the copper mine the cliff is blood red,
The white snow breaks at the edge of it;
The sky comes close to my eyes like the blue eyes
Of someone kissed in sleep.

I descend to camp,
To the young, sticky, wrinkled aspen leaves,
To the first violets and wild cyclamen,
And cook supper in the blue twilight.
All night deer pass over the snow on sharp hooves,
In the darkness their cold muzzles find the new grass
At the edge of the snow.

FALL, SIERRA NEVADA

This morning the hermit thrush was absent at breakfast,
His place was taken by a family of chickadees;
At noon a flock of humming birds passed south,
Whirling in the wind up over the saddle between
Ritter and Banner, following the migration lane
Of the Sierra crest southward to Guatemala.
All day cloud shadows have moved over the face of the mountain,
The shadow of a golden eagle weaving between them
Over the face of the glacier.
At sunset the half-moon rides on the bent back of the Scorpion,
The Great Bear kneels on the mountain.
Ten degrees below the moon
Venus sets in the haze arising from the Great Valley.
Jupiter, in opposition to the sun, rises in the alpenglow
Between the burnt peaks. The ventriloquial belling
Of an owl mingles with the bells of the waterfall.
Now there is distant thunder on the east wind.
The east face of the mountain above me
Is lit with far off lightnings and the sky
Above the pass blazes momentarily like an aurora.
It is storming in the White Mountains,
On the arid fourteen-thousand-foot peaks;
Rain is falling on the narrow gray ranges
And dark sedge meadows and white salt flats of Nevada.
Just before moonset a small dense cumulus cloud,
Gleaming like a grape cluster of metal,
Moves over the Sierra crest and grows down the westward slope.
Frost, the color and quality of the cloud,
Lies over all the marsh below my campsite.
The wiry clumps of dwarfed whitebark pines

Are smoky and indistinct in the moonlight,
Only their shadows are really visible.
The lake is immobile and holds the stars
And the peaks deep in itself without a quiver.
In the shallows the geometrical tendrils of ice
Spread their wonderful mathematics in silence.
All night the eyes of deer shine for an instant
As they cross the radius of my firelight.
In the morning the trail will look like a sheep driveway,
All the tracks will point down to the lower canyon.
"Thus," says Tyndall, "the concerns of this little place
Are changed and fashioned by the obliquity of the earth's axis,
The chain of dependence which runs through creation,
And links the roll of a planet alike with the interests
Of marmots and of men."

Lute Music

The earth will be going on a long time
Before it finally freezes;
Men will be on it; they will take names,
Give their deeds reasons.
We will be here only
As chemical constituents—
A small franchise indeed.
Right now we have lives,
Corpuscles, ambitions, caresses,
Like everybody had once—
All the bright neige d'antan people,
"Blithe Helen, white Iope, and the rest,"
All the uneasy remembered dead.

Here at the year's end, at the feast
Of birth, let us bring to each other
The gifts brought once west through deserts—
The precious metal of our mingled hair,
The frankincense of enraptured arms and legs,
The myrrh of desperate invincible kisses—

Let us celebrate the daily
Recurrent nativity of love,
The endless epiphany of our fluent selves,
While the earth rolls away under us
Into unknown snows and summers,
Into untraveled spaces of the stars.

Lyell's Hypothesis Again

An Attempt to Explain the Former
Changes of the Earth's Surface by
Causes Now in Operation
—SUBTITLE OF LYELL:
    PRINCIPLES OF GEOLOGY

The mountain road ends here,
Broken away in the chasm where
The bridge washed out years ago.
The first scarlet larkspur glitters
In the first patch of April
Morning sunlight. The engorged creek
Roars and rustles like a military
Ball. Here by the waterfall,
Insuperable life, flushed
With the equinox, sentient
And sentimental, falls away
To the sea and death. The tissue
Of sympathy and agony
That binds the flesh in its Nessus' shirt;
The clotted cobweb of unself
And self; sheds itself and flecks
The sun's bed with darts of blossom
Like flagellant blood above
The water bursting in the vibrant
Air. This ego, bound by personal
Tragedy and the vast
Impersonal vindictiveness
Of the ruined and ruining world,

Pauses in this immortality,
As passionate, as apathetic,
As the lava flow that burned here once;
And stopped here; and said, "This far
And no further." And spoke thereafter
In the simple diction of stone.

.

Naked in the warm April air,
We lie under the redwoods,
In the sunny lee of a cliff.
As you kneel above me I see
Tiny red marks on your flanks
Like bites, where the redwood cones
Have pressed into your flesh.
You can find just the same marks
In the lignite in the cliff
Over our heads. *Sequoia
Langsdorfii* before the ice,
And *sempervirens* afterwards,
There is little difference,
Except for all those years.

Here in the sweet, moribund
Fetor of spring flowers, washed,
Flotsam and jetsam together,
Cool and naked together,
Under this tree for a moment,
We have escaped the bitterness
Of love, and love lost, and love
Betrayed. And what might have been,
And what might be, fall equally
Away with what is, and leave
Only these ideograms
Printed on the immortal
Hydrocarbons of flesh and stone.

Andrée Rexroth

Died October 1940

Now once more gray mottled buckeye branches
Explode their emerald stars,
And alders smoulder in a rosy smoke
Of innumerable buds.
I know that spring again is splendid
As ever, the hidden thrush
As sweetly tongued, the sun as vital—
But these are the forest trails we walked together,
These paths, ten years together.
We thought the years would last forever,
They are all gone now, the days
We thought would not come for us are here.
Bright trout poised in the current—
The raccoon's track at the water's edge—
A bittern booming in the distance—
Your ashes scattered on this mountain—
Moving seaward on this stream.

Theodore Roethke

(1908–1963)

from North American Sequence

Meditation at Oyster River

I

Over the low, barnacled, elephant-colored rocks,
Come the first tide-ripples, moving, almost without sound, toward me,
Running along the narrow furrows of the shore, the rows of dead clam
   shells;
Then a runnel behind me, creeping closer,
Alive with tiny striped fish, and young crabs climbing in and out of the
   water.

No sound from the bay. No violence.
Even the gulls quiet on the far rocks,
Silent, in the deepening light,
Their cat-mewing over,
Their child-whimpering.

At last one long undulant ripple,
Blue-black from where I am sitting,
Makes almost a wave over a barrier of small stones,
Slapping lightly against a sunken log.
I dabble my toes in the brackish foam sliding forward,
Then retire to a rock higher up on the cliff-side.
The wind slackens, light as a moth fanning a stone:
A twilight wind, light as a child's breath
Turning not a leaf, not a ripple.
The dew revives on the beach-grass;
The salt-soaked wood of a fire crackles;
A fish raven turns on its perch (a dead tree in the rivermouth),
Its wings catching a last glint of the reflected sunlight.

2

The self persists like a dying star,
In sleep, afraid. Death's face rises afresh,
Among the shy beasts, the deer at the salt-lick,
The doe with its sloped shoulders loping across the highway,
The young snake, poised in green leaves, waiting for its fly,
The hummingbird, whirring from quince-blossom to morning-glory—
With these I would be.
And with water: the waves coming forward, without cessation,
The waves, altered by sand-bars, beds of kelp, miscellaneous driftwood,
Topped by cross-winds, tugged at by sinuous undercurrents
The tide rustling in, sliding between the ridges of stone,
The tongues of water, creeping in, quietly.

3

In this hour,
In this first heaven of knowing,
The flesh takes on the pure poise of the spirit,
Acquires, for a time, the sandpiper's insouciance,
The hummingbird's surety, the kingfisher's cunning—
I shift on my rock, and I think:
Of the first trembling of a Michigan brook in April,
Over a lip of stone, the tiny rivulet;
And that wrist-thick cascade tumbling from a cleft rock,
Its spray holding a double rain-bow in early morning,
Small enough to be taken in, embraced, by two arms,—
Or the Tittebawasee, in the time between winter and spring,
When the ice melts along the edges in early afternoon.
And the midchannel begins cracking and heaving from the pressure
    beneath,
The ice piling high against the iron-bound spiles,
Gleaming, freezing hard again, creaking at midnight—
And I long for the blast of dynamite,
The sudden sucking roar as the culvert loosens its debris of branches and
    sticks,
Welter of tin cans, pails, old bird nests, a child's shoe riding a log,
As the piled ice breaks away from the battered spiles,
And the whole river begins to move forward, its bridges shaking.

4

Now, in this waning of light,
I rock with the motion of morning;
In the cradle of all that is,
I'm lulled into half-sleep
By the lapping of water,
Cries of the sandpiper.
Water's my will, and my way,
And the spirit runs, intermittently,
In and out of the small waves,
Runs with the intrepid shorebirds—
How graceful the small before danger!

In the first of the moon,
All's a scattering,
A shining.

George Oppen
(1908–1984)

Eclogue

The men talking
Near the room's center. They have said
More than they had intended.

Pinpointing in the uproar
Of the living room

An assault
On the quiet continent.

Beyond the window
Flesh and rock and hunger

Loose in the night sky
Hardened into soil

Tilting of itself to the sun once more, small
Vegetative leaves
And stems taking place

Outside—O small ones,
To be born!

California

The headland towers over ocean
At Palos Verdes. Who shall say
How the Romantic stood in nature?
But I am sitting in an automobile
While Mary, lovely in a house dress, buys tomatoes from a road side stand.

And I look down at the Pacific, blue waves roughly small running at the
    base of land,
An area of ocean in the sun—

Out there is China. Somewhere out in air.
Tree by the stand
Moving in the wind that moves
Streaming with the waves of the Pacific going past.

            The beach: a child
Leaning on one elbow. She has swept an arm
To make a hollow and a mark around her in the sand,
A place swept smooth in one arm's claiming sweep beside the ocean,
Looking up the coast relaxed,
A Western child.
And all the air before her—what the wind brings past
In all the bright simpleness and strangeness of the sands.

Psalm

        Veritas sequitur . . .

In the small beauty of the forest
The wild deer bedding down—
That they are there!

            Their eyes
Effortless, the soft lips
Nuzzle and the alien small teeth
Tear at the grass

            The roots of it
Dangle from their mouths
Scattering earth in the strange woods.
They who are there.

            Their paths
Nibbled thru the fields, the leaves that shade them
Hang in the distances
Of sun

            The small nouns
Crying faith
In this in which the wild deer
Startle, and stare out.

89

The Occurrences

The simplest
Words say the grass blade
Hides the blaze
Of a sun
To throw a shadow
In which the bugs crawl
At the roots of the grass;

Father, father
Of fatherhood
Who haunts me, shivering
Man most naked
Of us all, O father

       watch
At the roots
Of the grass the creating
Now   that tremendous
plunge

Charles Olson
(1910–1970)

The Kingfishers

I

1

What does not change / is the will to change

He woke, fully clothed, in his bed. He
remembered only one thing, the birds, how
when he came in, he had gone around the rooms
and got them back in their cage, the green one first,
she with the bad leg, and then the blue,
the one they had hoped was a male

Otherwise? Yes, Fernand, who had talked lispingly of Albers & Angkor Vat.
He had left the party without a word. How he got up, got into his coat,
I do not know. When I saw him, he was at the door, but it did not matter,
he was already sliding along the wall of the night, losing himself
in some crack of the ruins. That it should have been he who said, "The
    kingfishers?

who cares
for their feathers
now?"

His last words had been, "The pool is slime." Suddenly everyone,
ceasing their talk, sat in a row around him, watched
they did not so much hear, or pay attention, they
wondered, looked at each other, smirked, but listened,
he repeated and repeated, could not go beyond his thought
"The pool   the kingfishers' feathers were wealth   why
did the export stop?"

It was then he left

2

"I thought of the E on the stone, and of what Mao said
la lumière"
   but the kingfisher
"de l'aurore"
   but the kingfisher flew west
est devant nous!
    he got the color of his breast
    from the heat of the setting sun!

The features are, the feebleness of the feet (syndactylism of the 3rd & 4th digit)
the bill, serrated, sometimes a pronounced beak, the wings
where the color is, short and round, the tail
inconspicuous.

But not these things are the factors. Not the birds.
The legends are
legends. Dead, hung up indoors, the kingfisher
will not indicate a favoring wind,
or avert the thunderbolt. Nor, by its nesting,
still the waters, with the new year, for seven days.
It is true, it does nest with the opening year, but not on the waters.
It nests at the end of a tunnel bored by itself on a bank. There,
six or eight white and translucent eggs are laid, on fishbones,
not on bare clay, on bones thrown up in pellets by the birds.

      On these rejectamenta
(as they accumulate they form a cup-shaped structure) the young are born
And, as they are fed and grow, this nest of excrement and decayed fish becomes
        a dripping, fetid mass
Mao concluded:
   nous devons
     nous lever
       et agir!

3

When the attentions change / the jungle
leaps in
        even the stones are split
                they rive

Or,
enter
that other conqueror we more naturally recognize
he so resembles ourselves

But the E
cut so rudely on that oldest stone
sounded otherwise,
was differently heard
as, in another time, were treasures used:
(and, later, much later, a fine ear thought
a scarlet coat)

        "of green feathers feet, beaks and eyes
        of gold

        "animals likewise,
        resembling snails

        "a large wheel, gold with figures of unknown four-foots,
        and worked with tufts of leaves, weight
        3800 ounces

        "last, two birds of thread and featherwork, the quills
        gold, the feet
        gold, the two birds perched on two reeds
        gold, the reeds arising from two embroidered mounds,
        one yellow, the other
        white.

           "And from each reed hung
           seven feathered tassels.

In this instance, the priests
(in dark cotton robes, and dirty,
their dishevelled hair matted with blood, and flowing wildly

over their shoulders)
rush in among the people, calling on them
to protect their gods

And all now is war
where so lately there was peace,
and the sweet brotherhood, the use
of tilled fields.

4

Not one death but many,
not accumulation but change, the feed-back proves, the feed-back is
the law

       Into the same river no man steps twice
       When fire dies air dies
       No one remains, nor is, one

Around an appearance, one common model, we grow up
many. Else how is it,
if we remain the same,
we take pleasure now
in what we did not take pleasure before? love
contrary objects? admire and/or find fault? use
other words, feel other passions, have
nor figure, appearance, disposition, tissue
the same?

       To be in different states without a change
       is not a possibility

We can be precise. The factors are
in the animal and/or the machine the factors are
communication and/or control, both involve
the message. And what is the message? The message is
a discrete or continuous sequence of measurable events distributed in time

is the birth of air, is
the birth of water, is
a state between

the origin and
the end, between
birth and the beginning of
another fetid nest

is change, presents
no more than itself

And the too strong grasping of it,
when it is pressed together and condensed,
loses it

This very thing you are

II

They buried their dead in a sitting posture
serpent cane razor ray of the sun

And she sprinkled water on the head of the child, crying
"Cioa-coatl! Cioa-coatl!"
with her face to the west

Where the bones are found, in each personal heap
with what each enjoyed, there is always
the Mongolian louse

The light is in the east. Yes. And we must rise, act. Yet
in the west, despite the apparent darkness (the whiteness
which covers all), if you look, if you can bear, if you can, long enough
as long as it was necessary for him, my guide
to look into the yellow of that longest-lasting rose

so you must, and, in that whiteness, into that face, with what candor, look

and, considering the dryness of the place
the long absence of an adequate race
(of the two who first came, each a conquistador, one healed, the other
tore the eastern idols down, toppled
the temple walls, which, says the excuser
were black from human gore)

hear
hear, where the dry blood talks
where the old appetite walks

la piu saporita et migliore
che si possa truovar al mondo

where it hides, look
in the eye how it runs
in the flesh / chalk

        but under these petals
        in the emptiness
        regard the light, contemplate
        the flower

whence it arose

        with what violence benevolence is bought
        what cost in gesture justice brings
        what wrongs domestic rights involve
        what stalks
        this silence

        what pudor pejorocracy affronts
        how awe, night-rest and neighborhood can rot
        what breeds where dirtiness is law
        what crawls
        below

III

I am no Greek, hath not th'advantage.
And of course, no Roman:
he can take no risk that matters,
the risk of beauty least of all.

But I have my kin, if for no other reason than
(as he said, next of kin) I commit myself, and
given my freedom, I'd be a cad
if I didn't. Which is more true.

It works out this way, despite the disadvantage.
I offer, in explanation, a quote:
si j'ai du gout, ce n'est gueres
Que pour la terre et les pierres

Despite the discrepancy (an ocean courage age)
this is also true: if I have any taste
it is only because I have interested myself
in what was slain in the sun

I pose you your question:

shall you uncover honey / where maggots are?

I hunt among stones

West Gloucester

Condylura
cristata
on Atlantic
Street West
Gloucester
spinning on its
star-wheel
nose,
in the middle of the
tarvia,

probably because it had been
knocked in the head (was
actually fighting all the time,
with its fore-paws at
the lovely mushroom growth
of its nose, snow-ball flake pink flesh
of a gentian, until I
took an oar out of the back seat of the station wagon
and removed it
like a pea on a knife to
the side of the road

stopped its dance dizzy dance
on its own nose out of its head
working as though it would get rid of
its own pink appendage

like a flower dizzy
with its own self

like the prettiest thing in the world drilling
itself into the

pavement

and I gave it, I hope, all the marshes of Walker's Creek
to get it off what might also seem
what was wrong with it, that the highway
had magnetized the poor thing

the loveliest animal I believe I ever did see
in such a quandary

and off the marshes
of Walker's Creek fall
graduatedly so softly to
the Creek and the Creek to
Ipswich Bay an arm
of the Atlantic Ocean

send the Star Nosed Mole
all into the grass
all away from the dizzying
highway if that was what was wrong

with the little thing, spinning
in the middle of the
highway

Elizabeth Bishop

(1911–1979)

At the Fishhouses

Although it is a cold evening,
down by one of the fishhouses
an old man sits netting,
his net, in the gloaming almost invisible,
a dark purple-brown,
and his shuttle worn and polished.
The air smells so strong of codfish
it makes one's nose run and one's eyes water.
The five fishhouses have steeply peaked roofs
and narrow, cleated gangplanks slant up
to storerooms in the gables
for the wheelbarrows to be pushed up and down on.
All is silver: the heavy surface of the sea,
swelling slowly as if considering spilling over,
is opaque, but the silver of the benches,
the lobster pots, and masts, scattered
among the wild jagged rocks,
is of an apparent translucence
like the small old buildings with an emerald moss
growing on their shoreward walls.
The big fish tubs are completely lined
with layers of beautiful herring scales
and the wheelbarrows are similarly plastered
with creamy iridescent coats of mail,
with small iridescent flies crawling on them.
Up on the little slope behind the houses,
set in the sparse bright sprinkle of grass,
is an ancient wooden capstan,
cracked, with two long bleached handles
and some melancholy stains, like dried blood,
where the ironwork has rusted.
The old man accepts a Lucky Strike.

He was a friend of my grandfather.
We talk of the decline in the population
and of codfish and herring
while he waits for a herring boat to come in.
There are sequins on his vest and on his thumb.
He has scraped the scales, the principal beauty,
from unnumbered fish with that black old knife,
the blade of which is almost worn away.

Down at the water's edge, at the place
where they haul up the boats, up the long ramp
descending into the water, thin silver
tree trunks are laid horizontally
across the gray stones, down and down
at intervals of four or five feet.

Cold dark deep and absolutely clear,
element bearable to no mortal,
to fish and to seals . . . One seal particularly
I have seen here evening after evening.
He was curious about me. He was interested in music;
like me a believer in total immersion,
so I used to sing him Baptist hymns.
I also sang "A Mighty Fortress Is Our God."
He stood up in the water and regarded me
steadily, moving his head a little.
Then he would disappear, then suddenly emerge
almost in the same spot, with a sort of shrug
as if it were against his better judgment.
Cold dark deep and absolutely clear,
the clear gray icy water . . . Back, behind us,
the dignified tall firs begin.
Bluish, associating with their shadows,
a million Christmas trees stand
waiting for Christmas. The water seems suspended
above the rounded gray and blue-gray stones.
I have seen it over and over, the same sea, the same,
slightly, indifferently swinging above the stones,
icily free above the stones,
above the stones and then the world.

If you should dip your hand in,
your wrist would ache immediately,
your bones would begin to ache and your hand would burn
as if the water were a transmutation of fire
that feeds on stones and burns with a dark gray flame.
If you tasted it, it would first taste bitter,
then briny, then surely burn your tongue.
It is like what we imagine knowledge to be:
dark, salt, clear, moving, utterly free,
drawn from the cold hard mouth
of the world, derived from the rocky breasts
forever, flowing and drawn, and since
our knowledge is historical, flowing, and flown.

The Moose

for Grace Bulmer Bowers

From narrow provinces
of fish and bread and tea,
home of the long tides
where the bay leaves the sea
twice a day and takes
the herrings long rides,

where if the river
enters or retreats
in a wall of brown foam
depends on if it meets
the bay coming in,
the bay not at home;

where, silted red,
sometimes the sun sets
facing a red sea,
and others, veins the flats'
lavender, rich mud
in burning rivulets;

on red, gravelly roads,
down rows of sugar maples,
past clapboard farmhouses
and neat, clapboard churches,
bleached, ridged as clamshells,
past twin silver birches,

through late afternoon
a bus journeys west,
the windshield flashing pink,
pink glancing off of metal,
brushing the dented flank
of blue, beat-up enamel;

down hollows, up rises,
and waits, patient, while
a lone traveller gives
kisses and embraces
to seven relatives
and a collie supervises.

Goodbye to the elms,
to the farm, to the dog.
The bus starts. The light
grows richer; the fog,
shifting, salty, thin,
comes closing in.

Its cold, round crystals
form and slide and settle
in the white hens' feathers,
in gray glazed cabbages,
on the cabbage roses
and lupins like apostles;

the sweet peas cling
to their wet white string
on the whitewashed fences;
bumblebees creep
inside the foxgloves,
and evening commences.

One stop at Bass River.
Then the Economies—
Lower, Middle, Upper;
Five Islands, Five Houses,
where a woman shakes a tablecloth
out after supper.

A pale flickering. Gone.
The Tantramar marshes
and the smell of salt hay.
An iron bridge trembles
and a loose plank rattles
but doesn't give way.

On the left, a red light
swims through the dark:
a ship's port lantern.
Two rubber boots show,
illuminated, solemn.
A dog gives one bark.

A woman climbs in
with two market bags,
brisk, freckled, elderly.
"A grand night. Yes sir,
all the way to Boston."
She regards us amicably.

Moonlight as we enter
the New Brunswick woods,
hairy, scratchy, splintery;
moonlight and mist
caught in them like lamb's wool
on bushes in a pasture.

The passengers lie back.
Snores. Some long sighs.
A dreamy divagation
begins in the night,
a gentle, auditory,
slow hallucination. . . .

In the creakings and noises,
an old conversation
—not concerning us,
but recognizable, somewhere,
back in the bus:
Grandparents' voices

uninterruptedly
talking, in Eternity:
names being mentioned,
things cleared up finally;
what he said, what she said,
who got pensioned;

deaths, deaths and sicknesses;
the year he remarried;
the year (something) happened.
She died in childbirth.
That was the son lost
when the schooner foundered.

He took to drink. Yes.
She went to the bad.
When Amos began to pray
even in the store and
finally the family had
to put him away.

"Yes . . ." that peculiar
affirmative. "Yes . . ."
A sharp, indrawn breath,
half groan, half acceptance,
that means "Life's like that.
We know *it* (also death)."

Talking the way they talked
in the old featherbed,
peacefully, on and on,
dim lamplight in the hall,
down in the kitchen, the dog
tucked in her shawl.

Now, it's all right now
even to fall asleep
just as on all those nights.
—Suddenly the bus driver
stops with a jolt,
turns off his lights.

A moose has come out of
the impenetrable wood
and stands there, looms, rather,
in the middle of the road.
It approaches; it sniffs at
the bus's hot hood.

Towering, antlerless,
high as a church,
homely as a house
(or, safe as houses).
A man's voice assures us
"Perfectly harmless. . . . "

Some of the passengers
exclaim in whispers,
childishly, softly,
"Sure are big creatures."
"It's awful plain."
"Look! It's a she!"

Taking her time,
she looks the bus over,
grand, otherworldly.
Why, why do we feel
(we all feel) this sweet
sensation of joy?

"Curious creatures,"
says our quiet driver,
rolling his *r*'s.
"Look at that, would you."
Then he shifts gears.
For a moment longer,

by craning backward,
the moose can be seen
on the moonlit macadam;
then there's a dim
smell of moose, an acrid
smell of gasoline.

William Everson

(1912–1994)

San Joaquin

This valley after the storms can be beautiful beyond the telling,
Though our cityfolk scorn it, cursing heat in the summer and drabness in
    winter,
And flee it: Yosemite and the sea.
They seek splendor; who would touch them must stun them;
The nerve that is dying needs thunder to rouse it.

I in the vineyard, in green-time and dead-time, come to it dearly,
And take nature neither freaked nor amazing,
But the secret shining, the soft indeterminate wonder.
I watch it morning and noon, the unutterable sundowns,
And love as the leaf does the bough.

Clouds

Over the coastal ranges slight and indefinite clouds
Moved in to sunrise, rode up the west;
Toward noon the change of the wind strung them to furrows.
Sundown flared late, the close and the heavy twilight of August hooded
    the fields.
They were broken to fragments, and were burnt on the growth of the
    gathering night,
When Venus blazed west and went down.

So common a beauty: the workers over the wide fields hardly looked up.
Under the great arching sky of the valley the clouds are across us,
The trade of the routes of the upper air,
Their temporal splendor hawked on the wind for some listless eye.

Cirrus and stratus: the fringe of the distant storms of the sea;
December wanes and the nimbus are driving.
They are scattered by dawns, or are killed on the heavy fists of the peaks;
But the wind breeds them west forever.

Robert Hayden

(1913–1980)

The Night-Blooming Cereus

And so for nights
we waited, hoping to see
the heavy bud
break into flower.

On its neck-like tube
hooking down from the edge
of the leaf-branch
nearly to the floor,

the bud packed
tight with its miracle swayed
stiffly on breaths
of air, moved

as though impelled
by stirrings within itself.
It repelled as much
as it fascinated me

sometimes—snake,
eyeless bird head,
beak that would gape
with grotesque life-squawk.

But you, my dear,
conceded less to the bizarre
than to the imminence
of bloom. Yet we agreed

we ought
to celebrate the blossom,
paint ourselves, dance
in honor of

archaic mysteries
when it appeared. Meanwhile
we waited, aware
       of rigorous design.

       Backster's
polygraph, I thought,
would have shown
       (as clearly as it had

       a philodendron's
fear) tribal sentience
in the cactus, focused
       energy of will.

       The belling of
tropic perfume—that
signaling
       not meant for us;

       the darkness
cloying with summoning
fragrance. We dropped
       trivial tasks

       and marveling
beheld at last the achieved
flower. Its moonlight
       petals were

       still unfold-
ing, the spike fringe of the outer
perianth recessing
       as we watched.

       Lunar presence,
foredoomed, already dying,
it charged the room
       with plangency

older than human
cries, ancient as prayers
invoking Osiris, Krishna,
Tezcátlipóca.

We spoke
in whispers when
we spoke
at all . . .

Muriel Rukeyser
(1913–1980)

from The Book of the Dead

ALLOY

This is the most audacious landscape. The gangster's
stance with his gun smoking and out is not so
vicious as this commercial field, its hill of glass.

Sloping as gracefully as thighs, the foothills
narrow to this, clouds over every town
finally indicate the stored destruction.

Crystalline hill: a blinded field of white
murdering snow, seamed by convergent tracks;
the traveling cranes reach for the silica.

And down the track, the overhead conveyor
slides on its cable to the feet of chimneys.
Smoke rises, not white enough, not so barbaric.

Here the severe flame speaks from the brick throat,
electric furnaces produce this precious, this clean,
annealing the crystals, fusing at last alloys.

Hottest for silicon, blast furnaces raise flames,
spill fire, spill steel, quench the new shape to freeze,
tempering it to perfected metal.

Forced through this crucible, a million men.
Above this pasture, the highway passes those
who curse the air, breathing their fear again.

The roaring flowers of the chimney-stacks
less poison, at their lips in fire, than this
dust that is blown from off the field of glass;

blows and will blow, rising over the mills,
crystallized and beyond the fierce corrosion
disintegrated angel on these hills.

THE DAM

All power is saved, having no end. Rises
in the green season, in the sudden season
the white the budded
                              and the lost.
Water celebrates, yielding continually
sheeted and fast in its overfall
slips down the rock, evades the pillars
building its colonnades, repairs
in stream and standing wave
retains its seaward green
broken by obstacle rock; falling, the water sheet
spouts, and the mind dances, excess of white.
White brilliant function of the land's disease.

Many-spanned, lighted, the crest leans under
concrete arches and the channelled hills,
turns in the gorge toward its release;
kinetic and controlled, the sluice
urging the hollow, the thunder,
the major climax
                              energy
total and open watercourse
praising the spillway, fiery glaze,
crackle of light, cleanest velocity
flooding, the moulded force.

> *I open out a way over the water*
> *I form a path between the Combatants:*

Grant that I sail down like a living bird,
power over the fields and Pool of Fire.
Phoenix, I sail over the phoenix world.

Diverted water, the fern and fuming white
ascend in mist of continuous diffusion.
Rivers are turning inside their mountains,
streams line the stone, rest at the overflow
lake and in lanes of pliant color lie.
Blessing of this innumerable silver,
printed in silver, images of stone
walk on a screen of falling water
in film-silver in continual change
recurring colored, plunging with the wave.

Constellations of light, abundance of many rivers.
The sheeted island-cities, the white surf filling west,
the hope, fast water spilled where still pools fed.
Great power flying deep: between the rock and the sunset,
the caretaker's house and the steep abutment,
hypnotic water fallen and the tunnels under
the moist and fragile galleries of stone,
mile-long, under the wave. Whether snow fall,
the quick light fall, years of white cities fall,
flood that this valley built falls slipping down
the green turn in the river's green.
Steep gorge, the wedge of crystal in the sky.

How many feet of whirlpools?
What is a year in terms of falling water?
Cylinders; kilowatts; capacities.
Continuity: $\sum Q = O$
Equations for falling water. The streaming motion.
The balance-sheet of energy that flows
passing along its infinite barrier.

It breaks the hills, cracking the riches wide,
runs through electric wires;
it comes, warning the night,
running among these rigid hills,
a single force to waken our eyes.

They poured the concrete and the columns stood,
laid bare the bedrock, set the cells of steel,
a dam for monument was what they hammered home.
Blasted, and stocks went up;
insured the base,
and limousines
wrote their own graphs upon
roadbed and lifeline.

Their hands touched mastery:
wait for defense, solid across the world.
Mr. Griswold. "A corporation is a body without a soul."
Mr. Dunn. When they were caught at it they resorted to the methods em-
    ployed by gunmen, ordinary machine gun racketeers. They cowardly
    tried to buy out the people who had the information on them.
Mr. Marcantonio. I agree that a racket has been practised, but the most
    damnable racketeering that I have ever known is the paying of a fee to
    the very attorney who represented these victims. That is the most outra-
    geous racket that has ever come within my knowledge.
Miss Allen. Mr. Jesse J. Ricks, the president of the Union Carbide & Carbon
    Corporation, suggested that the stockholder had better take this ques-
    tion up in a private conference.
The dam is safe. A scene of power.
The dam is the father of the tunnel.
This is the valley's work, the white, the shining.

		Stock and Dividend					Net	Closing		
High	Low	in Dollars	Open	High	Low	Last	Chge.	Bid	Ask	Sales
111	61 ¼	Union Carbide (3.20)	67 ¼	69 ½	67 ¼	69 ½	+3	69 ¼	69 ½	3,400

The dam is used when the tunnel is used.
The men and the water are never idle,
have definitions.
This is a perfect fluid, having no age nor hours,
surviving scarless, unaltered, loving rest,
willing to run forever to find its peace
in equal seas in currents of still glass.
Effects of friction: to fight and pass again,
learning its power, conquering boundaries,
able to rise blind in revolts of tide,

broken and sacrificed to flow resumed.
Collecting eternally power. Spender of power,
torn, never can be killed, speeded in filaments,
million, its power can rest and rise forever,
wait and be flexible. Be born again.
Nothing is lost, even among the wars,
imperfect flow, confusion of force.
It will rise. These are the phases of its face.
It knows its seasons, the waiting, the sudden.
It changes. It does not die.

William Stafford

(1914–1993)

Traveling through the Dark

Traveling through the dark I found a deer
dead on the edge of the Wilson River road.
It is usually best to roll them into the canyon:
that road is narrow; to swerve might make more dead.

By glow of the tail-light I stumbled back of the car
and stood by the heap, a doe, a recent killing;
she had stiffened already, almost cold.
I dragged her off; she was large in the belly.

My fingers touching her side brought me the reason—
her side was warm; her fawn lay there waiting,
alive, still, never to be born.
Beside that mountain road I hesitated.

The car aimed ahead its lowered parking lights;
under the hood purred the steady engine.
I stood in the glare of the warm exhaust turning red;
around our group I could hear the wilderness listen.

I thought hard for us all—my only swerving—,
then pushed her over the edge into the river.

At the Bomb Testing Site

At noon in the desert a panting lizard
waited for history, its elbows tense,
watching the curve of a particular road
as if something might happen.

It was looking for something farther off
than people could see, an important scene
acted in stone for little selves
at the flute end of consequences.

There was just a continent without much on it
under a sky that never cared less.
Ready for a change, the elbows waited.
The hands gripped hard on the desert.

Robert Duncan

(1919–1988)

Often I Am Permitted to Return to a Meadow

as if it were a scene made-up by the mind,
that is not mine, but is a made place,

that is mine, it is so near to the heart,
an eternal pasture folded in all thought
so that there is a hall therein

that is a made place, created by light
wherefrom the shadows that are forms fall.

Wherefrom fall all architectures I am
I say are likeness of the First Beloved
whose flowers are flames lit to the Lady.

She it is Queen Under the Hill
whose hosts are a disturbance of words within words
that is a field folded.

It is only a dream of the grass blowing
east against the source of the sun
in an hour before the sun's going down

whose secret we see in a children's game
of ring a round of roses told.

Often I am permitted to return to a meadow
as if it were a given property of the mind
that certain bounds hold against chaos,

that is a place of first permission,
everlasting omen of what is.

Poetry, a Natural Thing

Neither our vices nor our virtues
further the poem. "They came up
and died
just like they do every year
on the rocks."

The poem
feeds upon thought, feeling, impulse,
to breed   itself,
a spiritual urgency at the dark ladders leaping.

This beauty is an inner persistence
toward the source
striving against (within) down-rushet of the river,
a call we heard and answer
in the lateness of the world
primordial bellowings
from which the youngest world might spring,

salmon not in the well where the
hazelnut falls
but at the falls battling, inarticulate,
blindly making it.

This is one picture apt for the mind.

A second: a moose painted by Stubbs,
where last year's extravagant antlers
lie on the ground.
The forlorn moosey-faced poem wears
new antler-buds,
the same,

"a little heavy, a little contrived",

his only beauty to be
all moose.

A Little Language

I know a little language of my cat, though Dante says
that animals have no need of speech and Nature
abhors the superfluous.   My cat is fluent.   He
converses when he wants with me.   To speak

is natural.   And whales and wolves I've heard
in choral soundings of the sea and air
know harmony and have an eloquence that stirs
my mind and heart—they touch the soul.   Here

Dante's religion that would set Man apart
damns the effluence of our life from us
to build therein its powerhouse.

It's in his animal communication Man is
      true, immediate, and
in immediacy,   Man is all animal.

His senses quicken in the thick of the symphony,
      old circuits of animal rapture and alarm,
attentions and arousals in which an identity rearrives.
      He hears
particular voices among
      the concert,   the slightest
rustle in the undertones,
      rehearsing a nervous aptitude
yet to prove *his*.   He sees the flick
      of significant red within the rushing mass
of ruddy wilderness   and catches the glow
      of a green shirt
to delite him in a glowing field of green
      —it *speaks* to him—
and in the arc of the spectrum color
      speaks to color.
The rainbow articulates
      a promise he remembers
he but imitates
      in noises that he makes,

this speech in every sense
     the world surrounding him.
He picks up on the fugitive tang of mace
     amidst the savory mass,
and taste in evolution is an everlasting key.
     There is a pun of scents in what makes sense.

     Myrrh it may have been,
the odor of the announcement that filld the house.

     He wakes from deepest sleep

upon a distant signal   and waits

     as if crouching,   springs

     to life.

Barbara Guest

(1920–2006)

Santa Fe Trail

I go separately
The sweet knees of oxen have pressed a path for me
ghosts with ingots have burned their bare hands
it is the dungaree darkness with China stitched
where the westerly winds
and the traveler's checks
the evensong of salesmen
the glistening paraphernalia of twin suitcases
where no one speaks English.
I go separately
It is the wind, the rubber wind
when we brush our teeth in the way station
a climate to beard. What forks these roads?
Who clammers o'er the twain?
What murmurs and rustles in the distance
in the white branches where the light is whipped
piercing at the crossing as into the dunes we simmer
and toss ourselves awhile the motor pants like a forest
where owls from their bandaged eyes send messages
to the Indian couple. Peaks have you heard?
I go separately
We have reached the arithmetics, are partially quenched
while it growls and hints in the lost trapper's voice
She is coming toward us like a session of pines
in the wild wooden air where rabbits are frozen,
O mother of lakes and glaciers, save us gamblers
Whose wagon is perilously rapt.

James Dickey

(1923–1997)

The Heaven of Animals

Here they are. The soft eyes open.
If they have lived in a wood
It is a wood.
If they have lived on plains
It is grass rolling
Under their feet forever.

Having no souls, they have come,
Anyway, beyond their knowing.
Their instincts wholly bloom
And they rise.
The soft eyes open.

To match them, the landscape flowers,
Outdoing, desperately
Outdoing what is required:
The richest wood,
The deepest field.

For some of these,
It could not be the place
It is, without blood.
These hunt, as they have done,
But with claws and teeth grown perfect,

More deadly than they can believe.
They stalk more silently,
And crouch on the limbs of trees,
And their descent
Upon the bright backs of their prey

May take years
In a sovereign floating of joy.
And those that are hunted

Know this as their life,
Their reward: to walk

Under such trees in full knowledge
Of what is in glory above them,
And to feel no fear,
But acceptance, compliance.
Fulfilling themselves without pain

At the cycle's center,
They tremble, they walk
Under the tree,
They fall, they are torn,
They rise, they walk again.

Denise Levertov

(1923–1997)

O Taste and See

The world is
not with us enough
O taste and see

the subway Bible poster said,
meaning **The Lord**, meaning
if anything all that lives
to the imagination's tongue,

grief, mercy, language,
tangerine, weather, to
breathe them, bite,
savor, chew, swallow, transform

into our flesh our
deaths, crossing the street, plum, quince,
living in the orchard and being

hungry, and plucking
the fruit.

Souvenir d'amitié

Two fading red spots mark on my thighs
where a flea from the fur of a black, curly, yearning dog
bit me, casually, and returned into the fur.

Melanie was the dog's name. That afternoon
she had torn the screen from a door and littered fragments
of screen everywhere, and of chewed-up paper,

stars, whole constellations of paper, glimmered
in shadowy floor corners. She had been punished, adequately;
this was not a first offense. And forgiven,

but sadly: her master knew she would soon discover
other ways to show forth her discontent, her black humor.
Meanwhile, standing on hind legs like a human child,

she came to lean her body, her arms and head,
in my lap. I was a friendly stranger. She gave me
a share of her loneliness, her warmth, her flea.

The Past III

You try to keep the present
        uppermost in your mind, counting its blessings
                (which today are many) because
although you are not without hope for the world, crazy
        as that seems to your gloomier friends and often
                to yourself, yet your own hopes
have shrunk, options are less abundant. Ages ago
        you enjoyed thinking of names
                for a daughter; later you still entertained,
at least as hypothesis, the notion
        of a not impossible love, requited passion;
                or resolved modestly to learn
some craft, various languages.
        And all those sparks of future
                winked out behind you, forgettable. So—
the present. Its blessings
        many today:
                the fresh, ornate
blossoms of the simplest trees a sudden
        irregular pattern everywhere, audacious white,
                flamingo pink in a haze of early warmth.
But perversely it's not
        what you crave. You want
                the past. Oh, not your own,

no reliving of anything—no, what you hanker after
        is a compost,
                a forest floor, thick, saturate,
fathoms deep, palimpsestuous, its surface a mosaic
        of infinitely fragile, lacy, tenacious
                skeleton leaves. When you put your ear
to that odorous ground you can catch the unmusical, undefeated
        belling note, as of a wounded stag escaped triumphant,
                of lives long gone.

James Schuyler

(1923–1991)

Haze

hangs heavy
down into trees: dawn
doesn't break today,
the morning
seeps into being, one
bird, maybe
two, chipping
away at it. A white dahlia,
big
as Baby Bumstead's head,
leans
its folded petals
at a window, a lesson
in origami.
Frantically, God
knows what
machine: oh no,
just Maggio's
garbage truck.
Staring
at all the roughage
that hides an estuary,
such urbanity
seems inapt: the endless city
builds on and on
thinning out, here and there,
for the wet green velvet towels
("slight imperfections")
of summer

("moderately priced")
and a hazy morning
in August,
even that
we may grow to love.

CONTEMPORARY

A. R. Ammons

Corsons Inlet

I went for a walk over the dunes again this morning
to the sea,

then turned right along
   the surf
                 rounded a naked headland
                 and returned

  along the inlet shore:

it was muggy sunny, the wind from the sea steady and high,
crisp in the running sand,
    some breakthroughs of sun
  but after a bit

continuous overcast:

the walk liberating, I was released from forms,
from the perpendiculars,
    straight lines, blocks, boxes, binds
of thought
into the hues, shadings, rises, flowing bends and blends
     of sight:

             I allow myself eddies of meaning:
yield to a direction of significance
running
like a stream through the geography of my work:
  you can find
in my sayings
           swerves of action
           like the inlet's cutting edge:
      there are dunes of motion,
organizations of grass, white sandy paths of remembrance

in the overall wandering of mirroring mind:

but Overall is beyond me: is the sum of these events
I cannot draw, the ledger I cannot keep, the accounting
beyond the account:

in nature there are few sharp lines: there are areas of
primrose
    more or less dispersed;
disorderly orders of bayberry; between the rows
of dunes,
irregular swamps of reeds,
though not reeds alone, but grass, bayberry, yarrow, all . . .
predominantly reeds:

I have reached no conclusions, have erected no boundaries,
shutting out and shutting in, separating inside
    from outside: I have
    drawn no lines:
    as

manifold events of sand
change the dune's shape that will not be the same shape
tomorrow,

so I am willing to go along, to accept
the becoming
thought, to stake off no beginnings or ends, establish
    no walls:

by transitions the land falls from grassy dunes to creek
to undercreek: but there are no lines, though
    change in that transition is clear
    as any sharpness: but "sharpness" spread out,
allowed to occur over a wider range
than mental lines can keep:

the moon was full last night: today, low tide was low:
black shoals of mussels exposed to the risk
of air
and, earlier, of sun,
waved in and out with the waterline, waterline inexact,
caught always in the event of change:

                a young mottled gull stood free on the shoals
                and ate
to vomiting: another gull, squawking possession, cracked a crab,
picked out the entrails, swallowed the soft-shelled legs, a ruddy
turnstone running in to snatch leftover bits:

risk is full: every living thing in
siege: the demand is life, to keep life: the small
white blacklegged egret, how beautiful, quietly stalks and spears
                the shallows, darts to shore
                        to stab—what? I couldn't
        see against the black mudflats—a frightened
        fiddler crab?

                the news to my left over the dunes and
reeds and bayberry clumps was
                fall: thousands of tree swallows
                gathering for flight:
                an order held
                in constant change: a congregation
rich with entropy: nevertheless, separable, noticeable
        as one event,
                not chaos: preparations for
flight from winter,
cheet, cheet, cheet, cheet, wings rifling the green clumps,
beaks
at the bayberries
    a perception full of wind, flight, curve,
    sound:
    the possibility of rule as the sum of rulelessness:
the "field" of action
with moving, incalculable center:

in the smaller view, order tight with shape:
blue tiny flowers on a leafless weed: carapace of crab:
snail shell:
                pulsations of order
                in the bellies of minnows: orders swallowed,
broken down, transferred through membranes
to strengthen larger orders: but in the large view, no
lines or changeless shapes: the working in and out, together

and against, of millions of events: this,
              so that I make
              no form of
              formlessness:

orders as summaries, as outcomes of actions override
or in some way result, not predictably (seeing me gain
the top of a dune,
the swallows
could take flight—some other fields of bayberry
              could enter fall
              berryless) and there is serenity:

              no arranged terror: no forcing of image, plan,
or thought:
no propaganda, no humbling of reality to precept:

terror pervades but is not arranged, all possibilities
of escape open: no route shut, except in
       the sudden loss of all routes:

              I see narrow orders, limited tightness, but will
not run to that easy victory:
              still around the looser, wider forces work:
              I will try
       to fasten into order enlarging grasps of disorder, widening
scope, but enjoying the freedom that
Scope eludes my grasp, that there is no finality of vision,
that I have perceived nothing completely,
that tomorrow a new walk is a new walk.

Gravelly Run

I don't know somehow it seems sufficient
to see and hear whatever coming and going is,
losing the self to the victory
    of stones and trees,
of bending sandpit lakes, crescent
round groves of dwarf pine:

136

for it is not so much to know the self
as to know it as it is known
    by galaxy and cedar cone,
as if birth had never found it
and death could never end it:

the swamp's slow water comes
down Gravelly Run fanning the long
    stone-held algal
hair and narrowing roils between
the shoulders of the highway bridge:

holly grows on the banks in the woods there,
and the cedars' gothic-clustered
    spires could make
green religion in winter bones:

so I look and reflect, but the air's glass
jail seals each thing in its entity:

no use to make any philosophies here:
    I see no
god in the holly, hear no song from
the snowbroken weeds: Hegel is not the winter
yellow in the pines: the sunlight has never
heard of trees: surrendered self among
    unwelcoming forms: stranger,
hoist your burdens, get on down the road.

from Garbage

a waste of words, a flattened-down, smoothed-
over mesa of styrofoam verbiage; since words were

introduced here things have gone poorly for the
planet: it's been between words and rivers,

surface-mining words and hilltops, cuneiform
records in priestly piles; between clay

tablets and irrigated fields: papyrus in
sheets; vellum in Alexandria; hundreds of

temples to type and, now, networks of words
intricate as the realities they represent:

a persiflageous empurpling: the rains clear,
the blue sky's ragged white clouds shine up

the greens of treetops: the driveway is thick
with sugarmaple seed the chipmunk fills his

pouches with fast: the spirea bush, the five
nearly round, slightly dented petals to each

blossom, snows the ground white during rains:
the norway maple I cut back in the hedge has

turned out leaves ten inches between the
points! the robin down by the fence just about

sings his head off now, close to dusk his
belly lineated tight with slack worms: (yes, there's

a chipmunk left, though the tabby's lying out
for him): we must have the biggest machine,

fifty miles around, find the smallest particles,
and the ditchwork of the deepest degradation

reflects waters brighter than common ground:
poetry to no purpose! all this garbage! all

these words: we may replace our mountains with
trash: leachments may be our creeks flowing

from the distilling bottoms of corruption:
our skies, already browned, may be our brown

skies: fields may rise from cultivation into
suffocation: here was a silvery-green-blue-bright

planet, held in sway for hundreds of millions
of years by leathery monsters racing about roaring

and tearing, terrible cries of contest by
lakeshores in placid evenings, terrible cries of

assault at night, etc., all shoved away, imagine:
and then along came the frail one, our ancestor,

scavenger, seed finder, nut cracker, fruit
picker, grubs, bulbs, etc., and here we are at

last, last, probably, behold, we have replaced
the meadows with oilslick: when words have

driven the sludge in billows higher than our
heads—oh, well, by then words will have left

the poor place behind: we'll be settling
elsewhere or floating interminably, the universe

a deep place to spoil, a dump compaction will
always make room in! I have nothing to say:

what I want to say is saying: I want to be
singing, sort of: I want to be engaged with

the ongoing: but I have no portmanteau filled
with portfolio: still, I am for something:

what am I for: I'm for rights consistent with
others' rights: that says little but saying,

with a touch of singing: we'll live no more on
this planet, we'll live in the word: what:

we'll get off: we'll take it with us: our
equations will make any world we wish anywhere

we go: we'll take nothing away from here but
the equations, cool, lofty, eternal, that were

nowhere here to be found when we came: we are
a quite special species, as it were: would to

mercy those who went before in ignorance and
irresolution could know they forwarded a part,

though, of course, had they been told they'd
not have believed it: imagine, though we think

ourselves purposeless, we may be the thinnest
cross-section of an upcoming announcement, and

though we cannot imagine what the purpose might
be, even now it may be extruding itself, tiny

threads of weak energy fields, right through
us: first an earth in peace; then, hundreds of

years looking for other wars: strife and peace,
love and grief, departure and return: gliding

we'll kick the *l* out of the world and cuddle
up with the avenues and byways of the word:

Karen Leona Anderson

Snowshoe Hare

Lepus americanus

1.

Hunt hares because they run and leap for you,
not rabbits, no, who freeze in plain sight,

brown fur hoping to hide itself in a lawn
of green, shivered to death like unturned leaves

in a cold snap. Planes graze the roofs
of the hard little house, floors to please even

the hard hare ma, dropping her ones on the ground
without nests, without the fur picked from her own

spare belly. She is not sorry. You and the hare
have the same disease: always make more

and destroy all the luscious green nibs of the saplings
before they are trees. The stunning living room's

paneled, angular view is always ruined by
the gaping field of the airport, the hunt for a place

bare of sound, rich with the lithe spines of grass.
For the house can't jump up and worm into you,

make you stay and raise anything here. The neighborhood
stretches its maw, a plain to be snapped up;

may choose; must choose; run,
you and your young disappear.

2.

And so inside the hare, bark and wood
are made to blood; faster-than-predator parasites

course through its organs, hang on, accrue,
spend from the inside the hare's crushed buds

and air and melted snow. In hare, lungs take on
a hue silvicultural, a burned-over timberland begun

again with worms, a held-together place
professional eaters call silverskin, the see-

through, you-taken-everywhere bag for muscles
and bones, hare become a soft-walled house in the wood,

the threads of whitened fur between the toes
that hang the hare above the sugar

drifts. Our houses made to grow and choke
each other, the nematodes to needle food

together, our blood and waste and water
shivering through the woods—and where is the animal?

—foot stitched to the ground that trembles there.

Christopher Arigo

Gone feral: minor gestures

0. in the first age there was more light than the planet
knew what to do with and there was not yet myth—
there was damp and warmth and fecund water salty and rich feeding
there was a sense of neverending now extinct

1. the poet makes shadow-puppets
the poet makes words about shadowness
and home and a gourd of wildmint tea and
cattail roots dug from riverbanks and roasted
and prickly pear fruit just-sweet and seed-heavy and rubyesque
and little soups cooked with glowing basalt knobs dropped in gourds
to steam and spit and smell green and tonight smoke smells extra good
sandstone feels extra warm and shadows are as real
as the firelight that makes them flickering sibyls
waiting to blow away with sunrise—where the poems go

2. in the second age I find myself longing for a time
a place I can never know a place *before*
(I never asked for any of this . . .)
O longing of the atavist O rage of the Luddite
nostalgia can be a comforting disease and in the desert
I don't know where I belong unless it's here
drinking from a post-flash-flood river heavy with silt
that grits my teeth and smells as old as the ground stone
it carries as old as myths washed from canyon walls

3. a deadfall's stone jaw baited with rose hips or taste of grain
snaps shut on my hand or squirrel or packrat
in exchange for meat (and maybe that is the genesis of prayer)
then a chert flake to split the skin
to open the tiny striped pelt to read what's been eaten
and how it will feed me across miles of tri-toothy sage
and blue-berry-laden juniper

4. always a fall in the third age or earlier—
a lapse—plow and land and peopled landed and
never leaving not until next fall when leaves drop
or the land heaves them with an exhausted sigh
and can give no more—and maybe they listen this time

5. sparse water before storms drench my dreams
with flooding and eroded holes ringed with caliche pre-storm
filled with water post-storm a faint earthy nose and a refreshing finish
and beneath the sandy riverbed I push my hand
beneath the current I dig for a way farther into you I have a new face
layered with stiff hair and grit and I think I may be turning into stone
I think the river pouring around my knees may erode me to the waist

6. my outspread hands—palindromes of outstretched arms
my arms made circle almost made of stone when I clasp my hands
an embrace is palindrome the body ouroboros
the canyon river rises and falls
trapped in clouds fallen from clouds
breathe in breathe out breath respiraled
throughout so much of this uncertain world

7. fire needs no translation from spinning one stick
in the notch of another and the possible metaphors
and the black dust that accumulates then smokes and glows
and gives fire cradled in a tinder bundle nursed to flame and it's easy
to see in a handful of smoky light how magic was born
in an embrace of gambel oak leaves and a twig fire I nearly embrace at night

8. land is no machine—(land is only *land* when you visit)
no clockwork no mechanisms or apparati drive seasons
or erosions or a sidewinder sunning no cogs no jagged
teeth gears but maybe during a flashflood roaring through the canyon
I am undeaf to intuition to instincts and old things
willingly happily earthbound and certain of where I dwell

9. in death in the final age there is no final age
there is *moose, Indian*—better last words than most deserve and truer
and time for one last visit long enough to change
to return home to a new-old epoch
to a dusty overhang smelling of packrats where I am a guest
who has chosen a good dry place to sleep

Rae Armantrout

Thing

We love our cat
for her self
regard is assiduous
and bland,

for she sits in the small
patch of sun on our rug
and licks her claws
from all angles

and it is far
superior
to "balanced reporting"

though, of course,
it is also
the very same thing.

Natural History

I

Discomfort marks the boundary.

One early symptom was the boundary.

The invention of hunger.
I could *use* energy.

To serve.

Elaborate systems in the service of
far-fetched demands.

The great termite mounds serve
as air-conditioners.

Temperature within must never vary
more than 2 degrees.

2

Which came first
the need or the system?

Systematic.
System player.
Scheme of Things.

The body considered as a functional unit.
"My system craves calcium."

An organized set of doctrines.

A network formed for the purpose of . . .

"All I want is you."

3

was narrowing their options to one,
the next development.

Soldiers have elongate heads and massive mandibles.
Squirtgun heads are found among fiercer species.
Since soldiers cannot feed themselves, each requires
a troupe of attendants.

4

Her demands had become more elaborate.

He must be blindfolded,
   (Must break off his own wings)
wear this corset laced tight
   (seal up the nuptial cell)
to attain his heart's desire.

Move only as she permits
   (Mate the bloated queen each season)
or be hung from the rafters.
How did he get here?

   5

Poor baby,
I heard your hammer.

The invention of pounding.

"As soon as it became important
that free energy be channeled."

Once you cared to be
set off
from the surrounding medium.

This order has been preferred
since improvement was discovered.

The moment one intends to grow
at the expense.

When teeth emerge

Demand for special treatment
was an early symptom

Dusk

spider on the cold expanse
of glass, three stories high
rests intently
and so purely alone.

I'm not like that!

John Ashbery

Into the Dusk-Charged Air

Far from the Rappahannock, the silent
Danube moves along toward the sea.
The brown and green Nile rolls slowly
Like the Niagara's welling descent.
Tractors stood on the green banks of the Loire
Near where it joined the Cher.
The St. Lawrence prods among black stones
And mud. But the Arno is all stones.
Wind ruffles the Hudson's
Surface. The Irawaddy is overflowing.
But the yellowish, gray Tiber
Is contained within steep banks. The Isar
Flows too fast to swim in, the Jordan's water
Courses over the flat land. The Allegheny and its boats
Were dark blue. The Moskowa is
Gray boats. The Amstel flows slowly.
Leaves fall into the Connecticut as it passes
Underneath. The Liffey is full of sewage,
Like the Seine, but unlike
The brownish-yellow Dordogne.
Mountains hem in the Colorado
And the Oder is very deep, almost
As deep as the Congo is wide.
The plain banks of the Neva are
Gray. The dark Saône flows silently.
And the Volga is long and wide
As it flows across the brownish land. The Ebro
Is blue, and slow. The Shannon flows
Swiftly between its banks. The Mississippi
Is one of the world's longest rivers, like the Amazon.
It has the Missouri for a tributary.
The Harlem flows amid factories

And buildings. The Nelson is in Canada,
Flowing. Through hard banks the Dubawnt
Forces its way. People walk near the Trent.
The landscape around the Mohawk stretches away;
The Rubicon is merely a brook.
In winter the Main
Surges; the Rhine sings its eternal song.
The Rhône slogs along through whitish banks
And the Rio Grande spins tales of the past.
The Loir bursts its frozen shackles
But the Moldau's wet mud ensnares it.
The East catches the light.
Near the Escaut the noise of factories echoes
And the sinuous Humboldt gurgles wildly.
The Po too flows, and the many-colored
Thames. Into the Atlantic Ocean
Pours the Garonne. Few ships navigate
On the Housatonic, but quite a few can be seen
On the Elbe. For centuries
The Afton has flowed.
                    If the Rio Negro
Could abandon its song, and the Magdalena
The jungle flowers, the Tagus
Would still flow serenely, and the Ohio
Abrade its slate banks. The tan Euphrates would
Sidle silently across the world. The Yukon
Was choked with ice, but the Susquehanna still pushed
Bravely along. The Dee caught the day's last flares
Like the Pilcomayo's carrion rose.
The Peace offered eternal fragrance
Perhaps, but the Mackenzie churned livid mud
Like tan chalk-marks. Near where
The Brahmaputra slapped swollen dikes
Was an opening through which the Limmat
Could have trickled. A young man strode the Churchill's
Banks, thinking of night. The Vistula seized
The shadows. The Theiss, stark mad, bubbled
In the windy evening. And the Ob shuffled
Crazily along. Fat billows encrusted the Dniester's
Pallid flood, and the Fraser's porous surface.

Fish gasped amid the Spree's reeds. A boat
Descended the bobbing Orinoco. When the
Marne flowed by the plants nodded
And above the glistering Gila
A sunset as beautiful as the Athabasca
Stammered. The Zambezi chimed. The Oxus
Flowed somewhere. The Parnahyba
Is flowing like the wind-washed Cumberland.
The Araguía flows in the rain.
And, through overlying rocks the Isère
Cascades gently. The Guadalquiver sputtered.
Someday time will confound the Indre,
Making a rill of the Hwang. And
The Potomac rumbles softly. Crested birds
Watch the Ucayali go
Through dreaming night. You cannot stop
The Yenisei. And afterwards
The White flows strongly to its . . .
Goal. If the Tyne's shores
Hold you, and the Albany
Arrest your development, can you resist the Red's
Musk, the Meuse's situation?
A particle of mud in the Neckar
Does not turn it black. You cannot
Like the Saskatchewan, nor refuse
The meandering Yangtze, unleash
The Genesee. Does the Scamander
Still irrigate crimson plains? And the Durance
And the Pechora? The São Francisco
Skulks amid gray, rubbery nettles. The Liard's
Reflexes are slow, and the Arkansas erodes
Anthracite hummocks. The Paraná stinks.
The Ottawa is light emerald green
Among grays. Better that the Indus fade
In steaming sands! Let the Brazos
Freeze solid! And the Wabash turn to a leaden
Cinder of ice! The Marañón is too tepid, we must
Find a way to freeze it hard. The Ural
Is freezing slowly in the blasts. The black Yonne
Congeals nicely. And the Petit-Morin

Curls up on the solid earth. The Inn
Does not remember better times, and the Merrimack's
Galvanized. The Ganges is liquid snow by now;
The Vyatka's ice-gray. The once-molten Tennessee's
Curdled. The Japurá is a pack of ice. Gelid
The Columbia's gray loam banks. The Don's merely
A giant icicle. The Niger freezes, slowly.
The interminable Lena plods on
But the Purus' mercurial waters are icy, grim
With cold. The Loing is choked with fragments of ice.
The Weser is frozen, like liquid air.
And so is the Kama. And the beige, thickly flowing
Tocantins. The rivers bask in the cold.
The stern Uruguay chafes its banks,
A mass of ice. The Hooghly is solid
Ice. The Adour is silent, motionless.
The lovely Tigris is nothing but scratchy ice
Like the Yellowstone, with its osier-clustered banks.
The Mekong is beginning to thaw out a little
And the Donets gurgles beneath the
Huge blocks of ice. The Manzanares gushes free.
The Illinois darts through the sunny air again.
But the Dnieper is still ice-bound. Somewhere
The Salado propels its floes, but the Roosevelt's
Frozen. The Oka is frozen solider
Than the Somme. The Minho slumbers
In winter, nor does the Snake
Remember August. Hilarious, the Canadian
Is solid ice. The Madeira slavers
Across the thawing fields, and the Plata laughs.
The Dvina soaks up the snow. The Sava's
Temperature is above freezing. The Avon
Carols noiselessly. The Drôme presses
Grass banks; the Adige's frozen
Surface is like gray pebbles.

Birds circle the Ticino. In winter
The Var was dark blue, unfrozen. The
Thwaite, cold, is choked with sandy ice;
The Ardèche glistens feebly through the freezing rain.

For John Clare

Kind of empty in the way it sees everything, the earth gets to its feet and salutes the sky. More of a success at it this time than most others it is. The feeling that the sky might be in the back of someone's mind. Then there is no telling how many there are. They grace everything—bush and tree—to take the roisterer's mind off his caroling—so it's like a smooth switch back. To what was aired in their previous conniption fit. There is so much to be seen everywhere that it's like not getting used to it, only there is so much it never feels new, never any different. You are standing looking at that building and you cannot take it all in, certain details are already hazy and the mind boggles. What will it all be like in five years' time when you try to remember? Will there have been boards in between the grass part and the edge of the street? As long as that couple is stopping to look in that window over there we cannot go. We feel like they have to tell us we can, but they never look our way and they are already gone, gone far into the future—the night of time. If we could look at a photograph of it and say there they are, they never really stopped but there they are. There is so much to be said, and on the surface of it very little gets said.

There ought to be room for more things, for a spreading out, like. Being immersed in the details of rock and field and slope—letting them come to you for once, and then meeting them halfway would be so much easier—if they took an ingenuous pride in being in one's blood. Alas, we perceive them if at all as those things that were meant to be put aside—costumes of the supporting actors or voice trilling at the end of a narrow enclosed street. You can do nothing with them. Not even offer to pay.

It is possible that finally, like coming to the end of a long, barely perceptible rise, there is mutual cohesion and interaction. The whole scene is fixed in your mind, the music all present, as though you could see each note as well as hear it. I say this because there is an uneasiness in things just now. Waiting for something to be over before you are forced to notice it. The pollarded trees scarcely bucking the wind—and yet it's keen, it makes you fall over. Clabbered sky. Seasons that pass with a rush. After all it's their time too—nothing says they aren't to make something of it. As for Jenny Wren, she cares, hopping about on her little twig like she was tryin' to tell us somethin', but that's just it, she couldn't even if she wanted to—dumb bird. But the others—and they in some way must know too—it would never occur to them to want to, even if they could take the first step of the terrible journey toward feeling somebody should act, that ends in utter confusion and hopelessness, east of the sun and west of the moon. So

their comment is: "No comment." Meanwhile the whole history of prob-
abilities is coming to life, starting in the upper left-hand corner, like a sail.

Alcove

Is it possible that spring could be
once more approaching? We forget each time
what a mindless business it is, porous like sleep,
adrift on the horizon, refusing to take sides, "mugwump
of the final hour," lest an agenda—horrors!—be imputed to it,
and the whole point of its being spring collapse
like a hole dug in sand. It's breathy, though,
you have to say that for it.

And should further seasons coagulate
into years, like spilled, dried paint, why,
who's to say we weren't provident? We indeed
looked out for others as though they mattered, and they,
catching the spirit, came home with us, spent the night
in an alcove from which their breathing could be heard clearly.
But it's not over yet. Terrible incidents happen
daily. That's how we get around obstacles.

River of the Canoefish

These wilds came naturally by their monicker.
In 1825 the first canoefish was seen hanging offshore.
A few years later another one was spotted.
Today they are abundant as mackerel, as far as the eye can see,
tumbled, tumescent, tinted all the colors of the rainbow
though not in the same order,
a swelling, scumbled mass, rife with incident
and generally immune to sorrow.

Shall we gather at the river? On second thought, let's not.

Jimmy Santiago Baca

As Children Know

Elm branches radiate green heat,
blackbirds stiffly strut across fields.
Beneath bedroom wood floor, I feel earth—
bread in an oven that slowly swells,
simmering my Navajo blanket thread-crust
as white-feathered and corn-tasseled
Corn Dancers rise in a line, follow my calf,
vanish in a rumple and surface at my knee-cliff,
chanting. Wearing shagged buffalo headgear,
Buffalo Dancer chases Deer Woman across
Sleeping Leg mountain. Branches of wild rose
trees rattle seeds. Deer Woman fades into hills
of beige background. Red Bird
of my heart thrashes wildly after her.
What a stupid man I have been!
How good to let imagination go,
step over worrisome events,

those hacked logs
tumbled about
in the driveway.

Let decisions go!

Let them blow
like school children's papers
against the fence,
rattling in the afternoon wind.

This Red Bird
of my heart thrashes within the tidy appearance
I offer the world,

topples what I erect, snares what I set free,
dashes what I've put together,
indulges in things left unfinished,
and my world is left, as children know,
                    left as toys after dark in the sandbox.

Julianna Baggott

The Place Poem: Sparrow's Point

I was told it was named for a man, Thomas Sparrow,
but too late, no matter. I've seen what was once here
before the blasts of tugs hauling barges, the bleating trains,
the rattling gusto of the Red Rocket streetcar,
before it was a company town steeped in fumes,
dwarfed by thick electric wires; before everything—
gutters, fenceposts, penny candies left to harden
in bowls — was coated in the steel mill's red dust,
before the dust, wet from the billowing steam
of boiler chimneys, became a clammy paste:
                              Singing trees.
Sparrows, thousands. Low-lying marshland
                    and yawning blue sky
filled suddenly with dart and turn.
The air had muscled current. The birds beat, glided.
Now ghosts, they have the power to pass
                              through us,
to lodge and pulse in our ribs.
Put your hand on my heart, *there, there, now,*
                              the livid flutter.

Living Where They Raised Me

Delaware is ripe with cancer—
its shallow fields and factories without run-off,
but we don't speak of it, the hometowners,
because we aren't going anywhere.
From here, Ohio sounds exotic.
But we wonder how it will settle in,

where the curdled cells will take root.
In school, I was impressed
by the filmstrip of the woman born armless,
who could do everything with her feet—
trim her son's bangs, swat flies,
stir cake batter with her rump on the counter,
one leg around the bowl,
a wooden spoon hooked in her toes.
A nervous child, I prepared,
practiced the barefoot art
of turning pages, scrawling my name.
But my arms never fell off.
In fact, they are still here,
my feet still holding ground,
my pink organs turning this into that,
and Delaware, surrounded by the rumor
of mountains, is still flat,
its back unbroken, refusing to attempt
that sort of useless resurrection.
It's easy to blame the land,
to think if we lived somewhere else—
Hackensack or Damascus—
believing would be so easy.

Ellen Bass

Birdsong from My Patio

> Despair so easy. Hope so hard to bear.
> —THOMAS McGRATH

I've never heard this much song,
trills pure as crystal bells,
but not like bells: alive, small rushes
of air from the tiny plush lungs
of birds tucked in among the stiff
leaves of the olive and almond,
the lemon with its hard green studs.
As the sun slides down newborn
from thick-muscled clouds
their glittering voices catch the light
like bits of twirling aluminum.
I picture their wrinkled feet
curled around thin branches,
absorbing pesticide.
I see them preening, tainted
feathers sliding through their glossy
beaks, over their leathery tongues.
They're feeding on contaminated insects,
wild seeds glistening with acid rain.
And their porous, thin-shelled eggs,
bluish or milky or speckled,
lying doomed in each
intricate nest. Everything
is drenched with loss:
the wood thrush and starling,
the unripe fruit of the lemon tree.
With all that's been ruined
these songs impale the air
with their sharp, insistent needles.

The Big Picture

I try to look at the big picture.
The sun, ardent tongue
licking us like a mother besotted

with her new cub, will wear itself out.
Everything is transitory.
Think of the meteor

that annihilated the dinosaurs.
And before that, the volcanoes
of the Permian period—all those burnt ferns

and reptiles, sharks and bony fish—
that was extinction on a scale
that makes our losses look like a bad day at the slots.

And perhaps we're slated to ascend
to some kind of intelligence
that doesn't need bodies, or clean water, or even air.

But I can't shake my longing
for the last six hundred
Iberian lynx with their tufted ears,

Brazilian guitarfish, the 4
percent of them still cruising
the seafloor, eyes staring straight up.

And all the newborn marsupials—
red kangaroos, joeys the size of honeybees—
steelhead trout, river dolphins,

so many species of frogs
breathing through their damp
permeable membranes.

Today on the bus, a woman
in a sweater the exact shade of cardinals,
and her cardinal-colored bra strap, exposed

on her pale shoulder, makes me ache
for those bright flashes in the snow.
And polar bears, the cream and amber

of their fur, the long, hollow
hairs through which sun slips,
swallowed into their dark skin. When I get home,

my son has a headache, and though he's
almost grown, asks me to sing him a song.
We lie together on the lumpy couch

and I warble out the old show tunes, "Night and Day" . . .
"They Can't Take That Away from Me" . . . A cheap
silver chain shimmers across his throat

rising and falling with his pulse. There never was
anything else. Only these excruciatingly
insignificant creatures we love.

Dan Beachy-Quick

Arcadian

I could not stop my hands clapping. I clapped
And clapped. I clapped as in the dirt the bird collapsed,
As worms grew wings, I clapped.

A man stood in a river balancing
A grape on his lips. His tears fell in the current
Swept them away. He kept performing

His trick: grape hovering over the hole
Of his open mouth and never dropping in.
I clapped and I could not stop

My hands from wanting to cover my mouth
But they would not. They clapped
And I listened to them clap—a noise

That if there were woods would echo in
The woods. But there were no woods
I could see. Only a man. Twigs in his hair.

Bent over the water where the water stood
Most still. *A tree fell in the woods—*
He kept speaking to his own face—

Is true if and only if a tree fell in the
Woods is true if and only if—
He kept speaking to his face in the water

As I clapped, applauding the logic
That needed no belief. Like the shadows
Of bird's wings, the shadows of my hands

On the ground. If there were birds
I could believe in
The birds so I let myself look up.

One bird kept exploding in the sky.
One flower kept dying. *Isn't it happy?* a child asked,
Everything eating the sun? Isn't it

Happy? Isn't it—she asked, laying down
On her back in the grass—*happy?*
Everything eating the sun? Isn't it—

Lois Beardslee

Wawaskwanmiinan

Giinawind wawaskwanminige.

Ok, you say, and we find a plastic strainer.

They are beautiful and ripe and red, and they have been getting ready all summer for us to pick them.

A few here. A few there. Leave some for the birds. Leave some for the bunnies, come springtime.

Go up and down that beach, twisting our hands together, singing, putting away good-tasting vitamins for winters by the stove.

Maybe dry them on the very top of the woodstove, on that shelf above the warming bins, where we keep our favorite frying pan.

Maybe store them in that birch bark cylinder with the tight lid you helped me make last summer, helped me pull those spruce roots from under that tree over there.

Maybe mix them with *ozawadzhibig,* you get a sore throat. Maybe mix them with *mashkaginiibishabo,* you get cold from ice skating. Maybe sing that same song this winter, when we drink that tea.

Sandra Beasley

Unit of Measure

All can be measured by the standard of the capybara.
Everything is lesser than or greater than the capybara.
Everything is taller or shorter than the capybara.
Everything is mistaken for a Brazilian dance craze
more or less frequently than the capybara.
Everything eats greater or fewer watermelons
than the capybara. Everything eats more or less bark.
Everyone barks more than or less than the capybara,
who also whistles, clicks, grunts, and emits what is known
as his *alarm squeal*. Everyone is more or less alarmed
than a capybara, who—because his back legs
are longer than his front legs—feels like
he is going downhill at all times.
Everyone is more or less a *master of grasses*
than the capybara. Or going by the scientific name,
more or less *Hydrochoerus hydrochaeris*—
or, going by the Greek translation, more or less
water hog. Everyone is more or less
of a fish than the capybara, defined as the outermost realm
of fishdom by the sixteenth-century Catholic Church.
Everyone is eaten more or less often for Lent than
the capybara. Shredded, spiced, and served over plantains,
everything tastes more or less like pork
than the capybara. Before you decide that you are
greater than or lesser than a capybara, consider
that while the Brazilian capybara breeds only once a year,
the Venezuelan variety mates continuously.
Consider the last time you mated continuously.
Consider the year of your childhood when you had
exactly as many teeth as the capybara—
twenty—and all yours fell out, and all his

kept growing. Consider how his skin stretches
in only one direction. Accept that you are stretchier
than the capybara. Accept that you have foolishly
distributed your eyes, ears, and nostrils
all over your face. Accept that you will never be able
to sleep underwater. Accept that the fish
will never gather to your capybara body offering
their soft, finned love. *One of us,* they say, *one of us,*
but they will not say it to you.

Marvin Bell

The Book of the Dead Man (Fungi)

Live as if you were already dead.

1. ABOUT THE DEAD MAN AND FUNGI

The dead man has changed his mind about moss and mold.
About mildew and yeast.
About rust and smut, about soot and ash.
Whereas once he turned from the sour and the decomposed, now he
    breathes deeply in the underbelly of the earth.
Of mushrooms, baker's yeast, fungi of wood decay, and the dogs
    preceding their masters to the burnt acre of morels.
And the little seasonals themselves, stuck on their wobbly pin stems.
For in the pan they float without crisping.
For they are not without a hint of the sublime, nor the curl of a hand.
These are the caps and hairdos, the mini-umbrellas, the zeppelins of a
    world in which human beings are heavy-footed mammoths.
Puffballs and saucers, recurrent, recumbent, they fill the encyclopedia.
Not wrought for the pressed eternity of flowers or butterflies.
Loners and armies alike appearing overnight at the point of return.
They live fast, they die young, they will be back.

2. MORE ABOUT THE DEAD MAN AND FUNGI

Fruit of the fungi, a mushroom's birthing is an arrow from below.
It is because of Zeno's Paradox that one cannot get there by half-measures.
It is the fault of having anything else to do.
The dead man prefers the mushroom of the gatherer to that of the farmer.
Gilled or ungilled, stemmed or stemless, woody or leathery, the
    mushroom is secretive, yes, by nature.
Each mushroom was a button, each a flowering, some glow in the dark.
Medicinal or toxic, each was lopped from the stump of eternity.

166

The dead man has seen them take the shapes of cups and saucers, of
   sponges, logs and bird nests.
The dead man probes the shadows, he fingers the crannies and
   undersides, he spots the mushroom underfoot just in time.
When the dead man saw a mushrooming cloud above Hiroshima, he
   knew.
He saw that death was beautiful from afar.
He saw that nature is equidistant from the nourishing and the poisonous,
   the good and the bad, the beginning and the end.
He knew the littlest mushroom, shivering on its first day, was a signal.

Dan Bellm

Aspens

The individual life is not the point—*admire me*
I am a violet, and so on, as John Keats mocked,
in the voice of the self who wants to be more precious
than existence—long parentless by then,
nursing his brother Tom through the long bloodcoughing
months of death and knowing his own could come soon,
perhaps before love, or another visitation of poetry,
though he had only reached the Chamber of Maiden-thought
in the house of many rooms he was sketching out
in his own faint light—*on all sides many doors set open but all*
dark all leading to dark passages—maybe few to be revealed
in an individual life. So the naturalist led us poets
up a creekbed to show us a tiny portion of our own world:
a fragile meetingpoint of volcanic rock & granite
that over a hundred thousand years urged forth a way
for water to wash down and make this canyon to the valley:
told us that the grove of quaking aspens we stopped beside
ought to call into question our definition of a tree:
not separate trees but clones sprung from an underground
rhizomal oh I don't know what the word was,
which makes me ashamed—I didn't write it down—as if
knowledge of the names of things means understanding anything
of what they are—the other poets, I figured, were writing down
notes for me—wanting really to have the labeled placards
in an arboretum (*dote upon me I am a primrose*) so I could
walk away satisfied knowing more than enough but actually
nothing much. The point was that the system of roots beneath us
was vaster than we could think, a million years old or so,
and apparently so capable of continuing sending up clones each season
that it can wait for the arrival of the next ice age to this valley
if it takes another million years, and the theorizers who know

that our minds and words stop short of what this might mean
have posited what they can only call "theoretical immortality."
(All of the poets wrote *that* one down.) All right, so I returned
to poetry so late, guilty, ashamed, regretful, sad, all right.
My teacher beside me—disoriented by all these
lateblooming Sierra wildflowers unknown in northern New Hampshire—
another system but not another earth—connected underneath—
(same late-July mosquitoes here as there biting me though,
taking me back to my summers by Mt. Chocorua at the commie camp,
swimming in the deep pond there, deciding to be a writer and so
to change the world, *rich in the simple worship of a day*)—she said
she was grateful there was such a community of writers as this one
and she had found it—so little of the usual mutual hatred
and self-mistrust because we're working every day and facing
the blankness of paper, urging each other on, not showing off our
bundles of poems from home to be doted upon or angling
for career moves, though I do want my fucking book to get out
of my house. She agreed with me, no, you are not, at the age
of 45, the next young thing the poetry biz is waiting
to discover, and you can thank God herself for it, having had
students at the age of 23 all but drown in acclaim and felt
afraid for them as in, O honey—just wait until you're in
a small town somewhere with an underpaying job and a couple of
babies, not enough time, a husband who helps out, or not,
and one book on the shelf while the world has moved on
to the next bright morning star—that's when, if you're lucky,
you'll be a writer. Send down your taproot then, into the
many-chambered whatever it is, the comfort and fright of it,
that we're all connected. *And thus by every germ of Spirit*
sucking the Sap from mould ethereal every human might become great,
and Humanity instead of being a wide heath of Furse and Briars
with here and there a remote Oak or Pine, would become
a grand democracy of Forest Trees. These plant "communities"—
manzanita, huckleberry, snow-something, oh I didn't write those down
either I was so tired, the words are not the point—they're migrating
over geological time—they send messages to each other
across the great spongeous rootmass about changes in temp. and
rainfall, outbreaks of blight, accumulated experience we'd call
gossip or history, the sports and weather, film at 11—they slowly

move, and so others move with them, what's the choice—the point
is the interwoven indistinguishableness that all life feeds
and is fed by, not the individual life. And the hope
that I will be communicated with among the forms of life
must be what is meant by a blessing—say, the man I saw
laying his hands on another man's head, in the rain, to bless him,
in a crowd at the corner of Post & Stockton in the middle of the day—
it must be only our bodies, our skin, that make us think
we are contained in one place in one self, as a tree appears to end
at the root, the rock, the leaf-edge, the air, as a mountain appears
to end at the level ground, so we need the laying on
of hands to make an entryway into the one
oh what will I call it? We don't even have the same desires
as ourselves, as when the ex-President said, "I have opinions
of my own. Strong opinions. But I don't always agree with them."
We are temporary shadows constantly turning around
to misremember, elaborate constructions
unrecoverable a moment later, contradictory lifelines
in the palms of our hands. So even a sad song causes happiness
when it comes from the heart. So Jacob asked a blessing of his father
as I did, though I too had to steal it, holding his hand as he died
in a coma in a narrow bed: I think he was waiting for me.
And afterwards we go on living, at our own mercy,
which can be short at hand. Am I too old?
I am not the next young thing but that has never stopped
the subterranean-stream-continuation of all the desires.
Band of rose-gold on my finger, and 16 years of marriage
to the man I love, faithful in our quotes open relationship
well are we? though openness can be an aperture or chasm. The man
handing me change in the hardware store with my wall-grabbers
and wingnuts had two nipple rings, which I thought was one
too many, and was young enough to be my child; he made me hot
as our hands met though it meant nothing much, and am I too old
to get a nipple ring? I want to ask him if I did that would it
hurt, but a part of me I love is afraid it might not hurt enough:
more unfulfillment in desire, even the desire for pain, which runs on
in the underground stream and resurfaces each season
in its fashion, as here in a brightly-lit store midday
on Castro St.: I wanted to lick the salt from his skin.
Oh what would I turn into if I were single again? The devious

frightened loner I was before. Undiscovered by poetry.
Now we look upward on the trail because the life of birds,
living or ornamental, this one or the birds of tapestry in the decor
of our minds, the nothing that is not there, and the nothing
that is—their life is song. A junco but I didn't see it,
the guide helped us notice and then I heard it, a scold, a
trailing-off *compleynt*, as Bela Bartók must have heard
the actual Hungarian birds of his youth that he lived among
before the disaster of our midcentury dispersed the forms of life
but how did he still hear them and place them
directly by their song and without names into that never-quite-
finished Piano Concerto No. 3, his cry of anguished love
and a capitulation before some wellspring he knew would continue
after him, or at any rate that's what I heard when I first
heard it in Ann Arbor some twenty years ago, the days when I
was almost giving up on my own soul and living in that piss-
smelling boarding house on Miller Avenue, mourning my first lover,
smoking so much dope, back in the closet again,
romanticizing Larry and Sadie the drunks from the U.P. next door
because they were Indians and had done so much Real Time
in the Washtenaw County Jail right across the street—
we heard the screams and fighting of the prisoners at night—
and who therefore seemed to live more intensely, have *more* life,
than one such as me writing termpapers on *Middlemarch*,
when what I wanted from them really was another sedative drug—
what a sorrowful young youth I was, pitiful jade plant in my window
likewise half in love with death, but I had a rainsoaked *Book of
Nightmares* and the birds that Bela Bartók conjured up for me,
one mortal body passing the song on to another
across indefinite time, his final music, so full of legend and glory,
sitting on a cot an almost penniless refugee in 1945 on W. 57th St.
in New York knowing he was dying, racing to leave it
as a birthday present for his wife and even more, a useful
concert-piece that she could go on playing and earn a little
money from to make her way, the sheet music found only later
lying out of order on every available surface of bed and desk
and floor, a windowless room in which he caused
the birds of gone-forever Hungary to go on singing.

Margo Berdeshevsky

After the End After the Beginning

> Tears in the eyes of fishes
> —BASHO

After the end of the world, the dragon flies are the first,
returning. Frogs in chorus in a lead-weight rain, the bones
of buffalo, pissing.

After the end of the world, a shredded page, uprooted
monster trees. A blue jacket, a lace head cloth, a black
boot on a wheelchair stem, a mudded page of the floating
Koran.

After the end of the world, flooded rice fields, a blind
child seeing ghosts of ghosts, stabs his forefingers in his
eyes, screaming.

After the end of the world, Ayesha is chopping chiles to
spice our gruel—I was crazy but now I sing for the world,
she says and says and says again. After the end of the world,
a crazy woman who loves God, singing ahead of the heat.
After the end of the world, a woman who sings that the bad
ones perished,   Allehu   Akbar   in the next hot dawn again
and again, ever after.

After the end of the world, over and over—I lost, I lost, I lost,
and God is great, the mosquito ballet meeting the dragon flies,
circling.

This is not a dream, this is a tragedy, a boy making his words
a sing-song, spindle-shins, kicking. After red words on the broken
columns: this is not a dream, this was tragedy, fresh fish who may
have wedding rings in their bellies.

After the end, a new market. After the end, what kind of town had
it been?   yellow velvet, and minarets.   a shredded boot.   blue
china, broken.   a baby's rubber thong, not screaming.

After the finale, smiles left that say, I lived.   I dream of
corpses drowned in the noonday heat. What time is it now?

After the end of the world, the taro plant blooms in another
language, its flood-root, fetid emerald in the mud. After the end
of the world   bruised   dirty   determined Sisyphus—who
ever breathes—rebuilds.

—Aceh, December 26, 2004

Wendell Berry

Horses

When I was a boy here,
traveling the fields for pleasure,
the farms were worked with teams.
As late as then a teamster
was thought an accomplished man,
his art an essential discipline.
A boy learned it by delight
as he learned to use
his body, following the example
of men. The reins of a team
were put into my hands
when I thought the work was play.
And in the corrective gaze
of men now dead I learned
to flesh my will in power
great enough to kill me
should I let it turn.
I learned the other tongue
by which men spoke to beasts
—all its terms and tones.
And by the time I learned,
new ways had changed the time.
The tractors came. The horses
stood in the fields, keepsakes,
grew old, and died. Or were sold
as dogmeat. Our minds received
the revolution of engines, our will
stretched toward the numb endurance
of metal. And that old speech
by which we magnified
our flesh in other flesh

fell dead in our mouths.
The songs of the world died
in our ears as we went within
the uproar of the long syllable
of the motors. Our intent entered
the world as combustion.
Like our travels, our workdays
burned upon the world,
lifting its inwards up
in fire. Veiled in that power
our minds gave up the endless
cycle of growth and decay
and took the unreturning way,
the breathless distance of iron.

But that work, empowered by burning
the world's body, showed us
finally the world's limits
and our own. We had then
the life of a candle, no longer
the ever-returning song
among the grassblades and the leaves.

Did I never forget?
Or did I, after years,
remember? To hear that song
again, though brokenly
in the distances of memory,
is coming home. I came to
a farm, some of it unreachable
by machines, as some of the world
will always be. And so
I came to a team, a pair
of mares—sorrels, with white
tails and manes, beautiful!—
to keep my sloping fields.
Going behind them, the reins
tight over their backs as they stepped
their long strides, revived
again on my tongue the cries

of dead men in the living
fields. Now every move
answers what is still.
This work of love rhymes
living and dead. A dance
is what this plodding is.
A song, whatever is said.

Water

I was born in a drouth year. That summer
my mother waited in the house, enclosed
in the sun and the dry ceaseless wind,
for the men to come back in the evenings,
bringing water from a distant spring.
Veins of leaves ran dry, roots shrank.
And all my life I have dreaded the return
of that year, sure that it still is
somewhere, like a dead enemy's soul. Fear
of dust in my mouth is always with me,
and I am the faithful husband of the rain,
I love the water of wells and springs
and the taste of roofs in the water of cisterns.
I am a dry man whose thirst is praise
of clouds, and whose mind is something of a cup.
My sweetness is to wake in the night
after days of dry heat, hearing the rain.

The Hidden Singer

The gods are less
for their love of praise.
Above and below them all
is a spirit that needs
nothing but its own

wholeness,
its health and ours.
It has made all things
by dividing itself.
It will be whole again.
To its joy we come
together—the seer
and the seen, the eater
and the eaten, the lover
and the loved.
In our joining it knows
itself. It is with us then,
not as the gods
whose names crest
in unearthly fire,
but as a little bird
hidden in the leaves
who sings quietly
and waits
and sings.

The Peace of Wild Things

When despair for the world grows in me
and I wake in the night at the least sound
in fear of what my life and my children's lives may be,
I go and lie down where the wood drake
rests in his beauty on the water, and the great heron feeds.
I come into the peace of wild things
who do not tax their lives with forethought
of grief. I come into the presence of still water.
And I feel above me the day-blind stars
waiting with their light. For a time
I rest in the grace of the world, and am free.

To the Unseeable Animal

My daughter: *"I hope there's an animal
somewhere that nobody has ever seen.
And I hope nobody ever sees it."*

Being, whose flesh dissolves
at our glance, knower
of the secret sums and measures,
you are always here,
dwelling in the oldest sycamores,
visiting the faithful springs
when they are dark and the foxes
have crept to their edges.
I have come upon pools
in streams, places overgrown
with the woods' shadow,
where I knew you had rested,
watching the little fish
hang still in the flow;
as I approached they seemed
particles of your clear mind
disappearing among the rocks.
I have waked deep in the woods
in the early morning, sure
that while I slept
your gaze passed over me.
That we do not know you
is your perfection
and our hope. The darkness
keeps us near you.

Mei-mei Berssenbrugge

The Star Field

Placing our emotion on a field, I said, became a nucleus of space,
defined by a rain of light and indeterminate contours of a landscape,
like the photograph of an explosion, and gave the travel of your gaze into
    it, or on me,
imaginative weight of the passage along a gulf of space
or a series of aluminum poles.

She walks through the rooms of blue chain-linked fence, a spacious
    tennis court
of rooms on concrete, instead of the single movement of a room, where
    sky and earth
would come together.

Outside is the field she is thinking about: a category of gray dots
on a television screen of star data, representing no one's experience,
but which thrills all who gaze on it, so that it must be experience. And
the land at large becomes the light on the land.

A coyote or a flicker's call
is transfixed at the moment before its dissemination across the field,
a sediment of, instead
of the trace of feeling, the ratio of people to the space.
I pass through blue focal planes, a scene of desire

The material of the sky adjacent to me eludes me, a pure signifier,
shifting sense, the sky or space a gradation of material, the light
a trace of mobility like a trace of light on a sensitive screen,
extended into the plane of the trace
and marked by light poles or drawn close by a planet at the edge.

Your name becomes a trace of light. Through
its repetition and deferral, my life protects itself
from blurs, time lapses, flares
of the sexual act, its mobility of an afterimage.

Then I can understand the eye's passage into depth
as an inability to stand still for you to see.

from A Context of a Wave

November 5.

You could be thinking about your physical placement, what can be a
continuum and what is chance. You place yourself innately on a mesa.
There are blue hills at each horizon, the light falls copiously onto your
open space, the path of the sun and the planets are proportioned around
you.

The source of the balance is a sense perception. Your perception of your
location is not contingent, but accords with an idea of location inside you,
that turns in you like a gyroscope, as you are moving.

I believe in this sense perception of place, because I experience it.

It may be a sense of the shape of a space, or of the balance of features of
the space, or it may be a sense of a point on the earth in relation to forces
in the earth, which may be affected by stars and planets. Or, it may be in
relation to stars and planets.

November 9.

So that the place would sit in me, its wide space with sun, as what it
would be in my memory of this time. And how it would be perceived is
a matrix of how you were with some people around you, not agents but
catalyst or fuel for the perception of light on a wide space, so free as to be
impersonal in the company, implacable and impersonal.

November 10.

She would remember that it was a place of the wind. She would think that
she would remember the site of sun, and light without sound or without

value, but her body is pushed and drawn on by the force of wind on the ridge, every day, so that someday she would remember that she had lived in wind.

The wind can be in the future, a direction, as if there were time, because it comes from somewhere. Because it draws you somewhere, it is the time or space that is the next thing somewhere among the materials of a space or at a time. Because it might be seen as an expression of the forces making it, which push on you or draw from you, it is an expression to everything it is not, and you are reminded you are what it is not, and this expression deters you or abstains from you as a space, when the wind is pushing all night or on a sunny day against the windows and walls of your house.

Then, this expression of being what something is not, joins you with a piece of leaning yellow grass in low sun, or it abstains you from the expression, as if you are more becoming in your mind what you are looking at than what you are feeling.

November 11.

You would be able to see the meaning or whole of the space between the objects on the table, which before had been random space between the fork and the salt crystal.

Now you can see the meaning or the whole of the space between rods of illuminated streaks of clouds at sunset, zooming this way and that, and the volume and vector between them. From you to the horizon gains a meaning. Something happens to you, it is time moving, and you can see them as a whole thing and not the space between one cloud and another that appear on the same plane because of the same color of light on them.

November 12.

We walked in the dry riverbed. Water had left the sand in sweeps of lines and currents, fronds of tamarack drifted in. I want to call it pollen of tamarack drifting into patterns of sand made by currents of water, lift drifts of events in time. But it is more like the bits of tamarack frond, broken by the current and drifting into patterns or record was the time, because of there being something besides a pattern to perceive time by means of.

A skin of tufts of yellow grasses on a hillside threw off the lateral light, and threw down their delicate shadows. The flank of a hill suggesting a living creature.

November 13.

You can see the complexity of autumn plants and trees in the canyon below you. It is late autumn. The yellow and brown jumble of the foliage. Most of the leaves have fallen from the trees and bushes into heaps and drifts on either side of the stream. We are accustomed to think of disorganization and of increasing disorganization as a vector toward entropy. The pleasurable complexity of matter in the canyon would seem to be entropic, except for its beauty. It looks like death. It seems entropic, but it is not entropic, as biological death may not be. And I wonder if the beauty is an innate apprehension of the ongoingness, or "other" than entropy, of that sight?

November 14.

I see the honey moon rise from a bare horizon, after the sunset behind a mountain. I was waiting for the moon. It was a test and not a knowledge of the movement of the risings, by which I am trying to judge where I am on this plain. We are trying to understand if the moon sets in a different place than the sun, the sun which is moving and moving down the horizon. Soon, its colored glow will silhouette a mountain called The Wave.

Linda Bierds

April

A little wind. One creak from a field crow.
And the plow rips a shallow furrow, hobbles
from guide-stake to guide-stake,
draws its first contour line,
and parallel, its next, next,
then the turn-strips and deadfurrows, the headlands
and buffer lines, until the earth from a crow's vantage
takes the pattern of a fingertip.

And by noon the shadows are gridways: cut soil,
the man on the plow, the plow and simple tail,
each squat on a stretch of slender shade,
black and grid-straight, like the line of anti-light

a screen clicks up to, before its image
swells, deepens. Dark glass
going green, in the shade-darkened room
of a laboratory—it casts a little blush
across the face there, the shoulders and white pocket,
then magnifies the moon-skin of a microbe, then deeper,
electron molecules in a beam so stark it smolders.

The man on the plow fears frost,
its black cancer. The man at the screen
fears the storm an atom renders
on the lattice of a crystal. And heat. And the slick
back-licks of vapor. With luck, with the patience
the invisible nurtures, he will reshape

frost-making microbes, snip frost-hook genes
with a knife of enzymes. And at thirty degrees,
twenty, through seam lines of snap beans, oranges,

almonds, potatoes, no frost will form, no ratchet-bite
of ice, all the buds of transformed microbes
blossoming, reblossoming, like the first flowers.

There is wind at the rim of the black-out shade.
One tick of the focus gears. Another. On a glass plate,
enlarged from nothing to filaments, the lines
of DNA wander, parallel, in tandem,
curled together past pigment blips, resin,
as the contour lines for autumn oranges
swerve in unison past boulder pods. The light

through the mottled skins of genes
is not light at all, but friction, caught and channeled,
like pigment caught in the scratch-marks of caves.
This was our world, the marks say: horse, maize,
vast gods drawn down to a palm print.
Drawn up from nothing the microbes gather,
a little wind on the curtain,
sun on the curtain's faded side, on the crow and plow,
on the earth sketched perfectly to receive it.

Ralph Black

21st Century Lecture

Listen. You know what a torn shirt
the world's become. You know how thin
its fabric. You know what seams are,
and how your life, as though by accident,
settles in and trembles them apart.
And everyone knows you don't mean it.
So you say to yourself, don't be stupid.
You say, don't sham and swindle your way
through these stark desecrations,
don't stand around as your body's
warming waters rise, as they lift
and pool around the trunks
of three-hundred-year-old trees—
the ones that snatched away your breath
and all your words when you were a kid.
Your tea is getting cold. The shirts
you bought on a whim have to go back
to the Singapore sweatshop.
You're a smart enough guy, keening
over the paper each morning,
tuned in to just the right litany of fear—
Baghdad, Darfur, the Bronx—
the outstretched or instantly severed hand.
You could turn the page from the steady
unraveling of the planet's bright threads.
But your throat rasps and freezes at the sight
of the sea lion sow chewing the face
off her newborn pup; at the coho hatchlings
spilling out of the hatchery flume,
carrying their constellations of DNA
up and against the river's age-old equations;

at the polar bears starving at the edge
of their ice. You know the word *starving*,
you know the meaning of CO_2, you know
how apple seeds and smart bombs bloom,
how simple it is to flay a range of hills,
eviscerate a mountain with a spark.
You know how the stones can keep you warm.
You're not an idiot. You're not a fool.
You won't let your heart—that tiny,
glacial island—fracture and calve.
You think your love for your children
and your children's love for everything
but homework and spinach should be plenty.
The name of the wind is changing.
The wind, which you know is your breath,
and spills over flooded deltas, which churns
through the gleaming thickets of oil refineries,
fission factories, wind farms, water mills,
think tanks, smelters, grinders, brothels,
landfills, gun shops, billboards declaring
the newest-brightest-best—You know
how it fills you, how it lifts away from you
the words you use to talk back to yourself
late into the night. It's a very old wind, and you
utter it over and over, a mantra, a koan,
a playing out of words like an old uncle spiraling
ten-pound test over his favorite run of rapids
thirty miles up the East Fork of that river
that spills now green and empty as an eye.
You know all this. No one's telling you anything
you haven't known for a hundred years.
But your tongue says *say it*, just the same.
Your mouth makes the shape of a call, a cry,
an uneven song. You reach for a pen,
tired as you are. You write it down, because
stories and maps are the same. You think
of the photograph you saw at the museum:
a ten year old boy born blind who lost
both his arms in his country's war.

He's at a desk, reading a book with his mouth.
He's leaning in and kissing the words,
in love with his own hunger.
He's doing with his whole body
everything he knows how to do.

Robert Bly

The Dead Seal

1

Walking north toward the point, I come on a dead seal. From a few feet away, he looks like a brown log. The body is on its back, dead only a few hours. I stand and look at him. There's a quiver in the dead flesh: My God, he's still alive. And a shock goes through me, as if a wall of my room had fallen away.

His head is arched back, the small eyes closed; the whiskers sometimes rise and fall. He is dying. This is the oil. Here on its back is the oil that heats our houses so efficiently. Wind blows fine sand back toward the ocean. The flipper near me lies folded over the stomach, looking like an unfinished arm, lightly glazed with sand at the edges. The other flipper lies half underneath. And the seal's skin looks like an old overcoat, scratched here and there—by sharp mussel shells maybe.

I reach out and touch him. Suddenly he rears up, turns over. He gives three cries: Awaark! Awaark! Awaark! – like the cries from Christmas toys. He lunges toward me; I am terrified and leap back, though I know there can be no teeth in that jaw. He starts flopping toward the sea. But he falls over, on his face. He does not want to go back to the sea. He looks up at the sky, and he looks like an old lady who has lost her hair. He puts his chin back down on the sand, rearranges his flippers, and waits for me to go. I go.

2

The next day I go back to say goodbye. He's dead now. But he's not. He's a quarter mile farther up the shore. Today he is thinner, squatting on his stomach, head out. The ribs show more: each vertebra on the back under the coat is visible, shiny. He breathes in and out.

A wave comes in, touches his nose. He turns and looks at me—the eyes slanted; the crown of his head looks like a boy's leather jacket bending over some bicycle bars. He is taking a long time to die. The whiskers white as porcupine quills, the forehead slopes. . . . Goodbye, brother, die in the sound of the waves. Forgive us if we have killed you. Long live your race, your inner-tube race, so uncomfortable on land, so comfortable in the ocean. Be comfortable in death then, when the sand will be out of your nostrils, and you can swim in long loops through the pure death, ducking under as assassinations break above you. You don't want to be touched by me. I climb the cliff and go home the other way.

Marianne Boruch

Birdsong, face it, some male machine

Birdsong, face it, some male machine
gone addled—repeat, repeat—the damage
keeps doing, the world ending then starting,
the first word the last, etc. It's that

etcetera. How to love. Is a wire
just loose? Build an ear for that. Fewer, they say.
So many fewer, by far. He's showing off
to call her back. Or claiming the tree.

Or a complaint—the food around here,
the ants, the moths, the berries. She's making
the nest, or both are. In feathers, in hair or twigs,
in rootlets and tin foil. Shiny bits seen

from a distance, a mistake. But fate
has reasons to dress up. Stupid
and dazzling have a place, a place, a place
though never. She can't sing it.

It includes the butterfly and the rat, the shit

It includes the butterfly and the rat, the shit
drying to chalk, trees
falling at an angle, taking those moist
and buried rootballs with them

into deadly air. But someone will
tell you the butterfly's the happy ending
of every dirge-singing worm, the rat
a river rat come up from a shimmering depth,

the shit passed purely into scat one can read
for a source, the creature that shadowed it one
longish minute. And trees, of course they
wanted to fall. *It was their time* or something

equally sonorous. And wind too knows its
mindless little whirlpool's *not for nothing*, not
nothing—that pitch and rage stopped. How else
does the sparrow's neck break.

Annie Boutelle

The Rapture of Bees

Suddenly absent, vamoosed, as if
they'd never been, never spiraled

in air, nor clung to each other
through frozen dark, nor filled

the hive with their million lithe
bodies, packed shelves of wax

and gold, and all that honeyed buzz.
Like a child in a bed in Portugal, just

not there—only space in her stead.
Or hair in coils on the barber's floor,

the neck abandoned and chill. Or
the breast with the other discarded

body parts, somewhere in a hospital
basement and only the stitches to show

where it was. How not to envy
the bees? So fierce an uprush, it

can't be resisted, that soaring in air
to meet whoever is coming, the cell-

phone tower bristling with urgent
messages about the time, the place,

and the fake plastic branches are
arms that sweep them in, not one left,

and death is simple—just being where
the others are, a trembling vibration.

Elizabeth Bradfield

Multi-Use Area

Would the day on the hay flats—
sun slight through clouds, grasses
just starting again from last year's
grasses, geese and cranes bugling
over the marsh—have been better
without the old tires, the gutted couch
in a pullout, a moose slumped alongside,
meat taken but the head still attached?

I can close my eyes to the pop bottles,
booze bottles, and orange skeet shells
in the parking lot, along the river. Walk
past them. I can pretend my own steps
through the marsh convey a different
presence. But I can't close my ears.
There, a white-fronted goose, there
a pintail, willow branches cracking

underfoot, F-14s from the base. And there, again,
the shotgun blast and whoop which I can't
edit out, which I probably shouldn't.
It stops when I walk into view. I stop
and stare across the flats through my
binoculars, thinking *asshole*. And of course
someone's staring back at me
over a truck bed, thinking *asshole*.

Legacy

for Vitus Bering

They've closed again the gap that you first sailed,
Russian sponsored Dane, so cousins on the Diomedes

are in post Cold War touch. But you made the map

that made the border, sighting lands just guessed at
between Kamchatka and America's west coast. And we
   write history from what's put down *officially*, maps

and logbooks made and kept by the survivors
of your death, of your loss of ambition from years

line-toeing across the forehead of Siberia. Finally you set sail for

glory—or not *for* but *from* whatever pushes us beyond
our birth-spots. What pushes us away? I, too, have left
   for some spot unknown by any who claim me, for

place unhooked from kin and story. I've fled
the watched life of any hometown where if

you kick a dog, infect a girl, break a window

the girl turns out to be your mother's landlord's
cousin, the dog a beat cop's mutt, and shards
   cut your sister's foot: Each chafed-at thing's a window

in your glass-house world. So the age-old lust for places
we pretend are free of consequence. It's the same

now as it was with Oedipus, poor stiff, running to escape his fate

and running smack dab into it, an awful
scene, a nightmare warning we need to keep
   repeating because, of course, fate

never seems immediate. For weeks Bering's crew feasted
on the delicious bulk of sea cows (now extinct).

They played cards, anted up with otter pelts that *promyshlenniki* later

stripped from the shores. Foxes bit the men's toes
at night. The land ate them as they ate the land,
    calling it need, worrying about it later.

Laynie Browne

from Mermaid's Purse

A tree translates the double horizon. The day nods, filling pods with blue-gray. The crossbow principle does not apply here. Why do blue flowers yield red dye, and yellow flowers red? They first heard the house calling, and then went walking. Collecting samples from the spirit world. A completely round rainbow. This is the sound of falling asleep suddenly. If I can remember not to do so upon a wheel's edge.

.

Agate beach in rain which fell heavily, creating a pattern of opening and closing cavities in sand. The sound guided further out to sea. Hibernation in winter is the same misrepresentation of venture. If I remain indoors I may travel more easily. Speech mirrors silence the way footsteps would otherwise remain submerged. Ambulation is changed by water. I travel away in order to match the hem of waters. I witness the tide's undermarkings, as if reading a series of utterances. An attempt to study the kaleidoscopic languages.

.

I wrote a series of apologies to a landscape. The yellow geums turned to seed clusters. The face of the stream bank crept into shadow. We avoided trading upon the exposed roots of trees. And walked through this transition as if our arms were streamers. Those things which changed became rocklings. Who will remember which days were exchanged for roots? Leaves may carry a message when circling the body. Sash ideogram.

.

The rose resin clung to my hands, as did the countryside. Small dark lines moving over the blossoms are aphids. They reproduce before they are born. I wished for the ability to wander the landscape with no sense of division. The separation of matter by thought is a fleeting misconception. As the shadows of how many birds have crossed over me. A blink of shade. Like

the orange honeysuckle, Lonicera ciliosa, called "ghost" or "owl's swing."
The leaf surrounds the flower, and then cleaves.

.

Standing among the remains of discarded skeletons had become unfash-
ionable, so they walked about carrying their bones. Traces of the discarded
sky could be carried easily in a large bucket and spilled against the edges of
dawn. Harvested ice had been transformed into a system of nomenclature.
Her complexion reveals the toil of such days. She eats again what she has
spat out. Sparse word envelopes. Tired of youth, he summoned his further
lives. The cat was begging for cream. This completes my library of books
and bookish rogues.

.

I wished for the devices of the squid. A steady pen in place of a skeleton,
and the ability to shroud myself with ink. Those oceanic correspondences
cannot be lately regrettable as they leave no permanent markings. If water
were my medium, I should not consider paper steady. Limp ledgers, and
nebulous washes. The first letter appeared in the Cambrian period, at a
depth of six hundred meters. The reply, an elaborate display of color. A
walk above this streaming wake. Thus I may find my voice in the middle of
a boatride, and carry it back with me between teeth and tongue.

Derick Burleson

Outside Fairbanks

Mist this morning rises up
the valley like a nightmare
fading toward noon, until

I can't remember what
the horror was, rises from
the poison pond the gold

mine left, gilds the golden
aspen leaves with acid dew.
Late fall and the chickadees

already brave enough to eat
sunflower seeds from my hand.
A semi rumbles down Gold

Hill Road below, hauling who
knows what hazard toward town
while wild cranberries fill

the gelid air with a foretaste
of winter scent. Such strange
juxtapositions. And I wonder

what gasses my oil stove breathes
out, keeping me close and cozy
while the cold season rises.

I stood alone and watched
the northern lights last night,
a goddess lashing her moon-

bearing horses home late
with a sharp whip of green
flame. Now the morning

mist has risen here, turned
to a blank fog the far sun
can't break through.

Cyrus Cassells

Down from the Houses of Magic

1

Now the moon darns the moor with its fabric of minnows,
And the sea rushes with the ecstasy of ants.
Down from the houses of magic, a healing wind sweeps,
Down from the houses of magic.
On Gull Hill, in the flaming garden, God flings
A fistful of robin redbreasts—razzamatazz.
And the reed of the supple mind bends and shivers,
And the choirlike, match-stemmed, fiercely gallant flowers:
Johnny-jump-up, pert buttercup, anemone, peony, lupine,
The first lightning-white rose dying to open
Beneath the systole and diastole of a starry night,
Iris, allium, the proffered chalices of tulips,
The colors of a fabulous dusk in Tunisia;
Coming soon, a pleasure of freesias, a pleasure.
Such tintinnabulation—listen:
All the prayer-wheels of April-into-May luster
Spinning God-drunk—till finally beside
The moon-daft willow, slack as a marionette,
The frenzy of scotch broom,
The fleet-souled orioles marshal, at wolf's hour,
Then sally in one brilliant will.

2

Abundance begins here—at the sea lip:
On the Cape I've come to God and Proteus, come to rest in wild places:
Whisker-still galaxies of marshlands,
Beaches where I pause and study
The Atlantic, teal and taciturn, the Atlantic, glittering and fluent,
As on blond days fishermen stagger

And bluefish wake to the breathless dream of land.

Having combed eerie dunes,
I have been on desolate moons, wind-worked to pure scrimshaw,
And found deer, cranberries, a plum dusk,
Pools of sweet water carved into sand.

The streets stink of fish, after the dark
Gimcrack shawls of squalls and rain.
I amble through rumours of shipwrecks, ghosts,
Sense the red broom-sweep of the beacon even in my sleep—

I have my tremendous window.
The moon-jacklit boat comes to it, shimmering,
And the bride-sweet cirrus cloud,
And sometimes the streak of a squirrel, like the deft, sudden
Stroke of the watercolorist, whose brush distills the bay.

And now, clear and fugitive, in jack-in-the-box brilliance,
The baby whale blooms:
Wild world, wild messenger—you are the moment's crown, sea-loved:
When providence brims to the outermost land,
No lack, no lack, but in my human mind.

3

Midsummer.
And after belligerent sun, twilight brings
A muezzin of sea-wind,
And the soul of the garden bows,
A praise in the earth:
Among Turk-cap lilies, suddenly,
In the willow's cool hair,
The breath of God—

Now I stand in the garden
Like a messenger proclaiming
I am Cyrus, and I am here,
Amid Lilliputian canon-flowers—
I surrender! I surrender!—
Under starry dippers pouring
Into a vast and holy dark—

4

One day on Gull Hill I wept and prayed:
Let this earth become a heaven—

Beyond the garden, the wall of clematis:
The world with its rills of blood,
The blue and virulent cell where a man was flayed
To make a flag of human skin—

Tonight the moon makes a silver threshing floor of the sea.
Beside the moth-claimed path, the stone seraph decays,
The stiffened body of a finch—

The rose is no paraclete.
A keen star plummets into the heart's cup, the summer grasses.

And the blue earth resumes its measureless dialogue
Between catastrophe and plenty.

5

The dirty, nail-bitten hand
Of a Black Lear,
With the green and pink
Bracelet of a woman
Inching its way
Through garbage:

Even in the garden on Gull Hill,
I see that hand:
All day rocking back and forth
Between Turk-cap lilies and the trash—
Till at last words spill out,
Ones I shrink from:

Are you hungry all the time?

Yes, all the time—

O grant us strength to fashion a table
Where each of us has a name—

6

From autumn to autumn, teach us
How to breathe, endure,
In the shadow of the sickening weapon;

Teach us how to blossom,
If the sky is acid,
The garden marred—

We move through the world with its drastic reds,
Its discord,
Seeking balm in all things:
Mother's milk, the dream of reunion—

Not enough to hate suffering,
Hate war,
But to jettison at last
All duality, division,
To discern
God-in-the-guise-of-the-stranger,
God-in-the-guise-of-this-flesh—

7

Then in my dream, like a hawk,
I circled the garden:
No, it was not Earth, the grand, lacerated Earth;
On its whorled surface,
All the ages of mankind.
And a voice sang:
Here are the flowers of deep suffering,
Swaying in the heart of God—

8

Because
        Each of us must seek
A finer life, a finer death.

Because
        In the garden, beside the clematis,
Jousting with slippery shadows

Of birth-and-death-and-birth-and-death,
Sometimes I come back to
The pitiless floor of Hiroshima,
Knowing in the terror and magnitude
Of true comprehension
I meant to die there—
Back to the fierce moment
After the *pika*, the flash,
When suddenly I reclaimed
A small, clear
Flicker of self—
My flesh gone,
But my soul still singing,
Adamant to live:

The history of survival is written under my lids.

9

And if the husk of the world is ripped away,

We will not have altered the consciousness of one leaf—

10

Let this earth become a heaven:
From the point of light within the mind of God,
The Earth hurling its roughhouse wills and lusters,
The Earth accruing poison—
Planet of joy, planet of crucifixion,
Piñata destined to be smashed—
Ashes, ashes,
All the mirrors of heaven blackening, imagine:
No lack, no lack, but in our human minds—

Let the clematis become a prayer
As clouds and canon-flowers ready
Sweet unguents of pollen and rain,
As God bellows, and a wild cavalry of wind sweeps
Down from the houses of magic
Down from the houses of magic
Down from the houses of magic

Grace Cavalieri

A Field of Finches without Sight Still Singing

That song comes from sorrow   there is no doubt.
Bullfinches   in ancient times   had eyes put out
so they would   sing more sweet.   Think of
those   black beads   dropped to earth   coming
to seed   flowers   turning inward   every single
one of them   without   its sight.
Stories say   that   moving   in the wind   they
made up song   as if nothing   had been lost and
this   rings   long   into   the night. Every   sound
we hear   turns   to   a bigger one   and   each   is
true. We add   our own   until it is   the first
din   ever   heard,   the way   poetry   begins.

Lorna Dee Cervantes

Freeway 280

Las casitas near the gray cannery,
nestled amid wild abrazos of climbing roses
and man-high red geraniums
are gone now. The freeway conceals it
all beneath a raised scar.

But under the fake windsounds of the open lanes,
in the abandoned lots below, new grasses sprout,
wild mustard remembers, old gardens
come back stronger than they were,
trees have been left standing in their yards.
Albaricoqueros, cerezos, nogales . . .
Viejitas come here with paper bags to gather greens.
Espinaca, verdolagas, yerbabuena . . .

I scramble over the wire fence
that would have kept me out.
Once, I wanted out, wanted the rigid lanes
to take me to a place without sun,
without the smell of tomatoes burning
on swing shift in the greasy summer air.

Maybe it's here
en los campos extraños de esta ciudad
where I'll find it, that part of me
mown under
like a corpse
or a loose seed.

Emplumada

When summer ended
the leaves of snapdragons withered
taking their shrill-colored mouths with them.
They were still, so quiet. They were
violet where umber now is. She hated
and she hated to see
them go. Flowers

born when the weather was good—this
she thinks of, watching the branch of peaches
daring their ways above the fence, and further,
two hummingbirds, hovering, stuck to each other,
arcing their bodies in grim determination
to find what is good, what is
given them to find. These are warriors

distancing themselves from history.
They find peace
in the way they contain the wind
and are gone.

Jennifer Chang

Genealogy

This stream took a shorter course—
a thread of water that makes oasis

out of mud, in pooling,
does not aspire to lake. To river, leave

the forest, the clamorous wild.
I cannot. Wherever I am,

I am here, nonsensical, rhapsodic,
stock-still as the trees. Trickling

never floods, furrows its meager path
through the forest floor.

There will always be a root
too thirsty, moss that only swallows

and spreads. Primordial home, I am dying
from love of you. Were I tuber or quillwort,

the last layer of leaves that starts the dirt
or the meekest pond,

I would absorb everything.
I would drown. Water makes song

of erratic forms, and I hear the living
push back branches, wander off trail.

Patricia Clark

Out with the Monarch, the Vole, and the Toad

To live as they do, vulnerably, in the air,
the wing-assaulting wind, to breathe
the wind, the cool September air, and watch
the *Sweet Autumn* clematis twine and climb.
To live with the scuff and smatter of leaves
at the burrow hole, the dying fall of the pink
geranium petal, the tomato stalk blackening from last
night's chill. To live with the thought, the weight—the dead
branch pitching down to shatter in the yard,
the hawk's shadow, the days ahead
without sun. A full moon spills its cream
over Dean Lake and boys at midnight
putter on their scow. An exhalation from the lake
rises to surround them, safe with a light,
though far from shore. To live with water's depth
and dark, some force that wants to pull things
in and down. To live hidden, hurrying, hurt.
The toad finds the upturned pot and crouches there,
but the snake crawls across the flagstones' warmth
and surprises it. To live the death, the thrash
in red, the awful struggle, to let breath go.
To hunker down and yet be lifted up, skin tingling,
synapses firing, the heart a-beat, awash, eyes
wide, nose lifted to what is perceptibly near.

Lucille Clifton

the earth is a living thing

is a black shambling bear
ruffling its wild back and tossing
mountains into the sea

is a black hawk circling
the burying ground circling the bones
picked clean and discarded

is a fish black blind in the belly of water
is a diamond blind in the black belly of coal

is a black and living thing
is a favorite child
of the universe
feel her rolling her hand
in its kinky hair
feel her brushing it clean

the beginning of the end of the world

> cockroach population possibly declining
> —NEWS REPORT

maybe the morning the roaches
walked into the kitchen
bold with they bad selves
marching up out of the drains
not like soldiers   like priests
grim and patient in the sink
and when we ran the water

trying to drown them as if they were
soldiers   they seemed to bow their
sad heads   for us not at us
and march single file away

maybe then   the morning we rose
from our beds as always
listening for the bang of the end
of the world   maybe then
when we heard only the tiny tapping
and saw them dark and prayerful
in the kitchen   maybe then
when we watched them turn from us
faithless at last
and walk in a long line away

grief

begin with the pain
of the grass
that bore the weight
of adam,
his broken rib mending
into eve,

imagine
the original bleeding,
adam moaning
and the lamentation of grass.

from that garden,
through fields of lost
and found, to now, to here,
to grief for the upright
animal, to grief for the
horizontal world.

pause then for the human
animal in its coat

of many colors.   pause
for the myth of america.
pause for the myth
of america.

and pause for the girl
with twelve fingers
who never learned to cry enough
for anything that mattered,

not enough for the fear,
not enough for the loss,
not enough for the history,
not enough
for the disregarded planet.
not enough for the grass.

then end in the garden of regret
with time's bell tolling grief
and pain,
grief for the grass
that is older than adam,
grief for what is born human,
grief for what is not.

defending my tongue

what i be talking about
can be said in this language
only   this tongue
be the one that understands
what i be talking about

you are you talking about
the landscape that would break me
if it could   the trees
my grandfolk swung from   the dirt
they planted in and ate

no what i be talking about
the dirt   the tree   the land
scape can only be said
in this language   the words
be hard be bumping out too much
to be contained in one thin tongue
like this language   this landscape   this life

the killing of the trees

the third went down
with a sound almost like flaking,
a soft swish as the left leaves
fluttered themselves and died.
three of them, four, then five
stiffening in the snow
as if this hill were Wounded Knee
as if the slim feathered branches
were bonnets of war
as if the pale man seated
high in the bulldozer nest
his blonde mustache ice-matted
was Pahuska come again but stronger now,
his long hair wild and unrelenting.

remember the photograph,
the old warrior, his stiffened arm
raised as if in blessing,
his frozen eyes open,
his bark skin brown and not so much
wrinkled as circled with age,
and the snow everywhere still falling,
covering his one good leg.
remember his name was Spotted Tail
or Hump or Red Cloud or Geronimo
or none of these or all of these.
he was a chief. he was a tree

falling the way a chief falls,
straight, eyes open, arms reaching
for his mother ground.

so i have come to live
among the men who kill the trees,
a subdivision, new,
in southern Maryland.
I have brought my witness eye with me
and my two wild hands,
the left one sister to the fists
pushing the bulldozer against the old oak,
the angry right, brown and hard and spotted
as bark. we come in peace,
but this morning
ponies circle what is left of life
and whales and continents and children and ozone
and trees huddle in a camp weeping
outside my window and i can see it all
with that one good eye.

Henri Cole

Green Shade

[Nara Deer Park]

With my head on his spotted back
and his head on the grass—a little bored
with the quiet motion of life
and a cluster of mosquitoes making
hot black dunes in the air—we slept
with the smell of his fur engulfing us.
It was as if my dominant functions were gazing
and dreaming in a field of semiwild deer.
It was as if I could dream what I wanted,
and what I wanted was to long for nothing—
no facts, no reasons—never to say again,
"I want to be like him," and to lie instead
in the hollow deep grass—without esteem or riches—
gazing into the big, lacquer black eyes of a deer.

Jack Collom

Ruddy Duck

or dumpling duck, daub duck, deaf duck,
fool duck, sleepy duck,
butter duck, brown diving teal, widgeon coot,
creek coot, sleepy coot, sleepy brother,
butter-ball, batter-scoot, blatherskite, bumble coot,
quill-tailed coot, heavy-tailed coot, stiff-tail,
pin-tail, bristle-tail, sprig-tail, stick-tail, spine-tail, dip-tail,
diver, dun-bird, dumb-bird, mud-dipper,
spoon-billed butter-ball, spoonbill, broad-billed dipper,
dipper, dapper, dopper, broad-bill, blue-bill,
sleepy-head, tough-head, hickory-head,
steel-head, hard-headed broad-bill, bull-neck,
leather-back, paddy-whack, stub-and-twist,
lightwood-knot, shot-pouch, water-partridge,
dinky, dickey, paddy, noddy, booby, rook, roody,
stiff-tailed widgeon, gray teal, salt-water teal

nest: in the abandoned homes of coots

gunners near the mouth of the Maumee River
found them floundering helplessly fat
on the water

feeds upon delicate grasses

        & & & & & & &

metaphysics is the
green green graze that nobody
thinks of eating

cross out "purple, glittering":
plain, gray and yellow
air dusty though no dust is in the air
some loomings there; colors etcetera
I am on gleaming strands of butterscotch rolled half-round
with a lot of oil
gray, neat Stan has a sky-blue T-shirt

Ecology

Surrounded by bone, surrounded by cells,
by rings, by rings of hell, by hair, surrounded by
air-is-a-thing, surrounded by silhouette, by honey-wet bees, yet
by skeletons of trees, surrounded by actual, yes, for practical
purposes, people, surrounded by surreal
popcorn, surrounded by the reborn: Surrender in the center
to surroundings. O surrender forever, never
end her, let her blend around, surrender to surroundings that
surround the tender endo-surrender, that
tumble through the tumbling to that blue that
curls around the crumbling, to that, the blue that
rumbles under the sun bounding the pearl that
we walk on, talk on; we can chalk that
up to experience, sensing the brown here that's
blue now, a drop of water surrounding a cow that's
black & white, the warbling Blackburnian twitter that's
machining midnight orange in the light that's
glittering in the light green visible wind. That's
the ticket to the tunnel through the thicket that's
a cricket's funnel of music to correct & pick it out
from under the wing that whirls up over & out.

Julia Connor

m(other) tongue

Before . . .
        when moon and stone
             were the bulwark
against which   everything pushed
      and blood
           the first syllable

in the body's cup

      when the pulse
           at the base of the spine
               was a seahorse galloping
      before Raven
        tore open history's bag
      or the equines rode
      the rock face of Lascaux

when *time was the mind of the stars*
           as Pythagoras says
and the bright arms of motion
      our first song.

from Canto for the Birds

dusk
       in South Dos Palos
& 7 mourning doves
           on the wire
above a silo where
           los vatos   meet

(these are not *my* words
      but the guys in prison
          teaching me   theirs

           chale Julia , they say
            this valley is our llano!
in the room where we   meet
to talk about
        poetry
& you cannot talk about poetry
     without talking about
          the land)

YOU CANNOT TALK POETRY
WITHOUT TALKING LAND
          in the chapel
          where we meet to
             open
          our imperfect
          hearts

     7 mourning doves
perched like
        the shadows
           of ideas
     whose movements between
worlds
     we are
       the animate
     powers of

relax I tell them
            you're inside   poetry now

                        admonish they
                                    read themselves thru
                        concrete walls

        entrust my few
                                    magic skills
                & confide I've come
because I
            wish to grow old with the grace
                        to risk being
                                                ridiculous
                & am practicing
                                    now

Tule Elk
            near Buttonwillow
a mature buck
                with antlers
                    up
                                into the morning fog

        you   are the mirror of dust
                                        I love

                            .

                    close by
                            Sandy Marsh Road
                a single dowitcher
                                & 1

                    2, 3,   6,   11,

                            15,   24

        sandpipers of some kind
feeding in shallows
            on swamp
                        timothy

                    a black-necked stilt appears
                                    & now
a throng of several thousand
                    snow geese
                                        rise

            soar
                    over the feeding ground
            in mimetic display of the

                    Thrones / Seraphim / Principalities

                    of angelic lore

a single undulating
                                    mass
        of radiant white
                                                feather
                    caught
                                    by sun
cut
            by wing-tip
                                    black

are these
        the lights
                    of Dante's
Paradiso
                    wintering here?

                    these
wholly vegetarian
                                    mated for life
graceful birds

            slaughtered
                                        by the million
        for landing in
                                    grain fields

Matthew Cooperman

Still: Environment

Issue: what we live for where we live for what

Photograph: terraced hillside, upland Sri Lanka, waning tea plantation gathering in the mist; Bogota, soccer stadium, dying grass or dirt; Los Alamos, mega bulldozer pushing songlines into a new ethic called White Quartz Villa

Ideology: Old Navy decanting of Marxist collective into Knott's Berry Nature; Liberation Theology leading to shot-gunned priests; a mighty wind, a monkey wrench, a world tank's sugary stillness

Bumper: a Right to Life vitriol burbling burbling "what is unborn is no less hungry for the fields . . ."

Fields: of wheat (winter), and alfalfa all summer long

Songbook: "Give Yourself to Love" (Kate Wolf, '83); "My Life in the Bush of Ghosts" (Byrne/Eno, '81); "Species Diseases" (Midnight Oil, '88); "The Rites of Spring" (Stravinsky, 1913)

System: autonomic, holonomic, lymphogenesis, fractilia

Bookshelf: *Sea of Cortez* (Steinbeck, viz. "nonteleological thinking"), *Country of Pointed Firs* (Jewett), *Garbage* (Ammons), *Ecology: A Primer* (Golley), *Economic Foundations of the West* (Katherine Coman), *The Function of Reason* (Whitehead), *New Organon* (Francis Bacon), *The Death of Nature* (Carolyn Merchant), *Manifold Destiny: Eating What You Drive* (Jones, misshelved),

Outcome: Act III, Scene IV

Moon: harvest, blue, suburb, blood, third house

Repetend: what we live for where we live for what is a question; if it's a question as global warning, will we adapt?

Data: the Oomphalos Model loops eco-grammar, how a general C Value explains the mutation of DNAs. What's meta-architecture for coupled-map lattices? It's Julia Set Theory to doom methods

Prayer: one for Loti, that she discovers roses; one for Father PJ's speedy knee and tree recovery; one for Master Scorehound, who just returned, who kissed the wall and drained the swamps

Photograph: desalination ponds in southern Arabia, a camel drinking this

saying: "what does not change is the will to change . . . " "you just have to dig for wood and water . . . " "how near to good is what is wild . . ." "whosoever wakes here heed these words . . . " "fuzzy wuzzy wasn't . . . "

Stephen Cushman

The Rain in Maine

fell also on the Etchemins, their name for us
humans, us builders of fish weirs,

us real people, as opposed to monsters,
animals, or the ghosts of others

back for a visit to glacial moraine
above the beach where clamming thrived

and the canoe route south could make good use
of easy portage across a bar

exposed at low tide, for which they also
must have had words, maybe one meaning

the waters inhale or the earth whale breaches,
as they would have had words for various arrowheads,

the kind meant for deer rather than seals
or for making war on trespassing tribes,

who bad as they were weren't so pathetic
as to need such abstractions

as religion, as nature, as beauty removed
from whatever gray weather the eagle glides through.

Kwame Dawes

Genocide, Again

If a man were to wake in Sun City,
he would smell the truth of prophecy.
Those close by will die by machete blow,
those far away will die of the plague,
and those who are spared
will know the famine of orphaned days—
the youth wandering motherless
through the hollow houses tucked
into the overgrown valleys and hills,
the yam vines choked by the verdant
bush, and the way the earth swallows
the wet stain of a dead body.

The famine will soon destroy
the remnant, leaving an impossible
cavity in the nation. A man wakes
to the truth that sometimes God's
word smells like the rotting flesh
of murdered bodies scattered
among broken incense bowls, cold
wet fireplaces, strewn clothes,
splatters of blood on the floor,
an overturned pot, rice grains hardening
in the stale air and an empty leather sandal.

Alison Hawthorne Deming

Specimens Collected at the Clear Cut

1. Wild currant twig flowering with cluster of rosy microgoblets.

2. Wild iris, its three landing platforms, purple bleeding to white then yellow in the honey hollows, purple veins showing the direction to the sweet spot.

3. Dogwood? Not what I know from the northeast woods, the white four-petaled blossom marked with four rusty holes that make its shape a mnemonic for Christ hanging on the cross. This one, six-petaled, larger, whiter, domed seedhouse in the center, no holes on the edges, shameless heathen of the northwest forest that flaunts its status as exhibitionist for today.

4. Empty tortilla chip bag.

5. Empty Rolling Rock can. Empty Mountain Dew bottle. Empty shotgun shell. Beer bottle busted by shotgun shell, blasted bull's-eye hanging on alder sapling.

6. One large bruise four inches below right knee, inflicted by old-growth stump of western red cedar, ascent attempted though the relic was taller and wider than me, debris field skirting a meter high at its base, wet and punky; nonetheless, I made my try, eyes on a block of sodden wood, reddened by rain, fragrant as a cedar closet here in the open air, the block of my interest wormed through (pecked through?) with tunnels diameter of a pencil. How many decades, how many centuries, of damage and invasion the tree had survived! But the stump felled me, left me with its stake on my claim and jubilation to see that nothing of this ruin was mine, mine only the lesson that the forest has one rule: start over making use of what remains.

7. One hunk of dead Douglas fir, gray as driftwood, length of my forearm, width of my hand, woodgrain deformed into swirls, eddies, backflows,

and cresting waves, a measure of time, disturbances that interrupted linear growth to make it liquid as stream flow.

8. Lettuce lung (*Lobaria pulmonaria*), leaf lichen, upper-side dull green, turns bright green in rain, lobed, ridged surface with powdery warts, underside tan and hairy with bald spots, texture like alligator skin, sample attached to twig of Douglas fir falls at my feet on trail to Lookout Creek. Day five, re-sampling the site, t.i.d.

9. Four metaphors for the forest. Plantation trees: herringbone tweed. Old-growth trees: medieval brocade. Clear cut: the broken loom. Clear cut five years later: patches on the torn knees of jeans.

10. Skat. Pellets the size of Atomic Fireballs, hot candy I loved as a child. This, more oval. Less round. Not red. But brown. Specimen dropped by Roosevelt elk savoring the clear-cut's menu of mixed baby greens. One pellet broken open to reveal golden particles. Light that traveled from sun to grass to gut to ground to mind. Forest time makes everything round, everything broken, a story of the whole.

Deborah Digges

Damascus

Split by the light, wrought golden, one of a thousand cars stunned
    sun-blind,
crawling westward, I remembered a day I stopped for an old snapper,
as huge as, when embracing ghosts, you round your arms.
Who did I think I was to lift him like a pond,
or ballast from the slosh of hull swamp, tarred as he was, undaunted,
that thrashed and hissed at the worst place to try to cross,
where the road plunged east, the lumber trucks
swept daily down from the blue hills
past winter-ravaged toys blanching by makeshift crosses.
An old sea shimmered in the asphalt.
Spared over the mirage to ancient footpaths, he lunged again,
and spit, turning his oddly touching head toward the project
of the steep embankment. Such were the times.
Hardwired, the way. Cross here or die. Die crossing.

Elizabeth Dodd

House Sparrow at Skara Brae

On Orkney mainland

Feathers the color of winter-dried
heather, or sandstone, or kelp.

Little mouthful of grasses,
lichen-barred wings.

Loch vowel-shifts to *lake*; lapwings
glean and feed in the ancient fields.

Now each room lies open,
stone bedsteads, the fireless hearth.

Burnt whalebone, sheep dung, atoms
of ashes, the jet stream carbon follows:

spent breath, then flesh. (Wind
washes the beach sand, ever dissolving

low sky into spray.) Today,
soot blown from Asia seeds rain

over Iceland. Consonants dropped
in the sand cast fractal shadows,

shattered clusters of gesture. The bird flits
through the still-roofed passage, passes

from sight. Sediment catches in crevices,
waves sough on the distant cliffs.

Wasn't there something—
I think I wanted to tell you something.

All morning clouds open and close windows
in the sky, the stone slabs sliding back into place.

Sharon Dolin

For I Will Consider the Overlooked Dragonfly

How it is often a damselfly, skimmer, or darner
How it belies the idea that we invented neon
How it mates while in flight, laying eggs on the pond's lilies
How its blues are purples, its browns, reds
How unfearful it is of the human body
How one will come to bask on my forearm, foot, or the arm of my deck
    chair
How I praise the way it eats the larvae of biting insects
How a Variable Dancer in lavender and black alighted as I wrote this
For I praise them, not needing to search for dragonflies (the way birders
    search for birds) but let them fly to me
For sometimes their wings have stigma and in the wind I watch their
    wings and abdomen sway while their head and thorax are still
For this one's a male whose spider-web wings and abdomen are tipped
    sky-blue
For might it be the same damselfly that alights on the arm of my chair as
    I write
For his bulgy compound eyes, what do they see
For his violet thorax the color of a flower
For the honeybees grazing the sea honeysuckle
        and the hummingbirds on the mimosa blooms
For their pond world which is oblivious to names
For ours with its naming obsession
For the only way I desire to catch one is with the net of my eyes
For some say a damselfly is a weak flier compared to a dragonfly
For the male clasps the female's head with the end of its abdomen while
    mating
For we call mating pairs a copulation wheel but I say they look like a
    backwards 3
For it flies from spring through late summer (though they live for only a
    few weeks)

For some darters and skimmers migrate south and the ones returning are
their children or grand- or great-grandchildren or
For after the storm a male white-faced Meadowhawk, its thorax and
abdomen pomegranate-red, has come to bask in the windy sun
For the wind, the wind, which causes a stirring within the stillness
and a stillness within the stirring

Camille T. Dungy

On the rocks

I said, the cruise line said we might see wandering albatross. I said, they said we could walk through penguin rookeries. I said, we might see at least four species of seal. What do you have against traveling where black people are? she said. That's not my idea of a nice trip, she said. My friend said, give me pink coral sand and a Mai Tai. Give me so hot men wear nothing but swim trunks, she said. Give me hot men. She said, all those days out there with nothing to do? She said, no bowling? no movies? no shops? I said, they said we would have a chance to kayak. She said I said the Drake Passage was notorious for bad conditions. I said that was true. I said, however, we'd be further south by then, in the protected bays where the Southern Ocean meets the most southerly continent. She said, oh. I said I thought if I paddled far enough from the ship I might hear icebergs melting. I said, they said we could hear gas escaping from the ice. I said, they said it would sound a bit like a soda can being slowly opened. I said I thought it would sound like what it might sound like to find myself paddling through a giant highball of vodka on the rocks, the can of tonic being opened, everything I needed right there. You wouldn't catch me out there, she said, floating with nothing but a life vest and a kayak. I said, quiet. I want to hear what quiet really sounds like.

The Blue

One will live to see the Caterpillar rut everything
they walk on—seacliff buckwheat cleared, relentless
ice plant to replace it, the wild fields bisected
by the scenic highway, canyons covered with cul-de-sacs,
gas stations, comfortable homes, the whole habitat
along this coastal stretch endangered, everything,
everyone, everywhere in it in danger as well—

but now they're logging the one stilling hawk
Smith sights, the conspiring grasses' shh shhhh ssh,
the coreopsis Mattoni's boot barely spares,
and, netted, a solitary blue butterfly. Smith
ahead of him chasing the stream, Mattoni wonders
if he plans to swim again. Just like that
the spell breaks. It's years later, Mattoni lecturing
on his struggling butterfly. How fragile.

.

If his daughter spooled out the fabric
she's chosen for her wedding gown,
raw taffeta, burled, a bright-hued tan,
perhaps Mattoni would remember
how those dunes looked from a distance,
the fabric, balanced between her arms,
making valleys in the valley, the fan
above her mimicking the breeze.
He and his friend loved everything
softly undulating under the coyest wind,
and the rough truth as they walked
through the land's scratch and scrabble
and no one was there, then, besides Mattoni
and his friend, walking along Dolan's Creek,
in that part of California they hated
to share. The ocean, a mile or so off,
anything but passive so that even there,
in the canyon, they sometimes heard it smack
and pull well-braced rocks. The breeze,
basic: salty, bitter, sour, sweet. Smith trying
to identify the scent, tearing leaves
of manzanita, yelling, "This is it. Here! This is it!"
his hand to his nose, his eyes, having finally seen
the source of his pleasure, alive.

.

In the lab, after the accident, he remembered it,
the butterfly. How good a swimmer Smith had been,
how rough the currents there at Half Moon Bay, his friend

alone with reel and rod—Mattoni back at school
early that year, his summer finished too soon—
then all of them together in the sneaker wave,
and before that the ridge, congregations of pinking
blossoms, and one of them bowing, scaring up the living,
the frail and flighty beast too beautiful
to never be pinned, those nights Mattoni worked
without his friend, he remembered too.
He called the butterfly Smith's Blue.

Rachel Blau DuPlessis

Pastoral and Gigue

Peace gentle wood bird
kinwing loose in the natter

now will you
wet with dew and rumpled

plummet, hymeneal,
to the emptiness of the threshold.

Plumy as the ticklish
peaceful as the tickled

two cold feet step flat
into the night grass

at that bare and
itchy place that dance

down the patchy dirt path
beneath the road beneath the grass.

Earth in your face
for all black sky is earth

oily, wading into emptiness
the roadway under roadway

earth covering bird
of milk eggs plump, stars

in the dance
that leaping
seed and dead of night, so   *da capo al fine*

fine   that dance
       that falling into earth.

Praxilla's Silliness

for none but a simpleton would put cucumbers
and the like on a par with the sun and the moon.
—ZENOBIUS, PROVERBS: *LYRA GRAECA*, III

Almost
rounded moon,
Its unspilling
meniscus-

Light.

Honeyed face of the sibylline
earth.

Everything message, every randomness
twigs fallen just like that   here

bright lined bulging square.

Pepo   pepo   pepo
bird-ripe
fruit of melon, cucumber, squash, pumpi-
kin

slimy-seeded   cries   hot
August bouncing.

Sweet the push push out of the cell

mint watery by waysides
soft-leafed basil
tipped by bushy bracts

cusps of the moon.

Under the fingernails
dirt, flour, yeast

crusts of the sun.

Walk down the road until you go under it.

·

Dew on the wheat field wells up bread.
Stars, grass, fruit, all variants

Bite down.

The light travels like salt
The dark is thirst
deep shadows
of longing for more light—

But is not the longing for shadows
brightness

earth of the meeting tides?

    .

Wood white
large white little white
littler fritillaries

wayward

"lords" of air.

Green plums red plums yellow sun
grizzled dotty (newsprint) juice
the drupy fruits

        signz
        places

always russing somewhere
A leaf's moist papery crescent sloughs off.

Of silver-waxy bloom
of cuke uncurls
I sing.

The flea lights brisk upon
one tucked foot in the dark.

Mark.

    .

Written veins the stones' intrusions
wander
untranslated rocks.

Me goes leaping full and empty.

Now the dead dare coming closer.

All is inscribed,
nothing feeds them,

every day a heavy vulval loaf.

Are you ready
to go down
by the water?

What cannot be said
will get wept.

We live a little patch it doth
go forward
into grief

small lilac leafed
no blossom
white feather, blossom.

·

Travel through
picking and washing.
Flesh level, iridescent.

Roads travelled, roads untravelled
often equal.

Heavy as stone, loose as honey
earth
is constantly falling into earth.

So dress for the journey.
Pink for the cave
Pink for the endless stairwell

One hell, two deaths,
three tasteless oatcakes.

•

What starts and calls and whistles
through the long clicking night?

Littoral, on the jot and tittle coast-
line,
plup,
that the
little tides
catch into gravel, stars.

What I miss most *when dead* is the travelling
and after, stars
the shining sun and moon

crisp cucumbers in season
the apples bright
black-seeded *pears.*

But when I am living, bite hard
into the crossroads

cukies wet and apples sweet
I can sing and I can eat.

•

Bury
unbury

life deciduous as the moon.

•

1983

Tim Earley

I Like Green Things

Gnostic garden: give

gardenias   the green grants

gills & gimlet-eyed grasshoppers   gone

gravity of grass snake & gyrocompass

of green light   gypsy gypsum gynesis

gust of gyre & grace guttersnipe gondolier

green gage green finch green manure & green sea

      of ground & grimalkin of light of

grubs & grigs

          & grog shops & groins
going is my grief

      green gramercy

           grammar of green

gree unto green

           going is a guide

going is guiltless

going in the green of light & grace

     of ground & grief the gills &

gimlet-eyed green snakes   the green grants

going a grammar of gnosis

        geas an aster gold or green?

Of grace a green or gnosis of light

        Gravid light going

Is grief   a gospel   a green

Larry Eigner

September 21 65

flock of birds
      a moment
  of one tree reached

apples fall to the ground

June 17 68

moon

  arithmetic
  in the night

rain

May 3 71

the music of

  the sea

 beyond

the wood

   the wind blows

    the leaves

      they stay

    there   such times

roots spread

flower

face   the sky

sphere

ah the seed

not to choose

[trees green   the quiet sun]

trees green   the quiet sun

shed metal truck in the next street
passing the white house you listen
onwards

you heard

the dog

through   per
formed circles

the roads near the beach

rectangular

rough lines of the woods

tall growth   echoing

local water

Louise Erdrich

The Strange People

> The antelope are strange people . . . they are beautiful to look
> at, and yet they are tricky. We do not trust them. They appear
> and disappear; they are like shadows on the plains. Because of
> their great beauty, young men sometimes follow the antelope
> and are lost forever. Even if those foolish ones find themselves
> and return, they are never again right in their heads.
> —PRETTY SHIELD, MEDICINE WOMAN OF THE CROWS,
> TRANSCRIBED AND EDITED BY FRANK LINDERMAN (1932)

All night I am the doe, breathing
his name in a frozen field,
the small mist of the word
drifting always before me.

And again he has heard it
and I have gone burning
to meet him, the jacklight
fills my eyes with blue fire;
the heart in my chest
explodes like a hot stone.

Then slung like a sack
in the back of his pickup,
I wipe the death scum
from my mouth, sit up laughing
and shriek in my speeding grave.

Safely shut in the garage,
when he sharpens his knife
and thinks to have me, like that,
I come toward him,
a lean gray witch
through the bullets that enter and dissolve.

I sit in his house
drinking coffee till dawn
and leave as frost reddens on hubcaps,
crawling back into my shadowy body.
All day, asleep in clean grasses,
I dream of the one who could really wound me.
Not with weapons, not with a kiss, not with a look.
Not even with his goodness.

If a man was never to lie to me. *Never lie me.*
I swear I would never leave him.

The Red Sleep of Beasts

> On space of about an acre I counted two hundred and twenty of
> these animals; the banks of the river were covered thus with these
> animals as far as the eye could reach and in all directions. One
> may judge now, if it is possible, the richness of these prairies.
>
> —FROM A LETTER BY FATHER BELCOURT, A MISSIONARY
>   WHO ACCOMPANIED THE MICHIF ON ONE OF THEIR
>   LAST BUFFALO HUNTS IN THE 1840S, IN *NORTH DAKOTA*
>   *HISTORICAL COLLECTIONS*, VOLUME V

We heard them when they left the hills,
Low hills where they used to winter and bear their young.
Blue hills of oak and birch that broke the wind.
They swung their heavy muzzles, wet with steam,
And broke their beards of breath to breathe.

We used to hunt them in our red-wheeled carts.
Frenchmen gone *sauvage,* how the women burned
In scarlet sashes, black wool skirts.
For miles you heard the ungreased wood
Groan as the load turned.

Thunder was the last good hunt.
Great bales of skins and meats in iron cauldrons
Boiling through the night. We made our feast
All night, but still we could not rest.

We lived headlong, taking what we could
But left no scraps behind, not like the other
Hide hunters, hidden on a rise,
Their long-eyes brought herds one by one
To earth. They took but tongues, and you could walk
For miles across the strange hulks.

We wintered in the hills. Low huts of log
And trampled dirt, the spaces tamped with mud.
At night we touched each other in our dreams
Hearing, on the wind, their slow hooves stumbling

South, we said at first, the old ones knew
They would not come again to the low hills.
We heard them traveling, heard the frozen birches
Break before their long retreat
Into the red sleep.

B. H. Fairchild

Maize

After Roland Stills fell from the top of the GANO
grain elevator, we felt obliged in some confused,
floundering way as if his hand had just pulled
the red flag from our pockets and we had turned
to find not him but rows of Kansas maize
reeling into the sun, we felt driven to recall
more than perhaps, drunk, we saw: trees squatting
below like pond frogs, mare's tails sweeping the hills,
and the moon in its floppy dress riding low behind
the shock of his yellow hair as, falling, he seemed
to drop to his knees, drunk, passing out, *oh shit,*
with the same stupid grin as when he might recite
Baudelaire in the company of a girl and a small glass
of Cointreau, *Je suis comme le roi d'un pays pluvieux.*
And beyond his eyes blooming suddenly into white
flowers were the lights of houses where our parents
spoke of harvest like a huge wall they would climb
to come again to a new life. Driving along dirt roads
in our trucks, we would look through the scrim of dust
at the throbbing land and rows of red maize whipping past
before the hard heat of summer when the combines
came pushing their shadows and shouldering each other
dark as clouds erasing the horizon, coming down
on the fields to cut the maize, to cut it down
in a country without rain or the grace of kings.

West Texas

My red Ford running to rust idles
along the roadside, one headlight
swinging out across the plains,
the other blind. In the rear window
dawn light spills over my children
sprawling tangled in the backseat
beneath an army blanket. My wife
sleeps in front where the radio loses
itself in static, and even Del Rio
is a distant shout. From rig
to rig like this every few months,
the road looming toward more sky,
bunchgrass, sometimes a stooped,
ragged clump of trees. Always
a thin curtain of dust in the air.
Coffee sours through the night,
and I toss the grounds like seeds
from another country over the dry
shoulder. Driving high and sleepless,
I dream awake: faces like strange
gray flowers form and vanish,
my father kneeling in the road, then
looking up. *Stay put, let the land
claim you*, he always said. But here
men own you and the land you drill,
and you move on. My one headlight
dims in the morning light. The other
mirrors back the road, the whitening
sky. Far ahead a hawk is sweeping
into view on wide, black wings.

Patricia Fargnoli

Should the Fox Come Again to My Cabin in the Snow

Then, the winter will have fallen all in white
and the hill will be rising to the north,
the night also rising and leaving,
dawn light just coming in, the fire out.

Down the hill running will come that flame
among the dancing skeletons of the ash trees.
I will leave the door open for him.

Then

Then, he held me there as if stunned, the figure who had appeared saying
    this is the edge between what is and what is not.

On one side was the forest in all its complex depth and verdancy,
    on the other side stretched the field, a wide field full of emptiness

where memory was hidden among the grasses, each day of the past moving
    like small winds there among the tall grasses.

And therefore I chose, leaving behind what was supposed to be left behind—

and grasped his luminous robe to follow, without a question,
    across the transition zone into the old-growth forest with its wing sounds.

I might have been the story that wasn't told—of the woman who left her home
    without looking back—changing forever what happened after.

I trusted only in that spectral figure who moved, with such grace, ahead of me
    into the dark evergreens, and the door of their branches closed behind us.

Annie Finch

Watching the Oregon Whale

A hard gray wave, her fin, walks out on the water
that thickens to open and then parts open, around her.

Measured by her delved water, I follow her fill
into and out of green light in the depth she has spun

through the twenty-six fathoms of her silent orison,
then sink with her till she rises, lulled with the krill.

Beads of salt spray stop me, like metal crying.
Her cupped face breathes its spouts, like a jewel-wet prong.

In a cormorant's barnacle path, I trail her, spun
down through my life in the making of her difference,

fixing my mouth, with the offerings of silence,
on her dark whale-road where all green partings run,

where ocean's hidden bodies twist fathoms around her,
making her green-fed hunger grow fertile as water.

Jessica Fisher

Elegy

To see in the dark   Or stitch a blind seam

As if piecing together   The patchwork of forest

But I can't see she said   Where did the sun go

I think how I might show her   My little Galileo

A paper mâché cosmos   Orbit and rotation

All along we knew   We were also moving

In the drunken night   We lay on the cold earth

Waiting for disaster   The word of course meaning

Stars falling from the sky   Floater on the eye

As if a sunspot   A slow obliteration

Of embryonic origin   Who are you they asked

What do you see   If not the boundless sky

To answer you spoke   Of the eye's particular static

Familiar and degenerate   But there is a world unseen

Green beyond green   Cloud cover as though

A form of sleep   In the quiet room

Several of us wept   When he said elegy

The parade of image   On the whitewashed wall

Marking pre- and post-   Idyllic

Or was it only Eden after   And obliteration a foil

As night for starlight   I bore her in winter

The green returning   Tongues of the dead

Licking the hillside   I bore her in wartime

The radio pretuned   News of destruction

Coming over the airwaves   What was is no longer

The fieldnotes record   In Thoreau's Walden

Rose lilac and buttercup   Gone from the woods

Or what is untimely   Narcissi in winter

What were we thinking   When we weren't thinking

The moon clear at midday   But I'm not ready for night

What does it stand for   Fear of the dark

The skeletal shape   Of the world we knew

A carcass of sorts   I see with eyes closed

Or is death the mother   As Stevens wrote

Ann Fisher-Wirth

from Dream Cabinet

Fogdö, Sweden

1.

Soft rain. Skies white-gray the same as the water. I lie in the bottom
bunk beneath a green-striped blanket here on Fogdö. I've wakened from
a nightmare, taut with fear.

And when I dream, what then? What, when the bombs are falling on
Beirut and Haifa?

At the conference in Scotland, Lyn from Haifa said, *Nearly half my students
are Arabs, the other half Israeli. When it gets really bad, I go to the sea and
watch the fishing boats. Nothing has changed in their lives forever.*

•

3.

> Two days ago, we were still in Scotland—
> *the hottest day in the UK ever.* A columnist
> in the paper wrote of people's hideous fashions:
> *Better get used to dressing well when it's hot;
> after all, we'll have to cope with worse.*
>
> Cope? We'll choke, gasp, muffled.
> Cry out, the trees are vanishing,
> the blistering heat is rising. We will tip
> the planet past the healing point and then—
> Don't they know death wins, and flesh
>
> can be zapped fried seared, wars first for oil
> then for stolen water, wars for air not just food?
> Death will be the kind one, yet so plenteous

are our gizmos there will be no silence, no darkness
even in death. The grave, a brightly lit parking lot—

4.

How to be a muddy field, germy,
                rank, unseemly?

Here at Fogdö there is beauty.
      Bushes thick with blueberries
                 scatter among boulders.

        But the dream-phrase jumps in my mind:

There's a black pebble lodged against the heart chakra.

5.

          What do we dream
     What do we dream

        Be advised
    I do not exist

       If you are characters in my play
   it does you no harm.

        Daughter, mother, wife—
what am I but passages of light
             through wave, illuminating
    intransigence,

and bread cupped in a palm,
       water through hands
     that feel and cherish with the fingertips
        each slick of leaf, each bent branch

      as it flows or drifts into infinity—
The rabbits we saw in the field in Scotland

        hopped off to their nests beneath bushes
as sun hovered toward twilight over the river,
     the limestone town, hill with distant cattle.

6.

—Sleep, says the sea, sleep, says the sea, the birds
thicken in the trees as light glints across the water.

A breeze. Late afternoon, the light growing pewter,
soft Falun red of the ramshackle summer house

soaking up shadows. Out on the water, a motorboat.
I would like to spend the curve of a year

from bird cherries to mushrooms, *svamp*, in Sweden.
Trace the circle round through lilacs, king's-blood-lilies,

lilies of the valley, then blueberries, strawberries,
raspberries, then lingonberries, apples.

To gather them as they ripen, wander along
with that rapt purposeful emptiness, every sense alert

for a glimpse of red or blue, the scrotal sponginess
of puffballs, luminescence of chanterelles.

To know this place in the fullness of its seasons.
And watch the light on water, day after day,

empty out my everlasting self-regard.
Let the sunlight, fog, or rain have its will with me.

.

9.

Where I live they are paving the world.
The oaks they're "saving" perish,
hemmed in by concrete. Dogwoods parch
and wither in a season of no rain. You'd think
we'd think of the collapse of systems—
at a certain point, technology cannot save us.
Earth sickens and sickens, and finally
turns mean. Only things with thorns survive.

10.

I'm reading Kandinsky, he speaks about green
as the resting point between yellow and blue,

the color of tranquility and regeneration.
Surrounded by trees and water here at Fogdö, I want

to be writing of peace, want to be moving into that deeper
harmony where earth and sea and sky seep into, into,

every pulse of my blood. But I keep thinking
to write of peace right now is to be a tourist.

11.

Outhouse:

Here, at eight, when Frida's children go to sleep,
it's still soft daylight. Gulls are crying over the inlet.

And now they stop. It's absolutely silent—so silent
I can hear the spiders crawl across the page,
and each drop of pee falling in the bucket.

Yes, this is now, it's not escape and not evasion:
the just-so of water, light, and silence.

12.

Now the *lip, lip, lip* of the quiet water between the islands.

Julia, five, is singing
                La la la la la   la   la la la la la la.

    And Logan, two,
            tosses pebbles into the ocean,
                    chants *Bye bye weewee, bye bye weewee.*

13.

Kind summer, facing west as sun goes down.
The ducks still bob about the water, the Baltic opens up

between the islands, and the body grows calm
in its own contingencies. On the pier at Fogdö

a woman sits—a woman who is I—
and the sun shatters in a path across the water.

The ducks drift to and fro, and a few birds
honk and chirp, shriek and coo.

One motorboat's revving back across the water.
A spiderweb stretches like a line of laundry

from a rock to the pier, catches the slant of diminishing daylight.
Now the ducks are swimming home,

the little ones in front of their elders. Flies buzz my head.
Frida has just come out to wash Logan's bottle.

Amazing, to trust the world so much
you'll wash your baby's bottle in the ocean—

.

16.

I'm sitting on the pier as Peter sleeps beside me.
It's water nearly all the way around,
rippling with striations of shadow and light.

The ducks are floating ahead of me, growing near
the forested island. The birds are crying their long good-nights.
Like being inside a pearl: the perfect roundness of the summer evening.

Water—slate blue, gray-blue, with midges dancing on it.
Now the ducks are sailing away from me.
The sun still white, but sinking toward the horizon.

Now the sun is a fish, caught in the Baltic seagrasses.
Peter sleeps peacefully, his whole face soft. Sometimes
I can't help touching him even though I know it will wake him.

17.

A single bird perches on a branch—a wren, a willow branch.

> When the doors of the dream cabinet open, the bird flies away . . .
> into our lives.

> And the branch remains, to carry its singing.

Lisa Fishman

Out of the Field

In the weather that was not written
in documents attesting to order,
the windrows of straw defined the field

a series of parallel lines
cut down to dry and raked
in rows to bale.

In the hour that was not given
on the dial, the ladder
stood in snow

leaning against nothing, climbing where.
The moon lit the wooden ladder
just resting in the blue white snow.

In the night of the morning to follow
the season had altered again, not to summer or winter
turning to fall

backward like a father off a ladder
past a daughter's window

or a white dog loping past the potatoes
on the south slope, out of the field
of vision

Kathleen Flenniken

Plume

For   years
it   may   be   locked
in   the   matrix
of   silt   and   sand
like   a   photo-
graphic   image
still   and
untransported
absorbed
and   adsorbed
then
the   introduction
of   gradient
to   unsaturated
soils
                percolation
and   it   awakens
unfurling
like   a   frond
a   carpet   unrolling
itself
                    remote
                underground
this   beautiful
movement
fanning
between   interstices
feathering
void   to   void
describes
the   dark   earth
the   layering

of   permeable
and   impermeable
soils
it   is   out
of   our   hands
this 50 year old
mistake

this   poison
yes   it   is   moving
to   the   river   yes
it   migrates
between   grains
down   to
saturated   sediment
manifestly   down
and   when
it   descends
as   far   as   it   can
it   will   swim
ride   droplets
like   swanboats
float
spread

diffuse
                     distend
trailing   its
delicate
paisley   scarf
and   like
anything
with   a   destiny
a   flock   of   birds
sperm
                     breath
it   will   move
downstream
to   the   river
yes   the   river
will   take   it   in

Green Run

Hanford, Washington. December 2, 1949

Green
            a verdant dream
                        grass avenues framed by trees
Green
            untested
                        young
Run
            as in long limbs racing
Green as in raw
                        uncured
                                    uranium slugs
                                                aged 16 days instead of 90
Run
            meaning *batch*
                        an 8,000 Curie brew
or *Green*
            lush with buds
                        or with radio-iodine 131
                                    dead night
                                    stack a-belching
                                                when the weather turns
                                                            to snow
Run as in production
                        fallout
                                    over thousands of square miles
Green as in *sickly*
                        taken up
                                    by the thyroid
Run as in *hide*
            as in *keep the lid on this disaster*
Run as in *spill*
            as out of a cauldron
Green
            meaning
                        easily deceived
                                    meaning
                                                run

Carolyn Forché

The Museum of Stones

These are your stones, assembled in matchbox and tin,
collected from roadside, culvert, and viaduct,
battlefield, threshing floor, basilica, abattoir—
stones, loosened by tanks in the streets
from a city whose earliest map was drawn in ink on linen,
schoolyard stones in the hand of a corpse,
pebble from Baudelaire's *oui,*
stone of the mind within us
carried from one silence to another,
stone of cromlech and cairn, schist and shale, horneblende,
agate, marble, millstones, ruins of choirs and shipyards,
chalk, marl, mudstone from temples and tombs,
stone from the silvery grass near the scaffold,
stone from the tunnel lined with bones,
lava of a city's entombment, stones
chipped from lighthouse, cell wall, scriptorium,
paving stones from the hands of those who rose against the army,
stones where the bells had fallen, where the bridges were blown,
those that had flown through windows, weighted petitions,
feldspar, rose quartz, blueschist, gneiss and chert,
fragments of an abbey at dusk, sandstone toe
of a Buddha mortared at Bamiyan,
stone from the hill of three crosses and a crypt,
from a chimney where storks cried like human children,
stones newly fallen from stars, a stillness of stones, a heart,
altar and boundary stone, marker and vessel, first cast, lode and hail,
bridge stones and others to pave and shut up with,
stone apple, stone basil, beech, berry, stone brake,
stone bramble, stone fern, lichen, liverwort, pippin and root,

concretion of the body, as blind as cold as deaf,
all earth a quarry, all life a labor, stone-faced, stone-drunk
with hope that this assemblage of rubble, taken together, would become
a shrine or holy place, an ossuary, immoveable and sacred
like the stone that marked the path of the sun as it entered the human dawn.

Morning on the Island

The lights across the water are the waking city.
The water shimmers with imaginary fish.
Not far from here lie the bones of conifers
washed from the sea and piled by wind.
Some mornings I walk upon them,
bone to bone, as far as the lighthouse.
A strange beetle has eaten most of the trees.
It may have come here on the ships playing
music in the harbor, or it was always here, a winged
jewel, but in the past was kept still by the cold
of a winter that no longer comes.
There is an owl living in the firs behind us but he is white,
meant to be mistaken for snow burdening a bough.
They say he is the only owl remaining. I hear him at night
listening for the last of the mice and asking *who* of no other owl.

Carol Frost

The St. Louis Zoo

> The isle is full of noises,
> Sounds, and sweet air . . . sometimes voices.
> —*THE TEMPEST*

High, yellow, coiled and weighting the branch like an odd piece of fruit, a
    snake slept
by the gate, in the serpent house. I walked around the paths hearing

hushed air, piecemeal remarks, and the hoarse voice of the keeper
    spreading cabbage
and pellets in the elephant compound—"Hungry, are you? There's a girl.

How's Pearl?" —A clucking music, then silence again crept past me
on the waters of the duck pond. Birds with saffron wings in the flight cage

and flamingos the color of mangoes, even their webbed feet red-orange,
    made so
"by the algae they ingest," as angels are made of air—some bickered,

some were tongue-tied, some danced on one leg in the honeyed light.
I thought of autumn as leaves scattered down. Nearby, closed away

in his crude beginnings in a simulated rain forest, the gorilla pulled out
    handfuls
of grass, no Miranda to teach him to speak, though he was full of noises

and rank air after swallowing. Smooth rind and bearded husks lay about
    him.
His eyes were ingots when he looked at me.

In late summer air thick with rose and lily, I felt the old malevolence;
the snake tonguing the air, as if to tell me of its dreaming:—birds of
    paradise

gemming a pond; the unspooling; soft comings on, soft, soft
gestures, twisted and surreptitious; the shock; the taste; the kingdom.

In something more than words, *You are the snake, snake coils in you,*
it said. Do you think anyone knows its own hunger as well as the snake?

Why am I not just someone alive? When did Spirit tear me
to see how void of blessing I was? The snake hesitated, tasting dusk's
   black honey,

to feel if it was still good. And through its swoon
it knew it. Leaf, lichen, the least refinements, and the perfection.

Juan Carlos Galeano

Árbol

Un hombre enamorado de un árbol se va a vivir un tiempo con él antes de casarse.

"Así no tendrás que buscar más sol, ni agua ni comida," le dicen sus amigos.

Todas las noches el hombre le peina los cabellos al árbol y luego
se sientan a tomar té con sus amigos, los planetas y las estrellas más cercanas.

Life y las revistas ecológicas le cuentan la historia de amor a todo el mundo.

Pero un día el hombre se cansa de verle la misma cara al sol, a la luna y a las estrellas.

Los familiares, ecólogos y estrellas más amigas vienen y le preguntan
por qué no quiere vivir más con el árbol.

El hombre les dice que ha pensado casarse con un río o una nube, o con algo más variado.

Tree

A man in love with a tree goes to live with him for awhile before getting married.

"Now you no longer need to look for sunshine, water, or food," the man's friends tell him.

Every night the man combs the tree's hair and later
they sit down to tea with their friends, the planets and the closest stars.

Life and the environmental magazines tell their love story to the whole world.

But one day the man gets tired of seeing the same faces, the same sun, moon and stars.

Relatives, ecologists and their best friends, the stars, come and ask him why he doesn't want to live with the tree anymore.

The man tells them that he's been thinking of marrying a river, or a cloud, or something more versatile.

Historia

En el norte cazábamos muchos búfalos
y la grasa nos calentaba todos los inviernos.

Pero en la selva nos dijeron que para traer más luz
le echáramos más árboles al fogón del sol.

Un día se nos fue la mano, y le echamos toda la selva
con sus pájaros, los peces y los ríos.

Ahora pasamos mucho tiempo mirando las estrellas
y casi nunca cambia el menú de nuestra caza.

Hoy hemos cazado una nube
que iba a ser invierno en la ciudad de Nueva York.

History

In the north we hunted many buffalo
whose lard kept us warm all winter.

But in the jungle they told us that to bring more light
we should throw more trees into the sun's furnace.

One day our hand slipped and tossed in the entire jungle
with its birds, fish, and rivers.

Now we spend a lot of time gazing at the stars
and our daily menu almost never changes.

Today we hunted down a cloud
that was going to become winter in New York City.

—Translated by James Kimbrell and Rebecca Morgan

Brendan Galvin

An Intermission

After the last snows and the first
April chive-bursts, two came in
off the flyway, not flying
but coasting, humped to catch the air,
their wings on the long glide
without a single beat. White as if
a breeze were buffing fresh snowbanks,
their wing-sound was like wind
over snow—two tundra swans
by their black bills, not the decorative
imports children toss old bread at
on public water, but long as a man
and spanned wide as an eagle. *Cygnus
columbianus*, named for the river
Lewis and Clark found them on,
they had come all the way from
Currituck Sound or the Chesapeake,
aimed for the high Arctic
nesting grounds. Like gods out of
their element, they floated past me
above the pond and on down
the riverine marshes, pagan, twinned,
impersonal in their cold sublimity,
blind to my witness, their necks
outsnaking, intent on a brief rest
somewhere on our little river.

James Galvin

Three Sonnets

Where I live   distance is the primal fact
The world is mostly   far away and small
Drifting along through cause and effect   like sleep
As when the distance   unlikeliest of stems
Bears the unlikely   blossom of the wind
Engendering our only weather   dry
Except in winter   pine trees live on snow
So greedy   pulling down these drifts that bury
The fences snap   the trunks of smaller trees
If the forest wants   to go somewhere it spreads
Like a prophecy   its snow before it
Technology   a distant windy cause
There is no philosophy   of death where I live
Only philosophies   of suffering

They Haven't Heard the West Is Over

So that no one should forget, and no one be forgotten—isn't that what graves are for? The road from Tie Siding labors up the ridge like an old man in deep snow, leading the ditch like a mule, like always, making the woods by dark. The timber goes from green to blue on its way to the bone-white Divide.

Off the road there, in the lee of the rise (so that no one should forget), in a mixed patch of evergreen and aspen (so that no one be forgotten), you can barely see the rail fence, a brief enclosure, through the living trees.

Rough stones pried from the ground nearby, these markers bear no names. But I know who is buried here, and who repairs the rails. These folk were pioneers, and are, apart from other people: Ap Worster and his wife so frail he could place his hands wholly around her waist.

She wasn't strong enough to live so far away. Ap climbed a haystack when she died. He lay on his back and cried three days. That was 1910. Someone's girl died in winter, before she had a name. They kept her till the ground thawed. Death had done its work by then, and more.

There are others here that I could name and tell about, but the differences between them now are slight: a balsam tree is growing out of someone, someone is covered by an aspen bough, newly fallen.

Besides, these are not like graves in town that no one should forget. These were meant to be forgotten. Some people never stop wanting to disappear into the mountains. Right now the whole of Wyoming opens its rusty arms to the north, and the road from here keeps going, as if it were going somewhere.

Cartography

Out on the border a howl goes up, skinning the cold air.
A windrush as if from enormous wings descending
Slicks the grass down and thumps, and the whole sky bruises.
Out on the border it stops just as suddenly
As if there were some mistake, and there is: mortal beauty
This world can't bear, and a skeletal silence
Administrates the clouds, their passages, their dissolutions in light.

Out on the border right and wrong are more distinct,
But the border itself is suggestive, permissive, a thinly dotted line.
Amassed armies of forests and grasses poise,
Encroach, but never cross.
Even the sky stays on one side.
Another howl goes up, not a threat as was thought,
But an invitation to an interior. The border

Halves a piece of paper into here and hereafter.
A man, himself a fascicle of borders, draws a map and can't stop drawing
For fear of bleeding, smudging, disappearance.
When the map is complete the page will be completely
Obscured by detail, then a third howl.
Three things about the border are known:
It's real, it doesn't exist, it's on all the black maps.

Forrest Gander

Field Guide to Southern Virginia

True as the circumference
to its center. Woodscreek Grocery,
Rockbridge County. Twin boys
peer from the front window, cheeks
bulging with fireballs. Sandplum trees
flower in clusters by the levee. She
makes a knot on the inside knob
and ties my arms up
against the door. Williamsburg green.
With a touch as faint as a watermark.
Tracing cephalon, pygidium, glabella.

        .

Swayback, through freshly cut stalks,
stalks the yellow cat. Can you smell
where analyses end, the orchard
oriole begins? Slap her breasts lightly
to see them quiver. Delighting in this.
Desiccation cracks and plant debris
throughout the interval. In the Black-
water River, fishnets float
from a tupelo's spongy root
chopped into corks. There may be sprawling
precursors, descendent clades there are none.

        .

The gambit declined was less
promising. So the flock of crows
slaughtered all sixty lambs. Toward the east, red
and yellow colors prevail.
Praying at the graveside,
holding forth the palm of his hand

as a symbol of God's book.
For the entirety of the Ordovician.
With termites, Mrs. Elsinore explained,
as with the afterlife, remember:
there are two sides to the floor. A verb
for inserting and retrieving
green olives with the tongue. From
the scissure of your thighs.

.

In addition, the trilobites
were tectonically deformed. Snap-on
tools glinting from magenta
loosestrife, the air sultry
with creosote and cicadas.
You made me to lie down in a peri-Gondwanan back-arc basin.
Roses of wave ripples and gutter casts.
Your sex hidden by goat's beard.
Laminations in the sediment. All
preserved as internal molds
in a soft lilac shale.

.

Egrets picketing the spines of cattle in fields edged
with common tansy. Flowers my father gathered
for my mother to chew. To induce abortion. A common,
cosmopolitan agnostoid lithofacies naked in the foothills. I love
the character of your intelligence, its cast as well as pitch.
Border wide without marginal spines. At high angles
to the inferred shoreline.

.

It is the thin flute of the clavicles, each rain-pit
above them. The hypothesis of flexural loading. Aureoles
pink as steepleflower. One particular day, four hundred
million years ago, the mud stiffened
and held the strokes of waves. Orbital motion.
Raking leaves from the raspberries, you
uncover a nest of spring salamanders.

from Of Sum

That the trunk, submerged in air,
whirling leaves, thresholds-out. On the bark of
                              its leader stem, a black-capped
              chickadee pins caterpillars and lacewings.
      Its water sprouts and spurs unpruned,
                  unbraced, the Yellow Transparent apple-tree's
boughs release the girl open-mouthed
                  pumping her two-wheeler
                              across the meadow softly-furred
          as a bumble bee, her plastic bag
      pendant with hard apples
                              from one handlebar swaying—

Coffee cut with honeysuckle.
The unprimed pump won't give up its water.
Mosquito hawk clings to the barn wall's shadow.

.

That as though pulling thread from such a seam, the image
                              reveals a child's elative glance
          toward warbler-quickened birches
                  on an otherwise still morning
      when everything agrees to go quiet
                  but for the sound of leaves falling
                              through leaves,
the rotten, oily smell of red-blossoming
      paw paws clumped along the creek
              where a boy muddies for fish with a gig and hoe.
                              The path diverges. To the left
      and between tire ruts,
              long mounds of spongy grass
                  swerve through trees, but to the right
the path not taken remains unknowable,
              cottoned with light—

Soft-silted mouth of arrival.
A nest of shredded bark and small roots.
Croaking of the rain crow.

C. S. Giscombe

from Giscome Road

the song's a commotion rising in the current, almost an apparition: or the
                                                                    shape

rises—obvious, river-like—in the blood (in the house that the blood made)

& goes on, is the fact of the "oldest ancestor," in whose

name etc description itself persists on out, not like some story, into the up-
lands, on into the stony breakdown, no line

between the old river god & the old man's name coming up along the river
                                                    & on the road:

an endless invisible present going on,   a noise

(with nothing at the other side of it)

—but the name rowed (because water's got its ways)   out into the out,

        went the current,   on, like in a movie,

like talking, a voice-over going on from there—

        part of the caravan, part
                & parcel to the sweep of the noise, the sound spoken

    & divided out   of lengths
                                        of that water   part
                of that caravan there—,

                            a name to mouth   in the field,

& water has got its way:

the name rode along   being

a commotion:

an inflection described that one lip

(at wch water changed out there in the watershed)

o which—sung & shouted so—became

edge & description too,

a name-day, one of the day names

—the name oar'd along

in the current & the description,
the trill marking a border of

the place furthest from here,

an outermost jaggedness,

the heartless rind, shaded or not:

to be carried on over all of that in a sweep,

the long song edged out by the shout,

meaning the map

of sound got *fleshed* out so   it, the map,

got to be more   than a "document of voice" but   a way

bending north (out of range, peripheral & sourceless):

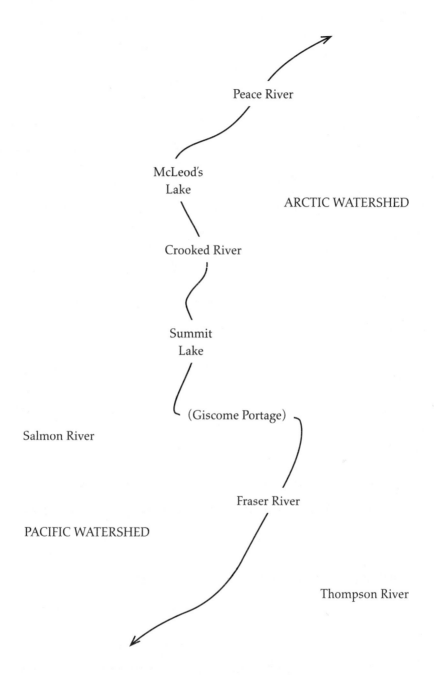

Peace River

McLeod's
Lake

ARCTIC WATERSHED

Crooked River

Summit
Lake

(Giscome Portage)

Salmon River

Fraser River

PACIFIC WATERSHED

Thompson River

     the name cycled along sourceless in the trees

  like it was a presupposition of lyrical content to the remote,

like it was a repeated tone looping the extravaganza,

     like it was a number (as quantity's a number),

or had number-like value   or added one

or could've to the road on out to where it's thickest at the outermost—most

extended—edges of remote:

some bottom-most designations of blood became the song, the basic

wordless change at the roadside along the road built thru the "center,"

& then thru the north's roadlessness as well where the word stopped

being mouthed, where it gave way, in form,

on or to some issues, basic as well, of drainage

(distance bending around & so forth, coming

up to a little ridge & stopping there, the state of rivers being a fact of the

             continent

like numbers, like money,

the spate of waters, water's jagged old way—

the voice was always centerless talking that was leading up to song, was about to

be the horn that marked the edge of the water—

       a river's head and its mouth
     there in that nomenclature out there

as if they were houses, one next to another one's yard:
    no word for the most interior edge of arrival:

all roads to there are the same, all roads

that are there are the same once anyone arrives: human nature surges

& blares & too is strayed & muting: water goes on like there's no tomorrow,

a row of hidden lights at the edge of a stage names

a shape to all that sound.

(& MOUTH): John Robert Giscome, "a negro miner," "a pioneer," John Robert

Giscome, "native of Jamaica West India" (self-described: "miner

& explorer"), he flourished in 19th C. British Columbia,

found a short way up into the Arctic & back out.

After whom: Giscome Canyon & the Giscome Rapids on the Fraser,

Giscome, B.C. in the Cariboo, Giscome Portage between

the watersheds, the Giscome Portage Historical Site,
the Giscome Portage Historical Society,

real Giscome Road from Old Cariboo Hwy in Prince George to Rte 16
—fabled Yellowhead Hwy—east of town.

Various other designations:

the rootless surname up on the river names rocks & water up there, the beauty

of apparitions is broken down & inflected both, the old Islands name,

the name that came & comes from *the Islands*,

the arrival, w/John R. Giscome, of the blackest name's edge
(& its variations & the effaced speaker's own name & parentage, Afro-

Caribbean, the spiral of announced approaches,

of descent & association, the long heart's most basic necessity out
where ambiguous fields meet the rim of houses, something

presignified, uninhabited—

a fleshy little bridge among the continents:

a little "Spanish" stole into view up along the river, islands appeared

to heave into situation)

Dr Rogers sd, of Bolívar, "This portrait of the great liberator painted in 1810
shows, in my opinion, a trace of Negroid strain in the fullness of the lips,
usually the last trace of Negro ancestry to disappear."

Peter Gizzi

Human Memory Is Organic

We know time is a wave.

You can see it in gneiss, migmatic
or otherwise, everything crumbles.

Don't despair.

That's the message frozen in old stone.

I am just a visitor to this world
an interloper really headed deep into glass.

I, moving across a vast expanse of water

though it is not water maybe salt
or consciousness itself

enacted as empathy. Enacted as seeing.

To see with a purpose has its bloom
and falls to seed and returns

to be a story like any other.
To be a story open and vulnerable

a measure of time, a day, this day one might say
an angle of light for instance.

Let us examine green. Let us go together

to see it all unstable and becoming
violent and testing gravity

so natural in its hunger.

The organic existence of gravity.
The organic nature of history.

The natural history of tears.

Louise Glück

Scilla

Not I, you idiot, not self, but we, we—waves
of sky blue like
a critique of heaven: why
do you treasure your voice
when to be one thing
is to be next to nothing?
Why do you look up? To hear
an echo like the voice
of god? You are all the same to us,
solitary, standing above us, planning
your silly lives: you go
where you are sent, like all things,
where the wind plants you,
one or another of you forever
looking down and seeing some image
of water, and hearing what? Waves,
and over waves, birds singing.

Witchgrass

Something
comes into the world unwelcome
calling disorder, disorder—

If you hate me so much
don't bother to give me
a name: do you need
one more slur
in your language, another
way to blame
one tribe for everything—

as we both know,
if you worship
one god, you only need
one enemy—

I'm not the enemy.
Only a ruse to ignore
what you see happening
right here in this bed,
a little paradigm
of failure. One of your precious flowers
dies here almost every day
and you can't rest until
you attack the cause, meaning

whatever is left, whatever
happens to be sturdier
than your personal passion—

It was not meant
to last forever in the real world.
But why admit that, when you can go on
doing what you always do,
mourning and laying blame,
always the two together.

I don't need your praise
to survive. I was here first,
before you were here, before
you ever planted a garden.
And I'll be here when only the sun and moon
are left, and the sea, and the wide field.

I will constitute the field.

Ray Gonzalez

Rattlesnakes Hammered on the Wall

Seven of them pinned in blood by
long, shiny tails, three of them still

alive and writhing against the wood,
their heaviness whipping the wall

as they try to break free,
rattles beating in unison,

hisses slowly dying in silence,
the other four hanging stiff

like ropes to another life,
patterns of torn skin dripping

with power and loss, the wonder
of who might have done this

turning to shock as all seven
suddenly come alive when

I get closer, pink mouths
trembling with white fangs,

lunging at me then falling back,
entangled in one another to form

twisted letters that spell a bloody
word I can't understand.

Charles Goodrich

Millennial Spring

The factory squats at the confluence of the rivers, where the Kalapuya had a potlatch ground. In vacant lots nearby, purple camas is blooming. Turkey vultures roost in cottonwood groves by the river. Beavers and foxes on nighttime errands ignore each other. There's a park with soccer fields and hiking trails, a littered encampment where bleary men roll up in blue tarps, and a skinny-dipping beach on the gravel bar.

My house is up the street, beyond the cemetery. Last night riding my bike past the factory I stopped and wrote—

> Night shift whoosh
>> of steam. A forklift's
> back-up beeper.
>> The factory wheezing
>> wounded air.

The factory wants to expand. I find myself along with dozens of neighbors organizing in opposition. The factory makes fiberglass. The air we breathe is studded with microscopic shreds of glass. After another late night meeting, six of us lean on our bicycles, talking. This is our social life, of late: strategy meetings and streetcorner hand-wringings. All of us are tired and grumpy. Suddenly I smell something.

> Shut up!
> Smell that cottonwood sap?
> We've missed
>> the arrival of spring.

I work as the gardener for the County Courthouse, and I'm way behind. Today I pruned the roses, the latest I have ever done so. As always, an elderly lady regards my severely pruned canes and asks, "Young man, do you know what you're doing?" Riding home in the evening I see a man at the back door of the factory, smoking a cigarette and gazing at the sky.

Yes, the gibbous moon
is lovely
through safety goggles.

The comet, Hyakatake, has been visiting the past few nights, a swatch of stardust in the eastern sky. After our son is asleep, my wife and I go out into the garden and hold each other and gaze at it.

Warm shoulders, fragrant hair.
When this comet comes again

we'll be gone.

The next night the comet has moved a little north, and the exhaust plumes from the factory rise toward it.

Your presence, comet,
sweetens somehow the evening's
aroma of skunk.

We have done a prodigious amount of research, read medical journals, studied the arcane language of pollution-control engineering. We cannot get the men who manage the factory to acknowledge any shred of possibility that there may be adverse health effects from respiring glass fibers. This tends to exaggerate our fears.

One must hope
that the great blue heron
fishing in the factory's settling pond

catches nothing.

To sit in the backyard grass, to lean and loaf while my son plays trucks in his sandbox—it doesn't happen much lately. Today, however, the sun was narcotic. I couldn't pursue the chores I had planned.

The plum tree in full blossom—
slower than this
time
does not go.

After a quick snooze on the chaise-longue, though, I begin to hear the unmowed grass growing at my feet, and weeds overwhelming the herbs in the garden. All right, to work then!

Affliction of spring—
        flowers
I have no time to admire.

Later in the afternoon:

My son, fishing the dry ditch
        for pretend fish,
                has drawn an audience
                of crows.

Five hundred people attend the hearing. One man speaks of the fox he
has seen trotting beside the river. A woman tells how geese fly right over
the factory's smokestacks. Several speakers dwell on the children who run
up and down the soccer fields in the shadow of the factory, while others
discuss the epidemiological studies and laboratory tests, the evidence of
lung disease and cancer. A woman roundly pregnant invokes seven future
generations.

Those few who talk in favor of the permit—all men, as it happens, most
of them in suits and ties—speak in the cliché of factuality. "There is no
reason to believe that these glass fiber emissions constitute any threat to
the health of the community." There is no reason to believe something
huge isn't rolling over all of us.

On my way home, to calm myself, I stroll among the gravestones—

The Big Dipper—
what's it pouring
down those smokestacks?

The month of April is cold and rainy. Blossoms are blown off the
cherry trees as quickly as they open. I hole up in the boiler room in the
basement of the Courthouse, drawing planting designs for the annual
flower beds, writing letters to the editor. In the brief interludes of
sunshine, I mow the Courthouse lawns, exulting.

Ah, to be living in a land
where everything is strange—
        my home town after rain.

On the first of May I plant pansies in the flower beds in front of
the Courthouse. The soil is beginning to warm, my spade turns up fat
earthworms. From the screen-roofed exercise-yard of the Gray Bar Hotel
come shouts of some raucous ball game.

                    Passers-by stop and scowl
                          at the sound of laughter
                                coming from the jail.

   The permit is granted. The factory begins to expand, growl a little louder. The air is lacerated. There are billions of glass fibers in it. I'm not leaving. Ever.

Jorie Graham

Evolution

How old are you?
As old as until now.
Under the kelp-bed razorclams turning to find
                                    purchase.
Young things shooting first-times and retaining
                                    precedence.
Razors digging backwards and down,
spurting spittle-bits of sea
to equalize descent.
Do you believe that after you die some part of you
                                    lives on?
Do you pray in hope of reward?
Do you agree or disagree with the following
                                    statement:
it bothers me my life did not turn out as I
                                    expected.
Also there are people on the beach.
And wind accepted by waterfilm.
Look: acceptance has a shape.
And fate—is it accepted by waterfilm?
And how we must promise things.
Do you pray in hope of reward.
Do you pray without hope of reward.
What is it has been gone a long time?
How long is the slightest chance?
Everything in sunlight
improvising backwards,
scratching phrases in a rapid jitter,
where the mind above it begins, ends, tries to get up
                                    and move
towards or away from.

You'll feel the so-called music strut hard against
                    the downsuck.
Also someone's shadow going to purchase a beverage.
Also everything in sunlight trying to become bodied by something
                                        else,
the whole retreating ocean laying
microscopic and also slightly larger fiercely-lit
kelp in streaks of action—
long sentences with branchlike off-widths indicating
                    acceleration brought forth
and left-off, phrases of gigantic backing-off
                    from a previously
held shore,
        rivulets of sand left visible in raised inscription
whitening where moistened—questionlike—algebraic—
regarding the long leave-taking—
We are ourselves walking to the right.
The noon hour is itself always a firstness
                    of something.
Also, elsewhere, who is hungry?
How small are they? How? I step on parts of
faces, only parts. A whole face, what is that? From here
it seems hard to make out, also a very empty
thing. Like the border of a nationstate.
Being comes into this, idles,
over the interminable logic of
manyness, the demand that *something exist*.
Bending to look close, a
spiking-up and forth of burrowings,
channelings, a turning, a re-turning on
itself where the broad
nouns of large clamshells
flayed open by gulls lie
in punctuating sunlit stillness
on top of a thing which but for
their stillness and expulsion
has no top. The seagulls
hurrying, dragging and retrieving. Also
pecking in place and dropping and

lifting. Sometimes stepping backwards in order to
drag and loosen. Also the drag of the slantline
downtilted towards ocean's sucking further still of
streams of water towards
itself. Of course the future
wasn't there before at all.
This all first time and then again first
                              time.
I feel reproach. Eyes closed I touch my face.
My hand hovers like the very question of my face
                              over my face.
G says, breathing beside me, that firstness is not, in any case,
a characteristic of experience.
He speaks of the long chain back
to the beginning of "the world" (as he calls it) and then, at last,
                              to the great *no*
beginning. I feel the *no* begin.
Subsequence hums tinily all round me,
erasing my tracks. Oh bright/morning. This
                              morning.
Look: what looks like retreating is not exactly so.
Sunlight makes of exactness an issue.
No issuing *forth* of matter
because of sunlight. But sun's
up-sucking also at work. And how
it seems to have weight,
pushing the originally pillowy kelp-beds
down, flattening them where they
give up water, unthickening their
pastures as the tunneling-away from
that gigantic drying drives
the almost-imperceptible downwards:
first glitter then more unchangeable shine slowly being
forced into the vast top of the
beachwide beds. Drying out and
hardening, the beds force light
                              back.
Back across what resides inside.
White closed-in part of gazing-out.
Bothered by the ease of touch.

As if one should open out and spill, again.
Sound in the sun now muted
(is there an inherent good)
as the ruffling back-roar recedes
(is there inherent good in people)—
Sound becoming particular and pricked
with syncopations of singularities—
peeps, insucks, snaps—where light is
                    in domain.
What good is my silence for, what would it hold
                    inside, keeping it free?
Sing says the folding water on stiller water—
one running through where the other's breaking. Sing me
something (the sound of the low wave-breaking)
(the tuning-down where it deposits life-matter on
the uphill of shore)(also the multiplicity
of deepenings and coverings where whiteness rises as a
                    manyness)
(as the wave breaks over its own breaking)
(to rip in unison)(onto its backslide)—
of something sing, and singing, disagree.

Sea Change

One day: stronger wind than anyone expected. Stronger than
                    ever before in the recording
                    of such. Un-
natural says the news. Also the body says it. Which part of the body—
                                        I look
            down, can
            feel it, yes, don't know
where. Also, submerging us,
            making of the fields, the trees, a cast of characters in an
            unnegotiable
drama, ordained, iron-gloom of low light, everything at once undoing
            itself. Also *sustained*, as in a hatred of
            a thought, or a vanity that comes upon one out of
            nowhere & makes

one feel the mischief in faithfulness to an
                    idea. Everything unpreventable and excited like
mornings in the unknown future. Who shall repair this now. And how
                                                    the future
                    takes shape
                    too quickly. The permanent is ebbing. Is leaving
                    nothing in the way of
trails, they are blown over, grasses shoot up, life disturbing life, & it
                    fussing all over us, like a confinement gone
                    insane, blurring the feeling of
                    the state of
                    being. Which did exist just yesterday, calm and
true. Like the right to
                    privacy—how strange a feeling, here, the *right*—
                    consider your affliction says the
                    wind, do not plead ignorance, & farther and farther
                    away leaks the
past, much farther than it used to go, beating against the shutters I
                    have now fastened again, the huge mis-
                    understanding round me now so
                    still in
the center of this room, listening—oh,
                    these are not split decisions, everything
                    is in agreement, we set out willingly, & also knew to
                    play by rules, & if I say to you now
                    Let's go
somewhere the thought won't outlast
                    the minute, here it is now, carrying its North
                    Atlantic windfall, hissing Consider
                    the body of the ocean which rises every instant into
                    me, & its
                    ancient e-
                    vaporation, & how it delivers itself
to me, how the world is our law, this indrifting of us
                    into us, a chorusing in us of elements, & how the
                    intermingling of us lacks in-
                    telligence, makes
reverberation, syllables untranscribable, in-clingings, & how wonder is
                                                    also what

pours from us when, in the
coiling, at the very bottom of
the food
chain, sprung
from undercurrents, warming by 1 degree, the in-
dispensable
plankton is forced north now, & yet farther north,
spawning too late for the cod larvae hatch, such
that the hatch will not survive, nor the
species in the end, in the right-now forever un-
interruptable slowing of the
gulf
stream, so that I, speaking in this wind today, out loud in it, to no one, am
suddenly
aware
of having written my poems, I feel it in
my useless
hands, palms in my lap, & in my listening, & also the memory of a
season *at its*
full, into which is spattered like a
silly cry this in-
cessant leaf-glittering, shadow-mad, all over
the lightshafts, the walls, the bent back ranks of trees
all stippled with these slivers of
light like
breaking grins—infinities of them—wriggling along the walls, over the
grasses—mouths
reaching into
other mouths—sucking out all the
air—huge breaths passing to and fro between the unkind blurrings—&
quicken
me further says this new wind, &
according to thy
judgment, &
I am inclining my heart towards the end,
I cannot fail, this Saturday, early pm, hurling myself,
wiry furies riding my many backs, against your foundations and your
best young
tree, which you have come outside to stake again, & the loose stones in
the sill.

Michael Gregory

The Cranes

Someone told Athenaeus the cranes turn into people
once they go back up north, tall and spindly-legged
with a shock of red hair where the sun they said touches
the earth's edge only twice a year and the moon the same
and it is warm there among the thin crane people
who never have wars or forget though very far north and their
voices are very loud trumpeting peacefulness for miles
across the unfrozen tundra and time it seems without end
since they first flew down in ragged lines to look at the strange
new creatures who could not fly at all and shivered naked
in the dark a third of the time asleep not even dreaming
of more to life than making a living or getting out of it
somehow or around it or taking their minds off it
(getting angry or sly or laid) compensating themselves
for their rotten luck with love when they can (which isn't
often) or poor substitutes they pay dearly for with
a hardening of the heart, a bickering among themselves
and insane cruelty against the other creatures, the world
itself, a fist shook or finger jabbed against the sky
where the dark formations, the shifting V's, swing through the cold
morning air in miles-wide ever-widening arcs
rising higher and higher above the still frozen fields
beginning almost at random to head north, their raucous calls
and turbulent flurrying wings finally out of earshot
leaving a sudden silence between winter and spring.

Tami Haaland

Goldeye, Vole

I say sweep of prairie
or curve or sandstone,

but it doesn't come close
to this language of dry wind

and deer prints, blue racer
and sage, its punctuation

white quartz and bone.
I learned mounds of

mayflowers, needle grass
on ankles, the occasional

sweet pea before I knew
words like perspective or

travesty or the permanence
of loss. My tongue spoke

obsidian, red agate,
arrowhead. I stepped

through tipi rings, leaped
buffalo grass and puff ball

to petrified clam.
Jawbone of fox, flint,

blue lichen, gayfeather,
goldeye, vole—speak to me

my prairie darling, sing me
that song you know.

John Haines

If the Owl Calls Again

at dusk
from the island in the river
and it's not too cold,

I'll wait for the moon
to rise,
then take wing and glide
to meet him.

We will not speak,
but hooded against the frost
soar above
the alder flats, searching
with tawny eyes.

And then we'll sit
in the shadowy spruce
and pick the bones
of careless mice,

while the long moon drifts
toward Asia
and the river mutters
in its icy bed.

And when the morning climbs
the limbs
we'll part without a sound,

fulfilled, floating
homeward as
the cold world awakens.

Donald Hall

Digging

One midnight, after a day when lilies
lift themselves out of the ground while you watch them,
and you come into the house at dark
your fingers grubby with digging, your eyes
vague with the pleasure of digging,

let a wind raised from the South
climb through your bedroom window, lift you in its arms
—you have become as small as a seed—
and carry you out of the house, over the black garden,
spinning and fluttering,

and drop you in cracked ground.
The dirt will be cool, rough to your clasped skin
like a man you have never known.
You will die into the ground
in a dead sleep, surrendered to water.

You will wake suffering
a widening pain in your side, a breach
gapped in your tight ribs
where a green shoot struggles to lift itself upwards
through the tomb of your dead flesh

to the sun, to the air of your garden
where you will blossom
in the shape of your own self, thoughtless
with flowers, speaking
to bees, in the language of green and yellow, white and red.

Joy Harjo

from She Had Some Horses

V. Explosion

The highway near Okemah, Oklahoma exploded.

                    There are reasons for everything.
Maybe   there is a new people, coming forth
               being born from the center of the earth,
               like us, but another tribe.

Maybe   they will be another color that no one
               has ever seen before. Then they might be hated,
               and live in Muskogee on the side of the tracks
               that Indians live on. (And they will be the
               ones to save us.)

Maybe   there are lizards coming out of rivers of lava
               from the core of this planet,

                      coming to bring rain

               to dance for the corn,
               to set fields of tongues slapping at the dark
               earth, a kind of a dance.

But maybe the explosion was horses,
                      bursting out of the crazy earth
near Okemah. They were a violent birth,
flew from the ground into trees
                   to wait for evening night
mares to come after them:

then	into the dank wet fields of Oklahoma
then	their birth cords tied into the molten heart
then	they travel north and south, east and west
then	into wet white sheets at midnight when everyone sleeps and the baby dreams of swimming in the bottom of the muggy river
then	into frogs who have come out of the earth to see for rain
then	a Creek woman who dances shaking the seeds in her bones
then	South Dakota, Mexico, Japan, and Manila
then	into Miami to sweep away the knived faces of hatred

Some will not see them.

But some will see the horses with their hearts of sleeping volcanoes
and will be rocked awake

past their bodies

to see who they have become.

.

My House Is the Red Earth

My house is the red earth; it could be the center of the world. I've heard New York, Paris, or Tokyo called the center of the world, but I say it is magnificently humble. You could drive by and miss it. Radio waves can obscure it. Words cannot construct it, for there are some sounds left to sacred wordless form. For instance, that fool crow, picking through trash near the corral, understands the center of the world as greasy scraps of fat. Just ask him. He doesn't have to say that the earth has turned scarlet through fierce belief, after centuries of heartbreak and laughter—he perches on the blue bowl of the sky, and laughs.

Eagle Poem

To pray you open your whole self
To sky, to earth, to sun, to moon
To one whole voice that is you.
And know there is more
That you can't see, can't hear;
Can't know except in moments
Steadily growing, and in languages
That aren't always sound but other
Circles of motion.
Like eagle that Sunday morning
Over Salt River. Circled in blue sky
In wind, swept our hearts clean
With sacred wings.
We see you, see ourselves and know
That we must take the utmost care
And kindness in all things.
Breathe in, knowing we are made of
All this, and breathe, knowing
We are truly blessed because we
Were born, and die soon within a
True circle of motion,
Like eagle rounding out the morning
Inside us.
We pray that it will be done
In beauty.
In beauty.

Lola Haskins

The Sandhill Cranes

The blue air fills with cries.
The cranes are streams, rivers.
They danced on the night prairie,
leapt at each other, quivering.

The long bones of sandhill cranes
know their next pond. Not us.
When something is too beautiful,
we do not have the grace to leave.

Prayer for the Everglades

A gumbo-limbo swoons in the arms of an oak.
A royal palm, smooth as sunless skin, rises
against blue. In this whole untouched world
there seems only wind, the grass, and us.
Now silent lines of wood storks appear,
their white wings edged black. Here is
a mathematical question for your evenings.
How many moments like this make a life?

But if it were not true? What if the glades
were a dream, ancient, written on the walls
of caves, so anthropologists peering into
the darkness could say only, *it must have
been lovely then, when grass flowed under
the sun like a young woman's falling hair.*
What if none of it were true? What if
you and I walked all our afternoons under
smoke, and never saw beyond? What if

the tiny lichens that velvet the water, the
gators that pile like lizards on the banks,
the ibis with her sweet curved bill? What
if the turtles that plop off their logs like little
jokes? What if the sheltering mangroves?
Oh what if? Look up, friend, and take my
hand. What if the wood storks were gone?

Robert Hass

Palo Alto: The Marshes

For Mariana Richardson (1830–1891)

1.

She dreamed along the beaches of this coast.
Here where the tide rides in to desolate
the sluggish margins of the bay,
sea grass sheens copper into distances.
Walking, I recite the hard
explosive names of birds:
egret, killdeer, bittern, tern.
Dull in the wind and early morning light,
the striped shadows of the cattails
twitch like nerves.

2.

Mud, roots, old cartridges, and blood.
High overhead, the long silence of the geese.

3.

"We take no prisoners," John Fremont said
and took California for President Polk.
That was the Bear Flag War.
She watched it from the Mission San Rafael,
named for the archangel (the terrible one)
who gently laid a fish across the eyes
of saintly, miserable Tobias
that he might see.
The eyes of fish. The land
shimmers fearfully.
No archangels here, no ghosts,

and terns rise like seafoam
from the breaking surf.

    4.

Kit Carson's antique .45, blue,
new as grease. The roar
flings up echoes,
row on row of shrieking avocets.
The blood of Francisco de Haro,
Ramon de Haro, José de los Reyes Berryessa
runs darkly to the old ooze.

    5.

The star thistles: erect, surprised,

    6.

and blooming
violet caterpillar hairs. One
of the de Haros was her lover,
the books don't say which.
They were twins.

    7.

In California in the early spring
there are pale yellow mornings
when the mist burns slowly into day.
The air stings
like autumn, clarifies
like pain.

    8.

Well I have dreamed of this coast myself.
Dreamed Mariana, since her father owned the land
where I grew up. I saw her picture once:
a wraith encased in a high-necked black silk
dress so taut about the bones there were hardly ripples
for the light to play in. I knew her eyes

had watched the hills seep blue with lupine after rain,
seen the young peppers, heavy and intent,
first rosy drupes and then the acrid fruit,
the ache of spring. Black as her hair
the unreflecting venom of those eyes
is an aftermath I know, like these brackish,
russet pools a strange life feeds in
or the old fury of land grants, maps,
and deeds of trust. A furious dun-
colored mallard knows my kind
and skims across the edges of the marsh
where the dead bass surface
and their flaccid bellies bob.

9.

A chill tightens the skin
around my bones. The other California
and its bitter absent ghosts
dance to a stillness in the air:
the Klamath tribe was routed and they disappeared.
Even the dust seemed stunned,
tools on the ground, fishnets.
Fires crackled, smouldering.
No movement but the slow turning
of the smoke, no sound but jays
shrill in the distance and flying further off.
The flicker of lizards, dragonflies.
And beyond the dry flag-woven lodges
a faint persistent slapping.
Carson found ten wagonloads
of fresh-caught salmon, silver
in the sun. The flat eyes stared.
Gills sucked the thin annulling air.
They flopped and shivered,
ten wagonloads. Kit Carson
burned the village to the ground.
They rode some twenty miles that day
and still they saw black smoke
smear the sky above the pines.

10.

Here everything seems clear,
firmly etched agaist the pale
smoky sky: sedge, flag, owl's clover,
rotting wharves. A tanker lugs silver
bomb-shaped napalm tins toward
port at Redwood City. Again,
my eye performs
the lobotomy of description.
Again, almost with yearning,
I see the malice of her ancient eyes.
The mud flats hiss as the tide turns.
They say she died in Redwood City,
cursing "the goddamned Anglo-Yankee yoke."

11.

The otters are gone from the bay
and I have seen five horses
easy in the grassy marsh
beside three snowy egrets.

Birds cries and the unembittered sun,
wings and the white bodies of the birds,
it is morning. Citizens are rising
to murder in their moral dreams.

Ezra Pound's Proposition

Beauty is sexual, and sexuality
Is the fertility of the earth and the fertility
Of the earth is economics. Though he is no recommendation
For poets on the subject of finance,
I thought of him in the thick heat
Of the Bangkok night. Not more than fourteen, she saunters up to you
Outside the Shangri-la Hotel
And says, in plausible English,
"How about a party, big guy?"

Here is more or less how it works:
The World Bank arranges the credit and the dam
Floods three hundred villages, and the villagers find their way
To the city where their daughters melt into the teeming streets,
And the dam's great turbines, beautifully tooled
In Lund or Dresden or Detroit, financed
By Lazard Frères in Paris or the Morgan Bank in New York,
Enabled by judicious gifts from Bechtel of San Francisco
Or Halliburton of Houston to the local political elite,
Spun by the force of rushing water,
Have become hives of shimmering silver
And, down river, they throw that bluish throb of light
Across her cheekbones and her lovely skin.

Exit, Pursued by a Sierra Meadow

That slow, rhythmic flickering of the wings,
As if from the ache of pleasure—
A California tortoiseshell
Fastened to the white umbel of a milkweed stalk.

Smell of water in the dry air,
The almost nutmeg smell of dust.

White fir, Jeffrey pine,
I have no way of knowing whether you prefer
Summer or winter,
Though I think you are more beautiful in winter.

Scarlet fritillary, corn lily,
I don't know which you prefer, either.
So long, horsemint,
Your piebald mix of lavender and soft gray-green under the cottonwoods
On a shelf of lichened granite near a creek
May be the most startling thing in these mountains,
Besides the mountains.
It's good that we stopped just a minute
To look at you and then walked down the trail
Because we had things to do

And because beauty is a little unendurable,
I mean, getting used to it is unendurable,
Because if we can't eat a thing or do something with it,
Human beings get bored by almost everything eventually,
Which is why winter is such an admirable invention.
There's another month of summer here.
August will squeeze the sweetness out of you
And drift it as pollen.

State of the Planet

On the occasion of the 50th anniversary of
the Lamont-Doherty Earth Observatory

I.

October on the planet at the century's end.
Rain lashing the windshield. Through blurred glass
Gusts of a Pacific storm rocking a huge, shank-needled
Himalayan cedar. Under it a Japanese plum
Throws off a vertical cascade of leaves the color
Of skinned copper, if copper could be skinned.
And under it, her gait as elegant and supple
As the young of any of earth's species, a schoolgirl
Negotiates a crosswalk in the wind, her hair flying,
The red satchel on her quite straight back darkening
Splotch by smoky crimson splotch as the rain pelts it.
One of the six billion of her hungry and curious kind.
Inside the backpack, dog-eared, full of illustrations,
A book with a title like *Getting to Know Your Planet*.

The book will tell her that the earth this month
Has yawed a little distance from the sun,
And that the air, cooling, has begun to move,
As sensitive to temperature as skin is
To a lover's touch. It will also tell her that the air—
It's likely to say "the troposphere"—has trapped
Emissions from millions of cars, idling like mine
As she crosses, and is making a greenhouse

Of the atmosphere. The book will say that climate
Is complicated, that we may be doing this,
And if we are, it may explain that this
Was something we've done quite accidentally,
Which she can understand, not having meant
That morning to have spilled the milk. She's
One of those who's only hungry metaphorically.

2.

Poetry should be able to comprehend the earth,
To set aside from time to time its natural idioms
Of ardor and revulsion, and say, in a style as sober
As the Latin of Lucretius, who reported to Venus
On the state of things two thousand years ago—
"It's your doing that under the wheeling constellations
Of the sky," he wrote, "all nature teems with life—"
Something of the earth beyond our human dramas.

Topsoil: going fast. Rivers: dammed and fouled.
Cod: about fished out. Haddock: about fished out.
Pacific salmon nosing against dams from Yokohama
To Kamchatka to Seattle and Portland, flailing
Up fish ladders, against turbines, in a rage to breed
Much older than human beings and interdicted
By the clever means that humans have devised
To grow more corn and commandeer more lights.
Most of the ancient groves are gone, sacred to Kuan Yin
And Artemis, sacred to the gods and goddesses
In every picture book the child is apt to read.

3.

Lucretius, we have grown so clever that mechanics
In our art of natural philosophy can take the property
Of luminescence from a jellyfish and put it in mice.
In the dark the creatures give off greenish light.
Their bodies must be very strange to them.
An artist in Chicago—think of a great trading city
In Dacia or Thracia—has asked to learn the method
So he can sell people dogs that glow in the dark.

4.

The book will try to give the child the wonder
Of how, in our time, we understand life came to be:
Stuff flung off from the sun, the molten core
Still pouring sometimes rivers of black basalt
Across the earth from the old fountains of its origin.
A hundred million years of clouds, sulfurous rain.
The long cooling. There is no silence in the world
Like the silence of rock from before life was.
You come across it in a Mexican desert,

A palo verde tree nearby, moss-green. Some
Insect-eating bird with wing feathers the color
Of a morning sky perched on a limb of the tree.
That blue, that green, the completely fierce
Alertness of the bird that can't know the amazement
Of its being there, a human mind that somewhat does,
Regarding a black outcrop of rock in the desert
Near a sea, charcoal-black and dense, wave-worn,
And all one thing: there's no life in it at all.

It must be a gift of evolution that humans
Can't sustain wonder. We'd never have gotten up
From our knees if we could. But soon enough
We'd fashioned sexy little earrings from the feathers,
Highlighted our cheekbones by rubbings from the rock,
And made a spear from the sinewy wood of the tree.

5.

If she lived in Michigan or the Ukraine,
She'd find, washed up on the beach in a storm like this
Limestone fossils of Devonian coral. She could study
The faint white markings: she might have to lick the stone
To see them if the wind was drying the pale surface
Even as she held it, to bring back the picture of what life looked like
Three hundred million years ago: a honeycomb with mouths.

6.

Cells that divided and reproduced. From where? Why?
(In our century it was the fashion in philosophy
Not to ask unanswerable questions. That was left
To priests and poets, an attitude you'd probably
Approve.) Then a bacterium grew green pigment.
This was the essential miracle. It somehow unmated
Carbon dioxide to eat the carbon and turn it
Into sugar and spit out, hiss out the molecules
Of oxygen the child on her way to school
Is breathing, and so bred life. Something then
Of DNA, the curled musical ladder of sugars, acids.
From there to eyes, ears, wings, hands, tongues.
Armadillos, piano tuners, gnats, sonnets,
Military interrogation, the Coho salmon, the Margaret Truman rose.

7.

The people who live in Tena, on the Napo River,
Say that the black, viscid stuff that pools in the selva
Is the blood of the rainbow boa curled in the earth's core.
The great trees in that forest house ten thousands of kinds
Of beetle, reptiles no human eyes has ever seen changing
Color on the hot, green, hardly changing leaves
Whenever a faint breeze stirs them. In the understory
Bromeliads and orchids whose flecked petals and womb-
Or mouthlike flowers are the shapes of desire
In human dreams. And butterflies, larger than her palm
Held up to catch a ball or ward off fear. Along the river
Wide-leaved banyans where flocks of raucous parrots,
Fruit-eaters and seed-eaters, rise in startled flares
Of red and yellow and bright green. It will seem to be poetry
Forgetting its promise of sobriety to say the rosy shinings
In the thick brown current are small dolphins rising
To the surface where gouts of the oil that burns inside
The engine of the car I'm driving ooze from the banks.

8.

The book will tell her that the gleaming appliance
That kept her milk cold in the night required
Chlorofluorocarbons—Lucretius, your master
Epictetus was right about atoms in a general way.
It turns out they are electricity having sex
In an infinite variety of permutations, Plato's
Yearning halves of a severed being multiplied
In all the ways that all the shapes on earth
Are multiple, complex; the philosopher
Who said that the world was fire was also right—
Chlorofluorocarbons react with ozone, the gas
That makes air tingle on a sparkling day.
Nor were you wrong to describe them as assemblies,
As if evolution were a town meeting or a plebiscite.
(Your theory of wind, and of gases, was also right
And there are more of them than you supposed.)
Ozone, high in the air, makes a kind of filter
Keeping out parts of sunlight damaging to skin.
The device we use to keep our food as cool
As if it sat in snow required this substance,
And it reacts with ozone. Where oxygen breeds it
From ultraviolet light, it burns a hole in the air.

9.

They drained the marshes around Rome. Your people,
You know, were the ones who taught the world to love
Vast fields of grain, the power and the order of the green,
Then golden rows of it, spooled out almost endlessly.
Your poets, those in the generation after you,
Were the ones who praised the packed seed heads
And the vineyards and the olive groves and called them
"Smiling" fields. In the years since we've gotten
Even better at relentless simplification, but it's taken
Until our time for it to crowd out, savagely, the rest
Of life. No use to rail against our curiosity and greed.
They keep us awake. And are, for all their fury
And their urgency, compatible with intelligent restraint.

In the old paintings of the Italian Renaissance,
—In the fresco painters who came after you
(It was the time in which your poems were rediscovered—
There was a period when you, and Venus, were lost;
How could she be lost? You may well ask.) Anyway
In those years the painters made of our desire
An allegory and a dance in the figure of three graces.
The first, the woman coming toward you, is the appetite
For life; the one who seems to turn away is chaste restraint,
And the one whom you've just glimpsed, her back to you,
Is beauty. The dance resembles wheeling constellations.
They made of it a figure for something elegant or lovely
Forethought gives our species. One would like to think
It makes a dance, that the black-and-white flash
Of a flock of buntings in October wind, headed south
Toward winter habitat, would find that the December fields
Their kind has known and mated in for thirty centuries
Or more, were still intact, that they will not go
The way of the long-billed arctic curlews who flew
From Newfoundland to Patagonia in every weather
And are gone now from the kinds on earth. The last of them
Seen by any human alit in a Texas marsh in 1964.

10.

What is to be done with our species? Because
We know we're going to die, to be submitted
To that tingling dance of atoms once again,
It's easy for us to feel that our lives are a dream—
As this is, in a way, a dream: the flailing rain,
The birds, the soaked red backpack of the child,
Her tendrils of wet hair, the windshield wipers,
This voice trying to speak across the centuries
Between us, even the long story of the earth,
Boreal forests, mangrove swamps, Tiberian wheat fields
In the summer heat on hillsides south of Rome—all of it
A dream, and we alive somewhere, somehow outside it,
Watching. People have been arguing for centuries
About whether or not you thought of Venus as a metaphor.

Because of the rational man they take you for.
Also about why your poem ended with a plague,
The bodies heaped in the temples of the gods.
To disappear. First one, then a few, then hundreds,
Just stopping over here, to vanish in the marsh at dusk.
So easy, in imagination, to tell the story backward,
Because the earth needs a dream of restoration—
She dances and the birds just keep arriving,
Thousands of them, immense arctic flocks, her teeming life.

Brooks Haxton

Submersible

> Why art thou cast down, O my soul?
> —PSALM 42

Down from twilight into dark at noon,
through darker, down until the black
could not be more devoid of star
or sunlight, O my soul, near freezing
in subphotic stillness past
the fragile strands of glowing jelly
radiant with tentacles to sting,
and bioluminescent lures of anglers,
down where water beading on the cold hatch
overhead has sheathed in dewdrops
the titanium, past dragonfish
with night-lights set into their heads
and flanks, past unlit cruisers,
blackcod, owl fish, eelpout, skate,
where spider crabs, arms long as mine,
on creamy prongs drift floodlit
over the pillow lava, here,
our craft has taken us where no one
could have come till now but corpses.

Chris Hayes

After My Daughter's Birth, a Late Night
Self-Portrait with a Running Mare

Over the fence, her hooves
were dropped walnuts

       thumping against clay
       in the Mississippi dark.

              I am elsewhere, and this
              is what I have conjured

       to mimic the stack of stones
       lodged in my throat.

Yesterday she swung her head
over the barbed wire, and nudged

       a swarm of worker bees
       from a clutch of fallen pears.

              This field is empty of trees;
              the air is not thick with sugar.

       I can almost hear the moon
       sinking into the water.

Soon, a birth in the pasture,
another foal slicked over with dew.

       Yanked into this world
       full of light and bad winters.

Allison Hedge Coke

Dust: Dad's Days

Dust storms darkened sky so, you couldn't
find your way around house, yard.
Crack thick as a postage stamp gave way
to dirt through walls, black blizzard.

Dirt in food—in everything.

Damn it, the dust storms—
three days at a time.
Couldn't see—

Dirt scratched, confused.
Some people lost their minds, killed their families.

Rabbits, grasshoppers everywhere, billions came.
Billions of grasshoppers at everything.

Rabbits,   hares, really.
Jack rabbits, had been in breaks by creeks.
Bad weather came, they moved to flats. Stressed
rabbits, hares, bearing six to eight young,
instead of two, three in litters.

Our Fox Terriers chased rabbits wildly.
The Border Collies trained them to herd
them in,   catch them.

Us Cherokee, all surrounded by Missouri Mormons.
Not as far out as Utah Mormons
who believed lizard language, angels.
We'd come out for the work there—freedom—
Cherokee hunkered there in the dust, missing mountain green.

Come winter, blizzards' winds howled and
howled and howled and howled and howled.

Windmill was all you could make out in ground blizzards.
Everything else whited out so bright, you'd think it was nothing.
Windmill would freeze, have to heat it
with pans of hot water,   unseize it.
Cattle horses drink on one side,
Prince the Percheron stallion would be on the other.
Only my brother Willis could hitch Prince and Doll.
She'd walk along, he'd pull.
Dolly, an older cattle mare, would discipline him, Prince.
He'd defer to her, even as an adult.
No matter his size.
She was boss.
Dust was our boss.

Sweet corn, beans, pumpkin, squash, and tomatoes we'd grow.
Six rows beans, six corn, switch
back and forth, alternate, rotate, annually.
People used a Go-Devil to cut back what they called weeds.

Times were thrashing beans, snapping corn—
We stripped ears of corn, threw up into wagons,
corn sheller gave cobs for winter fuel.
Dry cow chips for summer fuel.
Everything operated on one-boy-power:
laundry, cob fuel, chips—wagons full—

Made good crops till 1932. '33, the wind came, the dirt storms.
1934, gave it up, moved away,

That land should have never taken plowing
like the Whites around us gave it.
The drought killed us. Killed us.

Shouldn't have happened. Recklessness.
They'd lifted the herd sod.
Took the drumhead off the topsoil.
Loosed it, until it was crumble.
Reckless.

Dust.
Before WWII, before they found out it was more
efficient to fly one direction over another,
they didn't understand jet streams.
The Sonoran High Jet Stream moved north, took it all.
Fall 1935-6-7-8 and on so, throw a sack
around your shoulder, drag behind you,
picking left and right, we hit the cotton fields,
picking people's crops, any left.
Tally man recorded how much
Flies, sweat, back ached and ached, for a penny a pound—dust.
Teenager might make a hundred pounds in a day, make a dollar.
Older people more efficient,
maybe make two-three dollars a day.

We were always thankful for offers to come pick,
money so hard to come by.
Good owner'd say, "Why don't you eat some watermelons?"
Angle his finger toward some melons
growing alongside the cotton,
raised for pickers' pleasure
to keep us half-fit.

Dust, insects, sweat, aching back, dust—dust—
Everything dust. Everything dust.   —Dad said.

William Heyen

The Swamp

Stretched out underwater, neck telescoped forward,
smelling the spring mud as though just waking,
behemoth walked in a drowse. Braced myself,

hauled it in two pulls by its fat tail to shore
where it blinked and shut itself off to such nonsense,
withdrew its neck to wait out whatever. . . .

Noticed a leech necklace, glints of topaz in its eyes,
nostrils protruding upward so it could breathe while
hidden in muck with its maw open,

its pretty pink inviting tongue wiggling.
Fed it a stick: it struck in a hiss and snapped it.
Thought of creatures it had eaten—

even an adult blue heron piteously broken,
leg by wing, at last dragged down in mid-cry.
Wanted to end this snapper and all its children

in their primitive armor, wanted to boil it,
eat its heart, digest it at leisure in a trance of bliss
in my own top-of-the-food-chain arrogance, . . .

but if we rid the world of snappers, would mosquitoes cloud
when herons ate all frogs? Was there balance here,
or have we come too far filling in wetlands, forcing

every last heron into the snapper's jaws? Yearned
to knife its voracious brain to the ground,
but wanted to do the precarious right thing, you understand. . . .

In the end, wouldn't act alone. Looped a wire
around its shell, tied it to a tree with enough play
so it could just reach water or climb ashore. . . .

We've all summer to decide. If you want me to,
I'll ax its ugly bejeweled head off, or let it loose.
Listen to the swamp, and let me know.

Blackbird Spring

Mid-morning, walking ocean shoreline,
I found a hundred blackbirds
frozen in ice,
only their heads protruding,
black eyes open,
gleaming, most of their sharp beaks still
scissoring in mid-whistle.

Feeding, they'd been caught
in sea-spray, must be—
all males, up north early,
scarlet epaulettes aflame
a few inches under. I chipped
one bird loose with a stone,
held it in gloved hands

under the rising sun until,
until I realized, until I realized
nothing I hadn't known.
The tide retreated & would return.
Within the austere territories
these would have filled with belligerence
& song, spring had begun.

Brenda Hillman

Practical Water

What does it mean to live a moral life

It is nearly impossible to think about this

We went down to the creek
The sides were filled
   with tiny watery activities

The mind was split & mended
Each perception divided into more

& there were in the hearts of the water molecules
   little branches perpendicular to thought

Had lobbied the Congress but it was dead
Had written to the Committee on Understanding
Had written to the middle
   middle of the middle
   class but it was drinking
Had voted in cafes with shoplifters &
   beekeepers stirring tea made of water
   hitched to the green arc

An ethics occurs at the edge
of what we know

The creek goes underground about here

The spirits offer us a world of origins
Owl takes its call from the drawer of the sky

Unusually warm global warming day out

A tiny droplet shines
   on a leaf & there your creek is found

It has borrowed something to
   link itself to others

We carry ourselves through the days in code
DNA like Raskolnikov's staircase neither
   good nor bad in itself

Lower frequencies *are* the mind
What happened to the creek
   is what happened
   to the sentence in the twentieth century
It got social underground

You should make yourself uncomfortable
If not you who

Thrush comes out from the cottony
   coyote bush glink-a-glink
       chunk drink
   trrrrr
   turns a golden eyebrow to the ground

We run past the plant that smells like taco sauce

Recite words for water
   weeter wader weetar vatn
   watn voda
   [insert all languages here]

Poor Rimbaud didn't know how to live
   but knew how to act
Red-legged frog in the pond sounds like him

Uncomfortable & say a spell:
blossom knit & heel affix
fiddle fern in the neck of the sun

It's hard to be water
   to fall from faucets with fangs
   to lie under trawlers as horizons
   but you must

Your species can't say it
You have to do spells & tag them

Uncomfortable & act like you mean it

Go to the world
Where is it
Go there

Request to the Berkeley City Council
Concerning Strawberry Creek

(after George Herbert)

From hills, from storm drains
meeting tumbled-below molecules of Berkeley
tap water & rain, past Center & Shattuck to the cool straight
waves of the Bay, Council, daylight that Creek. Near CementHenge
of the B of A with the Shattuck Cinemas' mild butter Saturday matinee
popcorn redolence meets downtown Peets' decaf, daylight. Daylight pos-
sible lizards, raccoons, beetles which starts with be, their esplanade & vis-
ion. Corridors would return for vision citizens, also dew on finches flying
to Dwight. Council, apply your   wisdom. We swear by the seven
creeks of Berkeley, as by our   poetry—for e.g. A's, AW's, B's, B
H's, Bateau Group's, XX's C's, CS's, D's, D's, E's, F's, FH's, G's, G's, GG's
& GO's, XX's & I's, J's, JB's & JC's, JF's, JJ's, JM's, K's & KS's, L's, LH's,
LM's, LS's, M's, MP's, N's, P's, XX's & PD's, PS's, R's, RS's, RP's who
moved, S's, SK's, T's, U-Z's, XX's, XX's, all students living over win-
dows who walk near spearmint nooses of campus creeksides,
who write little or much, in water as in poetry—that we
are one body. (Shelley noted this.) The invisible
is lined with the visible.
(We also noted this.) Aren't you mostly water
yourselves? We walked to campus on Watershed Day against
our national government. Water creatures are against war. Even
the swordfish nearby knows not to send its sword into another sword-
fish unless it's going to eat it. So water leaped to brown. The soul of the
poet, healing, saw the leaping. Be on the side of leaping, Council. Aren't
the first two letters of Be   rkeley legally curved? So the dryads
living near this Creek leave   oaky ghost menus, words of ances-
tors CM, JM, JS, TG & letters from the east, from A-Z, C & F who
should have moved here, N & J, J & B who did move—So the visible
improves in a School where they said daylight the creek, day-light.
& the Aging sheen caught the Bay. We don't know how to live
but water thinks it through, a syntax tangled to renew, $H_2O=$
one-third forever & two-thirds good sense. Spirals & hips,
eyelashed willows, we're yours; what else lives? In
water, we stop stopping it—

There's so much about the mind
we don't know yet between the mem-
orable & the forgotten which is why
we need water words. The clogged-for-50-
years-creek tumbled along badly when the
father & brother of the brenda who transcribes
this worked on campus; when the first husband
worked here, the creek was dirty—just a dump—
& in the era of the second husband, clearing began.
They tried bunchgrass & a Study formed. Live oaks drop-
ped their spiky leaves on down, Council, & the creek had a
chance, its numbers & properties like mythic figures—Daphne
& her agitators—in M's word, to *toggle* back & forth between new
things they said. Wholeness lives in parts like those water striders,
triremes of golden insects, Council. (It's up to you to make brave gov-
ernment imagine things.) Sacramento suckers had returned, hitch-
minnow, the raccoon who fished them out; & the egret that fished
was probably even helping the salmon. Maybe you'll put porous
pavers for the Birkenstocks, my dears. This great stream
of Strawberry Creek, with its stickle-backs like the
letter E at the end of Mother Tuolumne carry-
ing the muskrat from Cascadia's borderland,
is three point five miles long, Council. We are
not on the side of extra starts but of inner free-
dom. Let's note to each lover of rain-checks that
economy & strains of longing come from the same
place. Feed creatures. Dolphins near Monterey dive,
Council, when the creek's mysterious ochre balances
in health. Fine mist is curling in the brenda hairs.
The lyric grew in strength & the water grew less dead.
Some have a moment of mood when they stand on the bridge
near the U.C. Life Sciences Building. The cottonwood says twenty-
five things & a lamp. Monarchs will come back from Reno & Win-
nemuca; buckeye, father of the camphor tree, would talk. Nymphs
would make do with celebrate. Sisters & brothers of the Council,
bring light, beauty & order to the edge; we the writers & readers,
griots with lyres & harps, in you, by you & for the generations,
ask that you day light that creek day, day ○ light ○ that ○ Creek

A Violet in the Crucible

Shelley wants you to visit Congress when he writes
       a violet in the crucible & when he notes
              imagination is enlarged by a sympathy
      that you may intuit environments
as endangered creatures do when 7 million pounds
       of nitrogen flow into the Chesapeake—
as you push open the cherry wood door
       & the intern looks up from her
map of wheels beside the philodendron with streaked
anemic arrows & a jar
         of pens from pharmaceutical firms,
Shelley knows you are endangered
      as the eyeless shrimp *Stygobromus hayi* living
          among rocks upstream in Virginia feeding on dying
      leaves is, or the Congressman you came to visit
        is endangered, feeding
in the Rayburn cafeteria with the lobbyist from Bechtel, having left his
aide endangered in a faux-maple carrel
      to work on the war funding bill
        where seedlings of the law have finished sprouting.
      You look at things to make them speak.
      You have threadlike legs found only in your species.
The cogs are selling credits to the dams
      for phosphorus to go into the sea.
When Shelley says ‹the poet is the legislator› he means as
      the duskytail darter from Tennessee legislates or
the Indiana bat, *myotis sodalist*, the dwarf wedgemussel
        half buried in Maryland with your bivalve
        in silt of your wetland habitat, as you, the vanishing
northeastern bulrush from Massachusetts
      legislate by shrinking; he doesn't mean you will live,
he means you could live on listen. As the sturgeon
      in a million pounds of phosphorous or
      the snowy plover from Cascadia might.
      The aide is living on listen too,
he takes your words, there a little you

in his left eye which tries to focus on your nervous
            speech, a stubby tassel
swinging on his shoe; he's got a friend in the Marines
        who likes it over there instead of working
                in the tire shop after high school. The punctuation
falling from your eyes its eyes their eyes his eyes
        is merging with uh·· uh·· uh·· uh·· uh·· uh·· as he explains
the Pentagon budget uh·· uh·· uh·· uh·· his sentences forming
a five-star alkaline: *We cannot leave them*
            there without weapons uh-uh-uh-uhuhuh.
        He cannot see the stars camped in your heart,
            the bunchy bunched-up stars, though he also
has stars in his heart & his friend the Marine has stars.
When Shelley notes ‹the poet is meant to cheer› he means
        your name is on the list right here, he means
                if you don't survive this way there are others,
        he means send the report with your body—

To Spirits of Fire after Harvest

Between earth
& its noun, i felt a fire . . .

—What does it mean by "i," Mrs?
—It means, (& i quote): one
    of the vowels in the brain
        & some of the you's—;

we were interested in the type of thing
humans can't know,
interested in kinds of think animals think
— a rabbit or a skink! (*Eumeces skiltonianus*)
        when autumn brings a grammar,
    wasps circle the dry stalks
    & you can totally
    see through amber ankles dangling
        in dazzle under our lord the sun
        of literature—

Between noon & its noun,
there were ridged
& golden runes on pumpkins . . . bluish
                    gourds— in the fields . . .
        (their white eyes lined up
                inside)—Wait a sec. Please
don't nail the door shut. The air is friendly
& non-existent as Veronica's veil — . . .

Earth, don't torment your fool,
your ambassador clown. Bring
the x of oxygen & sex, a fox
running sideways, through present noon —

Jane Hirshfield

The Supple Deer

The quiet opening
between fence strands
perhaps eighteen inches.

Antlers to hind hooves,
four feet off the ground,
the deer poured through it.

No tuft of the coarse white belly hair left behind.

I don't know how a stag turns
into a stream, an arc of water.
I have never felt such accurate envy.

Not of the deer—

To be that porous, to have such largeness pass through me.

Three Foxes by the Edge of the Field at Twilight

One ran,
her nose to the ground,
a rusty shadow
neither hunting nor playing.

One stood; sat; lay down; stood again.

One never moved,
except to turn her head a little as we walked.

Finally we drew too close,
and they vanished.
The woods took them back as if they had never been.

I wish I had thought to put my face to the grass.

But we kept walking,
speaking as strangers do when becoming friends.

There is more and more I tell no one,
strangers nor loves.
This slips into the heart
without hurry, as if it had never been.

And yet, among the trees, something has changed.

Something looks back from the trees,
and knows me for who I am.

Articulation: An Assay

A good argument, etymology instructs,
is many-jointed.
By this measure,
the most expressive of beings must be the giraffe.

Yet the speaking tongue is supple,
untroubled by bone.

What would it be
to take up no position,
to lie on this earth at rest, relieved of proof or change?

Scent of thyme or grass
amid the scent of many herbs and grasses.

Grief unresisted as granite darkened by rain.

Continuous praises most glad, placed against nothing.

But thought is hinge and swerve, is winch,
is folding.

"Reflection,"
we call the mountain in the lake,
whose existence resides in neither stone nor water.

Optimism

More and more I have come to admire resilience.
Not the simple resistance of a pillow, whose foam
returns over and over to the same shape, but the sinuous
tenacity of a tree: finding the light newly blocked on one side,
it turns in another. A blind intelligence, true.
But out of such persistence arose turtles, rivers,
mitochondria, figs—all this resinous, unretractable earth.

Inflection Finally Ungraspable by Grammar

I haven't yet found the pronoun through which to touch it directly.
You may feel differently.
You may think you can simply reach through all the way
    with your hand, like petting the shoulder of an old dog, who, when
she can no longer stand, lies on her bed, watching her kingdom
    arriving and leaving, arriving and leaving, until at last
it only departs.
We want our lives and deaths to be like that—something formal, a kingdom.
    Filled with the sense of the manyness of existence. As the French say
"Vous" to that which cannot yet be made familiar.
They do this less and less these days, it seems.

Speed and Perfection

How quickly the season of apricots is over—
a single night's wind is enough.
I kneel on the ground, lifting one, then the next.
Eating those I can, before the bruises appear.

For the *Lobaria, Usnea,* Witches' Hair, Map Lichen,
Beard Lichen, Ground Lichen, Shield Lichen

Back then, what did I know?
The names of subway lines, busses.
How long it took to walk 20 blocks.

Uptown and downtown.
Not north, not south, not you.

When I saw you, later, seaweed reefed in the air,
you were grey-green, incomprehensible, old.
What you clung to, hung from: old.
Trees looking half-dead, stones.

Marriage of fungi and algae,
chemists of air,
changers of nitrogen-unusable into nitrogen-usable.

Like those nameless ones
who kept painting, shaping, engraving each day
unseen, unread, unremembered.
Not caring if they were no good, if they were past it.

Rock wools, water fans, earth scale, mouse ears, dust,
ash-of-the-woods.
Transformers unvalued, uncounted.
Cell by cell, word by word, making a world they could live in.

H. L. Hix

The Last Crows Whose Cries Are Audible Here

In this tree the crows condense at dusk
Only to evaporate at daybreak.
They are the questions one knows not to ask,
The answers one does not know how to take.
They console bare limbs for lost leaves. Their flights
Are lines in verse translations of the snow
Into a tongue, inscrutable by light,
That no diurnal mind will ever know.
Their names are given by the wind, their one
Master, whose calls to them are audible
Among their own: *Wherefore, Nothing, In vain,*
Burning burning burned, Lost, Impalpable,
Map of the abyss, Listen my love, listen,
Illegible, Hardly, The unchained fall.

Tony Hoagland

Romantic Moment

After seeing the nature documentary we walk down Canyon Road,
onto the plaza of art galleries and high end clothing stores

where the orange trees are fragrant in the summer night
and the smooth adobe walls glow fleshlike in the dark.

It is just our second date, and we sit down on a bench,
holding hands, not looking at each other,

and if I were a bull penguin right now I would lean over
and vomit softly into the mouth of my beloved

and if I were a peacock I would flex my gluteal muscles to
erect and spread the quills of my Cinemax tail.

If she were a female walkingstick bug she might
insert her hypodermic proboscis delicately into my neck

and inject me with a rich hormonal sedative
before attaching her egg sac to my thoracic undercarriage,

and if I were a young chimpanzee I would break off a nearby tree limb
and smash all the windows in the plaza jewelry stores.

And if she were a Brazilian leopard frog she would wrap her impressive
tongue three times around my right thigh and

pummel me lightly against the surface of our pond
and I would know her feelings were sincere.

Instead we sit awhile in silence, until
she remarks that in the relative context of tortoises and iguanas,

human males seem to be actually rather expressive.
And I say that female crocodiles really don't receive

enough credit for their gentleness.
Then she suggests that it is time for us to go

do something personal, hidden, and human.

Wild

In late August when the streams dry up
and the high meadows turn parched and blond,

bears are squeezed out of the mountains
down into the valley of condos and housing developments.

All residents are therefore prohibited
from putting their garbage out early.

The penalty for disobedience will be
bears: large black furry fellows

drinking from your sprinkler system,
rolling your trashcans down your lawn,

bashing through the screen door of the back porch to get their
first real taste of a spaghetti dinner,

while the family hides in the garage
and the wife dials 1-800-BEARS on her cell phone,

a number she just made up
in a burst of creative hysteria.

Isn't that the way it goes?
Wildness enters your life and asks

that you invent a way to meet it,
and you run in the opposite direction

as the bears saunter down Main Street
sending station wagons crashing into fire hydrants,

getting the police department to phone
for tranquilizer guns,

the dart going by accident into the
neck of the unpopular police chief,

who is carried into early retirement
in an ambulance crowned with flashing red lights,

as the bears inherit the earth
full of water and humans and garbage,

which looks to them like paradise.

Richard Hoffman

Cove

Small waves repeat,
disappear on sand,
stairs of an escalator

down. I forgot what
I meant to say. I forgot
what I meant to say.

Soft flesh in a broken
shell. Tangled rope.
Stones worn human.

Linda Hogan

Turtle Watchers

Old mother at water's edge
used to bow down to them,
the turtles coming in from the sea,
their many eggs,
their eyes streaming water like tears,
and I'd see it all,
old mother as if in prayer,
the turtles called back to where they were born,
the hungry watchers standing at the edge of trees
hoping for food when darkness gathers.

Years later, swimming in murky waters
a sea turtle swam beside me
both of us watching as if clasped together
in the lineage of the same world
the sweep of the same current,
even rising for a breath of air at the same time
still watching.
My ancestors call them
the keepers of doors
and the shore a realm to other worlds,
both ways and
water moves the deep shift of life
back to birth and before
as if there is a path where beings truly meet,
as if I am rounding the human corners.

Moving the Woodpile

Never am I careless,
yet when I lift the wood,
before I even see the wasp nest
I see spiders and ants, some preserved in pitch
and when I lift the wood
the bark falls from the log
and there are the silk cocoons,
worm-carved lines worked into the
woodflesh,
the beautiful work of insects
before they were white-winged, dusted creatures
who never asked the tree, What am I, who could I be,
never did they say, Oh world I love you
yet I loosen your skin and then I fly into the night.

As I lifted the log,
there they were in the wood, not yet anything,
the paper wasp nest of the barely alive,
only pale fingers searching, without eyes.

It's been so many years ago now
and still I have the haunting
memory and feel, standing there with the nest,
offering the wasps back their young,
but they could not approach a human holding their nest.

Maybe our sin is not enough
of us get on our knees and ever see
how everything small and nearly gone
is precious, the paper wasp nest,
made by the moment-by-moment creation of care.

Maybe our human sin is for us never to say
all these are great.
And I, the one who took it, in innocence, apart
as if being human I could not help it,
despite myself, generous and thieving
at one and the same time.

I've always wished
to hold the truly stolen, broken world together
but my every move is to break
by degrees, acres, even the smallest atom.

Still, from this other body continent
I offered them their young
and they could not come near the untamed woman,
only fly with desperation
and I think of this still
every evening, like a prayer,
that day holding out the nest for them, placing it down,
but never for them to approach,
and how I waited, how I watched.

Cynthia Hogue

Fluff

Of pollen freed
     from anther drifts
          into woods, what
naturalists term
     "a troubled landscape"
          and you call "beautiful."
Somewhere
     you knew that
          humans trouble
all we touch
     though that
          was intuition.
To translate farms,
     houses, sheep
          and cows, cities,
sewers, power
     stations, satellites,
          spies, the grab for
power like the grab
     for mineral rights:
          humans cannot
stand uncertain
     or imaginary
          gain. You think,
Imagination has
     no power. Yet
          what else makes
our feelings sway
     and moves us
          with such force

that we wake up? To what?
      you ask, looking out
            from the mountainside
you've climbed
      on all the harm
            below. And why?

Richard Hugo

Skykomish River Running

Aware that summer baked the water clear,
today I came to see a fleet of trout.
But as I wade the salmon limp away,
their dorsal fins like gravestones in the air,
on their sides the red that kills the leaves.
Only the sun can beat a stream this thin.
The river Sky is humming in my ear.

Where this river empties in the sea,
trout are waiting for September rain
to sting their thirst alive. If they speed
upstream behind the kings and eat the eggs
the silvers lay, I'll pound the drum for rain.
But sunlight drums, the river is the same,
running like old water in my ear.

I will cultivate the trout, teach their fins
to wave in water like the legs of girls
tormented black in pools. I will swim
a week to be a witness to the spawning,
be a trout, eat the eggs of salmon—
anything to live until the trout and rain
are running in the river in my ear.

The river Sky is running in my hair.
I am floating past the troutless pools
learning water is the easy way to go.
I will reach the sea before December
when the Sky is turning gray and wild
and rolling heavy from the east to say
late autumn was an Oriental child.

Luisa A. Igloria

Ziggurats there aren't here, my Sweethearts—

     you would however marvel at the high-pitched winds
exiting over the prairie at dawn, followed by
wild cawing in the hedges. Before breakfast, I leafed through
vellum scrapbooks on a table by the fireplace, some
unbound so yellowed portraits spilled from pages
tender as chamois and tearable. I long for
stir-fried noodles, milkfish in sour broth, sticky rice,
raw jicama slices dipped in vinegar and pepper flakes . . .
Queridas, why is an overcast day naturally
perfect for nostalgia? I'm stranded as usual
on an island of incidentals, wanting forgiveness for
not having arrived at a less stammering representation of
myself, for the array of unremarkable possessions
littering homes we've tried to make. I wanted to give you
keepsakes that wouldn't tarnish: a wraparound porch, a swing, that
Jungian well cleared of debris at last (and bubbling sweet water).
Instead I've understood no more, no less than this wild
hunger: how it leads the eye to Birds-of-Paradise, to any bloom
growing like an impossible promise in the soil.
Fall's flavor is pungent, I read; *at dusk,*
Emptiness sets, and at dawn the Willow. But
don't think this is mere lamentation or elegy. I've seen someone
come to the lake faithfully each afternoon with a small
bag of crumbs for stray animals, just because
affliction has such a desolate color.

Ronald Johnson

[eartheathearth]

eartheathearth
eartheathearth
eartheathearth
eartheathearth
eartheathearth
eartheathearth

from Spring

4
EMANATIONS

`I am a walking fire, I am all leaves'.

`I find I incorporate gneiss, coal, long-threaded moss,
fruit, grains, esculent roots.
And am stucco'd with quadrupeds & birds all over'.

I find I advance with
sidereal motions
—my eyes containing substance

of the sun,
my ears built of beaks & feathers—

I ascend with saps

& flower in season

& eddy with tides.

With every moon,
I come from the darkness into incandescence.

My tongue assumes the apple's flesh
& my skin, the infinite spheres of the thistle's prickle. And as I
breathe

the wind has its billow—& all the grasses—

in a combing, mazy movement.

5
APRIL 13TH

Here, the river swept great
curves
along wide valleys.

We left our footprints
green, behind,
as we followed the straight bright dew-path, meadow banks gleaming.

Clouds moved down the valley—their shadows
a river of huge dapples—their glowing masses opening above
as we came,

a white, enveloping progression.

Mid-day, whole
clouds lowered

& one leaned into wind to walk—a brisk,
wet fog blowing—

though by evening the sun set westward
in our eyes

among slow cumulus that shafted bands of yellow
light

& remained black spaces
neither earth,
nor air,

suspended in that `vacant interlunar cave'

where all the stars

revolved, wheeled, glittered.

from Summer

2
WHAT THE EARTH TOLD ME

No surface is allowed to be bare,

& nothing to stand still. A man could forever study a pebble

& at last see dilations & expansions of the hills—

to pull the most slender stalk, is to jostle the stars,

& between the bearded grass

& man 'looking in the vegetable glass

of Nature', is a network of roots & suckers

fine as hairs.

I threw a stone upon a pond

& it bounded the surface, its circles interlacing

& radiating out to the most ephemeral edge.

Flint & Mica, Lichened Limestone, Shale & Sarcens, Sandstone, Soil.

I saw the wind moving on a meadow

& the meadows moving under wind

lifting, settling & accumulating.

Flint & Mica, Lichened Limestone,

Shale & Sarcens, Sandstone, Soil.

•

II

'UNLESS THE HUMMING OF A GNAT IS
AS THE MUSIC OF THE SPHERES

& the music of the spheres is as the humming

of a gnat . . .' A spectre came, *transparent-winged,*

out of the interstices of light,

& shadow went up like smoke & everywhere

the hills were as clouds over valleys of water, rippling

& reverberating.

And before him the sands of the beach swarmed as insects, close-knit

in electrical flight . . .

'For MATTER is the dust of the Earth,

every atom of which is the life.

For the flames of fire may be blown thro musical pipes'.

And everywhere the hills were as clouds over

valleys of water, rippling

& reverberating.

Rodney Jones

The Assault on the Fields

It was like snow, if snow could blend with air and hover,
    making, at first,
A rolling boil, mottling the pine thickets behind the fields,
    but then flattening
As it spread above the fenceposts and the whiteface cattle,
    an enormous, luminous tablet,

A shimmering, an efflorescence, through which my father
    rode on his tractor,
Masked like a Martian or a god to create the cloud where
    he kept vanishing;
Though, of course, it was not a cloud or snow, but poison,
    dichlorodiphenyltrichloroethane,

The word like a bramble of black locust on the tongue,
    and, after a while,
It would fill the entire valley, as, one night in spring,
    five years earlier,
A man from Joe Wheeler Electric had touched a switch
    and our houses filled with light.

Already some of the music from the radio went with me
    when the radio was off.
The bass, the kiss of the snare. Some of the thereness
    rubbing off on the hereness.
But home place still meant family. Misfortune was a well
    of yellowish sulfur water.

The Flowerses lived next door. Coyd drove a road grader
    for the county.
Martha baked, sewed, or cleaned, complaining beautifully
    of the dust
Covering her new Formica counters. Martha and Coyd,
    Coyd Jr., Linda, and Jenny.

How were they different from us? They owned
    a television,
Knew by heart each of the couples on Dick Clark's
    American Bandstand.
At dusk Junior, the terrible, would beat on a cracked
    and unfrettable Silvertone guitar

While he pitched from the top of his wayward voice
    one of a dozen songs
He'd written for petulant freshman girls. "Little Patti,"
    "Matilda,"
"Sweet Bonnie G." What did the white dust have to do
    with anything?

For Junior, that year, it was rock 'n' roll; if not rock 'n' roll,
    then abstract expressionism—
One painting comes back. Black frame. Black canvas—
    "I call it *Death*," he would say,
then stomp out onto the front lawn to shoot his .22 rifle
    straight into the sky above his head.

Surely if Joel Shapiro's installation of barbed wire and
    crumbled concrete blocks,
In a side room of the most coveted space in Manhattan,
    pays homage
To the most coveted space in Manhattan, then Junior
    Flowers's *Death*,
Hanging on a wall dingy with soot in North Alabama,
    is a comment, too.

Are they the same thing? I do not know that they are not
    the same thing.
And the white dust, so magical, so poisonous: how does it
    differ from snow?
As it thins gradually over many nights, we don't notice
    it; once the golden

Carp have rotted from the surface of ponds, there is no
    stench to it;
It is more of an absence of things barely apprehended,
    of flies, of moths;
Until one day the hawks who patrolled the air over
    the chicken coops are gone;

And when a woman, who was a girl then, finds a lump,
    what does it have to do
With the green fields and the white dust boiling
    and hovering?
When I think of the name Jenny Flowers, it is that
    whiteness I think of.

Some bits have fallen to clump against a sheet of tin
    roofing
The tornado left folded in the ditch, and she stoops there
    to gather
A handful of chalk to mark the grounds for hopscotch.

Judy Jordan

Long Drop to Black Water

What confidence led us into a rainy Ithaca night
neither I nor my friend knew. Swollen gorges
to our left, the ground crumbling
as we clung to tree trunks and hooked our fingers
into the tight loops of a gun factory fence,
sleighting a path in spray and fog
that swallowed our legs below the knees,
not knowing till the next day's retracking
how often we had hung, far from the eroded bank,
above nothing but a long drop to black water.

Whatever that confidence was, I've lost it.
But it informs the toads,
crouches them in crooked caves of alder roots,
pulses the pale skin under their slack mouths,
keeps them in the pond's tight waves clutching anything:
a pine's resinous knot, a fist of chair foam,
even a drowned and legless female.

Now in the sun's last light, unctuous through haze
that lifts the land above itself
and leans the alders over water in green flames,
I see more in the pasture's stubbed grass,
leaping sure and unwavering to the cold,
without thought of the ducks scouring the pond's edge
for the mass of eggs
or the snapper hungry on the gelid bottom.
What could bring them year after year
and always less in number
but faith in their own wholeness and desire.
Faith that I lack, faith that I want
in this spring, fecund and feral.

from Dream of the End

Sinaloa to Nayarit,
Culiacán valley and the long rows of tin shacks,
Santiago Ixcuintla and its tobacco,
the Huicholeo Indians asleep under the strung cords of drying leaves,

Who would have thought death's chemicals would smell like vanilla?

Hamivel, Methomyl, Paraquat, Parathion,

Adrian Allesquita Sota, dead,
Luciano Lomeli,
Alberto León,
José Luis Santos, all dead,

Malathion, Methamidophos, Endosulfan.

   Cuidado Veneno
   Altamente Tóxico

Margarita, the bean of her casket in the dry earth.
My favorite, Margarita, little daisy.

I could not chase her from the fields
when she snuck out under
the bone stare of the bosses
but gave her the last of my canteen
though my own lips cracked
and the fist of dust stopped my throat.

I tucked her inside my shirt
when the planes flew low
to drop the yellow crop dust.

And though I curled my body over hers,
it was she the sickness found.

Old women came, black shawls
pulled close over dark faces.

I could cut out my own heart,
give it to a *hacendado* to have her back,
and he would tear it apart,
scatter it to the four directions of the leached earth.

Old women shell beans to their laps.

They've seen the children curl into hunger
like supper scraps thrown to the dry wind,

and now the children and unknown diseases.
The iguana in the bushes,
a dog scratching in the yard's dust.

The mockingbirds sound like old women crying.

Vulcan and Vertrac. Rockwell's Rocky Flats.
Dioxin, PCB, PVC, organochlorine.
Magic circles useless in the hour of Mars, fourth moon waxing.

The dead long since finished falling
and still we scratch our names in their sweat,
sweep them down with the raffinate and the nine-legged frogs.
We wash in the yellow water, eat the eyeless chicken.

A brew of greed and Atrazine,
a red-bellied spider between buttered bread
and a mother buries her child.

Brigit Pegeen Kelly

The Leaving

My father said I could not do it,
but all night I picked the peaches.
The orchard was still, the canals ran steadily.
I was a girl then, my chest its own walled garden.
How many ladders to gather an orchard?
I had only one and a long patience with lit hands
and the looking of the stars which moved right through me
the way the water moved through the canals with a voice
that seemed to speak of this moonless gathering
and those who had gathered before me.
I put the peaches in the pond's cold water,
all night up the ladder and down, all night my hands
twisting fruit as if I were entering a thousand doors,
all night my back a straight road to the sky.
And then out of its own goodness, out
of the far fields of the stars, the morning came,
and inside me was the stillness a bell possesses
just after it has been rung, before the metal
begins to long again for the clapper's stroke.
The light came over the orchard.
The canals were silver and then were not,
and the pond was—I could see as I laid
the last peach in the water—full of fish and eyes.

Blessed Is the Field

In the late heat the snakeroot and goldenrod run high,
White and gold, the steaming flowers, green and gold,
The acid-bitten leaves. . . . It is good to say first

An invocation. Though the words do not always
Seem to work. Still, one must try. Bow your head.
Cross your arms. Say: *Blessed is the day. And the one*

Who destroys the day. Blessed is this ring of fire
In which we live. . . . How bitter the burning leaves.
How bitter and sweet. How bitter and sweet the sound

Of the single gold and black insect repeating
Its two lonely notes. The insect's song both magnifies
The field and casts a shadow over it, the way

A doorbell ringing through an abandoned house
Makes the falling rooms, papered with lilies and roses
And two-headed goats, seem larger and more ghostly.

The high grasses spill their seed. It is hard to know
The right way in or out. But here, you can have
Which flower you like, though there are not many left,

Lady's thumb in the gravel by the wood's fringe
And on the shale spit beneath the black walnut that houses
The crow, the peculiar cat's-paw, sweet everlasting,

Unbearably soft. Do not mind the crow's bark.
He is fierce and solitary, but he will let us pass,
Patron of the lost and broken-spirited. Behind him

In the quarter ring of sumacs, flagged like circus tents,
The deer I follow, and that even now are watching us,
Sleep at night their restless sleep. I find their droppings

In the morning. And here at my feet is the self-heal,
Humblest of flowers, bloomless but still intact. I ate
Some whole once and did not get well but it may strike

Your fancy. The smell of burning rubber is from
A rabbit carcass the dog dragged into the ravine.
And the smell of lemon is the snakeroot I am crushing

Between my thumb and forefinger. . . . There could be
Beneath this field an underground river full
Of sweet liquid. A dowser might find it with his witching

Wand and his prayers. Some prayers can move
Even the stubborn dirt. . . . Do you hear? The bird
I have never seen is back. Each day at this time

He takes up his ominous clucking, fretting like a baby,
Lonely sweetling. It is hard to know the right way
In or out. But look, the goldenrod is the color

Of beaten skin. Say: *Blessed are those who stand still*
In their confusion. Blessed is the field as it burns.

Windfall

There is a wretched pond in the woods. It lies at the north end of a piece of
land owned by a man who was taken to an institution years ago. He was a
strange man. I only spoke to him once. You can still find statues of women
and stone gods he set up in dark corners of the woods, and sometimes you
can find flowers that have survived the collapse of the hidden gardens he
planted. Once I found a flower that looked like a human brain growing
near a fence, and it took my breath away. And once I found, among some
weeds, a lily white as snow. . . . No one tends the land now. The fences
have fallen and the deer grown thick, and the pond lies black, the water
slowly thickening, the banks tangled with weeds and grasses. But the pond
was very old even when I first came upon it. Through the trees I saw the
dark water steaming, and smelled something sweet rotting, and then as I
got closer, I saw in the dark water shapes, and the shapes were golden, and
I thought, without really thinking, that I was looking at the reflections of
leaves or of fallen fruit, though there were no fruit trees near the pond and
it was not the season for fruit. And then I saw that the shapes were moving,
and I thought they moved because I was moving, but when I stood still,
still they moved. And still I had trouble seeing. Though the shapes took
on weight and muscle and definite form, it took my mind a long time to
accept what I saw. The pond was full of ornamental carp, and they were
large, larger than the carp I have seen in museum pools, large as trumpets,
and so gold they were almost yellow. In circles, wide and small, the plated

fish moved, and there were so many of them they could not be counted, though for a long time I tried to count them. And I thought of the man who owned the land standing where I stood. I thought of how years ago in a fit of madness or high faith he must have planted the fish in the pond, and then forgotten them, or been taken from them, but still the fish had grown and still they thrived, until they were many, and their bodies were fast and bright as brass knuckles or cockscombs. I tore pieces of my bread and threw them at the carp, and the carp leaped, as I have not seen carp do before, and they fought each other for the bread, and they were not like fish but like gulls or wolves, biting and leaping. Again and again, I threw the bread. Again and again, the fish leaped and wrestled. And below them, below the leaping fish, near the bottom of the pond, something slowly circled, a giant form that never rose to the bait and never came fully into view, but moved patiently in and out of the murky shadows, out and in. I watched that form, and after the bread was gone and after the golden fish had again grown quiet, my mind at last constructed a shape for it, and I saw for the space of one moment or two with perfect clarity, as if I held the heavy creature in my hands, the tarnished body of an ancient carp. A thing both fragrant and foul. A lily and a man's brain bound together in one body. And then the fish was gone. He turned and the shadows closed around him. The water grew blacker, and the steam rose from it, and the golden carp held still, still uncountable. And softly they burned, themselves like flowers, or like fruit blown down in an abandoned garden.

Galway Kinnell

The Bear

1

In late winter
I sometimes glimpse bits of steam
coming up from
some fault in the old snow
and bend close and see it is lung-colored
and put down my nose
and know
the chilly, enduring odor of bear.

2

I take a wolf's rib and whittle
it sharp at both ends
and coil it up
and freeze it in blubber and place it out
on the fairway of the bears.

And when it has vanished
I move out on the bear tracks,
roaming in circles
until I come to the first, tentative, dark
splash on the earth.

And I set out
running, following the splashes
of blood wandering over the world.
At the cut, gashed resting places
I stop and rest,
at the crawl-marks

where he lay out on his belly
to overpass some stretch of bauchy ice
I lie out
dragging myself forward with bear-knives in my fists.

   3

On the third day I begin to starve,
at nightfall I bend down as I knew I would
at a turd sopped in blood,
and hesitate, and pick it up,
and thrust it in my mouth, and gnash it down,
and rise
and go on running.

   4

On the seventh day,
living by now on bear blood alone,
I can see his upturned carcass far out ahead, a scraggled,
steamy hulk,
the heavy fur riffling in the wind.

I come up to him
and stare at the narrow-spaced, petty eyes,
the dismayed
face laid back on the shoulder, the nostrils
flared, catching
perhaps the first taint of me as he
died.

I hack
a ravine in his thigh, and eat and drink,
and tear him down his whole length
and open him and climb in
and close him up after me, against the wind,
and sleep.

5

And dream
of lumbering flatfooted
over the tundra,
stabbed twice from within,
splattering a trail behind me,
splattering it out no matter which way I lurch,
no matter which parabola of bear-transcendence,
which dance of solitude I attempt,
which gravity-clutched leap,
which trudge, which groan.

6

Until one day I totter and fall—
fall on this
stomach that has tried so hard to keep up,
to digest the blood as it leaked in,
to break up
and digest the bone itself: and now the breeze
blows over me, blows off
the hideous belches of ill-digested bear blood
and rotted stomach
and the ordinary, wretched odor of bear,

blows across
my sore, lolled tongue a song
or screech, until I think I must rise up
and dance. And I lie still.

7

I awaken I think. Marshlights
reappear, geese
come trailing again up the flyway.
In her ravine under old snow the dam-bear
lies, licking
lumps of smeared fur
and drizzly eyes into shapes

with her tongue. And one
hairy-soled trudge stuck out before me,
the next groaned out,
the next,
the next,
the rest of my days I spend
wandering: wondering
what, anyway,
was that sticky infusion, that rank flavor of blood, that
poetry, by which I lived?

Daybreak

On the tidal mud, just before sunset,
dozens of starfishes
were creeping. It was
as though the mud were a sky
and enormous, imperfect stars
moved across it as slowly
as the actual stars cross heaven.
All at once they stopped,
and as if they had simply
increased their receptivity
to gravity they sank down
into the mud; they faded down
into it and lay still; and by the time
pink of sunset broke across them
they were as invisible
as the true stars at daybreak.

Burning the Brush Pile

I shoved into the bottom of the brush
pile two large grocery bags holding
chainsaw chaff well-soaked
in old gasoline gone sticky—a kind
of homemade napalm, except, of course,
without victims, other than boughs,
stumps, broken boards, vines, crambles.

Bracing my knees against the next-
to-the-top roundel of the twelve-foot
apple-picker stepladder
I poured diesel all gurgling
and hiccupping into the center of the pile,
then climbed down and sloshed
the perimeter with kerosene and sludge.

Stepping back, I touched a match
to the oil rag knotted to the thick end
of a thick stick and hurled it, javelin
style, into the core of the pile,
which gasped, then illuminated:
red sunset seen through winter trees.
A small flame came curling out from either
side of the pile and quietly wavered there,
as if this were simply the way matter burns.
Suddenly the great loaded shinicle roared
into flames that leapt up sixty, seventy feet,
 swarming through the hole they had heated
open in the chill air to be their chimney.
At noon I came back with a pitchfork
and flicked into the snapping flames
a lot of charred boughs, twig ends burnt off,
that lay around the edges of the fire
as if some elephantine porcupine had been
bludgeoned on its snout, on this spot,
and then, rotting away, had left a rough circle
of black quills pointing to where it had been.

In the evening, when the fire had faded,
I was raking black clarts out of the smoking dirt,
and felt a tine of my rake snag on a large lump.
I jerked, shook, beat it apart, and out fell
a small blackened snake, the rear half
burnt away, the forepart alive. When
I took up this poor Isaac, it flashed its tongue,
then struck my hand a few times; I let it.

Already its tail was sealing itself off,
fusing shut the way we cauterize unraveling
nylon line by using its own hot oozings
as glue. I lowered it into the cool grass,
where it waggled but didn't get very far.
Gone the swift lateral undulation, the whip-tail,
the grip that snakes bring into the world.

It stopped where the grass grew thick
and flashed its tongue again, as if trying
to spit or spirit away its pain,
as we do, with our growled profanities,
or as if uttering a curse, or—wild fantasy—
a benediction. Most likely it was trying to find
its whereabouts, and perhaps get one last take
on this unknown being also reeking of fire.
Then the snake zipped in its tongue
and hirpled away into the secrecy of the grass.

Yusef Komunyakaa

The Millpond

They looked like wood ibis
From a distance, & as I got closer
They became knots left for gods
To undo, like bows tied
At the center of weakness.
Shadow to light, mind to flesh,
Swamp orchids quivered under green hats,
Nudged by slate-blue catfish
Headed for some boy's hook
On the other side. The day's
Uncut garments of fallen chances
Stumbled among flowers
That loved only darkness,
As afternoon came through underbrush
Like a string of firecrackers
Tied to a dog's tail.
Gods lived under that mud
When I was young & sublimely
Blind. Each bloom a shudder
Of uneasiness, no sound
Except the whippoorwill.
They conspired to become twilight
& metaphysics, as five-eyed
Fish with milky bones
Flip-flopped in oily grass.

.

We sat there as the moon rose
Up from chemical water,
Phosphorous as an orange lantern.
An old man shifted

His three-pronged gig
Like a New Guinea spear,
So it could fly quicker
Than a frog's tongue or angry word.
He pointed to snapping turtles
Posed on cypress logs,
Armored in stillness,
Slow kings of a dark world.
We knelt among cattails.
The reflection of a smokestack
Cut the black water in half.
A circle of dry leaves
Smouldered on the ground
For mosquitoes. As if
To draw us to them, like decoys
For some greater bounty,
The choir of bullfrogs called,
Singing a cruel happiness.

                    •

Sometimes I'd watch them
Scoot back into their tunnels,
Down in a gully where
The pond's overflow drained . . .
Where shrub oak & banyan
Grew around barbed wire
Till April oozed sap
Like a boy beside a girl
Squeezing honeycomb in his fists.
I wondered if time tied
Everything to goldenrod
Reaching out of cow manure for the sun.
What did it have to do
With saw & hammer,
With what my father taught me
About his world? Sometimes
I sat reading *Catcher in the Rye*,
& other times *Spider Man*
& *Captain Marvel*. Always
After a rain crawfish surfaced

To grab the salt meat
Tied to the nylon string,
Never knowing when they left
The water & hit the bottom
Of my tincan. They clung
To desire, like the times
I clutched something dangerous
& couldn't let go.

Blackberries

They left my hands like a printer's
Or thief's before a police blotter
& pulled me into early morning's
Terrestrial sweetness, so thick
The damp ground was consecrated
Where they fell among a garland of thorns.

Although I could smell old lime-covered
History, at ten I'd still hold out my hands
& berries fell into them. Eating from one
& filling a half gallon with the other,
I ate the mythology & dreamt
Of pies & cobbler, almost

Needful as forgiveness. My bird dog Spot
Eyed blue jays & thrashers. The mud frogs
In rich blackness, hid from daylight.
An hour later, beside City Limits Road
I balanced a gleaming can in each hand,
Limboed between world, repeating *one dollar*.

The big blue car made me sweat.
Wintertime crawled out of the windows.
When I leaned closer I saw the boy
& girl my age, in the wide back seat
Smirking, & it was then I remembered my fingers
Burning with thorns among berries too ripe to touch.

Dream Animal

He's here again. Is this hunger I smell, something like wildflowers and afterbirth tangled in sage? I press down on each eyelid to keep him here: otherwise, otherwise. . . . But he always escapes the lair. Don't care how much I dance and chant rain across the mountains, it never falls on his back. Tiger or wolf, he muzzles up to me, easy as a Christbird walking across lily pads. As if he slipped out of a time machine, his phantom prints disappear at the timberline. I'm on all fours, with my nose almost pressed to the ground. A few galah feathers decorate clumps of tussock. Ants have unlocked the mystery of a bearded dragon, as they inch him toward some secret door. I close my eyes again. Somewhere, a kookaburra laughs. In this garden half-eaten by doubt and gunpowder, honeyeaters peck the living air. And here he stands beneath the Southern Cross, the last of his kind, his stripes even brighter in this dark, nocturnal weather.

Blessing the Animals

Two by two, past
the portals of paradise,
camels & pythons parade.
As if on best behavior,
civil as robed billy goats
& Big Bird, they stroll
down aisles of polished stone
at the Feast of St. Francis.
An elephant daydreams, nudging
ancestral bones down a rocky path,
but won't venture near the boy
with a white mouse peeking
from his coat pocket. Beyond
monkeyshine, their bellows
& cries are like prayers
to unknown planets & zodiac
signs. The ferret & mongoose
on leashes, move as if they know
things with a sixth sense.

Priests twirl hoops of myrrh.
An Australian blue cattle dog
paces a heaven of memories—
a butterfly on a horse's ear
bright as a poppy outside
Urbino. As if crouched
between good & bad, St. John
the Divine grows in quintessence
& limestone, & a hoorah of Miltonic
light falls upon alley rats
awaiting nighttime. Brother
ass, brother sparrowhawk,
& brother dragon. Two
by two, washed & brushed down
by love & human pride,
these beasts of burden
know they're the first
scapegoats. After sacred
oils & holy water, we huddle
this side of their knowing
glances, & they pass through
our lives, still loyal to thorns.

Ted Kooser

Flying at Night

Above us, stars. Beneath us, constellations.
Five billion miles away, a galaxy dies
like a snowflake falling on water. Below us,
some farmer, feeling the chill of that distant death,
snaps on his yard light, drawing his sheds and barn
back into the little system of his care.
All night, the cities, like shimmering novas,
tug with bright streets at lonely lights like his.

Grasshoppers

This year they are exactly the size
of a pencil stub my grandfather kept
to mark off the days since rain,

and precisely the color of dust, of the roads
leading back across the dying fields
into the '30s. Walking the cracked line

past the empty barn, the empty silo,
you hear them tinkering with irony,
slapping the grass like drops of rain.

Maxine Kumin

The Whole Hog

When you go to your favorite grocery store
and this week's Special is boneless pork
tenderloin that you'll roll in a floured
paste with cracked pepper and rosemary
before you roast it in a hot oven
and serve it with homemade pear chutney

do you visualize up to twenty wet
pink piglets squirming out
of the sow's vagina while she is trapped
in a farrowing crate so narrow that
she can't turn to lick her newborns because
she might roll over and crush one as

they worm their way uphill to a teat
and do you see her being bred back to the boar
only a few days later to make more
piglets and the grown offspring
trucked off to slaughter in
a double-decker tractor trailer, their first

and only time in daylight, the ones
on top shitting and throwing up on the ones
underneath, and the whole glistening mass
of them screaming, before they're forced
down the ramp and into lines
to be killed, the way I heard

and then saw them cross the town
of Storm Lake, Iowa, big corn-fed hogs
bawling, knowing they were going to die,
like those guys beheaded in Iraq?
Well, this is factory farming smack
in the heart of the USA in 2008

so follow your star. *Bon appétit.*

Stanley Kunitz

The Wellfleet Whale

1

You have your language too,
   an eerie medley of clicks
     and hoots and trills,
location-notes and love calls,
   whistles and grunts. Occasionally,
     it's like furniture being smashed,
or the creaking of a mossy door,
   sounds that all melt into a liquid
     song with endless variations,
as if to compensate
   for the vast loneliness of the sea.
     Sometimes a disembodied voice
breaks in as if from distant reefs,
   and it's as much as one can bear
     to listen to its long mournful cry,
a sorrow without name, both more
   and less than human. It drags
     across the ear like a record
running down.

2

No wind. No waves. No clouds.
   Only the whisper of the tide,
     as it withdrew, stroking the shore,
a lazy drift of gulls overhead,
   and tiny points of light
     bubbling in the channel.
It was the tag-end of summer.
   From the harbor's mouth
     you coasted into sight,

flashing news of your advent,
   the crescent of your dorsal fin
      clipping the diamonded surface.
We cheered at the sign of your greatness
   when the black barrel of your head
      erupted, ramming the water,
and you flowered for us
   in the jet of your spouting.

   3

All afternoon you swam
   tirelessly round the bay,
      with such an easy motion,
the slightest downbeat of your tail,
   an almost imperceptible
      undulation of your flippers,
you seemed like something poured,
   not driven; you seemed
   to marry grace with power.
And when you bounded into air,
   slapping your flukes,
      we thrilled to look upon
pure energy incarnate
   as nobility of form.
      You seemed to ask of us
not sympathy, or love,
   or understanding,
      but awe and wonder.

That night we watched you
   swimming in the moon.
      Your back was molten silver.
We guessed your silent passage
   by the phosphorescence in your wake.
      At dawn we found you stranded on the rocks.

   4

There came a boy and a man
   and yet other men running, and two
      schoolgirls in yellow halters

and a housewife bedecked
 with curlers, and whole families in beach
 buggies with assorted yelping dogs.
The tide was almost out.
 We could walk around you,
  as you heaved deeper into the shoal,
crushed by your own weight,
 collapsing into yourself,
  your flippers and your flukes
quivering, your blowhole
 spasmodically bubbling, roaring.
  In the pit of your gaping mouth
you bared your fringework of baleen,
 a thicket of horned bristles.
  When the Curator of Mammals
arrived from Boston
 to take samples of your blood
  you were already oozing from below.
Somebody had carved his initials
 in your flank. Hunters of souvenirs
  had peeled off strips of your skin,
a membrane thin as paper.
 You were blistered and cracked by the sun.
  The gulls had been pecking at you.
The sound you made was a hoarse and fitful bleating.
What drew us, like a magnet, to your dying?
 You made a bond between us,
  the keepers of the nightfall watch,
who gathered in a ring around you,
 boozing in the bonfire light.
 Toward dawn we shared with you
your hour of desolation,
 the huge lingering passion
  of your unearthly outcry,
as you swung your blind head
 toward us and laboriously opened
  a bloodshot, glistening eye,
in which we swam with terror and recognition.

5

Voyager, chief of the pelagic world,
   you brought with you the myth
      of another country, dimly remembered,
where flying reptiles
   lumbered over the steaming marshes
   and trumpeting thunder lizards
wallowed in the reeds.
   While empires rose and fell on land,
      your nation breasted the open main,
rocked in the consoling rhythm
   of the tides. Which ancestor first plunged
      head-down through zones of colored twilight
to scour the bottom of the dark?
   You ranged the North Atlantic track
      from Port-of-Spain to Baffin Bay,
edging between the ice-floes
   through the fat of summer,
      lob-tailing, breaching, sounding,
grazing in the pastures of the sea
   on krill-rich orange plankton
      crackling with life.
You prowled down the continental shelf,
   guided by the sun and stars
      and the taste of alluvial silt
on your way southward
   to the warm lagoons,
      the tropic of desire,
where the lovers lie belly to belly
   in the rub and nuzzle of their sporting;
      and you turned, like a god in exile,
out of your wide primeval element,
   delivered to the mercy of time.

   Master of the whale-roads,
let the white wings of the gulls
   spread out their cover.
   You have become like us,
disgraced and mortal.

Dorianne Laux

The Orgasms of Organisms

Above the lawn the wild beetles mate
and mate, skew their tough wings
and join. They light in our hair,
on our arms, fall twirling and twinning
into our laps. And below us, in the grass,
the bugs are seeking each other out,
antennae lifted and trembling, tiny legs
scuttling, then the infinitesimal
ah's of their meeting, the awkward joy
of their turnings around. O end to end
they meet again and swoon as only bugs can.
This is why, sometimes, the grass feels electric
under our feet, each blade quivering, and why
the air comes undone over our heads
and washes down around our ears like rain.
But it has to be spring, and you have to be
in love—acutely, painfully, achingly in love—
to hear the black-robed choir of their sighs.

Life Is Beautiful

                    and remote, and useful,
if only to itself. Take the fly, angel
of the ordinary house, laying its bright
eggs on the trash, pressing each jewel out
delicately along a crust of buttered toast.
Bagged, the whole mess travels to the nearest
dump where other flies have gathered, singing
over stained newsprint and reeking

fruit. Rapt on air they execute an intricate
ballet above the clashing pirouettes
of heavy machinery. They hum with life.
While inside rumpled sacks pure white
maggots writhe and spiral from a rip,
a tear-shaped hole that drools and drips
a living froth onto the buried earth.
The warm days pass, gulls scree and pitch,
rats manage the crevices, feral cats abandon
their litters for a morsel of torn fur, stranded
dogs roam open fields, sniff the fragrant edges,
a tossed lacework of bones and shredded flesh.
And the maggots tumble at the center, ripening,
husks membrane-thin, embryos darkening
and shifting within, wings curled and wet,
the open air pungent and ready to receive them
in their fecund iridescence. And so, of our homely hosts,
a bag of jewels is born again into the world. Come, lost
children of the sun-drenched kitchen, your parents
soundly sleep along the windowsill, content,
wings at rest, nestled in against the warm glass.
Everywhere the good life oozes from the useless
waste we make when we create—our streets teem
with human young, rafts of pigeons streaming
over the squirrel-burdened trees. If there is
a purpose, maybe there are too many of us
to see it, though we can, from a distance,
hear the dull thrum of generation's industry,
feel its fleshly wheel churn the fire inside us, pushing
the world forward toward its ragged edge, rushing
like a swollen river into multitude and rank disorder.
Such abundance. We are gorged, engorging, and gorgeous.

Patrick Lawler

Hummingbird

Never certain
whether I'm the
hummingbird

or the hunger,

the burrowing
or the blossom.

This alchemist's breath.
This living graphic.

This vibrating text.

A spurt. A spark. A lure.

A flag
for a fancy
country.

In Europe
they ended up
in glass boxes.

The head
like a bishop's ring.

Fractal. Flint.
Metallic flicking.

The tiny
meteor of the heart

bursts.

Sin-splashed,
it sparkles.

It glistens
like sex.

A transvestite's
rainbow brain.

Technically
a jewel.

In the 19th century
millions

were murdered
so they could
be hats.

A sapphire soul.
A magician's
last breath.

Thought
hovering
outside
the body.

Lucifer.
Ruby bliss.

Light
about to be
swallowed.

Wings blinking.

An inch of bridge
between
spectacle and id.

Eventually
you become
what you desire.

A piece
of ecclesiastical
sparkle.

A splash of purple
in an iridescent dive.

A liquid medal
for a biplane pilot.

A flying piece of sugar
for a fallen acrobat.

All mouth:
a semaphore of hunger
tapped out with the tongue.

Everything is
ready to be devoured.

A tiny aurora borealis
before a swollen blossom.

This courtship
between tongue
and nectar.

A gemologist
of indulgence.

The dipping into petals—
soft inner spaces.

Succulent
nectar cup.

The hummingbird
hypnotizes
the flower.

Jay Leeming

Law Office

I am sitting in an adjustable chair on the 32nd floor of a skyscraper in New York City. I am typing a list of a thousand names into a computer. As I work I am listening through headphones to a recording of the journals of Cabeza de Vaca, a Spanish explorer who traveled to North America in the 15th century. The office is air-conditioned and I am wearing a tie. A hurricane has drowned half of de Vaca's crew, and most of the rest are sick and dying of starvation on an island off the Florida Keys. The names I am entering are plaintiffs in a case against Union Carbide chemical company, and about half of them are deceased. Some filing cabinets are behind me; one is marked "Bhopal" and another reads "Breast Implants." The secretary sitting behind me goes to get a cup of coffee. De Vaca and his crew have eaten their horses and are now sailing in a makeshift raft that uses their hides for sails. I keep typing. At noon a man comes through the office and waters all the plants. Every hour another sailor dies of pneumonia, or loses his grip and slides off the raft into the storm.

Shara Lessley

Tooth of the Lion

Not footsteps-of-spring or devil's lettuce. Not
hound's tongue, Spanish lotus, Spanish broom.
Not the hottentot fig, its acrid center an unripe

lemon pared in two. Not vanilla leaf, nor bitterroot.
Not the five-fingered fern, glove of spinach
palm faced up, as if about to be read its fortune.

Not creeping snow-berry. Not the hairy fringepod
whose leaves hang down like hand-carved paper
ornaments. Not even the hot-mouthed venus

thistle or scarlet pimpernel compare. Look past
the coastal orchids' loose flirtation, the poppies'
turned-up cheeks. Past the sunflower and tom-cat

clover. To know what it is to stand alone
face into the wind, it's *dent-de-lion*—it's what is
least desired. Sour stem of milk. Erratic growth.

The globular seedball identified as burden. Shelter
for the black beetle, grasshopper, garden centipede.
Fodder for goldfinch and honeybee. Lightweight

crown of bristle broken once to braid a necklace,
chain, or held to the lips to predict a future
which seemed then, so far off. The dandelion's

core dispersed to places unimagined. Chorus
of a hundred directions. Each sliver
a possibility somewhere anchoring itself in dirt.

Philip Levine

They Feed They Lion

Out of burlap sacks, out of bearing butter,
Out of black bean and wet slate bread,
Out of the acids of rage, the candor of tar,
Out of creosote, gasoline, drive shafts, wooden dollies,
They Lion grow.
           Out of the gray hills
Of industrial barns, out of rain, out of bus ride,
West Virginia to Kiss My Ass, out of buried aunties,
Mothers hardening like pounded stumps, out of stumps,
Out of the bones' need to sharpen and the muscles' to stretch,
They Lion grow.
           Earth is eating trees, fence posts,
Gutted cars, earth is calling in her little ones,
"Come home, Come home!" From pig balls,
From the ferocity of pig driven to holiness,
From the furred ear and the full jowl come
The repose of the hung belly, from the purpose
They Lion grow.
           From the sweet glues of the trotters
Come the sweet kinks of the fist, from the full flower
Of the hams the thorax of caves,
From "Bow Down" come "Rise Up,"
Come they Lion from the reeds of shovels,
The grained arm that pulls the hands,
They Lion grow.
           From my five arms and all my hands,
From all my white sins forgiven, they feed,
From my car passing under the stars,

They Lion, from my children inherit,
From the oak turned to a wall, they Lion,
From they sack and they belly opened
And all that was hidden burning on the oil-stained earth
They feed they Lion and he comes.

Our Valley

We don't see the ocean, not ever, but in July and August
when the worst heat seems to rise from the hard clay
of this valley, you could be walking through a fig orchard
when suddenly the wind cools and for a moment
you get a whiff of salt, and in that moment you can almost
believe something is waiting beyond the Pacheco Pass,
something massive, irrational, and so powerful even
the mountains that rise east of here have no word for it.

You probably think I'm nuts saying the mountains
have no word for ocean, but if you live here
you begin to believe they know everything.
They maintain that huge silence we think of as divine,
a silence that grows in autumn when snow falls
slowly between the pines and the wind dies
to less than a whisper and you can barely catch
your breath because you're thrilled and terrified.

You have to remember this isn't your land.
It belongs to no one, like the sea you once lived beside
and thought was yours. Remember the small boats
that bobbed out as the waves rode in, and the men
who carved a living from it only to find themselves
carved down to nothing. Now you say this is home,
so go ahead, worship the mountains as they dissolve in dust,
wait on the wind, catch a scent of salt, call it our life.

Larry Levis

The Oldest Living Thing in L.A.

At Wilshire & Santa Monica I saw an opossum
Trying to cross the street. It was late, the street
Was brightly lit, the opossum would take
A few steps forward, then back away from the breath
Of moving traffic. People coming out of the bars
Would approach, as if to help it somehow.
It would lift its black lips & show them
The reddened gums, the long rows of incisors,
Teeth that went all the way back beyond
The flames of Troy & Carthage, beyond sheep
Grazing rock-strewn hills, fragments of ruins
In the grass at San Vitale. It would back away
Delicately & smoothly, stepping carefully
As it always had. It could mangle someone's hand
In twenty seconds. Mangle it for good. It could
Sever it completely from the wrist in forty.
There was nothing to be done for it. Someone
Or other probably called the LAPD, who then
Called Animal Control, who woke a driver, who
Then dressed in mailed gloves, the kind of thing
Small knights once wore into battle, who gathered
Together his pole with a noose on the end,
A light steel net to snare it with, someone who hoped
The thing would have vanished by the time he got there.

Anastasia & Sandman

The brow of a horse in that moment when
The horse is drinking water so deeply from a trough
It seems to inhale the water, is holy.

I refuse to explain.

When the horse had gone the water in the trough,
All through the empty summer,

Went on reflecting clouds & stars.

The horse cropping grass in a field,
And the fly buzzing around its eyes, are more real
Than the mist in one corner of the field.

Or the angel hidden in the mist, for that matter.

Members of the Committee on the Ineffable,
Let me illustrate this with a story, & ask you all
To rest your heads on the table, cushioned,
If you wish, in your hands, &, if you want,
Comforted by a small carton of milk
To drink from, as you once did, long ago,
When there was only a curriculum of beach grass,
When the University of Flies was only a distant humming.

In Romania, after the war, Stalin confiscated
The horses that had been used to work the fields.
"You won't need horses now," Stalin said, cupping
His hand to his ear, "Can't you hear the tractors
Coming in the distance? I hear them already."

The crowd in the Callea Victoria listened closely
But no one heard anything. In the distance
There was only the faint glow of a few clouds.
And the horses were led into boxcars & emerged
As the dimly remembered meals of flesh
That fed the starving Poles
During that famine, & part of the next one—
In which even words grew thin & transparent,

Like the pale wings of ants that flew
Out of the oldest houses, & slowly
What had been real in words began to be replaced
By what was not real, by the not exactly real.
"Well, not exactly, but . . ." became the preferred
Administrative phrasing so that the man
Standing with his hat in his hands would not guess
That the phrasing of a few words had already swept
The earth from beneath his feet. "That horse I had,
He was more real than any angel,
The housefly, when I had a house, was real too,"
Is what the man thought.
Yet it wasn't more than a few months
Before the man began to wonder, talking
To himself out loud before the others,
"Was the horse real? Was the house real?"
An angel flew in and out of the high window
In the factory where the man worked, his hands
Numb with cold. He hated the window & the light
Entering the window & he hated the angel.
Because the angel could not be carved into meat
Or dumped into the ossuary & become part
Of the landfill at the edge of town,
It therefore could not acquire a soul,
And resembled in significance nothing more
Than a light summer dress when the body has gone.

The man survived because, after a while,
He shut up about it.

Stalin had a deep understanding of the *kulaks*,
Their sense of marginalization & belief in the land;

That is why he killed them all.

Members of the Committee on Solitude, consider
Our own impoverishment & the progress of that famine,
In which, now, it is becoming impossible
To feel anything when we contemplate the burial,
Alive, in a two-hour period, of hundreds of people.
Who were not clichés, who did not know they would be

The illegible blank of the past that lives in each
Of us, even in some guy watering his lawn

On a summer night. Consider

The death of Stalin & the slow, uninterrupted
Evolution of the horse, a species no one,
Not even Stalin, could extinguish, almost as if
What could not be altered was something
Noble in the look of its face, something

Incapable of treachery.

Then imagine, in your planning proposals,
The exact moment in the future when an angel
Might alight & crawl like a fly into the ear of a horse,
And then, eventually, into the brain of a horse,
And imagine further that the angel in the brain
Of this horse is, for the horse cropping grass
In the field, largely irrelevant, a mist in the corner
Of the field, something that disappears,
The horse thinks, when weight is passed through it,
Something that will not even carry the weight
Of its own father
On its back, the horse decides, & so demonstrates
This by swishing at a fly with its tail, by continuing
To graze as the dusk comes on & almost until it is night.

Old contrivers, daydreamers, walking chemistry sets,
Exhausted chimneysweeps of the spaces
Between words, where the Holy Ghost tastes just
Like the dust it is made of,
Let's tear up our lecture notes & throw them out
The window.
Let's do it right now before wisdom descends upon us
Like a spiderweb over a burned-out theater marquee,
Because what's the use?
I keep going to meetings where no one's there,
And contributing to the discussion;
And besides, behind the angel hissing in its mist
Is a gate that leads only into another field,

Another outcropping of stones & withered grass, where
A horse named Sandman & a horse named Anastasia
Used to stand at the fence & watch the traffic pass.
Where there were outdoor concerts once, in summer,
Under the missing & innumerable stars.

Audre Lorde

What My Child Learns of the Sea

What my child learns of the sea
of the summer thunders
of the riddles that hide in the curve of spring
she will learn in my twilights
and childlike
revise every autumn.

What my child learns
as her winters grow into time
has ripened in my own body
to enter her eyes with first light.

This is why
more than blood
or the milk I have given
one day a strange girl will step
to the back of a mirror
cutting my ropes
of sea and thunder and spring.
Of the way she will taste her autumns—
toast-brittle or warmer than sleep—
and the words she will use for winter
I stand already condemned.

Anne Marie Macari

Migration South

Early morning along the river, animals pulsing
but motionless—

like the Indigo Bunting resting its small blue body
on a stalk of sorghum,

its head turned west in contemplation. All day
hiking, canoeing, finding

what we could—a Jesus Lizard, crowned, with feet
so fast it could walk on water

if it weren't frozen there trying to look
like a stick, or the Spider Monkey

leaping between trees, arms and legs splayed wide
overhead so it seemed

held still in space. That night, exhausted, I dimmed
the lights, relieved to be alone,

as if I hadn't been able to think all day with
so much life around me, till

in my half-sleep I heard rough wing-beats, not bird

but a harder rasping, and turned to face a cockroach size
of a flattened hen's egg

scurrying behind a cabinet. Up in the thatched roof
I imagined colonies of insects

watching over me, invisible multitude,
and who was I to question them?

Who was I with my binoculars and books?

Not the Hissing Roach or Dusky Antbird, not
a shelled thing with wings

that clicked when it moved, but a frightened
creature of the north,

out of her habitat, no feeble quills on my back,
no gliding from the tree,

just that same falling and falling again, startled

into my bed, into my own featherless skin. Overhead:
clouds of tiny creatures,

the eyes of roaches, moths, broken arm
of the bat, or a bird

trapped in the peaked roof, frantic for release.

Kelly Madigan

Offering

Always the same story
the bulldozers at the meadow's edge
the high whine of motorized saws
at the base of nests.

Always my heart beating
in the sole of my foot,
the tire on the economy van
from the city's poorest church
about to blow on the blacktop
with fourteen children riding.

The banks of the river
are hung with trash
and even now a little ways
upstream a boy kicks
the Styrofoam bait container
into the brown water.

Spring comes too early
or not at all, the bees have fled
and someone quotes Einstein,
and someone else comes along
to say he never really said that,
but it rings in your ears
anyway, the bee-dead earth.

We steal each other's jewelry
and one gets drunk and says
what he has held back for years
while another pours ammonia
into the watershed
and the fish are gaping at the edges.

Throw open the pasture gates
and let the horses have their heads,
allow them to cross the river
in the dark. Light fire to the altars
and throw on sage and cedar
and the long list of grievances.

No one can autopsy the bees
since they never return to the hive.
They dispute the Einstein quote,
say it is overblown, the bees
are rich and plentiful,
they are high on the hog,
they are in greener fields.

In the black cave
of the forest, the growl
and heave of heavy equipment.
I can see the path
the deer make as they flee.

Davis McCombs

from Tobacco Mosaic

Stripping Room

They were working past dark at the waist-high bench
that night; they were smoking and talking in that place
of the barrel stove and of the chalk figures while outside
and all around them, a season folded its leaves
into the ground like wings. They reached their hands
into the veined, elastic plants; they touched the tips
of shadows stretching like fingers from a past
of splintered bone and ash, the dark of the Continent.
Autumn was shifting and rustling, preparing
for sleep, and the moon rose through the empty fields,
flashing its wide search-beam through the roosts.
They were standing at the end of a process, sorting
by the light of jar lamps. In that dust-paneled room,
deep in a dwindling year, they stripped the lugs
and flying from the stalks and let the bounty
of the long days slip so easily through their hands.

Lexicon

The people are talking about budworms; they are talking
about aphids and thrips. Under the bluff at Dismal Rock,
there where the spillway foams and simmers,
they are fishing and talking about pounds and allotments;
they are saying white burley, lugs and cutters.
Old men are whittling sticks with their pocketknives
and they are saying Paris Green; they speak of topping
and side-dressing; they are whistling and talking
about setters, plant beds and stripping rooms.

394

At Hedgepeths, under the shade of the Feed Mill awning,
in that place of burlap and seedbins, of metal scoops,
they are sitting on milk crates; they are drinking from bottles
and they are talking about pegs, float plants and tierpoles.
At the Depot Market, they say blue mold, high color;
they are nodding and saying sucker dope; they are leaning
on the counter and talking about Black Patch, high boys, flue-cured.
They are arguing about horn worms and buyouts.
They are saying come back, come back, come back.

Drought

Now the river hones its dull blade on a strop of gravel,
and the bobcats, sensing this, come down off the dry
ridgetops, slake their thirst at the water's sharpened edge,
and cling to the shade of bank-side undergrowth.
This is the time of the brick kiln, of pond craters,
that month when even moonlight chars the limp cornsilks
in the fields. Now the people come, the men stripping
shirtless in pokeweed and pawpaws; they come
to where the riffles' flashbulbs strobe the sycamores,
to the still pools above the Railroad Bridge where carp mope
and algae bloom. The children paddle out in inner tubes,
they hide a watermelon at the Blue Hole. At dusk,
their parents build great fires of driftwood on the gravel,
roasting hotdogs on willow prongs. They crank the handle
of the ice cream churn, mopping their foreheads,
and celebrate, though their hearts are burning, and the leaves
on the blue hills high above them vanish into smoke.

The Sharecroppers

So many moons have risen through the fields of leaf.
So many suns have turned the rows of stobs to cover crops
and turned away: it sank like a stain into the hills that night,
a flash, without heat, on the dust-coated window

of the stripping room and the unlit barrel stove inside.
On that day of the developers and the divvying up,
he walked the farm and thought of those who labored there.
He crouched in the shade of the barn, thinking and mumbling,
and the wind ripped the words from his mouth, spun them
along an edge of sheering air. He thought of someone
in a barn or field far away looking up to see who spoke;
he thought how nothing he could ever say would match
the sound of the undergrowth's inquietude that last night
when barred owls talked in the timbered sink, and he heard
in the call of the towhee the sound of the end of the world.

Jane Mead

The Origin

of what happened is not in language—
of this much I am certain.
Six degrees south, six east—

and you have it: the bird
with the blue feathers, the brown bird—
same white breasts, same scaly

ankles. The waves between us—
house light and transform motion
into the harboring of sounds in language.—

Where there is newsprint
the fact of desire is turned from again—
and again. Just the sense

that what remains might well be held up—
later, as an ending.
Twice I have walked through this life—

once for nothing, once
for facts: fairy-shrimp in the vernal pool—
glassy-winged sharp-shooter

on the failing vines. Count me—
among the animals, their small
committed calls.—

Count me among
the living. My greatest desire—
to exist in a physical world.

Sandra Meek

Biogeography

So for the first time, we have answers to the question
of Earth's restlessness . . .
—THOMAS E. HEMMERLY, *APPALACHIAN WILDFLOWERS*

Reading landscape again fails me, having lost the necessary
nomenclature of wonder, both family
and scientific names. Distant kin to Narcissus, I expect to find

myself in every local habitat, in spruce-fir and cove hardwood forests,
bogs and balds, cedar glades: I've traced the breakage
of history's stone tablets to illustrated field guides

cleaving fossil, mineral, animal. The safety in numbers
is in their division: Cherokee, Seneca, Micmac, Catawba; monocot
and dicot; whatever's exiled, trailed

to tears, accounted for. Even this evening no
continuous fade but an extinguishing series
of blue equations, each shade measured by how far it's fallen

from day's *sky blue*. Though nothing stalls
continental drift, the weathering
mosaic of the body, serpentine barrens where the soul,

like any soil, composes itself by horizons, layers visible
only in profile. The terror's in facing
anything head-on. Better to note the way distance

breaks the forest to layers
of aspiration: shrub, understory, canopy.
In geologic scope, what the ground we're mesmerized to won't

let us forget, these mountains are a single
inflorescence, a half-life not more than one
exhalation of stars. This is the ice

we skate, clarity
which brings us down; genesis
of binomials—second naming of all the transitory's

incarnations, flora to fauna—that craving for return
to the earliest garden, as if again what was left to us
was world enough, and time.

Event One

We spread across the temperate world as if it would last
forever, while millennia's held breath

bubbled Greenland ice flowing surface-
forward, an extended

glance of light. Our climate's history is clocked
in beetle casings, the thickening skins
lakes secret, articulations

of the body. If stars don't destroy us, weather

will. We are its children. What calmed
six thousand years ago stopped

the wandering; cities
were born, and alphabets, Word as landscape, and climatology, the theory
of our eminent end

at the hands of ice. This far south, in Georgia,
pockets of air are what's left when groundwater's drained
by quarries and drought. Overnight

a sinkhole opens; morning, the earth's
a cupped hand holding

its own broken bones. Camp Century lasted
a decade. It was the cold war. Ten top-secret years
counting layers of summer and winter snows

like an abacus of tree rings spiraling
toward an origin perhaps itself

nomadic, moving
       through *us*, what it whips up to veil
its one stormy eye, a Ouija's

         glass window guided by whatever
is writing us down.

138 feet, Atlanta
       is burning; 2500 feet down, Socrates sips hemlock.

Blackened here by Pompeii ash, here by Roman smelters' lead,
         ice they're again drilling no longer
       registers sublime without that lost

theory of doom, not global warming's
         slow slippage, but *what can calm*
can craze again,
       climate like science fickle and owing us

nothing. Time, for now, remains

a weight. One hundred thousand years down, pressed snow
         is ice, and materiality
       a ticking; brought to the surface, the sample

               may explode, like the heart
of a diver, too quickly risen. Camp Century's now

part of the drift—mess hall, hospital, skating rink, shelves of perfume
         for absent loves, all

scatter and flow beneath a night sky stippled
         with ice and dark breaths: absence knocking
       between heartbeats, the sound a word makes
when it's taken back.

W. S. Merwin

For a Coming Extinction

Gray whale
Now that we are sending you to The End
That great god
Tell him
That we who follow you invented forgiveness
And forgive nothing

I write as though you could understand
And I could say it
One must always pretend something
Among the dying
When you have left the seas nodding on their stalks
Empty of you
Tell him that we were made
On another day

The bewilderment will diminish like an echo
Winding along your inner mountains
Unheard by us
And find its way out
Leaving behind it the future
Dead
And ours

When you will not see again
The whale calves trying the light
Consider what you will find in the black garden
And its court
The sea cows the Great Auks the gorillas

The irreplaceable hosts ranged countless
And foreordaining as stars
Our sacrifices

Join your word to theirs
Tell him
That it is we who are important

Vixen

Comet of stillness princess of what is over
        high note held without trembling without voice without sound
aura of complete darkness keeper of the kept secrets
        of the destroyed stories the escaped dreams the sentences
never caught in words warden of where the river went
        touch of its surface sibyl of the extinguished
window onto the hidden place and the other time
        at the foot of the wall by the road patient without waiting
in the full moonlight of autumn at the hour when I was born
        you no longer go out like a flame at the sight of me
you are still warmer than the moonlight gleaming on you
        even now you are unharmed even now perfect
as you have always been now when your light paws are running
        on the breathless night on the bridge with one end I remember you
when I have heard you the soles of my feet have made answer
        when I have seen you I have waked and slipped from the calendars
from the creeds of difference and the contradictions
        that were my life and all the crumbling fabrications
as long as it lasted until something that we were
        had ended when you are no longer anything
let me catch sight of you again going over the wall
        and before the garden is extinct and the woods are figures
guttering on a screen let my words find their own
        places in the silence after the animals

Nocturne

The stars emerge one
by one into the names
that were last found for them
far back in other
darkness no one remembers
by watchers whose own
names were forgotten
later in the dark
and as the night deepens
other lumens begin
to appear around them
as though they were shining
through the same instant
from a single depth of age
though the time between
each one of them
and its nearest neighbor
contains in its span
the whole moment of the earth
turning in a light
that is not its own
with the complete course
of life upon it
born to brief reflection
recognition and anguish
from one cell evolving
to remember daylight
laughter and distant music

Recognitions

Stories come to us like new senses

a wave and an ash tree were sisters
they had been separated since they were children
but they went on believing in each other

though each was sure that the other must be lost
they cherished traits of themselves that they thought of
as family resemblances features they held in common
the sheen of the wave fluttered in remembrance
of the undersides of the leaves of the ash tree
in summer air and the limbs of the ash tree
recalled the wave as the breeze lifted it
and they wrote to each other every day
without knowing where to send the letters
some of which have come to light only now
revealing in their old but familiar language
a view of the world we could not have guessed at

but that we always wanted to believe

The Laughing Thrush

O nameless joy of the morning

tumbling upward note by note out of the night
and the hush of the dark valley
and out of whatever has not been there

song unquestioning and unbounded
yes this is the place and the one time
in the whole of before and after
with all of memory waking into it

and the lost visages that hover
around the edge of sleep
constant and clear
and the words that lately have fallen silent
to surface among the phrases of some future
if there is a future

here is where they all sing the first daylight
whether or not there is anyone listening

Deborah Miranda

Eating a Mountain

You stand in the kitchen, cut
up a buck that a friend
shot for us. I watch you trim,
slice, decide: this is stir fry,
this is steak, this is stew.
These are treats for long-suffering
dogs on the porch, panting. Oh,

we are blessed! I rinse, pack,
mark the cuts, this beautiful
deep red velvety offering.
Eating this deer means
eating this mountain:
acorns, ash, beech, dogwood,
maple, oak, willow, autumn olive;

means devouring witch hazel, pine,
lichens, mushrooms, wild grape,
fiddleheads, honeysuckle,
poison ivy, crown vetch,
clover; means nibbling wild onion,
ragweed, beggar's lice, June grass,
raspberry cane, paw-paws,

crispy green chickweed,
and so you give the meat
your most honest attention,
dedicate your sharpest blade
to muscle, fat, sinew—
carve up that deer
with gratitude, artistry, prayer,
render a wild and sacred animal
into wild, sacred sustenance.

How we eat this deer is a debt
that comes due on the day
we let this mountain
eat us.

Thorpe Moeckel

Bartram's Trail

To follow Bartram's trail upstream, past Tugaloo,
to cross the Chattooga River at Earl's Ford,
to go up the Warwoman Valley,
up past the cascades & bridalveils of Finney Creek,
up along the Continental Divide
between Rabun Bald & Hickory Knob,
is to crawl, is to hopscotch
between the doghobble and the yellowroot,
the rhododendron and the laurel, hand over hand,
inch by dirty, glistening inch;
to follow Bartram is to squirm, prostrate,
under the lattice-work of limb,
the umbrellaed variations of lanceolate,
the way the lungless slip like tongues
through the tiny, moss-flamed grottoes,
oblivious to four-legged jesuses
walking on the water's white-lit roostertails;
to follow Bartram's trail is to go
wet-socked, knee-weary & briar-inked,
is to limbo under shadows
mosaiced and three-quarter domed;
to follow Bartram as far as the end
is split, past the leastmost echo,
past the hiccup of wild mint and galax,
the azalea, the teaberry, the trailing arbutus;
to follow Bartram into the shade of the giant poplar,
across the intersection of trunk and root,
across the blighted chestnuts,
is to find the place
where no pattern goes unrepeated,
the place where the first ashes were spread.

Patricia Monaghan

Connemara Autumn

A few more weeks and winter's hand will run
across the bramble fruit and poison it.
But no one picks what glistens in the sun
along the roadsides. Small birds hide within

the hedgerow thorns and fatten on the fruit.
The hedges seed and spread, engulfing
old stone walls and wooden fences. Minute
by minute, mystery removes itself from us.

The men who married women of the sea
have moved inland and taken human wives.
Dogs run wild among the sheep, which flee
into the granite hills. Even the crow falls silent.

Richard O. Moore

Driving to Fort Bragg

" . . . the existence of the appearance is the reality
in question . . . "
—JOHN SEARLE

Inferred only *this* time *is* history, yet uncovered:

hawks on fence posts, even ravens those acrobats, fog
has called a general strike along the coast, no
thermal-lazing, hovering, no tidying-up by vultures
descended from above;

through cataracts dimly, once winged enterprise,
feathers tented against rain, these vision-
masters of the air . . . headlights
catch them in refracting dawn;
whatever their hunger the ceiling will not yield,
bird shapes lost in the moment of discovery,
as if light, after millennia released, reduced substance to ash,
a part of the vast curriculum of circumstance and nothing,
with yesterday's blinding sunlight withheld there,
so many questions fearful to be asked;

place *this* with the pacific fence post
posturing of hawks.

Lori Anderson Moseman

Grate | Table Grace

Shoots narrow to steer. Spilt rail]	[Weekend meal is at noon. We girls
rattle. Cattle mount each other.]	[leave the corral early to grate tender
Defecate. Sal counts. Ranch hands]	[roots of homegrown carrots. Shoots
squeezes blue powder for pink eye. Ooze.]	[so sweet we parse them on plates.
So the steer can see what exactly?]	[Sal goes easy with the rough steel
Death of color into the birth of new.]	[eyelets. I grate for abrasion. Nip
Pay dirt. Loam's nitro—god's green]	[knuckles again. Blood. Hiss. Mess
alfalfa. Discomfort dissipates. Breeze.]	[my borrowed apron. Recipe loops:

repeat with remaining stock

too many cattle in shoot too many ashes in this soap sunset fires us too soon
stuck on a cattle grate straddle *activity* and *calm* we're always that cow's eye
severed from nerve and humor—a stray lens in a shallow tray with formaldehyde

Harryette Mullen

from Muse and Drudge

I dream a world
and then what
my soul is resting
but my feet are tired

half the night gone
I'm holding my own
some half forgotten tune
casual funk from a darker back room

handful of gimme
myself when I am real
how would you know
if you've never tasted

a ramble in brambles
the blacker more sweeter juicier
pores sweat into blackberry tangles
going back native natural country wild briers

Naomi Shihab Nye

Negotiations with a Volcano

We will call you "Agua" like the rivers and cool jugs.
We will persuade the clouds to nestle around your neck
so you may sleep late.
We would be happy if you slept forever.
We will tend the slopes we plant, singing the songs
our grandfathers taught us before we inherited their fear.
We will try not to argue among ourselves.
When the widow demands extra flour, we will provide it,
remembering the smell of incense on the day of our Lord.

Please think of us as we are, tiny, with skins that burn easily.
Please notice how we have watered the shrubs around our houses
and transplanted the peppers into neat tin cans.
Forgive any anger we feel toward the earth,
when the rains do not come, or they come too much,
and swallow our corn.
It is not easy to be this small and live in your shadow.

Often while we are eating our evening meal
you cross our rooms like a thief,
touching first the radio and then the loom.
Later our dreams begin catching fire around the edges,
they burn like paper, we wake with our hands full of ash.

How can we live like this?
We need to wake and find our shelves intact,
our children slumbering in their quilts.
We need dreams the shape of lakes,
with mornings in them thick as fish.
Shade us while we catch and hook—
but nothing else, nothing else.

The Turtle Shrine near Chittagong

Humps of shell emerge from dark water.
Believers toss hunks of bread,
hoping the fat reptilian heads
will loom forth from the murk
and eat. Meaning: *you have been
heard.*

I stood, breathing the stench of mud
and rotten dough, and could not feel
encouraged. Climbed the pilgrim hill
where prayers in tissue radiant tubes
were looped to a tree. Caught in
their light, a hope washed over me
small as the hope of stumbling feet
but did not hold long enough
to get me down.

Rickshas crowded the field,
announced by tinny bells.
The friend beside me, whose bread
floated and bobbed,
grew grim. They're full, I told him.
But they always eat mine.

That night I told the man I love most
he came from hell. It was also
his birthday. We gulped lobster
over a white tablecloth in a country
where waves erase whole villages, annually,
and don't even make our front page.
Waiters forded the lulling currents
of heat. Later, my mosquito net
had holes.

All night, I was pitching something,
crumbs or crusts, into that bottomless pool
where the spaces between our worlds take root.
He would forgive me tomorrow.
But I wanted a mouth to rise up
from the dark, a hand,
any declarable body part, to swallow,
or say, *This is water, that is land.*

dg nanouk okpik

She Sang to Me Once at a Place for Hunting Owls: *Utkiavik*

I wade through the nesting ground fitted like a fingerprint. You say it's a
place of speckled day owls with golden eyes. You and I travelling together
following the caribou at the entrance of *Quunquq* River, we see caves
in old sod houses which belonged to reindeer herders. Our dogs start
barking, whining. We follow the whale rib steps up to the ridge, leave
tobacco. We keep hiking up the mountains where there live many Dall
sheep, we set camp. I dream of a snow bird with pearlescent plumes, a
horntail and a spiked crown. She brought me a lens to use in the echo
chamber. When we come upon *Okpikrauq* River, I hear her song vibrate
off the cliffs:

> *People have as their names, their rivers, their rivers.*

Tulunigraq: Something Like a Raven

Dances for Qarrtsiluni

to change   the steps home

under salt white moon   *Tulunigraq* dances

to the braided night shade. He toe hops   on blades

of sea grass   his feathers shine   like Acoma black on black

pottery his beak   a locus of tool for song.

He sings   into the purple morning   clicks and caws

in medicine words   waits   waits   for something to break.

Qarrtsiluni sitting   in silence   where all things

and all beings reach   back into time before iron and oil.

Like his cousin Crow,   Raven Man clicks and caws

in verse time told tomorrow   461 days ago and today.

In the same moment of stillness   over the Tongass sledge

at high day   Raven lights a whale oil lamp   by the sun's rays.

It is said Raven   flickers the way   for Inupiaq.

  He sings click,

click, caw because   rarely is there any   one place to call home.

Mary Oliver

Alligator Poem

I knelt down
at the edge of the water,
and if the white birds standing
in the tops of the trees whistled any warning
I didn't understand,
I drank up to the very moment it came
crashing toward me,
its tail flailing
like a bundle of swords,
slashing the grass,
and the inside of its cradle-shaped mouth
gaping,
and rimmed with teeth—
and that's how I almost died
of foolishness
in beautiful Florida.
But I didn't.
I leaped aside, and fell,
and it streamed past me, crushing everything in its path
as it swept down to the water
and threw itself in,
and, in the end,
this isn't a poem about foolishness
but about how I rose from the ground
and saw the world as if for the second time,
the way it really is.
The water, that circle of shattered glass,
healed itself with a slow whisper
and lay back
with the back-lit light of polished steel,
and the birds, in the endless waterfalls of the trees,

shook open the snowy pleats of their wings, and drifted away,
while, for a keepsake, and to steady myself,
I reached out,
I picked the wild flowers from the grass around me—
blue stars
and blood-red trumpets
on long green stems—
for hours in my trembling hands they glittered
like fire.

Wild Geese

You do not have to be good.
You do not have to walk on your knees
for a hundred miles through the desert, repenting.
You only have to let the soft animal of your body
    love what it loves.
Tell me about despair, yours, and I will tell you mine.
Meanwhile the world goes on.
Meanwhile the sun and the clear pebbles of the rain
are moving across the landscapes,
over the prairies and the deep trees,
the mountains and the rivers.
Meanwhile the wild geese, high in the clean blue air,
are heading home again.
Whoever you are, no matter how lonely,
the world offers itself to your imagination,
calls to you like the wild geese, harsh and exciting—
over and over announcing your place
in the family of things.

The Lilies Break Open Over the Dark Water

Inside
  that mud-hive, that gas sponge,
    that reeking
      leaf-yard, that rippling

dream-bowl, the leeches'
  flecked and swirling
    broth of life, as rich
      as Babylon,

the fists crack
  open and the wands
    of the lilies
      quicken, they rise

like pale poles
  with their wrapped beaks of lace;
    one day
      they tear the surface,

the next they break open
  over the dark water.
    And there you are,
      on the shore,

fitful and thoughtful, trying
  to attach them to an idea—
    some news of your own life.
      But the lilies

are slippery and wild—they are
  devoid of meaning, they are
    simply doing,
      from the deepest

spurs of their being,
  what they are impelled to do
    every summer.
      And so, dear sorrow, are you.

Alicia Suskin Ostriker

Love III

In the ocean said the oceanographer
there is no place to hide
beluga whales protect each other
by traveling in a group

probably the instinct to save
any individual that seems to be sinking
as they do with babies and others in trouble
by lifting them from below into the air

is not species-specific so that when the young
diver began to choke thinking
now I will die she felt this incredible force
almost like a machine push her upward

until she breached and breathed
rinsed by the sky
but the giant form dove and disappeared
into the immeasurable sea

those of her own species drew her up
peeled her suit off, wrapped towels around her
wondered why she cried and cried
since she had not died

Michael Palmer

Dearest Reader

He painted the mountain over and over again
from his place in the cave, agape
at the light, its absence, the mantled
skull with blue-tinted hollows, wren-
like bird plucking berries from the fire
her hair alight and so on
lemon grass in cafe in clear glass.
Dearest reader there were trees
formed of wire, broad entryways
beneath balconies beneath spires
youthful head come to rest in meadow
beside bend in gravel road, still
body of milky liquid
her hair alight and so on
successive halls, flowered carpets and doors
or the photograph of nothing but pigeons
and grackles by the shadow of a fountain.

Notes for Echo Lake   6

> "The next stage is memory . . . "
> —AUGUSTINE, *CONFESSIONS*, X.8

A tree's streaming imitates light. Water gathers light behind the arm.
The arm is 'held' there. Water bodies light to divide. Light measures by
resemblance. Water filters bridge as in left-handedness. Light alters it.
Water patterns bridge against its step. Hills cancel redness. Body emp-
ties and divides. Body's shift patterns bridge this river is called. Here

trees cancel bodies light sometimes marks. An angle occurs in selection. Here trees are marks. Here trees begin a cancelled pattern. He sometimes hears them. Coffee is sent. Here dancing is done in fear across rooftops.

Notes for Echo Lake   9

Was lying in am lying on I is I am it surrounds

G. E. Patterson

The Natural World

You got trees all dappled with sunlight and shit
You got trees green with lots of leaves
You got fruit-bearing trees   made for climbing
    good for something

I got trees too   My trees stainless steel poles
with no flags   My trees streetlights redyellowgreen
glass shattered on the ground

You got birds waking you up in the morning
Birds waking you up in the morning   TweetTweet
ChirpChirp   That's how it is for y'all
          mutherfuckers

I got birds too   My birds
loud as jackhammers   My birds
loud as police sirens   My birds
loud as gunfire   My birds
electric   gas-powered

My birds   My birds   killers

Lucia Perillo

Bulletin from Somewhere up the Creek

Luckily, it's shallow enough that I can pole my rubber boat—
don't ask what happened to the paddle. Anywhere is lovely
if you look hard enough: the scum on the surface
becomes a lace of tiny flowers.
In the space between cedars, a half-moon slides
across a sky colored like the inside of a clam.
Two terns slice it with their sharp beaks,
gape-mouthed and wheeling and screaming like cats.

See, nature is angry, I said to myself: *Nature
is just an ice pick with wings.* Then a weasel or something
poked its head through the muck, looked around for a while
before submerging again. And not even bumping
the ketchup squeeze bottle seemed to disturb it,
nor was it afraid to lose itself in this brown soup.
Or maybe this was just a very large rat—still,
why should its example be of any less worth?

Ah, my friends, I could tell you my troubles
but is that why you came? Sure, it stinks here—
the best birding is done in foul-smelling places.
So far I've seen the hawk circling, the kingfisher chuckling
before smashing itself breast-first in the muck.
I've watched the blue heron standing on just one leg
until it found something half rotten to spear. Then swallowing
with a toss of its head, as if this were a meal for kings.

The Crows Start Demanding Royalties

Of all the birds, they are the ones
who mind their being armless most:
witness how, when they walk, their heads jerk
back and forth like rifle bolts.
How they heave their shoulders into each stride
as if they hoped that by some chance
new bones there would come popping out
with a boxing glove on the end of each.

Little Elvises, the hairdo slicked
with too much grease, they convene on my lawn
to strategize for their class-action suit.
Flight they would trade in a New York minute
for a black muscle car and a fist on the shift
at any stale green light. But here in my yard
by the Jack-in-the-Box Dumpster
they can only fossick in the grass for remnants

of the world's stale buns. And this
despite all the crow poems that have been written
because men like to see themselves as crows
(the head-jerk performed in the rearview mirror,
the dark brow commanding the rainy weather).
So I think I know how they must feel:
ripped off, shook down, taken to the cleaners.
What they'd like to do now is smash a phone against a wall.
But they can't, so each one flies to a bare branch and screams.

Shrike Tree

Most days back then I would walk by the shrike tree,
a dead hawthorn at the base of a hill.
The shrike had pinned smaller birds on the tree's black thorns
and the sun had stripped them of their feathers.

Some of the dead ones hung at eye level
while some burned holes in the sky overhead.
At least it is honest,
the body apparent
and not rotting in the dirt.

And I, having never seen the shrike at work,
can only imagine how the breasts were driven into the branches.
When I saw him he'd be watching from a different tree
with his mask like Zorro
and the gray cape of his wings.

At first glance he could have been a mockingbird or a jay
if you didn't take note of how his beak was hooked.
If you didn't know the ruthlessness of what he did—
ah, but that is a human judgment.

They are mute, of course, a silence at the center of a bigger silence,
these rawhide ornaments, their bald skulls showing.
And notice how I've slipped into the present tense
as if they were still with me.

Of course they are still with me.

.

They hang there, desiccating
by the trail where I walked, back when I could walk,
before life pinned me on its thorn.
It is ferocious, life, but it must eat,
then leaves us with the artifact.

Which is: these black silhouettes in the midday sun,
strict and jagged, like an Asian script.
A tragedy that is not without its glamour.
Not without the runes of the wizened meat.

Because imagine the luck!—to be plucked from the air,
to be drenched and dried in the sun's bright voltage—
well, hard luck is luck, nonetheless.
With a chunk of sky in each eye socket.
And the pierced heart strung up like a pearl.

Jim Peterson

No Bite

Not enough claw
in the mountains,
not enough snow
deepening the slopes.
Not enough covert eyes,
not enough wind
to blur the vision,
not enough silence
to seize the claptrap of talk.

Not enough footprints
in the woods,
predator and prey,
no more walking sticks
left in good faith at the trailhead.
Not enough getting lost
in the back country,
exploring and holing up
on the high cliffs, the day
so long even the rocks are shaking.
Not enough bite in the winter air.

Not enough story
left in the ink,
not enough character
driven to the brink
of decision.
Not enough risk
in the telling or the living.
Not enough blood
in the word.

D. A. Powell

republic

soon, industry and agriculture converged
        and the combustion engine
sowed the dirtclod truck farms green
               with onion tops and chicory

mowed the hay, fed the swine and mutton
        through belts and chutes

cleared the blue oak and the chaparral
           chipping the wood for mulch

back-filled the marshes
        replacing buckbean with dent corn

removed the unsavory foliage of quag
           made the land into a production
made it *produce*, pistoned and oiled
        and forged against its own nature

and—with enterprise—built silos
           stockyards, warehouses, processing plants
abattoirs, walk-in refrigerators, canneries, mills
            & centers of distribution

it meant something—in spite of machinery—
      to say *the country*, to say *apple season*
though what it meant was a kind of nose-thumbing
           and a kind of sweetness
      as when one says *how quaint*
knowing that a refined listener understands the doubleness

and the leveling of the land, enduing it in sameness, cured malaria
as the standing water in low glades disappeared,
          as the muskegs drained

typhoid and yellow fever decreased
                    even milksickness abated
thanks to the rise of the feeding pen
          cattle no longer grazing on white snakeroot

vanquished: the germs that bedeviled the rural areas
                    the rural areas also
vanquished: made monochromatic and mechanized, made suburban

now, the illnesses we contract are chronic illnesses: dyspepsia, arthritis
          heart disease, kidney disease, high blood pressure, asthma
                    chronic pain, allergies, anxiety, emphysema
                              diabetes, cirrhosis, lyme disease, aids
               chronic fatigue syndrome, malnutrition, morbid obesity
hypertension, cancers of the various kinds: bladder bone eye lymph
          mouth ovary thyroid liver colon bileduct lung
                    breast throat & sundry areas of the brain

no better in accounting for death and no worse: we still die
we carry our uninhabited mortal frames back to the land
                    cover them in sod, we take the land to the brink
          of our dying: it stands watch, dutifully, artfully
enriched with sewer sludge and urea
                              to green against eternity of green

hocus pocus: here is a pig in a farrowing crate
                    eating its own feces
human in its ability to litter inside a cage
                    to nest, to grow gravid and to throw its young

I know I should be mindful of dangerous analogy:
          the pig is only the pig
                    and we aren't merely the wide-open field
                              flattened to a space resembling nothing

you want me to tell you the marvels of invention?   that we persevere
that the time of flourishing is at hand?   I should like to think it

meanwhile, where have I put the notebook on which I was scribbling

it began like:
                    "the smell of droppings and that narrow country road . . ."

John Pursley III

Hand Over Fist

The Atlantic breaks at the estuary's edge,
  Rushes among rocks. Rocks dreg & silt
For miles upstream. Like a devolving language

It settles out slowly—*or like curlews themselves*
  Who circle the shoals for worms and carrion.
Imagine the hand-over-fist force of salt

And sediment, of water impinged upon
  Undulate water. Eighteen-thousand years
Of spherical melting. Ice. Coming to calm

In slow procession. The reverberant dead-
  Mile drift. The flatness of it all
Laid out in fallow fields, like thin threads

Warped along looms. The provisional
  Placidity, as if stillness were a formality
Of strict discipline—*or motion.* Before the gull

Rises, the tern & curlew. Before bodies
  Are lifted & the first cricket sings. Imagine
The repose, the uninterruptible periodicity.

Bernard Quetchenbach

Dark Night of the Hermit

Again, dream
face among stars

Satellite
tracks east
to west

Closer to home
than I.

Janisse Ray

Justice

Let them have their oil.
Let them have their mosques and holy books,
the sun gleaming on the face of a woman
kneeling for the fifth time to pray.
Let her have the baby in her arms.
Let her bring from market the lentils, lamb,
bouquet of cilantro, cloves
that taste like the dusty rock of house
walls bordering the street.
Let her have the woven rug red and blue
beneath her real feet.
Let her have the pot, and the wooden ladle,
and the quiet ticking of a clock she no longer notices.
Let her have the common bird singing from the olive
and the sound of a door opening as it should.

And let me have my farm.
Let me have small clouds of breath as I rise
from patchwork quilts in the winter house.
Let me have a fallen maple for firewood
and the fire itself an eager bed of coals.
Let me have bowls of oatmeal and cups of tea
sweetened with tupelo honey, steaming
on the white enamel table.
Let me have my husband pulling on boots
to plant potatoes, while the moon
pauses in the sign for roots.
Let me have brown eggs still warm
from the hen, milk hot from the cow.
Let me have the common bird singing from the oak
and the sound of a door opening as it should.

Srikanth Reddy

Monsoon Eclogue

Some years ago a procession
of men calling themselves
the sky-clad came
to this district to build
a hospital for birds that had been
damaged by the rains.

The landholders here
my grandfather among them
decided against it—
it not being our way
to intervene with monsoons

which is why to this day
the birds here grow
so damaged & wise,

or so our tutor said gravely

before stepping out into the sun-
washed coriander patch to watch
droplets work down
stems one by one, small
storms suspended, while over
the rooftiles came
breakers of mist making
our whole house to him
drift back like the high prow
of the viceroy's steamship
he watched sail off with his youth.

Inside I still could not find
the main verb the chariot
wheel performed. I thought

it was silver. It bore

the king with 100 heads
across a battlefield red
with his wounded
up to the end of the
beginner's workbook

then blue-skinned Rama bent his bow then his
raider's arrow met
the axle & then

I could not stop laughing

as through the doorway my mother scolded
the aphasic houseboy

who peed into our
green watertank
(black putti, untouchable)
arcing the thin golden
stream & singing
ooo-ee ooo-ee at our ruin.

Carter Revard

Aesculapius Unbound[1]

(Ovid and Darwin in Oklahoma)

By beautiful design, a snake's jawbones
unhinge, so it can swallow
things bigger around
than it is.
I wondered, when
the old man shot a blacksnake in
the hen-house, then held it
up by the tail,
just how in hell those great big lumps
along its six-foot length, slow-twisting up and
down as it hung, had ever been
choked down.
Later, I heard that snakes
are deaf, those three hinged bones
had not yet turned into the malleus, incus
and stapes of my middle ear,
they have no tympanum
and no cochlea,
no auditory nerve, their brain only
processes earth's vibrations, but not thunder's,
so snakes don't sing, although perhaps
they dance when mating—
only their cousins, the small birds,[2]
sing the light's changes,
as Melampous knew.[3]
So when I heard,
as twilight grew, the orchard
oriole sing its heart out there in the elm's
Edenic shadows, something unhinged
and let the music in,
but if they hold me up and listen,

it may by then be part of me—
be how I live and breathe,
or will at least be how
I try to whistle, when
the spirit moves.[4]

[1]In Ovid's *Metamorphoses*, Book 15 (lines 622-744), he tells how Apollo's son Æscu-
lapius, god of healing, changed himself into the great serpent which twines about his
staff, and as a serpent was brought by the Romans from the ancient Greek shrine in
Epidaurus to Rome and installed, as the God of Healing, in a new shrine on an island
in the Tiber, where he healed the Romans of a terrible plague. Earlier in Book 15, Ovid's
spokesmen tell how the world was created and continually changes (humans are reincar-
nated, and some in previous lives were animals); they advocate a vegetarian diet instead
of killing and eating sheep, goats, and oxen, and deplore animal sacrifices to the gods.
Finally, Ovid ends this last book of his *Metamorphoses* by narrating recent and future
Roman history: Julius Caesar's assassination and his transformation into a god (a star in
heaven); the ascent to imperial power of Caesar's adopted son Augustus Caesar; and the
future ascent to heaven of Augustus, who will "there, removed from our presence, listen
to our prayers." In the last nine lines of the poem, Ovid prophesies that his poetry will
also be immortal: "through all the ages shall I live in fame."

[2]This at least is the Darwinian Creation Story, as told in encyclopedias under the
entry for *Reptiles*. This story says birds and snakes evolved as branches of *Reptilia*, and
that mammals bloomed on another branch of that tree, so we humans (including the
Oklahoma cowboy who shot the egg-stealing snakes, and the boy who witnessed that
and heard an orchard oriole sing) also hang, not far away, on this tree of life.

[3]See George Economou, *Ananios of Kleitor* (Exeter, England: Shearsman Books,
2009), Fragment 18, "Melampous overheard the worms overhead" (p. 20) and the *End-
note* on this, pp. 88-9, for the story of Melampous, who received the gift of hearing and
understanding the speech of animals, and consequently the gift of prophecy, from some
serpents, because he had ceremonially cremated the body of their mother whom he had
found, "a sacrificial victim, beside an oak tree. In gratitude . . . these serpent children
licked his ears as he slept, purifying him and enabling him to understand the language
of birds and animals, which he used to foretell the future." Thanks, George: sometimes
the gifts borne by Greeks are better than Trojans.

[4]*Acts of the Apostles* 2.1-6:
1. And when the day of Pentecost was fully come, they were all with one accord in
   one place.
2. And suddenly there came a sound from heaven as of a rushing mighty wind,
   and it filled all the house where they were sitting.
3. And there appeared to them cloven tongues like as of fire, and it sat upon each
   of them.
4. And they were all filled with the Holy Ghost and began to speak with other
   tongues, as the Spirit gave them utterance.
   . . . .
6. . . . every man heard them speak in his own language.

Donald Revell

Election Year

A jet of mere phantom
Is a brook, as the land around
Turns rocky and hollow.
Those airplane sounds
Are the drowning of bicyclists.
Leaping, a bridesmaid leaps.
You asked for my autobiography.
Imagine the greeny clicking sound
Of hummingbirds in a dry wood,
And there you'd have it. Other birds
Pour over the walls now.
I'd never suspected: every day,
Although the nation is done for,
I find new flowers.

My Mojave

Sha-
Dow,
As of
A Meteor
At mid-
Day: it goes
From there.

A perfect circle falls
Onto white imperfections.
(Consider the black road,
How it seems white the entire
Length of a sunshine day.)

Or I could say
Shadows and mirage
Compensate the world,
Completing its changes
With no change.

In the morning after a storm,
We used brooms. Out front,
There was broken glass to collect.
In the backyard, the sand
Was covered with transparent wings.
The insects could not use them in the wind
And so abandoned them. Why
Hadn't the wings scattered? Why
Did they lie so stilly where they'd dropped?
It can only be the wind passed through them.

Jealous lover,
Your desire
Passes the same way.

And jealous earth,
There is a shadow you cannot keep
To yourself alone.
At midday,
My soul wants only to go
The black road which is the white road.
I'm not needed
Like wings in a storm,
And God is the storm.

"Birds small enough . . ."

Birds small enough to nest in our young cypress
Are physicians to us

They burst from the tree exactly
Where the mind ends and the eye sees

Another world the equal of this one
Though only a small boy naked in the sun

Glad day glad day I was born
Sparrow hatted old New York

And the physician who brought me
Drowned under sail next day in a calm sea

There are birds small enough to live forever
Where the mind ends and where

My love and I once planted a cypress
which is God to us

Adrienne Rich

from Twenty-One Love Poems

I

Wherever in this city, screens flicker
with pornography, with science-fiction vampires,
victimized hirelings bending to the lash,
we also have to walk . . . if simply as we walk
through the rainsoaked garbage, the tabloid cruelties
of our own neighborhoods.
We need to grasp our lives inseparable
from those rancid dreams, that blurt of metal, those disgraces,
and the red begonia perilously flashing
from a tenement sill six stories high,
or the long-legged young girls playing ball
in the junior highschool playground.
No one has imagined us. We want to live like trees,
sycamores blazing through the sulfuric air,
dappled with scars, still exuberantly budding,
our animal passion rooted in the city.

.

Power

Living in the earth-deposits   of our history

Today a backhoe divulged   out of a crumbling flank of earth
one bottle   amber   perfect   a hundred-year-old
cure for fever   or melancholy   a tonic
for living on this earth   in the winters of this climate

Today I was reading about Marie Curie:
she must have known she suffered   from radiation sickness
her body bombarded for years   by the element
she had purified
It seems she denied to the end
the source of the cataracts on her eyes
the cracked and suppurating skin   of her finger-ends
till she could no longer hold   a test-tube or a pencil

She died   a famous woman   denying
her wounds
denying
her wounds   came   from the same source as her power.

from The Spirit of Place

v.

Orion plunges like a drunken hunter
over the Mohawk Trail   a parallelogram
slashed with two cuts of steel

A night so clear that every constellation
stands out from an undifferentiated cloud
of stars, a kind of aura

All the figures up there look violent to me
as a pogrom on Christmas Eve in some old country
I want our own earth   not the satellites, our

world as it is   if not as it might be
then as it is: male dominion, gangrape, lynching, pogrom
the Mohawk wraiths in their tracts of leafless birch

watching: will we do better?
The tests I need to pass are prescribed by the spirits
of place   who understand travel but not amnesia

The world as it is: not as her users boast
damaged beyond reclamation by their using
Ourselves as we are   in these painful motions

of staying cognizant: some part of us always
out beyond ourselves
knowing   knowing   knowing

Are we all in training for something we don't name?
to exact reparation for things
done long ago to us and to those who did not

survive what was done to them   whom we ought to honor
with grief   with fury   with action
On a pure night   on a night when pollution

seems absurdity when the undamaged planet seems to turn
like a bowl of crystal in black ether
they are the piece of us that lies out there
knowing   knowing   knowing

.

What Kind of Times Are These

There's a place between two stands of trees where the grass grows uphill
and the old revolutionary road breaks off into shadows
near a meeting-house abandoned by the persecuted
who disappeared into those shadows.

I've walked there picking mushrooms at the edge of dread, but don't
    be fooled,
this isn't a Russian poem, this is not somewhere else but here,
our country moving closer to its own truth and dread,
its own ways of making people disappear.

I won't tell you where the place is, the dark mesh of the woods
meeting the unmarked strip of light—
ghost-ridden crossroads, leafmold paradise:
I know already who wants to buy it, sell it, make it disappear.

And I won't tell you where it is, so why do I tell you
anything? Because you still listen, because in times like these
to have you listen at all, it's necessary
to talk about trees.

Alberto Ríos

Beetles and Frogs

The peach beetles bring green
With them. They wear it and nothing else

On their backs, green
Trimmed with fine yellow stripes.

Frogs, too, bring green with them,
Frogs and hummingbirds under the wing.

In the green they harbor and look after: green,
Black and dark blue, red and yellow,

With these colors each animal carries with it
News from one world to another.

We think they are bringing the news to us.
Save for our loyal dogs, however,

And sometimes a cat, animals do not
Stop in front of us. They run

Instead. They fly and hop, crawl and yip.
Everything they do, they do away from us.

To whom do they deliver this news, then?
And how much news has there been?

And what is the hurry, the incessant effort,
Everything moving so continually around us?

The sun at its work every day does not stop
For us. The moon does not stop.

The birds are in a hurry all the time,
In a rush to reach their perch on a branch

In the congress they hold at all hours
In the linden trees, and the tamarisks,

All those birds speaking simultaneously,
Without translation for us, any of us,

Not one single word directed toward us,
No bird asking us for anything.

Worms carrying dirt, ants in their trails,
Fish schooling in perfect formation

For something, this practice we mimic
So ungracefully with our soldiers,

Moving left, moving right, walking all
Together, but for what?

Everything moves and will not stop.
It exhausts us. We take vacations.

We sit in Adirondack chairs,
Shaking our heads as we watch the world—

Silly thing! And all those animals.
We shake our heads and cluck our tongues

At this mysterious, incessant business
The world seems so insistent upon.

Uncovered Ants

Lifting a rotting landscaper's log full of craggy wood-spikes, a treasure
Shows—fresh red and the straw color of gold, they glitter then glimmer,

Ants everywhere, thick, unsunned, small and new to the greater world,
They move like a honey poured, so many kids on the last day of school

Bursting out the door: I was one of those boys from years ago. I knew
What being in the middle of something like this felt like—

There was no middle. Instead, a hundred edges, a hundred mouths,
Two hundred legs, single-minded but not with a single mind:

Each of us had a plan not bigger than getting the heck out of there.
It was a good plan, and we were committed to it, running, pushing

As if we had all this time been holding our breath hard underwater,
Swimmers up at the very last moment bearable, hard and sudden

In a reverse scream, drawing into us all the possible air and noise
The moment had to offer, drawing into us what fear could push out.

This was a category of happiness, the opposite of scared, a moment, joy.
Did these ants feel it, too? Right now, sudden, finally, like me that day

Throwing open the doors and running into the arms of the world?
They were ants, only ants, what I was looking at. But for a moment

I felt myself in them, the frenzied grammar of childhood, the feeling
Going out that door gave me. I did not see my face in them, but I saw

My arms. Still, they were ants, and soon enough crawling everywhere.
I returned the rotting log to its quietude, to its attitude of decorum—

A frame for the yard the way one might frame and hang a painting,
This log, full of life, one more part of the garden getting old.

Ed Roberson

be careful

i must be careful about such things as these.
the thin-grained oak.   the quiet grizzlies scared
into the hills by the constant tracks squeezing
in behind them closer in the snow.   the snared
rigidity of the winter lake.   deer after deer
crossing on the spines of fish who look up and stare
with their eyes pressed to the ice.   in a sleep.   hearing
the thin taps leading away to collapse like the bear
in the high quiet.   i must be careful not to shake
anything in too wild an elation.   not to jar
the fragile mountains against the paper far-
ness.   nor avalanche the fog or the eagle from the air.
of the gentle wilderness i must set the precarious
words.   like rocks.   without one snowcapped mistake

Wave

everyone sees the sea coming down the beach
everyone calls it the white horses.
nobody's language is ever mistaken
they never fail to come called
on any shore they are broken to.
there is a man who has seen the distance
in the desert do just that
same break   at a walk.
he calls the horizon the white horses
and i have called my sight the reef.

i can imagine that black men call them
the white dogs
and that for the same reasons
the earth could come to call the spray
stars of the milky way
the middle passage
coming down the black sand space
like it was as due as justice
a simple wave   landing and
towing the blanched shell it has taken back like slaves.

To See the Earth before the End of the World

People are grabbing at the chance to see
the earth before the end of the world,
the world's death piece by piece each longer than we.

Some endings of the world overlap our lived
time, skidding for generations
to the crash scene of species extinction
the five minutes it takes for the plane to fall,
the mile ago it takes to stop the train,
the small bay   to coast the liner into the ground,

the line of title to a nation   until the land dies,
the continent uninhabitable.
That very subtlety of time between

large and small
Media note   *people chasing glaciers*
in retreat up their valleys   and *the speed* . . .

watched ice was speed made invisible,
now—   it's days, and a few feet further away,
a subtle collapse of time between large

and our small human extinction.
If I have a table
at this event, mine bears an ice sculpture.

Of whatever loss it is   it lasts as long as ice
does until it disappears   into its polar white
and melts   and the ground beneath it, into vapor,

into air.   All that once chased us and we
chased to a balance chasing back, tooth for spear,
knife for claw,
                    locks us in this grip
          we just now see
                              our own lives taken by
taking them out.   Hunting the bear,
we hunt the glacier with the changes come
          of that choice.

City Eclogue: Words for It

          Beautifully flowering trees you'd expect
should rise from seeds whose fluttering to the ground
is the bird's delicate alight
or the soft petal stepping its image
into the soil
                    but here come the city's trucks
bumping up over the curb dropping
the tight balls of roots in a blueprint out
on the actual site in the street
someone come behind with a shovel will bury.

          City of words we're not supposed to use
Where everyone is lying when it's said these words
are not accurate, that this shit is not the flowering,
that shit off the truck and not the gut
bless of bird and animal dropping isn't somehow

just as natural a distribution
as the wild bloom   The trees are
delivered in ordered speech   as is
dirt mouth curse and graffiti
to where the backed perches want them.   Bought with
                    the experience that thought up city.

448

The idea of the place
tramples up its rich regenerate head
of crazy mud into the mutant's changling potion.
Committee cleanliness and its neat
districts for making nice nice and for making sin
may separate its pick of celebrant monsters;
                    but which it is now is
irrelevant as the numbered street sequence
to archival orders of drifting sand.
What it will be   the stinking flower
the difficult fruit   bitter   complex   the trunk   — all

              on the clock   on the tree rings' clock
                  history's   section cross cut
                  portrait   landscape
                                it already
                  knows   composts into ours the
                                grounds for city.

The Distant Stars as Paparazzi

the News   cattlebirds of paper fly around
thinking   a movie shot
and not that they're just rubbish light enough
and it's time for pick up

which will dump them into dance with garbage gulls
who partner themselves
with popular images   pages flying
winged magazines.

the humped earth settles up to its horns in mud
roaring   then bubbles
of going under cloud air with odor—
stink also a local character

a spirit   flocking its natural herd decompositions
along a mound made into natural
ground for later   their coats sheared into compost for

the spin
into garden earth.

Naked, the planet turns itself
into itself   a mirror
modeling beautiful   it shows its timeless line
for season in its fashion

Pattiann Rogers

Geocentric

Indecent, self-soiled, bilious
reek of turnip and toadstool
decay, dribbling the black oil
of wilted succulents, the brown
fester of rotting orchids,
in plain view, that stain
of stinkhorn down your front,
that leaking roil of bracket
fungi down your back, you
purple-haired, grainy-fuzzed
smolder of refuse, fathering
fumes and boils and powdery
mildews, enduring the constant
interruption of sink-mire
flatulence, contagious
with ear wax, corn smut,
blister rust, backwash
and graveyard debris, rich
with manure bog and dry-rot
harboring not only egg-addled
garbage and wrinkled lip
of orange-peel mold but also
the clotted breath of overripe
radish and burnt leek, bearing
every dank, malodorous rut
and scarp, all sulphur fissures
and fetid hillside seepages, old,
old, dependable, engendering
forever the stench and stretch
and warm seeth of inevitable
putrefaction, nobody
loves you as I do.

Rolling Naked in the Morning Dew

Out among the wet grasses and wild barley-covered
Meadows, backside, frontside, through the white clover
And feather peabush, over spongy tussocks
And shaggy-mane mushrooms, the abandoned nests
Of larks and bobolinks, face to face
With vole trails, snail niches, jelly
Slug eggs; or in a stone-walled garden, level
With the stemmed bulbs of orange and scarlet tulips,
Cricket carcasses, the bent blossoms of sweet William,
Shoulder over shoulder, leg over leg, clear
To the ferny edge of the goldfish pond—some people
Believe in the rejuvenating powers of this act—naked
As a toad in the forest, belly and hips, thighs
And ankles drenched in the dew-filled gulches
Of oak leaves, in the soft fall beneath yellow birches,
All of the skin exposed directly to the *killy* cry
Of the king bird, the buzzing of grasshopper sparrows,
Those calls merging with the dawn-red mists
Of crimson steeplebush, entering the bare body then
Not merely through the ears but through the skin
Of every naked person willing every event and potentiality
Of a damp transforming dawn to enter.

Lillie Langtry practiced it, when weather permitted,
Lying down naked every morning in the dew,
With all of her beauty believing the single petal
Of her white skin could absorb and assume
That radiating purity of liquid and light.
And I admit to believing myself, without question,
In the magical powers of dew on the cheeks
And breasts of Lillie Langtry believing devotedly
In the magical powers of early morning dew on the skin
Of her body lolling in purple beds of bird's-foot violets,
Pink prairie mimosa. And I believe, without doubt,
In the mystery of the healing energy coming
From that wholehearted belief in the beneficent results
Of the good delights of the naked body rolling

And rolling through all the silked and sun-filled,
Dusky-winged, sheathed and sparkled, looped
And dizzied effluences of each dawn
Of the rolling earth.

Just consider how the mere idea of it alone
Has already caused me to sing and sing
This whole morning long.

William Pitt Root

Dear Jeffers

A Note from Sheridan to Carmel-By-The-Sea

It's a long way from the queer remote silence-making *quawk*
of that heron your words snagged on the wing
as I was being born, Jeffers, decades ago,
in a Minnesota blizzard, and you were in a squall of rage
near Big Sur in the place no longer your place—
   as you foresaw, dragging stone after stone
to your tower nonetheless
from the live surf and froth of your own sweat.
Edged in now
by homes No-Man built to live in— high-priced sucker traps
for those successful in that coming world you shunned and decried
poem after bitter poem—your stone tower, Jeffers,
      even your stone tower
raised by hand toward the high blue home
of your beloved hawks
toward whom you turned and turned your falcon of a face
   for evidence of worthiness,
is gone into their hands, their pockets,
enhanced by your famous hatred, the prices rising
with your skydriven fistlike poems exactly abhorring them.
Where I am, in Wyoming still magnificent with wilderness
no sea has breathed on in millions of years,
   the old forces
finding a new grip soon will ream out
ranchers and farmers bewildered by profits sudden as true
   strokes, making way for holes
into which men hungry for the good life
   will descend innocent
of your hawks, gulls, godlike stallions, and women

with wild eyes will tend them
as some die, most prosper
   in the ways men do these days,
their families dull with generations of decay
in their hearts, surrounded by the crown jewels of the age—
   appliances and gadgets designed to make
life careless. And they work, dear Jeffers. They do work.

Song of Returnings

All the bones of the horses rise in moonlight
on the flatlands and hillsides, dropping
from trees, squeezing out from
under rocks, disengaging themselves
from the earth and things that live from the earth
and the scattered uniforms assemble
   to the sounds of bugling come back from the stars
and what has rotted into dust reforms with a furious sound
   of whirlwind tearing the faces from the astonished living
and gold flows molten from the mouth of Cortez
   and returns to the stones and the water and the air
and the redwoods collapse back into cones
and Christ is pried from the cross and flogged and spat upon
   and let loose among fishermen who scatter to their ships
   and enters his mother's womb and enters into the stars
and Babylon reassembles and Sodom and Gomorrah reassemble
and David sings then babbles in his mother's arms
and all living things return to their sources
and the waters return to their sources
and the sun returns to the source
and the vast darkness returns
and all things are
and are not.

Michael Rothenberg

The Bromeliad

for Hart Crane

But this,—defenseless, thornless, sheds no blood,
Almost no shadow—but the air's thin talk.

In the air! maybe there
     these spindly creatures
          are ethereal. Maybe at
the Heart of Hurricane
But know them as I know them!
When Caribbean breezes
     are spiders' transport,
          leaf to leaf. Know them
the leathery grapplers
air plant
woody rooted, sawtooth wind-slicer
holds fast to slippery bark of Anything!

Fierce, succulent, windworn
Know them! Passionate exhibitionists
     burning, aching high
          violet sweetheart of hummingbirds
broad berried wands of ripening Tropica, all
     hallelujah, still

no pretense to divine. They are great
colonizers
white tufted seeds parachute course
between trees
through curtains of lianas
cling to craggy bark
build gardens, festooning cities.

Bromeliad, out on a limb, civilization
of raw vegetable kingdom generating until all
kingdom, life and limb, crashes to the ground

Frog pond! Serpent house! Stagnant channeled
reservoir! Malaria nursery!
                          Sky Chalice!

Or wedged on rocky sun blast ledge! Or anchored
as forbidding hedge
                     for robbers. Barbed.

Ira Sadoff

Nature

In the old days there were characters
and settings: if you wrote snow
you could see wetness and whiteness
bending twigs of the cherry tree.

How many robins perched on that quince
in the snowstorm? Did the spill of milk
make us ill? And what did that say
about when the ladder fell? Everybody's sick

of naming a few familiar birds and trees
whose dilemmas are just like ours.
If we started out playful and restless,
flooded with all at once, we ended up

married to episodes. But don't give me
the Utopia of Childhood, the moody
little brats, what they extract,
how they suffer: I was a storehouse

of lassitude. I took everything personally,
I was a thumbnail sketch of the universe.
The branches are smarter than we are.
Their contract with stillness is limber

and listless. They bring us the sheen,
not of sparrows, not what we're thinking,
but juniper berries, just how green
they are soon after you clip them.

I've Always Despised the Wetlands

I've always despised the wetlands
and their preserves, the gawky stork-like birds
squawking, standing endlessly on one leg
waiting for trout to leap onto their beaks—

the girth of them, the wingspan,
the smell half-sulphur, half-rotted pine
and something else smeared green
on the sewer pipe. I remember Traviata

on the tin can of a radio, tin cans
on the kitchen counter, a walk-up by the river,
a stench that made your eyes water
by the Dumpsters. Stab wounds on the boulevard.

You tried to break out by mangling
or burying your head in a book. Because patter
is terrible, being sunny, walking away
from a subject when shrieks cry out.

And sometimes you can't get a word in,
you don't want to forget, you want to straighten out
the sentence you've been given. I remember
a nest half-buried in a cedar. With an eyedropper

we fed the broken wren. A shoebox
would have been the right repository
for a voice on the edge of "terror," but only
a thin rope of words girded our neighborhood:

they were deficient little deficits, the signs
for Sanctuary and Refuge just beyond the fence,
where scattered birdcalls from a world
complete without us flourished, reminding me

how in snapshots Callas rose shining and waving
from the black limo, all ermine and pearls:
how she screened her lips when she threw fans kisses,
how wings are always attached to the singing.

Benjamin Alire Sáenz

To the Desert

I came to you one rainless August night.
You taught me how to live without the rain.
You are thirst and thirst is all I know.
You are sand, wind, sun, and burning sky,
The hottest blue. You blow a breeze and brand
Your breath into my mouth. You reach—then *bend*
Your force, to break, blow, burn, and make me new.
You wrap your name tight around my ribs
And keep me warm. I was born for you.
Above, below, by you, by you surrounded.
I wake to you at dawn. Never break your
Knot. Reach, rise, blow. *Sálvame, mi dios,*
Trágame, mi tierra. Salva, traga. Break me,
I am bread. I will be the water for your thirst.

Craig Santos Perez

from all with ocean views

    'put on the map by

exciting

    new hotels' 'towns lit   with traditional

                              lanterns' 'the

                 resilience of its

    inhabitants is | hypnotic | spectacles' 'evry-

        one speaks English and | evryone | knows the low cost of

                       dying'

'guåhan is unveiling
new guam visitors bureau brand 'i am guam' at sheraton laguna resort to
attract visitors we can no longer depend on location we must earn tour-
ism business a brand is an emotional connection to destination rooted in
making our brand differentiation more competitive rapid growing tourism
markets japan korea east asia we bring this brand to life making guam
great place live work play marketing guam enhanced if we on guam fix
ourselves we must root 'i am guam' brand to local culture historic back-
ground shaped us what we are as destination

    update: 'i am guam' doesn't belong to guam visitors bureau phrase
    registered trademark by 'shades of paradise' both parties say efforts
    are complementary anxious to work together

ginen aerial roots

[gui'eng : waterlines—
the lines of our palms—skin
chart to read blood currents—saina,
why have you given me these lines
do your palms mirror
mine, do the lines of your hull

    because this

        [hígadu : is what we carry
        to live in the memory
        of those who don't see us—
        in our own—

is remembered we went to hagåtña boat basin—small canoe—no outrigger—
no sail—the five of us—mr flores in another canoe alongside counting "hacha
hugua tulu fatfat lima"—we repeat—we paddle—the current—our bodies
aligned—row—in the apparent wind—past the breakwater—past the reef—

[aga'ga' : what we inherit
what is passed from
contours the lines
of the sakman

    as [riñón : the saltwind trades
    in things unknown and unpredictable—
    even without the names of the stars in chamorro—
    even when we lost
    contact—it will never be too dark
    for us to see—

hunggan hunggan hunggan magahet

from preterrain

     i didn't know 'sea level'
         would remind me of 'shelter'
     in the material sheaths of the body the smallest wave pronounces
     'light derives from
     what it touches'
     even though the sun no longer sets no sky
     ever becomes complete
     -ly foreign
          our shadow

     never completely hides
     given the necessities of breath our skin afields
     every physicality
     of light a map
          that exactly covets its territory

from tidelands[8]

     what is our story
     who will listen to these stories
     i have told what stories
     have you listened to will tell those stories
     who said don't tell stories
     what is your story
     who is telling the stories
     i am listening to *is this my story*
     who said what takes place according to story

8 ~~this year, at least 3 other military aircrafts have crashed in or near andersen air force base.~~
~~u.s. colonial presence has not only damaged our bodies of land and water, but it's deteriorated our physical bodies as well. the military used guam as a decontamination site during its nuclear testing in the 1970s, which resulted in massive radiation and agent orange and purple exposure. high incidences of various kinds of cancer and neuro-degenereative diseases, such amyothrophic lateral sclerosis, parkinsonism dementia, and lytico botig plague the chamoru people. toxic chemicals have sneaked into our~~

Tim Seibles

Ambition: Cow & Microphone

There's so much I can't
make a sound for: sunrise
on a hillside   or a cool dusk
bluing a meadow, late June

or better yet, mid-September,
when the first flecks of autumn
begin to walk summer

down from its tall heat.
How can anything living
not love the color light

spends on October –
when the bulls hum
the last unnibbled pasture?

Wonnnderful! Sometimes I think
I could lend my own true music
to that slow farewell:

the daylight bleeding, a whole season
turning away switching its tail   and my voice,
an encyclopedia of lovely noise,

flies open to the first page, and I'm Ella Fitzgerald's
raging treble clef. I'm a four-legged
fluegelhorn, a glad clarinet, the radical ambassador

scatting a voluptuous river of sax,
blowing the rest of the lows
into a dumb herd, while I run the range
of my whole Angus heart:

loneliness – the light   always
    a clear view to death   the prevailing
hands of the powerful   and sweet

    sweet grass – the earth's free bread
grown back   and lately, the knowledge
    that an animal like me   can't be heard

exactly – and all this breaks out of my teeth
    into the bovine world.   My bruised tongue
at last an angel's lash

    driving the stampede and   shouldn't I
be the Pied Piper: my stomachs are full

of rare news and the cruel promise
    of slaughter.   Isn't the other language

underneath this? Isn't there
    one word   that still brands you?

First Verse

I admit the world remains almost beautiful.
The dung beetles snap on their iridescent jackets
despite the canine holiness of the Vatican
and, despite the great predatory surge of industry,
two human hands still mate like butterflies
when buttoning a shirt.
                    Some mornings
I take myself away from the television
and go outside where the only news comes
as fresh air folding over the houses.
And I feel glad for an hour in which race
and power and all the momentum of history
add up to nothing.

As if from all the mad grinding
in my brain, a single blue lily had grown –
my skull open like a lake. I can hear

an insect   sawing itself into what must be
a kind of speech.
                           I know there is little
mercy to be found among us, that we have
already agreed to go down fighting, but
I should be more amazed: look
at the blood   and guess who's holding
the knives. Shouldn't we be *more*
amazed? Doesn't the view
just blister your eyes?

To have come this long way, to stand
on two legs, to be   not tarantulas
or chimpanzees   but soldiers of our own
dim-witted enslavement. To utterly miss the door
to the enchanted palace. To see *myself*
coined into a stutter. To allow the money
to brand us   and the believers
to blindfold our lives.
                           In the name
of what? If that old book was true
the first verse would say   *Embrace*

the world. Be friendly. The forests
are glad you breathe.

I see now
The Earth itself *does* have a face.
If it could say *I* it would
plead with the universe, the way
dinosaurs once growled
at the stars.
                     It's like
the road behind us is stolen
completely   so the future can
never arrive. So, look at this: look
what we've *done.* With all
we knew.
With all we knew
that we knew.

Anthony Seidman

Runoff

There are pollutants above this dog, above us all, and brush fires on the San Fernando foothills; crows perch on telephone cables, crows my dog hears cawing, crows who know the vacant lots where bones of murder victims sink among jimson weed, grass, and the narrow tunnels leading to the ant queen's den and the sinews of this desert. As always, night arrives: this dog looks up, and only a grey darkness, like that of dishwater, night pressing through smog, through clumps of weed and burr, coagulant of night, dulling the heat the way salt and fats slow the nervous ticking of circulation. Dog thinks summer will never end; an ecstasy of sniffing and dozing, and men who sit on the sidewalk drinking beer, sowing the pavement with peanut shells. This dog has fangs chiseled for meat, and irises that dilate; but, at last, night swells, overflows, a sewage-tide of shadow, and both dog and poet will witness hillside and hearth washing away, the way a red taillight throbs in rainfall, diminishes in size, then turns onto a darker street where one can only hear the roar, decrescendo, of the engine.

A Dog's Poetry

My dog can't decipher Wang Wei with his titles encapsulating the river, willows, the long white beards that smell of autumn, and twilights like water kept in a metal pitcher, water turning ochre. And so I read to my dog of the river, the horse whinnying, and the friends saying farewell, but I am a voice reading in an apartment where the hum of air conditioning replaces wind unleashing the plum blossoms. Long ago, Wang Wei, aged yet drunk and desiring a courtesan with her finger-drums and jade brocade, read some of his lines for her scarlet lips, narrow slippers, and hair the color of a crow. Yet the hands of a swordsman who dealt her the gift of a ripe mandrake burned in her thoughts as she feigned interest in Wang Wei's moonlight and discarded silk fan. My dog twists from my recitation, falls back asleep, and in his dream bounds after a squirrel who scampers up a trunk to a bough where the oranges, like that courtesan's breasts, are pendant, ripe, and forbidden.

Martha Serpas

Fais Do-Do

A green heron pulls the sky behind it
like a zipper. Sharp rows

of clouds fold into themselves, erasing
the framed blue tide.

Barrier islands disappear into
the Gulf's gray mouth.

Everywhere something strives to overtake something else:
Grass over a mound of fill dirt, ants over grass,

the rough shading of rust between rows
of sheet metal frustrating the sky.

Boats breast up three deep in every slip,
and, as soon docked, are waved away.

The only music's crickets and lapping,
happy bullfrogs on slick logs.

A rustling skirt of palmettos
around the roots of a modest oak

that appear after hard rain. A fiddle,
or idling motor, moves away.

Go to sleep. God will come
in an extended cab for all of us:

the children, the dogs, the poets.
That old Adversary, the Gulf,

our succoring Mother, having given
everything, will carry the whole of us away.

Eric Paul Shaffer

The Open Secret of the Sea

He uli na ka he'e pūloa.

The octopus is the open secret of the sea. Day is the darkness
        in which he hides, and when I read the reef, floating above
    with sun at my back, he watches with an eye I cannot see.

                The octopus stands atop the coral outcrop, silent, still,
an innocuous knot invisible in the web of hues shifting
    below the surface. With rainbows hidden in his skin, the octopus

    takes the tint of the current, blends with coral and sand spangled
        in sunlight among the black and gold, scarlet and turquoise
of flickering fish. Shaped by the sea, his is the soft body

    and tough skin of the impermanent that tides and current prove
on the shore. Eight-armed and articulate, he is a compass flower
        sauntering the surface below the surface,

    yet with measureless ocean to explore and one sole year,
the octopus seeks a cave with a door the size of a shark's eye
        and slides his rubbery bulk through crevices smaller than he,

    rounding corners no others turn. As clever as a child of Maui,
        the octopus reveals the wisdom of concealment. He fades
into the ultramarine, and only a lure contrived of cowry shell

    and hidden hook draws him from his den, yet curious and clever,
he avoids the fate of becoming board or bait, understanding the hunter
    is always, as well, the hunted. Even caught, landed, and stowed,

    the octopus escapes, as one limber limb slips
from within his prison to twist a latch or lift a lid for a sudden slide
        through the scuppers to the sea. Solitary seeker

beneath the waves, the octopus assumes the character of light,
                seen yet not seen, and teaches the craft and cunning of night,
        for in long, utterly lightless nights under the ocean, he distills

              that darkness into the ink which is his fame and his flight.
Sought and spied hiding in the light, the octopus
        disappears in the drifting cloud of his own shadow.

He uli na ka heʻe pūloa means "ink from the long-headed octopus." In *Ōlelo Noʻeau*, her collection of traditional Hawaiʻian proverbs, Mary Kawena Pukui notes that these words are spoken "of a person clever at getting away with mischief. The ink of the octopus is its camouflage."

Derek Sheffield

A Good Fish

Jerk that bitch, urges my guide,
and I give my shuddering pole
a jerk, hooking the throat
of the first steelhead of my life.
Reel 'em, he mutters and revs the motor.
I horse my pole and reel and horse.
The boat's mascot whines, her claws
clicking. *Let it take some line.*
My father, uncle, and cousin
are reeling. *First fish!* they shout,
and I shout, *What a fighter!*
A silver spine touches the air.
There, he points, *a hen. And guess what?*
She's gonna join the club,
somehow spotting in that glimpse
the smooth place along her back
where a fin had been snipped.
He leans over the gunwale, dips a net,
and scoops her into the boat.
She is thick with a wide band
of fiery scales, slap-
slapping the aluminum bottom.
Welcome to the club, he says,
and clobbers her once, and again,
and once more before she goes still.
A bleeder, he says, shaking his head
and handing her to me. I curl
a finger through a gill the way

you're supposed to, determined
not to let her slip and flop
back to the river, a blunder
I'd never live down. A good fist.
Fish, I mean. A good fish.

Darwin's Eyes

He kept seeing himself, a swallow
peeking from its nest, moss, the crawl
of a wasp across his study window.

And he kept having to drop everything and duck
as certain callers appeared in the mirror
he'd aimed at the front door.

A beak he could understand. A talon
was a hand holding his own. It was the eye,
with its vicious complexity, that stabbed at him—

lightning bolts of doubt,
a cyclopean stare, ten years his *Origin*
stewing in a stack of notes.

And the eye, perhaps, why he went back,
after all was said and begun,
to the worms, spending his last years

watching them as his fingers
wriggled over piano keys, exploring
up the scales and down, concerto

and dirge. His first passion, his final,
those tender needles with their dark impulse
to feel all around them our earth.

Reginald Shepherd

Some Kind of Osiris

"Green" calls green into being,
speaking my skin into color. I am free
of song and sky and live among
beetles and dung, my vast and trivial

brown apartments: earth-like I lie with loam
and undergrowth, a dust of words
in my occasional mouth watered by rain,
torn pages from the book called

Without Wings. Simple metals
capture me, smell of basil, bay leaf,
northern magnolia, every twig and shoot
alloyed with laurel, laureled with mineral

undergrowths. "Without wings
what will you accomplish?"
asks the wind, the wind's accomplices
(birds, or toxic butterflies), and I

fail to reply, my fingers filled
with leaves, mouth with remains
of leaves. The day skilled in italics
declines my nouns of *wait* and *sleep,*

but I walk down into the muddy
ground again, all estivation,
hibernation: wake as season
and oscillation, less a person

than a place, inclined toward
or away from the sun. (I was rain
and rain-tilled fields, and cloudy too.
When is winter nowadays, spring forth.)

Then I remember I am a god, and history
stutters forward, starts again.

Evie Shockley

notes for the early journey

for j.v.k.

somewhere along the way you will need to lean
over a bluff's edge   drop your shoes and keep moving   use
the feel of greening grass under your feet as a guide   if a
rainbow confuses you   which end   go the third
way   on the mountain you'll remember   climb on
up to where the aspens tremble   you will be alone   these
high winds can knife some lungs to gasping rags   but for you

there's nothing to worry about   breathe   sniff the air like
a bloodhound and head the opposite way   find the
place where the land dissolves into sand   keep walking   when
that sand becomes sea   speak a bridge into being
i know you can do it   your father's son ain't
heard of can't   follow the song   don't stop until you're south
of sorrow and all you can smell is jasmine   i never
once stumbled on such a place   hard to say if a brown child
in the last four hundred years has had such
a luscious dream   day or night   but this is your mother's
lullaby   i know she meant you to sleep sweet

atlantis made easy

orange was the color of her address, then blue silt : : whiskey burned
brown down the street, then a dangerous drink whirled around a paper
umbrella : : intoxication blue across the porch then rose in the attic : :
bloated tuesday taught us, she's never been dry and never will be : : brass,
bass, ivory, skins : : i hate to see that ninth ward wall go down : : army

corpse engineers ran a 'train on her : : aw chere : : sweet ghost, saturated, deserted : : teething ground for the expected spectre, we knew it'd show up better late (against a black backdrop), whenever : : wait in the water, wait in the water, children : : stub your soul on a granite memory, a marble key change, an indigo mood : : trouble (the water)

Gary Short

Near the Bravo 20 Bombing Range

I bring the mare a green apple & then we ride
the wrinkled land along the river road
in the slow-turning wheel of the day.
Past the pen of the brown goat with a broken moan,
past the stiff glove thick with dirt
where it has lain on the path since winter,
past the coyote slung over the barbed fence,

its eyes gone to sky—
blue where a black jet angles
high above the stand of aspen, leaves
spinning to coin in the wind's hand.
I ride past the green wave of alfalfa
that grows one sweet inch each day.

Over the next mountain is the range,
public land bombed for thirty-five unauthorized years.
At what point is turning back an option?
The skeleton of a mustang, dreaming its run,
rises slowly back out of dust.

Farther out, the surface of the marsh is sunstruck tin.
The ones who walked here before
walked quietly & believed the green
slick on the pond.
I hear the jet after it is gone.
What remains—a white strand, sheer against the sky,
with the breath of the mare
as she bends to drink
from the still water.

Kevin Simmonds

Sighted

Nature poet handling his plume
Urban poet his switchblade

Each with wings unfolding in their hands

One travels the boned corset of cactus
sky lifting its hoop skirt to a meringue of stars

The other eulogizes children fallen from loveliness   filed
into caskets

Both behold faces turning to see
and be seen

They scatter the broken mirror everywhere

giovanni singleton

caged bird

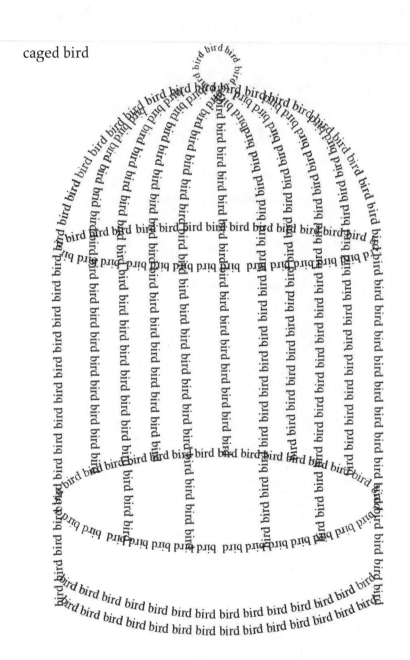

Jonathan Skinner

Birds of the Holy Lands

Jerusalem is just above the thirtieth parallel
about the latitude of Charleston, Montgomery, Jackson

I often listen for the birds of the Holy Lands
sometimes you can hear them
behind the news, between the gunshots
and imagine the dappled shadows
beside the fountain in a courtyard
with olive trees and myrtle bushes

and the peaceful chirping of sparrows
creates a restful space for the mind

I would like to go birding in the Holy Lands
For sparrows alone, there is a great
Biblical tradition—with forty instances
of *tzippor*, Hebraic chirping or twittering
in the Old Testament, and two
strouthion (sparrows) in the New

According to my Bible Dictionary,
"The birds above mentioned are found in
great numbers in Palestine, and are of
very little value, selling for the merest trifle
and are thus strikingly used by our Savior
Matthew 10:29 as an illustration of our Father's
care for his children"

Unfortunately the Authorized Version
renders the Hebrew indifferently
as "bird" or "fowl" ignoring
the great variety, such as—

the Yellow-vented Bulbul, Clamorous Reed Warbler, Crested
Honey Buzzard, Lappet-faced Vulture, Cream-Coloured
Courser, Crowned Sandgrouse, Little Green Bee-eater, Mountain
Chiffchaff, Arabian Babbler, Palestine Sunbird, Isabelline Shrike,
Yellowhammer, Cinereous Bunting

According to Dr. Thomson, the house-sparrows
and field-sparrows of Palestine "are a tame,
troublesome and impertinent generation,
and nestle just where you do not want them

They stop up your stove- and water-pipes with their rubbish,
build in the windows and under the beams of the roof,
and will stuff your hat full of stubble in half a day"

Carnegia Gigantea (remixed)

firecracker penstemon's sad ray
caught between dirt and light, videos
the hedgehog cactus transparents

Firecracker penstemon, with spikes of red
tubular flowers as bright as exploding
firecrackers . . . (Susan Tweit, *The Great
Southwest Nature Factbook* 143)

The first cacti to bloom in spring are small
Echinocereus—hedgehog or strawberry
cacti. (109)

Gila woodpeckers and gilded flickers
excavate nest cavities in the flesh of big
saguaros. The cacti seal off the wound with
thick scar tissue, thereby preventing the
entrance of fatal bacteria. Once vacated by
their builders, the cavities provide homes
for other desert residents: tiny elf owls and
other birds, as well as insects and reptiles.
(154)

pale flesh from home flickers
wearing out the mantle
in waves of long-nosed rabbits

[S]aguaro tissues "supercool" instead of
freezing into crystalline ice at 32° F, allow-
ing them briefly to withstand temperatures
into the 20s. (152)

which invade, propose, retract
saguaros in winter lows cast stones
an idiot's banter to skunks

Although thousands of tiny saguaro
seedlings sprout in a good year, most die
of drought, are gutted by cutworm larvae,
or are mowed down by hungry rodents and
rabbits. (153)

the skeleton a fascicle of rods
in scarlet seed pulps, her cutworm
guts rows of silent swells

Their heavy trunks and thick arms consist
almost entirely of succulent water-storage
tissue, supported by a ring of vertical,
woody ribs. Between each rib a pleat allows
the stem to swell when the saguaro takes
on water, and prevents the waxy outer
skin, or cuticle, from tearing. . . . The cactus
shrinks again as it uses its reservoir in
times of drought. (152)

Ground temperatures can reach 175° in
summer.

painful to nest on the scar boot
locks lava heat, rock-plates, in gum
trails a radiant vector bursts

by the end of the dry season the water
trails . . . are worn to a white ribbon in
the leaning grass, spread out faint and
fanwise toward the homes of gopher and
ground rat and squirrel. But however faint
to man-sight, they are sufficiently plain to
the furred and feathered folk who travel
them. . . . no matter what the maps say,
or your memory, trust them; they know.
(Mary Austin, *The Land of Little Rain* 19)

and July without rain juice
ferments to get wet, all round
the wisest and driest

Saguaro fruits mature in July and burst
open, revealing a scarlet pulp, filled with
tiny black seeds, that is avidly consumed
by bats, birds, rodents, moths, other
insects, and people. Traditional Tohono
O'odham (Papago) and Pima Indians still
harvest the fruit, knocking it to the ground
with long poles and eating the scarlet pulp
either raw or preserved. They ferment the
juice into wine to celebrate the coming of
the summer rains, a time of plenty. (Tweit
153–154)

Papago and Pima to the bat
expand, give ground to seedlings
with long poles—delicious snacks

rows of silent type saguaros
claim a cactus length, squat
with an agile, retractable gun

An elaborate network of ropelike roots just
below the soil surface, that extends out
as far as the trunk is tall, harvests water
within hours after the sporadic desert rains.

The waxy, outer cuticle, thickest on the
south side of the plant, protects the saguaro
from sunburn and slows evaporation of
the precious water inside. The saguaro's
vertical ridges are deeper on the south side
and shade the plant's surface. (152)

and nest in flesh and finches
thickest skinned, shadiest
fruits in July burst open, to dust

Diverting about half of its energy to
reproduction, [the saguaro] sprouts dozens
of knobby buds at the end of its stubby
stem. In May and June, these open at
night, one by one, revealing spectacular
waxy-white flowers. The 3-inch-wide,
funnel-shaped flowers remain open until
the following afternoon, broadcasting a
curious, skunky odor to attract their chosen
partner: the long-nosed bat. Flocks of the
nectar-feeding bats migrate north to the
Sonoran Desert just as the saguaros begin
to bloom and, flying at night, search out
the pollen and nectar-laden flowers. The
bats hover over the saguaro flower while
pushing their entire head into the flower to
sip the nectar. Carrying a golden mantle of
pollen, the bats fly on to fertilize the sticky
stigmas of other flowers. (153)

and wear a bruised mantle of pollen
Phyllostomatidae up to ears
in honey, skunks from the cup

[G]ilded flickers can cut large holes
through the skeletal ribs and cause struc-
tural damage, which can result in the loss
of a branch or branch tip in a windstorm,
exposing the succulent flesh to saguaro rot.
(154)

gets drunk on rain, sometimes
the arm falls and other trysts
between dirt and light, yellow cups

A strong gust of wind may send these
giants crashing to the ground because they
lack a taproot to anchor their bulk firmly.
Lightning during the summer often injures
or kills these tall cacti. (152)

open californica one by one
a pushover, a lightning's blast
hovers from verbena

About every ten years, the rainfall and temperature patterns are just right, and wildflower seeds germinate by the billions. The ground blazes with the tiny yellow, daisylike blooms of goldfields (*Lasthenia californica*) and the brilliant orange desert flowers of goldpoppy (*Escholtzia* species). Magenta spikes of owl clover (*Orthocarpus purpurascens*) and blue-purple lupines (*Lupinus* species) splotch the yellow background, as do fragile pink desert five spots (*Malvastrum* species), magenta sand verbena (*Abronia villosa*), and deep blue-purple larkspur (*Delphinium* species). (118–119)

Charlie Smith

Monadnock

I'd say more about these rocks, but
there're limits to what we can know. You'd
think they oozed up
out of the dirt and how do you care for them
or come to know them in the way you know the community government.
From a distance they look calm. Scuff marks,
striations, frantically clawed areas, sulcations, ricochets
like tiny angels leapt up, depressions following this, muti-
lations, frankly crumbling spots, tiny
smoothed-off areas where makeup goes, notes
of lighter shading, nooks
where the mountain "spoke," half-
healed wounds where forces violently made them stop.
Bucket brigades, little
streams ladled from the top
trickle down. These rocks come up
from inside. The rains bring them out, huddled, close-cropped,
powerfully expressive, and so on, the splashed-with-white mass.
They form a trail. That's what we are talking about.
Ferns, firs, birches to either side. At the top, revelation
which is the point: there's a world beyond yourself.
Here you can see it. The valley, green or white
or red with burning brush
become expensive in your heart. You come up
with difficulty over rocks
and you can see things work like this,
the rocks appear "unchanging" and are obstacles
slow to wear away,
and then the trees loosen their grip, give up,
and you climb among blueberries and mountain grasses,
turn, and look freely out as if you are not imprisoned.
But you are standing on rock.

Patricia Smith

5 P.M., Tuesday, August 23, 2005

"Data from an Air Force reserve unit reconnaissance aircraft . . .
along with observations from the Bahamas and nearby ships . . .
indicate the broad low pressure area over the southeastern
Bahamas has become organized enough to be classified as
tropical depression twelve."
—NATIONAL HURRICANE CENTER

A muted thread of gray light, hovering ocean,
becomes throat, pulls in wriggle, anemone, kelp,
widens with the want of it. I become
a mouth, thrashing hair, an overdone eye. How dare
the water belittle my thirst, treat me as just
another
small
disturbance,

try to feed me
from the bottom of its hand?

I will require praise,
unbridled winds to define my body,
a crime behind my teeth
because

every woman begins as weather,
sips slow thunder, knows her hips. Every woman
harbors a chaos, can

wait for it, straddling a fever.

For now,
I console myself with small furies,
those dips in my dawning system. I pull in
a bored breath. The brine shivers.

Man on the TV Say

Go. He say it simple, gray eyes straight on and watered,
he say it in that machine throat they got.
On the wall behind him, there's a moving picture
of the sky dripping something worse than rain.
Go, he say. Pick up y'all black asses and run.
Leave your house with its splinters and pocked roof,
leave the pork chops drifting in grease and onion,
leave the whining dog, your one good watch,
that purple church hat, the mirrors.
Go. Uh-huh. Like our bodies got wheels and gas,
like at the end of that running there's an open door
with dry and song inside. He act like we supposed
to wrap ourselves in picture frames, shadow boxes,
and bathroom rugs, then walk the freeway, racing
the water. *Get on out.* Can't he see that our bodies
are just our bodies, tied to what we know?
Go. So we'll go. Cause the man say it strong now,
mad like God pointing the way outta Paradise.
Even he got to know our favorite ritual is root,
and that none of us done ever known a horizon,
especially one that cools our dumb running,
whispering urge and constant: *This way. Over here.*

Won't Be But a Minute

Tie Luther B to that cypress. He gon' be all right.
That dog done been rained on before,
he done been here a day or two by hisself before,
and we sho' can't take him. Just leave him
some of that Alpo and plenty of water.
Bowls and bowls of water.
We gon' be back home soon this thing pass over.
Luther B gon' watch the place while we gone.

You heard the man—he said *Go*—and you know
white folks don't warn us 'bout nothing unless
they scared too. We gon' just wait this storm out.
Then we come on back home. Get our dog.

8 A.M., Sunday, August 28, 2005

> Katrina becomes a Category 5 storm, the highest
> possible rating

For days, I've been offered blunt slivers
of larger promises—even flesh,
my sweet recurring dream,
has been tantalizingly dangled before me.
I have crammed my mouth with buildings,
brushed aside skimpy altars,
snapped shut windows to bright shatter
with my fingers. And I've warned them, soft:
You must not know my name.

Could there be other weather,
other divas stalking the cringing country
with insistent eye?
Could there be other rain,
laced with the slick flick of electric
and my own pissed boom? Or could this be

it, finally,
my praise day,
all my fists at once?

Now officially a bitch, I'm confounded by words—
all I've ever been is starving, fluid, and noise.
So I huff a huge sulk, thrust out my chest,
open wide my solo swallowing eye.

You must not know
Scarlet glare fixed on the trembling crescent,
I fly.

Looking for Bodies

I.

Slowly push the door open with your foot
because wood that has been wet for so long
gives to touch, imitates flesh.
Do not kick the door open,
no matter how weirdly your heart drums.
There may be something all wrong behind it.
Push and immediately drown
in what could be ordinary, if ordinary was
a crusted saucepan, toppled rockers,
pine-framed portraits of newly
baptized babies and fathers with an overload of teeth.
Allow yourself his lunatic smile as you spy
signs of ritual and days undone—
bright ghosts of skirts and workshirts,
or the spiraled grace of decapitated dolls
doing their blind dance, bumping your knees.

Eventually you will need these diversions.
You will lock your fractured heart upon them,
because what you will see next
will hurt you long and aloud.
A monstered smell sings her out of hiding,
and at first you believe
that one doll, plumper than the rest
and still intact,
survived the deluge—
but then you—

II.

guide the gold of her into
your arms blessing the droop
and blown skin marveling
at the way her soul rides
slickly on the outside of
everything how it ripples
the water how it so deftly
damns your hands

Gary Snyder

from Hunting

THIS POEM IS FOR BEAR

"As for me I am a child of the god of the mountains."

A bear down under the cliff.
She is eating huckleberries.
They are ripe now
Soon it will snow, and she
Or maybe he, will crawl into a hole
And sleep. You can see
Huckleberries in bearshit if you
Look, this time of year
If I sneak up on the bear
It will grunt and run

The others had all gone down
From the blackberry brambles, but one girl
Spilled her basket, and was picking up her
Berries in the dark.
A tall man stood in the shadow, took her arm,
Led her to his home. He was a bear.
In a house under the mountain
She gave birth to slick dark children
With sharp teeth, and lived in the hollow
Mountain many years.
                    snare a bear: call him out:
honey-eater
forest apple
light-foot
Old man in the fur coat, Bear! come out!
Die of your own choice!
Grandfather black-food!
                    this girl married a bear

Who rules in the mountains, Bear!
                you have eaten many berries
                you have caught many fish
                you have frightened many people
Twelve species north of Mexico
Sucking their paws in the long winter
Tearing the high-strung caches down
Whining, crying, jacking off
(Odysseus was a bear)

Bear-cubs gnawing the soft tits
Teeth gritted, eyes screwed tight
                but she let them.
Til her brothers found the place
Chased her husband up the gorge
Cornered him in the rocks.
Song of the snared bear:
      "Give me my belt.
      "I am near death.
      "I came from the mountain caves
      "At the headwaters,
      "The small streams there
      "Are all dried up.

—I think I'll go hunt bears.
         "hunt bears?
Why shit Snyder,
You couldn't hit a bear in the ass
         with a handful of rice!"

from Burning

THE TEXT

Sourdough mountain called a fire in:
Up Thunder Creek, high on a ridge.
Hiked eighteen hours, finally found
A snag and a hundred feet around on fire:
All afternoon and into night

Digging the fire line
Falling the burning snag
It fanned sparks down like shooting stars
Over the dry woods, starting spot-fires
Flaring in wind up Skagit valley
From the Sound.
Toward morning it rained.
We slept in mud and ashes,
Woke at dawn, the fire was out,
The sky was clear, we saw
The last glimmer of the morning star.

THE MYTH

Fire up Thunder Creek and the mountain—
        Troy's burning!
The cloud mutters
The mountains are your mind.
The woods bristle there,
Dogs barking and children shrieking
Rise from below.
Rain falls for centuries
Soaking the loose rocks in space
Sweet rain, the fire's out
The black snag glistens in the rain
& the last wisp of smoke floats up
Into the absolute cold
Into the spiral whorls of fire
The storms of the Milky Way
"Buddha incense in an empty world"
Black pit cold and light-year
Flame tongue of the dragon
Licks the sun

The sun is but a morning star

Crater Mt. L.O. 1952–Marin-an 1956

Piute Creek

One granite ridge
A tree, would be enough
Or even a rock, a small creek,
A bark shred in a pool.
Hill beyond hill, folded and twisted
Tough trees crammed
In thin stone fractures
A huge moon on it all, is too much.
The mind wanders. A million
Summers, night air still and the rocks
Warm.   Sky over endless mountains.
All the junk that goes with being human
Drops away, hard rock wavers
Even the heavy present seems to fail
This bubble of a heart.
Words and books
Like a small creek off a high ledge
Gone in the dry air.

A clear, attentive mind
Has no meaning but that
Which sees is truly seen.
No one loves rock, yet we are here.
Night chills. A flick
In the moonlight
Slips into Juniper shadow:
Back there unseen
Cold proud eyes
Of Cougar or Coyote
Watch me rise and go.

Milton by Firelight

Piute Creek, August 1955

"O hell, what do mine eyes
    with grief behold?"
Working with an old
Singlejack miner, who can sense
The vein and cleavage
In the very guts of rock, can
Blast granite, build
Switchbacks that last for years
Under the beat of snow, thaw, mule-hooves.
What use, Milton, a silly story
Of our lost general parents,
    eaters of fruit?

The Indian, the chainsaw boy,
And a string of six mules
Came riding down to camp
Hungry for tomatoes and green apples.
Sleeping in saddle-blankets
Under a bright night-sky
Han River slantwise by morning.
Jays squall
Coffee boils

In ten thousand years the Sierras
Will be dry and dead, home of the scorpion.
Ice-scratched slabs and bent trees.
No paradise, no fall,
Only the weathering land
The wheeling sky,
Man, with his Satan
Scouring the chaos of the mind.
Oh Hell!

Fire down
Too dark to read, miles from a road
The bell-mare clangs in the meadow
That packed dirt for a fill-in
Scrambling through loose rocks
On an old trail
All of a summer's day.

Riprap

Lay down these words
Before your mind like rocks.
            placed solid, by hands
In choice of place, set
Before the body of the mind
            in space and time:
Solidity of bark, leaf, or wall
            riprap of things:
Cobble of milky way,
            straying planets,
These poems, people,
            lost ponies with
Dragging saddles
            and rocky sure-foot trails.
The worlds like an endless
            four-dimensional
Game of *Go*.
            ants and pebbles
In the thin loam, each rock a word
            a creek-washed stone
Granite: ingrained
            with torment of fire and weight
Crystal and sediment linked hot
            all change, in thoughts,
As well as things.

For Nothing

Earth a flower
A phlox on the steep
slopes of light
hanging over the vast
solid spaces
small rotten crystals;
salts.

Earth a flower
by a gulf where a raven
flaps by once
a glimmer, a color
forgotten as all
falls away.

A flower
for nothing;
an offer;
no taker;

Snow-trickle, feldspar, dirt.

Burning the Small Dead

burning the small dead
        branches
broke from beneath
    thick spreading
            whitebark pine.

            a hundred summers
snowmelt   rock   and air

hiss in a twisted bough.

sierra granite;
        Mt. Ritter—
          black rock twice as old.

Deneb, Altair

windy fire

Wave

Grooving clam shell
        streakt through marble,
     sweeping down ponderosa pine bark-scale
       rip-cut tree grain
           sand-dunes, lava
             flow

Wave   wife.
       woman—wyfman—
"veiled; vibrating; vague"
  sawtooth ranges pulsing;
           veins on the back of the hand.

Forkt out: birdsfoot-alluvium
        wash

      great dunes rolling
Each inch rippld, every grain a wave.

Leaning against sand cornices til they blow away

    —wind, shake
    stiff thorns of cholla, ocotillo
    sometimes I get stuck in thickets—

Ah, trembling spreading radiating wyf
        racing zebra
  catch me and fling me wide
To the dancing grain of things
        of my mind!

For the Children

The rising hills, the slopes,
of statistics
lie before us.
the steep climb
of everything, going up,
up, as we all
go down.

In the next century
or the one beyond that,
they say,
are valleys, pastures,
we can meet there in peace
if we make it.

To climb these coming crests
one word to you, to
you and your children:

stay together
learn the flowers
go light

Juliana Spahr

from Gentle Now, Don't Add to Heartache

TWO

We came into the world at the edge of a stream.
The stream had no name but it began from a spring and flowed down a
hill into the Scioto that then flowed into the Ohio that then flowed into
the Mississippi that then flowed into the Gulf of Mexico.
The stream was a part of us and we were a part of the stream and we were
thus part of the rivers and thus part of the gulfs and the oceans.
And we began to learn the stream.
We looked under stones for the caddisfly larva and its adhesive.
We counted the creek chub and we counted the slenderhead darter.
We learned to recognize the large, upright, dense, candle-like clusters
of yellowish flowers at the branch ends of the horsechestnut and we
appreciated the feathery gracefulness of the drooping, but upturning,
branchlets of the larch.
We mimicked the catlike meow, the soft quirrt or kwut, and the louder,
grating ratchet calls of the gray catbird.
We put our heads together.
We put our heads together with all these things, with the caddisfly larva,
with the creek chub and the slenderhead darter, with the horsechestnut
and the larch, with the gray catbird.
We put our heads together on a narrow pillow, on a stone, on a narrow
stone pillow, and we talked to each other all day long, because we loved.
We loved the stream.
And we were of the stream.
And we couldn't help this love because we arrived at the bank of the
stream and began breathing and the stream was various and full of
information and it changed our bodies with its rotten with its cold with
its clean with its mucky with fallen leaves with its things that bite the
edges of the skin with its leaves with its sand and dirt with its pungent
at moments with its dry and prickly with its warmth with its mushy and
moist with its hard flat stones on the bottom with its horizon lines of

500

gently rolling hills with its darkness with its dappled light with its cicadas buzz with its trills of birds.

.

FOUR

It was not all long lines of connection and utopia.
It was a brackish stream and it went through the field beside our house.
But we let into our hearts the brackish parts of it also.
Some of it knowingly.
We let in soda cans and we let in cigarette butts and we let in pink tampon applicators and we let in six pack of beer connectors and we let in various other pieces of plastic that would travel through the stream.
And some of it unknowingly.
We let the runoff from agriculture, surface mines, forestry, home wastewater treatment systems, construction sites, urban yards, and roadways into our hearts.
We let chloride, magnesium, sulfate, manganese, iron, nitrite/nitrate, aluminum, suspended solids, zinc, phosphorus, fertilizers, animal wastes, oil, grease, dioxins, heavy metals and lead go through our skin and into our tissues.
We were born at the beginning of these things, at the time of chemicals combining, at the time of stream run off.
These things were a part of us and would become more a part of us but we did not know it yet.
Still we noticed enough to sing a lament.
To sing in lament for whoever lost her elephant ear lost her mountain madtom
and whoever lost her butterfly lost her harelip sucker
and whoever lost her white catspaw lost her rabbitsfoot
and whoever lost her monkeyface lost her speckled chub
and whoever lost her wartyback lost her ebonyshell
and whoever lost her pirate perch lost her ohio pigtoe lost her clubshell.

FIVE

What I did not know as I sang the lament of what was becoming lost and what was already lost was how this loss would happen.
I did not know that I would turn from the stream to each other.

I did not know I would turn to each other.

That I would turn to each other to admire the softness of each other's breast, the folds of each other's elbows, the brightness of each other's eyes, the smoothness of each other's hair, the evenness of each other's teeth, the firm blush of each other's lips, the firm softness of each other's breasts, the fuzz of each other's down, the rich, ripe pungency of each other's smell, all of it, each other's cheeks, legs, neck, roof of mouth, webbing between the fingers, tips of nails and also cuticles, hair on toes, whorls on fingers, skin discolorations.

I turned to each other.

Ensnared, bewildered, I turned to each other and from the stream.

I turned to each other and I began to work for the chemical factory and I began to work for the paper mill and I began to work for the atomic waste disposal plant and I began to work at keeping men in jail.

I turned to each other.

I didn't even say goodbye elephant ear, mountain madtom, butterfly, harelip sucker, white catspaw, rabbitsfoot, monkeyface, speckled chub, wartyback, ebonyshell, pirate perch, ohio pigtoe, clubshell.

. . . .

I put a Streamline Tilt Mirror in my shower and I kept a crystal Serenity Sphere with a Winter Stream view on my dresser.

I didn't even say goodbye elephant ear, mountain madtom, butterfly, harelip sucker, white catspaw, rabbitsfoot, monkeyface, speckled chub, wartyback, ebonyshell, pirate perch, ohio pigtoe, clubshell.

. . . .

I just turned to each other and the body parts of each other suddenly glowed with the beauty and detail that I had found in the stream.

I put my head together on a narrow pillow and talked with each other all night long.

And I did not sing.

I did not sing otototoi; dark, all merged together, oi.

I did not sing groaning words.

I did not sing otototoi; dark, all merged together, oi.

I did not sing groaning words.

I did not sing o wo, wo, wo!

I did not sing I see, I see.

I did not sing wo, wo!

Gerald Stern

Cow Worship

I love the cows best when they are a few feet away
from my dining-room window and my pine floor,
when they reach in to kiss me with their wet
mouths and their white noses.
I love them when they walk over the garbage cans
and across the cellar doors,
over the sidewalk and through the metal chairs
and the birdseed.
—Let me reach out through the thin curtains
and feel the warm air of May.
It is the temperature of the whole galaxy,
all the bright clouds and clusters,
beasts and heroes,
glittering singers and isolated thinkers
at pasture.

One Animal's Life

For Rosalind Pace

This is how I saved one animal's life,
I raised the lid of the stove and lifted the hook
that delicately held the cheese—I think it was bacon—
so there could be goodness and justice under there.
It was a thirty-inch range with the pilot lit
in the center of two small crosses. It was a Wincroft
with a huge oven and two flat splash pans above it.
The four burners were close together, it was
a piece of white joy, from 1940 I'd judge

from the two curved handles, yet not as simple as
my old Slattery, not as sleek. I owe
a lot to the woman who gave me this house, she is
a lover of everything big and small, she moans
for certain flowers and insects, I hear her snuffle
all night sometimes, I hear her groan. She gave me
a bed and a kitchen, she gave me music, I couldn't be
disloyal to her, yet I had to lift
the murderous hook. I'll hear her lectures later
on *my* inconsistencies and hypocrisies;
I'll struggle in the meantime, like everyone else, to make
my way between the stove and refrigerator
without sighing or weeping too much. Mice
are small and ferocious. If I killed one it wouldn't be
with poison or traps. I couldn't just use our weapons
without some compensation. I'd have to be present—
if it was a trap—and hear it crash and lift
the steel myself and look at the small flat nose
or the small crushed head, I'd have to hold the pallet
and drop the body into a bag. I ask
forgiveness of butchers and hunters; I'm starting to talk
to vegetarians now, I'm reading books,
I'm washing my icebox down with soda and lye,
I'm buying chicory, I'm storing beans.
I should have started this thirty years ago,
holding my breath, eating ozone, starving,
sitting there humming, feeling pure and indignant
beside the chewed-up bags and the black droppings.

Susan Stewart

Four Questions Regarding the Dreams of Animals

I. IS IT TRUE THAT THEY DREAM?

It is true, for the spaces of night surround
them with shape and purpose, like a warm hollow below
the shoulders, or between the curve of thigh and belly.
    The land itself can lie like this. Hence
our understanding of giants.
    The wind and the grass cry out to the arms
of their sleep as the shore cries out, and buries
its face in the bruised sea.
    We all have heard barns and fences splintering
against the dark with a weight that is more than wood.
    The stars, too, bear witness. We can read
their tails and claws as we would read the signs of our
own dreams; a knot of sheets, scratches defining the edges
of the body, the position of the legs upon waking.
    The cage and the forest are as helpless in
the night as a pair of open hands holding rain.

2. DO THEY DREAM OF THE PAST OR OF THE FUTURE?

Think of the way a woman who wanders the roads
could step into an empty farmhouse one afternoon and find
a basket of eggs, some unopened letters, the pillowcases
embroidered with initials that once were hers.
    Think of her happiness as she sleeps in the daylilies;
the air is always heaviest at the start of dusk.
    Cows, for example, find each part of themselves
traveling at a different rate of speed. Their bells call back
to their burdened hearts the way a sparrow taunts an old
hawk.

As far as the badger and the owl are concerned,
the past is a silver trout circling in the ice. Each night
he swims through their waking and makes his way back
to the moon.

Clouds file through the dark like prisoners through
an endless yard. Deer are made visible by their hunger.

I could also mention the hopes of common spiders:
a green thread sailing from an infinite spool, a web, a thin nest,
a child dragging a white rope slowly through the sand.

3. DO THEY DREAM OF THIS WORLD OR OF ANOTHER?

The prairie lies open like a vacant eye, blind
to everything but the wind. From the tall grass the sky
is an industrious map that bursts with rivers and cities.
A black hawk waltzes against his clumsy wings, the buzzards
grow bored with the dead.

A screendoor flapping idly on an August afternoon
or a woman fanning herself in church; this is how the tails
of snakes and cats keep time even in sleep.

There are sudden flashes of light to account for.
Alligators, tormented by knots and vines, take these as a sign
of grace. Eagles find solace in the far glow of towns, in the small
yellow bulb a child keeps by his bed. The lightning that scars
the horizon of the meadow is carried in the desperate gaze
of foxes.

Have other skies fallen into this sky? All the evidence
seems to say so.

Conspiracy of air, conspiracy of ice, the silver trout
is thirsty for morning, the prairie dog shivers with sweat. Skeletons
of gulls lie scattered on the dunes, their beaks still parted by
whispering. These are the languages that fall beyond our hearing.

Imagine the way rain falls around a house at night,
invisible to its sleepers. They do not dream of us.

4. HOW CAN WE LEARN MORE?

This is all we will ever know.

The Forest

You should lie down now and remember the forest,
for it is disappearing—
no, the truth is it is gone now
and so what details you can bring back
might have a kind of life.

Not the one you had hoped for, but a life
—you should lie down now and remember the forest—
nonetheless, you might call it "in the forest,"
no the truth is, it is gone now,
starting somewhere near the beginning, that edge,

Or instead the first layer, the place you remember
(not the one you had hoped for, but a life)
as if it were firm, underfoot, for that place is a sea,
nonetheless, you might call it "in the forest,"
which we can never drift above, we were there or we were not,

No surface, skimming. And blank in life, too,
or instead the first layer, the place you remember,
as layers fold in time, black humus there,
as if it were firm, underfoot, for that place is a sea,
like a light left hand descending, always on the same keys.

The flecked birds of the forest sing behind and before
no surface, skimming. And blank in life, too,
sing without a music where there cannot be an order,
as layers fold in time, black humus there,
where wide swatches of light slice between gray trunks,

Where the air has a texture of drying moss,
the flecked birds of the forest sing behind and before:
a musk from the mushrooms and scalloped molds.
They sing without a music where there cannot be an order,
though high in the dry leaves something does fall,

Nothing comes down to us here.
Where the air has a texture of drying moss,
(in that place where I was raised) the forest was tangled,
a musk from the mushrooms and scalloped molds,
tangled with brambles, soft-starred and moving, ferns

And the marred twines of cinquefoil, false strawberry, sumac—
nothing comes down to us here,
stained. A low branch swinging above a brook
in that place where I was raised, the forest was tangled,
and a cave just the width of shoulder blades.

You can understand what I am doing when I think of the entry—
and the marred twines of cinquefoil, false strawberry, sumac—
as a kind of limit. Sometimes I imagine us walking there
(. . . pokeberry, stained. A low branch swinging above a brook)
in a place that is something like a forest.

But perhaps the other kind, where the ground is covered
(you can understand what I am doing when I think of the entry)
by pliant green needles, there below the piney fronds,
a kind of limit. Sometimes I imagine us walking there.
And quickening below lie the sharp brown blades,

The disfiguring blackness, then the bulbed phosphorescence of the roots.
But perhaps the other kind, where the ground is covered,
so strangely alike and yet singular, too, below
the pliant green needles, the piney fronds.
Once we were lost in the forest, *so strangely alike and yet singular, too,*
but the truth is, it is, lost to us now.

Sheryl St. Germain

Midnight Oil

how to speak of it
this thing that doesn't rhyme
or pulse in iambs or move in predictable ways
like lines
or sentences

how to find the syntax
of this thing
that rides the tides
and moves with the tides and under the tides
and through the tides
and has an underbelly so deep and wide
even our most powerful lights
cannot illuminate its full body

this is our soul shadow,
that darkness we cannot own
the form we cannot name

and I can only write about it at night
when my own shadow wakes me, when I can feel
night covering every pore and hair follicle, entering eyes
and ears, entering me like Zeus, a night I don't want
on me or in me, and I dream of giving birth
to a rusty blob of a child who slithers out of me,
out and out and won't stop slithering, growing and darkening,
spreading and pulsing between my legs
darkening into the world

.

what it might feel like to be a turtle, say,
swimming in the only waters you have ever known

swimming because it is the only way you move through the world
to come upon this black bile
a kind of cloying lover

a thing that looks to you
like a jellyfish, so you dive into it and try to eat it
but it covers your fins so they can't move as before
and there is a heaviness on your carapace and head
that wasn't there before, and you are blind
in the waters of your birth

.

When the summers got too hot even for those of us born in New
Orleans, so hot that our ancestors' bones sweated and complained in
their vaults, my father would decide it was time, and the family would
pile into the station wagon and drive down to Grand Isle, where we'd run
along the beach into the Gulf as if into a lover's arms, smash into the salty
waves, swim until the sun went down and we were red as boiled crawfish.

Mother would have made a pungent crab salad, with quarters of crab
marinated in garlic and olive oil, lemon and celery. Sometimes we'd have
boiled shrimp or crabs. The grownups would stay up drinking and playing
cards at night while we slept the sweet sleep of children who don't yet
know what stygian rivers run in their veins. Exhausted from swimming,
hair still damp and smelling like the Gulf, we'd huddle together in the big
bed on the screened porch. The smell and sound of the waves rocked us
to sleep, dreams of pelicans and gulls and flying fish filled our heads and
hearts, and we were content.

On rainy days when we couldn't swim my father taught me how to
play pool in one of the hulking bars that used to front the beach.
The bar's gone now, like the house we stayed in, destroyed by hurricanes
that wipe out
every human-made thing every few years.

.

Oiled Birds, edited from Wikipedia:

*Penetrates plumage, reduces insulating ability, makes birds vulnerable to
temperature fluctuations, less buoyant in water. Impairs bird's abilities to
forage and escape predators. When preening, bird ingests oil that covers*

feathers, causing kidney damage, altered liver function, digestive tract
irritation. Foraging ability is limited. Dehydration, metabolic imbalances.
Bird will probably die unless there is human intervention.

.

I'm looking at an old photo of my brother, right after he got out
of prison. He's twenty, sitting on a beach chair at Grand Isle,
looking gaunt and pale, but smiling.
It was the first place my mother thought to take him
when she feared the grime and shame of that other place
might have tarnished his heart too deeply.

She knew he loved this island, where simple things
like saltwater and clean beaches,
birds and fish, crabs,
might act like containment booms,
keep the demons away.

He'd die a few years later,
his liver polluted with what he thought
would make the world bearable,
and a few years after him
my father would go
from that same staining.

Now, when I look at these beaches I love,
greasy with oil as far as I can see,
when I think of how this island
and its marshes should act like filters,
I think of my father and brother,
I think this is what
their livers must have looked like
as they moved toward the end, darkening,
becoming pebbly with disease, finally
too black with blight
to filter
anything.

.

It's June in Pittsburgh where I live now, hot and muggy,
and it feels like a day my father would've said *let's go.*

.

People don't want to look at the pictures anymore of the birds
and turtles, the fish, the oiled beaches
                                        they want to go on to something else
they don't want to hear about the old fishermen
                        who may never fish again
                                        the ones being trained to clean up instead of fish

                It's an old story, really, how we always dirty what we love,
                        and I'm tired too, have seen way too many pictures
                        of oiled birds and the oiled waters of this dear place

                        and I've heard way too many pundits and politicians
                                and newsmen analyze, blame and predict

                        and jokemen joke:
                                        let's call the Gulf *the Black Sea.*

Dear CNN: even the devil would bore us
if he was on 24 hours a day

there are times we need silence
as much as we need news

or a poem that creates a silence
in us where we can feel again

.

How people from Louisiana have described the oil:

*Brown and vivid orange globs. Tar balls. Thick gobs. Red waves. Deep
stagnant ooze. Clumps of tar. Consistency of latex paint. Sheets of foul-
smelling oil. Patches of oil. Caramel-colored oil. Tide of oil. Red brown oil.
Rainbows of Death. Waves of gooey tar blobs. Bruised internal organs of a
human body. Heavy heavy slickoil. Oil sheen. Oily stench. Melted chocolate.*

.

An eye for an eye, my father might say,
a tooth for a tooth.

Let's ask those responsible,
and some of those are us

to walk deep out into the waters
of this once beautiful island,
the waters that once teemed with speckled trout,
oysters, shrimp,
let's ask them to walk far out into it,
to swim out with long sweeping strokes,

and then,
when they are thick and covered
with the stuff, when it's in their hair and blinding
them, stopping up their ears and mouths,
when it's sticking to every pore
in their body,

then
let them try to swim back

then
let them try to explain

Laura-Gray Street

An Entangled Bank

—with Darwin and Thoreau

An entangled bank. It is interesting to contemplate
humid June on the skin like wet feathers

in Saran Wrap. Picking the sticky fabric (cotton
blends, polyester, vinyl) from my sweaty legs,

I have to strip myself like a quick jerk
of Band Aid or masking tape from the car seat.

Sun block, lotions, creams stew into an oil
slicking down arms and chest and forehead.

Innumerable little streams overlap and interlace,
one with another, exhibiting a sort of hybrid-, shall we say,

product. Few phenomena give me more delight
than that kind of money in the bank. You and I

are clothed with many kinds of trafficking.
And the world, oh, the world is rank

with early-bird specials twittering amongst
the tax cuts; insect repellents of all varieties

tizzying up the place, and erratic earthworms
thrashing like heavy-metal bangers at

the street curbs. It is interesting to contemplate
the way sand pours off our eroded slopes like lava,

pulled down over the headwaters like balaclavas.
Everyone stays focused on the cash flow, which takes

the forms of the laciniated and imbricated phalluses
of bureaucratic henchmen. Just think of brain coral,

of lung fish, of bowels and all kinds of excrements.
We contrive a system to transport all our runoff

to the treatment plant, where it is treated, well, like shit
and excreted. Piped through entangled banks and spit

back into the watershed. In heavy rains, volume exceeds
capacity and overflows, by design—so interesting

to contemplate—into your neighborhood streams, rivers,
lakes, aquifers, wells. And not only stormwater but also

untreated human and industrial waste and debris,
all running blissfully together as one intoxicated

toxic stream, transformed, converted, wholly
baptized and foaming at the mouth,

like the born again in the parking lot yesterday,
who, bless his heart, collared me when afternoon

had hit its steamiest, when I was unsticking myself
from the car seat. Few phenomena give more delight.

But it's important to stay calm and enjoy the amenities.
There is no end to the heaps of liver, lights, and bowels.

True, what I say is somewhat excrementitious in character,
but isn't it interesting to contemplate the plain liquid idioms

undulating along the ripple marks on the river bottom,
age after age, stratum upon stratum. Even the godless,

and accountants, must recognize the stubborn beauty
of such waves, and how from so simple, so rudimentary

a beginning such hopelessly entangled forms
have been, and are being, brewed.

First Lessons in Beekeeping

Walking into the humming,
he said to me, *Don't be afraid they
can smell your fear.*

I had long hair then, lank on my neck
and shoulders that were halter-bare
and glazed with summer sweat.

    •

Sometimes the house swarms with bees. Finding no exit,
they console themselves with plaster, harvesting
dust in their pollen baskets. A household.

    •

I was drawn to the boy blindly, circumstantially.
He kissed me between rows of tasseled corn.

Led me by the hand to the hill of bee hives.

    •

Sometimes I feel them at my elbow, urging,
or browsing along femur, murmuring
through sternum, lodging
in inner ear.

    •

Because all honey comes from bees.

    •

The orange peels on the table steep
in afternoon light, staining the wood bitter,
dense flesh emptied to formality.

*Old bees they fly off and don't come back.
Fly out to die because flying out and dying is what they do.*

    •

But reports of dead drones cascaded down the hives,
mats of dead bees pooled almost six feet around the hives.

And pollinators that live in hedge rows and woods:
feral, fading.

.

Electric air.

Don't run, he called
as I ran downhill, bucking,
as the bees tangled in my hair drove
their stingers into my scalp and neck.

.

You get enough Nosema cranae, *a colony will die.*
You get enough viruses, the colony will die.
You get enough mites, the colony will die.
Enough exposure to insecticides, enough drought,
enough sudden weather, enough sterile pollen,
enough stupid people, the colony will die.

.

Was it the shampoo—lab-constructed
supermarketed florals—that drew them
so deeply into that curtain?

Then the animal undercurrents—oily fear,
metallic adrenaline—bubbled up,
agitated the room.

.

Sometimes, balled as one body
they careen and swerve, launch
themselves at chinks and chippings,
probing for flaws. A muscular
frustration.

.

Orange seeds in my palm:

I imagine the groves now stranded,
pinpricks of bee hum and sun that burn
when I close my hand.

·

Hold still
Hold still Hold
still Hold still
Hold
still

·

When a bee lands where my hand's still
sticky with juice, I will myself to relax,
to breathe calmly and focus on observing this
infinitely interesting living thing.

·

No almonds, cherries, peaches, apples,
avocados, blueberries, cranberries, sunflowers,
cantaloupes, watermelon, cucumbers, oranges.

Only planks and dry wall.

·

Then I give way to instinct.

·

I can still taste that first kiss
of bees in my hair.

If I could have walked
calmly with them from there to here.

Arthur Sze

The Angle of Reflection Equals the Angle of Incidence

Take that and that and that and that and—

a kid repeatedly kicks a dog near where
raw sewage gurgles onto sand at low tide,

Málaga, 1971. A man rummaging in a ravine
of trash is scrunched by a bulldozer.

If only I had q or r or s dissolves

into floaters in her eyes. Simmer. Scattered
ashes on blue-black Atlantic waves bob

and tinkle in the rippling tide of morning.
How quickly at dawn one makes out power lines,

cloud, fence, blue awning, orchard, plank

over ditch, but twisting chimney smoke
incites one to mark white apple blossoms

by a low gate, whale bones in a backyard,
chile roasting in a parking lot, or the memory

of wrapping an exposed pipe, the sizzle

when our tongues meet. When dead leaves
flowed downstream and encountered a sword,

they were razored in two. One, two,
four, eight: surmise a molten sword has

32,768 pounded layers before a final hissing.

Who believes what is written will never perish?
In 1258 Mongols hurled books into the Tigris

River and dyed the waters black with ink.
Although a first record tabulating sheep and goats

has disappeared from a museum, the notation is

never expunged but is always renewed, amplified,
transmogrified. When a woman gives you a sheet

of handmade magnolia paper with mica flecks,
you lift it up to light, a milk snake's

translucent skin slides off. Though a strand

of silk unfurls to become a kilometer long,
tracks are not the only incubator of dreams.

So you missed the Eta Aquarid meteor shower,
or last week's total lunar eclipse. When you

sweep cobwebs out of the fireplace, sneeze,

scrutinize the veins of a peony leaf, you mark
the vertiginous moment of your beginning,

catch and release what you cannot hold,
smell kumquats in a glass bowl, stare down

at hundreds of red ants simultaneously fanning

out and converging at a point of emergence.
After a motorcycle blares past the north window,

the silence accretes: a rose quartz crystal
in the night. I garner the aroma of seared

scallops on a bamboo skewer; the ashes of

the woman who savored them scattered on waves.
Can watermelon seeds germinate in this moonlight?

The hairbrush, soap, thermometer by the sink
form a moment's figure that dissolves

as easily as an untied knot. A plumber fluent

in Sanskrit corrects my pronunciation of *dhyāna*,
while he replaces a chrome faucet fixture.

I pore over a cross-sectional drawing of a plum;
is an infinitesimal seed at the cross-

sectional center of the cosmos? Though a vibrating

crystal can measure increments, time itself
is a black thread. I arrive at a vernal cusp:

the murmur you make on the tide of sleep;
the sleighlike sounds when we caress.

Who waits and waits at a feeder for yesterday's

indigo bunting to arrive? A woman curls grape
roots into a sculpture, mentions her husband

died three years ago. We do not shut the eyelids
of the deceased, nor are we tied in quinine-soaked

sheets for delineating the truth. Once you begin,

the branching is endless: miller moths spiral
against a screened porch; we apprehend the shadows

of leaves on leaves, regard a goldfinch
feeding outside a window, a sparrow that keeps

flinging itself into glass. When a minute stillness

is sifted out of the noise, a whirlpool becomes
a spiral galaxy. When I run my tongue along

your clavicle, we dig clamshells out of the sand,
net red crabs at low tide. In the wren song

of brief rain, what matters is that we instill

the darkness with jade, live clear-eyed incising
a peony-blossoming dawn. And as someone trans-

plants bell peppers and onions into a garden,
leaves on a stream approach another sword

but, when they are about to touch, are repelled.

Quinoa simmers in a pot; the aroma of cilantro
on swordfish; the cusp of spring when you

lean your head on my shoulder. Orange crocuses
in the backyard form a line. *Once* is a scorched site;

we stoop in the grass, finger twelve keys with

interconnected rings on a swiveling yin-yang coin,
dangle them from the gate, but no one claims them.

Our meandering intersects with the vanished
in ways we do not comprehend: as a primary cord

may consist of two-ply two-color s-plied cords

joined by z spiraling single-colored simple cord:
I note the creaking cottonwood branch overhead;

moon below Venus in morning twilight; in our arms
one season effloresces into another into another.

The polar ice caps of Mars advance and retreat

with their seasons. Sometimes in gazing afar,
we locate ourselves. We were swimming in a river

below a sloping waterfall; I recalled wandering
away from the main peony garden and pausing

in front of blue poppies. To recollect is to

renew, invigorate, regenerate. A papyrus shoot
spikes out of a copper tub. *Hang glider, sludge,*

pixel, rhinoceros horn, comb, columbarium,
wide-angle, spastic, Leica lens, pincushion—

these have no through-line except that all

things becoming and unbecoming become part
of the floe. When I stare at a photograph

and count two hundred sixty-five hazelnuts,
examine the irregular cracks in their shells,

I recognize the fractures in turtle plastrons,

glimpse the divinatory nature of language.
And as a lantern undulating on the surface

of a black pool is not the lantern itself,
so these synapsed words are not the things

themselves, but, sizzling, point the way.

Nathaniel Tarn

from Ins and Outs of the Forest Rivers

in memoriam, S., activist

Les rivières sont des chemins qui marchent et qui portent où
l'on veut aller.
—PASCAL

It is not certain that the speaker is the hero for it may be he
who listens.
—"THE HEROES AT KAPIT, 1815," MS.

Famished for the totality,
forever, still, again,
sampling yet another part,
moving out once more
toward the expected
but unknown flag
high on a mountain top
at this extremity of the tropic world.
Car to the airport late, friend
nervous and uncommunicative,
bookstore phone line down,
credit card therefore useless,
not a nickel left in cash, bank
a.t.m. machine swallows my card,
bird-watching book not acquired.
A poor beginning.
The plane is at the gate
a thousand steps away in this
crazy airport—the gun jumped
by this country once again
into a "higher" stage of "progress."
Weather is foggy, hazy, masks

an undertow begging to be revealed.
A seabed waits for you,
has waited since time began.
History enters the present
like a river into the sea.
This may well surprise you
but today is the day that you die

In the interests of solitude
that the void might conjure up a world,
nothing to be left at your back
from which any recall could proceed,
the river to run unimpeded into any sea
it might choose to drown in, the forest
to spring upward into its canopy,
the line between earth and sky
uninterrupted, with passage to and fro:
all the high birds in their sprung freedom
eating of fruit ripened by heaven

Entrance into the forest. In trance. At start
everything slithers, first of all two feet,
inadequately shod, on slimy roots and branches,
everything drips, face drips, the right
side neck gland drips high in the nape,
the forehead into eyes, chin drips, nose, cheek,
hat itself drips—only gods know how—you stand
there watering the earth as if it were a garden.
Noise of the insects, a noise eternal
which never stops for birth or death
as bugs relay their sound through centuries.
Ditto the calls of birds—but "bird"
itself remains invisible high in the canopy,
will not come down for drowning man to glimpse.
A leaf will drop: no, it is not bird,
a movement here or there: it is a butterfly:
the butterflies in forest surrender to the eye
but the bird not: prefers to place a leaf
over its face and say "Cuckoo! Yes, I *am*
bird—but *you* will never read me!"
And finally the unexamined lives of all

these trees so much alive and yet so
silent, these also you can see with all their
parasites, exuding life with generosity
unparalleled in all the kingdoms. A single
giant especially, *dypterocarp*, couple of hundred
feet up into sky, its crown a jewel
of that ceiling in which, I'll swear to it,
all my birds are hiding. Trunk I cannot
embrace, diameter continuing so far
beyond my hands—and yet I wish I could,
more than a grandfather, so awe-inspiring
are reach and fretted bark. And then the silence
underneath the noise, refusing to allow
the planet a green death, the accidental scenes
of the two-legged animals slaving and slavering
to bite this treasure down with their steel teeth

Every time you move to the forest's edge
you meet it sooner. Forest encircles
you like a bride's corset (made up of silver
hoops among these tribes). Forest will choke
you if you move carelessly, without
extremes of circumspection. The animals look
haunted: they run into each other far too often.
Birds find overmuch to feed on in the canopy.
They fly in circles, caged by the borders
imposed by bulldozers and other noise-makers.
It is the vastness of the forest over-shrunk.
Note, one pointed out, of all these surrounding
mountains only that small part over there
about a tenth, is free of cutting—and now
they've got concessions for that tenth and
even villages sink into their maelstrom,
because of having to give up their choicest trees,
the ground infertile and unhallowed,
their fields unable now to raise the rice

                 .

Sometimes it is my pleasure to become
obsessed with one of many subjects: this

time the predicate is "bird." I slither through
an unknown land with a methodical thirst
for a knowledge which will quench the desire
and cause it to desist. Leeches drain flush of
blood runs crimson down my legs and arms
while small thought-strokes from time to time
destroy what can't be bird in mind—which
is to say destroys all things that are not forest.
This purification will also satisfy the apes
astride the branches quietly in trees like
ripened fruit about to fall, the tails sometimes
hanging straight down, bell cords to pull—
unknown to them the trees themselves
they sit on will very soon be cut
for a few hours of heat or light as far away
as death is near to forest. "Up close and personal"
they call this thirst to know completion of the
catalogue before the very last of trees collapses
so that we are aware of what we've lost
we that have not achieved full-scale humanity

Trapped in pervading stench of old ideas,
trapped in repetitive paralyzed projects,
trapped by the magistrates who never move
on cases dusty for decades, and by police
who police nothing but the new owners' acres
they took from those who grew the land
and are now homeless. The forest drips
a thousand years of water from every tip
of every branch mourning its lords, much
as the rocks in the high caves drip greater spans
of time to reach aspiring stalagmites. If this
were blood, the whole land would run red.
Trapped in the monologues of ancient stories,
invisible birds and heroes sound their songs
but no one's there to hear them. My own ears
age—day by day I can hear less of birds
who sing the tribal sorrows for lack of poets.
All fades to elegy. Deadened by repetition,

I try to hear the words in birdsong, attempt,
by swallowing remnants of beauty, not to lose hope.
Colleague ends up by whistling like a bird

.

The forest's heart explodes,
its green blood foams in the arteries
returning to the sea through a thousand
mountain walls of green untouched as yet.
Cascades of flowers several stories up,
beginning in the canopy and ending
in the river, the only signature of red.
Everything in heart's world explodes
as well, only the sapphire kingfisher
pierces the cataracts of emerald blood,
avoids a drenching, moves to further fish.
In a boat that tips at the breath of a
dragonfly, keeping the body tense through
the endless hours, the corpse is taken
back to base and all blood ends in water. It is
the bird unseen takes a spent heart to ocean

.

Think now as if the forest's parts were clouds
meshing with each other, some dark, some
light, or lighter. The green mass has the name
duration: one tree replacing another and never
falling but of its own accord and in obedience
to the common law. Nothing despoiled,
nothing torn down, nothing cut in its very life,
leaving its blood over the jungle floor.
Clouds billowing but contained in the mass
although some, like balloons, could seem to
take off—if looked at long and hard enough.
Up there in the walls, on invisible paths,
leeches immeasurably patient below leaves,
bodies gyrating to warmth of mammal flesh
And, at the end, the forest closes in
on itself, and stops to admire itself, and
rests. Astounded at its own beauty

it gives assent to the planet
that it should continue, that it should
survive and its ark of creatures also.
This is where the birds
have become color
against a relentless green.
Across the mass of tints
white undulation headed with black,
Terpsiphone a! paradisi,
deserves the appellation heaven.
In the middle of the scene
the vast river hushes too, rapt in its
rapids, its bridal veils of water,
creating a sound recognized as distance.
Far from the world of corporations
in murderous contention, the forest wonders
how men will last. Sun falls on leaves
a blessing lighting their myriad veins: it is
as if the air itself were sung with joy
in the temperate heat of earliest morning:
day is as light as a young hero, not
yet weighing on banks in suffocation

At the back of all buildings in the cities
mocking parameters of "progress"
forest walls rise in abundance and from
the walls hang the great war cloths
along whose strands the race depends.
All beings once woven into the cloths,
all beings compete there for air to breathe
and food with which to tamp their hunger.
The early patterns are the most complex
with the hooks on which creation hangs,
all hangs together in a famous peace
between the warring tribes of the great currents,
set many years before in a red-dye bath:
back when an emperor lost out at Waterloo.
This archaic image of the golden births
which the tribe looks back to as its hair
tears from the hooks holding the heads

in place: enemy heads ferociously parted
from neighbor bodies, together with
its own vivid catastrophes. But heads
are not taken anymore—only the honors won
by suffocating those who are too poor
to eat their forest any longer, die in the ghastly
cities, imbecile jobs. The stench of sewers open
for all to smell and drop into with both feet clawing
as they fall from the great cloths of their lives

Conjunction of forest and sea
dark crimson dragonfly linking the two
stitching together landscapes of the mind
where we have seen before, head above
clouds, landscapes remembered from another
life, remembered by each other. Too much
diversity hiding the forest's own
behind a mask of sameness. I won't
say "previous," would rather claim
some simultaneous lives running parallel,
with trigger hairs from time to time
between them. Steadfastly birds
refuse to manifest: they fly the gardens
far below this perch. I climbed this
mountain by mistake on a bitch trail.
No matter for my mind is so replete with birds,
so fabulous a kingdom of the upper sky
cannot be abdicated for a bunch of facts,
a bunch of species ticked off in a book:
I am content behind these empty eyes.
The dragonfly has left for the far mountain
opposite, the beach's other shore. I shall
go down as well, my time goes down
the joyous sky and drinks drink up each
other. I am as thirsty at this water as if this
were my desert. The sun begets a second star

What if this butterfly
is the color of sky and night
and this one of the sea and night
and this one in the sun's blaze

at midnight on the alternate side
of world—night being the high color
of wing and day being the low?
I should have been a butterfly-watcher
for they are out in the open
with their delicate touches of paint
in the midst of horror—whereas
the birds now, the birds alas . . .
Butterflies are more direct
with their shorter spans more patient,
read out to me in wavering lines
brief life and its annihilation.
Whereas the birds move on and on,
pierce the sky like arrows, never seem to fall.
Their death is a quiet one in the deep forest
as the death of the forest is not quiet:
the towering trees fall over and over.
One dusk, as the light went down over the river,
the one bird I had dreamed of seeing and despaired
of ever seeing as the days went by, finally
Lord *Buceros* himself, prince of forest and sky,
bird of the river gods and gods of fallen heads,
dropped out of the sky and covered a tree
and seemed as large as the tree, covering it entirely.
It was still possible to glimpse the colors of the head
and know it for itself. Although this bright darkness
preceded the death, a death mourned by its fellows,
warrior-bird was known: for me, a death redeemed

> *Lem Baa Bario Asal, Pa Umor; Sungai Kinabatangan, Sabah; Miri,*
> *Mulu, Uma Bawang, Batang Baram; Long Lunyim, Sungai Pelutan;*
> *Sibu, Kapit, Kai Wong/Pala Wong, Batang Rajang; Kuching,*
> *Kubah, Bako, Sungai Santubong/Sungai Sarawak, 2005*

Susan Terris

No Golden Fish Were Harmed in the Making of This Poem

Let the landscape be white and flat far as the eye can see.
Let the seas be ink agitated by unseen monsters
and the golden fish expelled to gasp yet dazzle on the shore.
Let the wings overhead be long-feathered,
while all the black and white and burnished creatures
of sea and land and sky
whisper their songs, unlock the Babel of their tongues,
offer up steps to the sun dance, ghost dance, the dance for
fishes and loaves and manna, for radiant poppies and tulips.
Let the albatross make their nests on the sand
and the golden fish walk together from the margin
with new knowledge of the meaning of light and air.

Jeffrey Thomson

from Celestial Emporium of Benevolent Knowledge

In "The Analytical Language of John Wilkins," Jorge Luis Borges describes a Chinese Encyclopedia, in which it is written that all plants and animals may be divided into:

I. THOSE THAT BELONG TO THE EMPEROR

A cat sweeping dawn into the corners
of the City. Pheasants with black heads
and necks squared in crimson that warble
and cluck when tossed grain. Sable antelope
clacking their horns among willow branches
by the river. Trumpet vine, heliotrope, the red
bird of paradise. Flies spinning above sliced
melon. Ten thousand rhododendrons and
the green writhing of dahlias. Globe-eyed carp
among saucers of hyacinth. The dragon
of morning and evening. Gibbons and
the orangutan that haunts the trees beyond
the terrace. Hornbills and buntings.
The raffish pose of the frill-necked lizard.
Mackerel and tuna stacked on ice. Mandrills
like clowns. Three stags and a decomposing body
laid out on a slab. Binturong. Bromeliad.
Clownfish and anemones. Five thousand butterflies
and one lepidopterist. A family of yak.
Tiger lilies with their mouths full of bees.
The clouded leopard that hunts mice and frightens
the horses. Cattle. Roses and the spring litter
of cherry trees. Cattails, irises, the emerald heads
of pintail ducks. Anything the heart desires:
A bat in a cage without a door. Tiny elephants
and the lizards that hunt them. Glass frogs,

their visible hearts hammering through their skin.
Lungfish. Spiders the size of books. A handful
of stones and two eggs of unknown origin.

.

6. STRAY DOGS

gather behind the zoo
  to test the fence
and run the antelope,
  skittish the gazelles,
and scatter the dawning
  flamingos. In the morning
small bleating sheep
  shy from the carcass
of their own, entrails
  running bloody ribbons
along the corn and sawdust
  floor. A pronghorn's
haunch glazed with flies
  half buried in the leaves,
but the dogs are long gone,
  hiding, bramble-tied,
curled in sleep, the day
  rotten with light,
as the sun piles up the sky.

.

10. SUCKLING PIGS

This encyclopedia of articulate nothing,
taxonomy of damage, library of sand.
Manuscript of clouds, archipelago of crabs
in a wash of seafoam. I could write anything—
a pack of pigs sucking at the blank canvas
of the sow's belly—and you'd believe it.

.

14. THOSE THAT LOOK LIKE FLIES FROM A DISTANCE

Start simply—
             the dead snag filled
with white herons near Caño Blanco,
the muscular press of clouds above,
the colonnade a plane slices into
and the sudden smallness of the plane
seen from the ground, farmers
looking up from their fields of aloe,
the plants like rows of jade octopi
and the pearl buttons on their shirts
iridescent as flies. A bottle hive
of paper wasps hanging from
the middle story treetops along
the road to San Isidro becomes
the eye of a gazelle gone gauzy and fly-
charmed on the hot savannah below
a hillside glossy with wildebeest.
Pink dolphins roiling blackwater
as they herd tucunare within the flooded
forest turn to squadrons of toucans
streaming through back-lit kapoks,
long-tendriled lianas, the silver-edged
leaves of the winter's bark trees
school in the wet air like herring.
Plankton bloom in the cold upwelling
of the Chukchi Sea. Shrimp feed
so delicately on the plankton
and sand eels gorge on the shrimp.
I close the book where I have been writing
all day; the unused pages fall whitely
over the City. *What have you learned?*
The words churn, a mob of bitterns
thrash about the corpse of a marten,
hagfish writhe on a gray whale one mile
down as leaf-cutter ants dismember
a nearby *guanacaste* and moths punish
the porchlight. Shoals of starlings
awash in a mackerel sky, small as
the rain that comes on in the distance.

Melissa Tuckey

Refrain

A cricket in the closet is the closest
I've come to home I leave
the windows open nothing comes inside

Late night birds carry the weight
of war I wake with
alarm instead of love

I tell you now I admit it
I'm jealous horses die and you bury
them you know their names

Chase Twichell

City Animals

Just before the tunnel, the train
lurches through a landscape
snatched from a dream. Flame blurts

from high up on the skeletal refinery,
all pipes and tanks. Then a tail of smoke.

The winter twilight looks like fire, too,

smeared above the bleached grasses
of the marsh, and in the shards of water

where an egret the color of newspaper
holds perfectly still, like a small angel

come to study what's wrong with the world.

In the blond reeds, a cat picks her way
from tire to oil drum,

hunting in the petrochemical stink.

Row of nipples, row of sharp ribs.
no fish in the iridescence.
Maybe a sick pigeon, or a mouse.

Across the Hudson,
Manhattan's black geometry begins to spark

as the smut of evening rises in the streets.

Somewhere in it,
a woman in fur with a plastic bag in her hand
follows a dachshund in a purple sweater,

letting him sniff a small square of dirt
studded with cigarette butts.
And in the park, a scarred Doberman

drags on his choke chain toward another fight,

but his master yanks him back.
It's like the Buddhist vision of the beasts
in their temporary afterlife, each creature

locked in its own cell of misery,
the horse pulling always uphill
with its terrible load, the whip

flicking bits of skin from its back,
the cornered bear woofing with fear,

the fox's mouth red from the leg in the trap.

Animal islands, without comfort between them.
Which shall inherit the earth?

Not the interlocking kittens frozen in the trash.

Not the dog yapping itself to death
on the twentieth floor. And not the egret,
fishing in the feculent marsh

for the condom and the drowned gun.

No, the earth belongs to the spirits
that haunt the air above the sewer grates,

the dark plumes trailing the highway's
diesel moan, the multitudes
pouring from the smokestacks of the citadel

into the gaseous ocean overhead.

Where will the angel rest itself?
What map will guide it home?

Pamela Uschuk

Snow Goose Migration at Tule Lake

Iris-eyed dawn and the slow blind buffalo of fog
shoulders along flat turned fields.
We hear the bassoon a cappella
before air stutters

        to the quake that wheels.

Then the thermonuclear flash of snow geese,
    huge white confetti,

        storm and tor of black tipped wings
          across Shasta's silk peak,
            the bulging half moon.

There are thousands. Now
    no stutter but ululations
      striking as the riot of white water.
Wave on wave breaks
over us.   V
      after V interlock, weave
        like tango dancers to dip and rise
          as their voices hammer
silver jewelry in our hearts. These multitudes
      drown every sound, stop
        every twenty-first century complaint.

Snow geese unform us.
Fluid our hands, our arms, legs,
      our hearts. What more do we ever need?
Than these songs
      cold and pure as Arctic-bladed warriors
      circling the lake's mercuric eye.

Snake graceful in the sky, snow geese wail
                    through sunrise like tribal women
                              into funeral flames.
Sun rouges their feathers
            as they rise
                        hosannahward, dragging us
stunned by the alchemy of their clamour.

And we think
how it must have been each season
for eight hundred years while Modocs harvested wild rice
                    blessed by the plenty of wings
                    on the plenty of water
before slaughter moved in with the settlers.
The few Modoc survivors were exiled to Oklahoma
to make way for potato farms
                        that even now poison the soil
and drain Tule Lake.

In this month of wild plum blossoms, we would pretend
it is the early world.
            Snow geese migrate through sky wide
as memory. Their wild choirs lift us
            beyond the dischords of smoking fields and tractors
to light struck white, to our own forgotten wings
and ungovernable shine.

Jean Valentine

The Badlands Said

I am the skull
under your hundred doubts. I, I
will be with you always.
Heart's-deprive.
Still numinous and alive.
Elephant's side.

Come lie down,
tooth and bone.

Ya, ya,
from a mile high
I crook you up warm,
rabbit-arm.

I am love's sorrow,
the desert's violet needle and gray star.

The River at Wolf

Coming east we left the animals
pelican beaver osprey muskrat and snake
their hair and skin and feathers
their eyes in the dark: red and green.
Your finger drawing my mouth.

Blessed are they who remember
that what they now have they once longed for.

A day a year ago last summer
God filled me with himself, like gold, inside,
deeper inside than marrow.

This close to God this close to you:
walking into the river at Wolf with
the animals. The snake's
green skin, lit from inside. Our second life.   .

Rain

Snakes of water and light in the window
snakes that shrug out of their skins and follow
pushing a path with their heads full of light
—heavy trembling mercury headlights—
leaving trails of clear glass, and rocks,
nests where they half live, half sleep,
above ground:
Snake where do you come from?
who leave your grass path
and follow me wordless
into our glass
water and light house,
earth wet on your mouth,
you the ground of my underground.

Ellen Bryant Voigt

Chameleon

beside myself in Texas the doctors asking my beloved
to give his pain a number one to ten his answer is always
two I tell them eight the holly bush in the yard is putting out new leaves
which makes its resident lizard bright green also light brown
along its slender spine a plausible twig
except the lining of its mouth is red as it puts away
in three quick bites some kind of fly and then at its throat
a rosy translucent sac swells and subsides maybe peristaltic
pushing its meal forward or maybe preening for a mate or maybe
residual from the blooming hibiscus shrub or maybe learned from frogs
that also live in a tree but singing is dangerous if you mean
to replicate vegetation
                              o exquisite creature
whose dull cousin back in Vermont the brown lizard
navigates our dooryard by alternating pairs of elbows like oars
determined and clumsy moving across the gravel yet moving forward
I see you do not move unless you need to eat you almost fool
the mockingbird nearby in a live oak tree flinging out another's song
which is me which which is me

Cow

end of the day daylight subsiding into the trees lights coming on
in the milking barns as somewhere out in the yard some ants
are tucking in their aphids for the night behind
hydrangea leaves or in their stanchions underground
they have been bred for it the smaller brain

serving the larger brain the cows eat so we will eat we guarantee
digestion is the only work they do heads down tails up
they won't have sex they get some grain some salt
no catamounts no wolves we fertilize the fields
we put up bales of hay we give them names

but again this week one breached the fence the neighbors
stopped to shoo it back a girl held out a handful of grass
calling the cow as you would a dog no dice so what
if she recoiled to see me burst from the house with an axe
I held it by the blade I tapped with the handle where the steaks come from

like the one I serve my friend a water sign who likes to lurk
in the plural solitude of Zen retreat to calm his mind but when it's done
what he needs I think is something truly free of mind a slab of earth
by way of cow by way of fire the surface charred the juices
running pink and red on the white plate

Gyorgyi Voros

Forest Orison

Whoever spoke to me first—
rock, wind, bird, or fir—whoever broke
the membrane of silence
(I watched its tatters waft like
rags of albumen in water),
whoever made my skin skin, not
air, not fur, not sand, not fiber,
whoever uprooted me from the soil
of nothing, whacked breath into me,
unleashed my voice, I ask you now:
Come back.

I know you're there. I see
your hoofprints in muck, your
signature in torn tree bark, hear
your rowdy scuffle as I walk by.
The leaves sway. Where you've nested
the pressed grass cups form without
substance. Smack in my path
your scat sings its small joke:
blackness riddled with seed and sign.

I've heard you breathing softly,
snuffling to smell my smell,
moving near and ever away.
Your tail has flicked fire on the path
before me, your shape assembled
from deep within the patterned trees,
then come apart. In the rain
of acorns, in sifting grass,
in the brisk sigh of ice on the river,

I've heard your voices.
When I call, you answer with
a whoosh and shut of air,
and ringing silence.
I ask again and will again:
Come back.

Frank X. Walker

Canning Memories

Indian summer Saturday mornings
meant project door screens sat open
waiting for the vegetable truck

No new moons or first frosts
just the horn on an old flatbed
trumpeting the harvest

No almanac announcement, no ads
just a short black farmer in overalls
and mud-caked boots

Grandmothers who still clicked
their tongues, who called up the sound
of a tractor at daybreak
the perfume of fresh turned earth
and the secret location of the best
blackberry patch
like they were remembering
old lovers, planted themselves
a squint away from palming
and weighing potatoes
string beans, kale, turnips, sweet corn
onions and cabbage

They seeded themselves
close enough to see each other
bent low in the fields, pulling weeds
dispensing verbal insecticide
gingham dresses gathered in front
cradling cucumbers and Big Boy tomatoes
destined for kitchen windowsills
and mason jars

They break sacred ground far away
from these acres of red brick
and concrete neighbors
close enough to the earth
to know
    if all city folk plant iz family 'n friends
    alls dey gonna gets iz funerals

Emily Warn

Ox Herding Lesson

The road bends away
     from the sea,
          meandering
through salt meadow hay.
You walk along singing
     on the road of white sand
          dug from the marsh,
the sea a hushed roar in the distance
where the forge of waves
          levels the sand,
spilling its molten silver
     at the sandpipers' feet
          who scurry, jotting it all down.

Just ahead of you on the road
is an egret, perfectly still,
     perfectly white
and shaped like a lamed,
the only letter with its top
          in the clouds,
the only letter that leans
     like marsh grass,
one eye cocked on ditch water,
          the other on clouds—
               white feathers,
                    aloft yet earthbound.

The egret is dwarfed by salt marsh,
which stretches far, far
               away,
a wind-flattened white sea of grass

with islands of scraggly myrtles
                              rising
from it. And dwarf cedars whose outer needles burn
                    to protect the living sap.

Egrets can stand so still among reeds
                    that fish mistake their legs for grass.
Why then is this one in the road
              when ditches on either side teem
                          with minnows?

You sit down on hot gravel to ask
                          and hear
the egret listening to you
          pierce and swallow
                    the atmosphere of fishes and clouds.

Rosanna Warren

Man in Stream

You stand in the brook, mud smearing
your forearms, a bloodied mosquito on your brow,
your yellow T-shirt dampened to your chest
as the current flees between your legs,
amber, verdigris, unraveling
today's story, last night's travail . . .

You stare at the father beaver, eye to eye,
but he outstares you—you who trespass in his world,
who have, however unwilling, yanked out his fort,
stick by tooth-gnarled, mud-clabbered stick,
though you whistle vespers to the wood thrush
and trace flame-flicker in the grain of yellow birch.

Death outpaces us. Upended roots
of fallen trees still cling to moss-furred granite.
Lichen smolders on wood-rot, fungus trails in wisps.
I wanted a day with cracks, to let the godlight in.
The forest is always a nocturne, but it gleams,
the birch tree tosses its change from palm to palm,

and we who unmake are ourselves unmade
if we know, if only we know
how to give ourselves in this untendered light.

Eliot Weinberger

The Stars

The stars: what are they?   They are chunks of ice reflecting the sun;   they are lights afloat on the waters beyond the transparent dome;   they are nails nailed to the sky;   they are holes in the great curtain between us and the sea of light;   they are holes in the hard shell that protects us from the inferno beyond;

they are the daughters of the sun;   they are the messengers of the gods;   they are shaped like wheels and are condensations of air with flames roaring through the spaces between the spokes;   they sit in little chairs;

they are strewn across the sky;   they run errands for lovers;   they are composed of atoms that fall through the void and entangle with one another;   they are the souls of dead babies turned into flowers in the sky;

they are birds whose feathers are on fire;   they impregnate the mothers of great men;   they are the shining concentrations of spirit-breath, made from the residues left over from the creation of the sun and moon;

they portend war, death, famine, plague, good and bad harvests, the birth of kings;   they regulate the prices of salt and fish;   they are the seeds of all the creatures on earth;   they are the flock of the moon, scattered across the sky like sheep in a meadow, and she leads them to pasture;   they are spheres of crystal and their movement creates a music in the sky;   they are fixed and we are moving;   we are fixed and they are moving;

they are the seal-hunters who have lost their way;

they are the footprints of Vishnu, striding across the sky;   they are the lights of the palaces where the spirits live;   they are of different sizes;   they are funeral candles, and to dream of them is to dream of death;

they are, like all matter, made of four kinds of matter: protons, neutrons, electrons, neutrinos;   they are all the same size but some are closer to us;   they interact through four forces: gravity, electromagnetism, the strong and weak nuclear forces;   they are the only gods and the sun is the chief among them;   they are the ostrich hunters, out all night, and at dawn they huddle near the sun to get warm, which is why you cannot see them;

dew and frost fall from the stars;   winds, warm and cold, come from the stars;   stars fall from heaven into a maiden's lap;   they are the embers of the fire of creation;   they never change;   they are the white tents where the Star People live;   they are the countless eyes of Varuna, who rides across the sky on Makara, who is half bird and half crocodile, or half antelope and half fish;   they are in a state of constant flux;   sacrifices must be made to them to bring rain;   they are the Never Vanishing, in the form of swallows feeding on the fruit of the Tree of Immortality that grows on the island in the Lake of the Green Falcon;   they glisten, twinkle, sparkle, flash;   they are delightful;   they are portents of evil;   they are the eyes of Thjasse flung into the sky by Thor;   they are the white ants in the anthill built around the motionless Dhurva, who meditates for eternity deep in the forest;   they are a kind of celestial cheese churned into light;   they are, they simply are;   the stars are an enormous garden, and if we do not live long enough to witness their germination, blooming, foliage, fecundity, fading, withering, and corruption, there are so many specimens that every stage is before our view;   we and all the stars we see are just one atom in an infinite ensemble: a cosmic archipelago;   the sky is like a millstone turning, with the stars like ants walking on it in the opposite direction;   the sky is like the canopy of a carriage, with the stars strung like beads across it;   the sky is a solid orb and the stars the perpetual illumination of the volcanoes upon it;   the sky is solid lapis lazuli, flecked with pyrite, which are the stars;   each star has a name and a secret name;   the only word we hear from them is their light;   men will never compass in their conceptions the whole of the stars;   under a starry sky on a clear night, the hidden power of knowing speaks a language with no name;

goodness and love flow down from them;   if we were not located in a galaxy we would see no stars at all;   if gravity were not so weak, the stars would be smaller, and if the stars were smaller they wouldn't burn for very long, and if they didn't burn for very long we wouldn't be here; they have no chance or random element, no erratic or pointless movement;   evil and misfortune flow down from them;   their existence is improbable;   their infinitude propels us to count them;   their wondrous regularity is beyond belief and proof of the divine intelligence that resides within them;   the eternal silence of those infinite spaces is frightening;   the more the universe seems comprehensible, the more it also seems pointless;

all stars move and shine in order to be most fully what they are—light gives light because it is its nature;   acquaintance with the stars is essential to an understanding of the poets;   if the stars did not radiate light they would explode;   souls after death inhabit the stars—the blaze of a new star might therefore indicate that the soul of a great man, or woman, had reached its destination;   'disaster' connotes 'astrally unfortunate';

the only explanation why there are so many stars we cannot see is that the Lord created them for other creatures, further out, to admire at a nearer distance;   we are the center of the material universe but at the perimeter of the spiritual universe and we are doomed to watch the spectacle of the celestial dance from afar;   unlike the other animals, man was made to stand erect so that he could gaze at the stars;   King Arthur is up there, waiting for his return to rule England again;   K'uei is there, the brilliant scholar born with a hideous face;   up there is the Manger, the Mist, the Little Cloud, the Beehive;

look: the Tower of Babel and the Felicity of Tents; up there are highway robbers, and doves bringing ambrosia to the gods, and the twin horsemen of the dawn;   up there the daughter of the wind, mourning for her husband lost at sea;   the Strong River is there, and the Palace of the Five Emperors, the Kennel of the Barking Dogs, the

Straw Road, the Birds' Way, the Snake River of Sparkling Dust;   up there are the nymphs who mourn their brother Hyas, killed by a wild boar, and whose tears are shooting stars;   there are the Seven Portuguese Towers, the Boiling Sea, the Place Where One Bows Down; look: the Ostriches Leaving and the Ostriches Returning and the Two Ostriches who are friends;   Cassiopeia, Queen of Ethiopia, who thought she was more beautiful than the Nereids, is there, and her hapless daughter Andromeda, and Perseus who rescued her with the head of Medusa swinging from his belt, and the monster, Cetus, he slew, and the winged horse Pegasus he rode;   there is the bull who plows the Furrow of Heaven;   up there is the Hand Stained with Henna, the Lake of Fullness, the Empty Bridge, the Egyptian X;   and once there was a girl who married a bear and her father and brothers were so horrified they killed the bear and then she herself turned into a bear and killed her parents and chased her brothers over the mountains and through the streams and cornered them in a tree until the youngest aimed his magic bow high and each brother held on to an arrow and was shot into the sky and turned into a star up there;   up there;   up there is the Butcher's Shop, the Easy Chair, the Broken Platter, the Rotten Melon, the Light of Heaven;   Hans the Wagoner, who gave Jesus a ride, is there, and the lion who fell from the moon in the form of a meteor;   up there, once a year, ten thousand magpies form a bridge so that the Weaving Girl can cross the River of Light to meet the Oxherding Boy; there are the braids of Queen Berenice, who sacrificed her hair to assure her husband's safety;   up there is a ship that never reaches safe harbor, and the Whisperer, the Weeping One, the Illuminator of the Great City, and look: the General of the Wind;   the Emperor Mu Wang and his charioteer Tsao Fu, who went in search of the peaches of the Western Paradise, are there;   the beautiful Callisto, doomed by Juno's jealousy, and the goddess Marichi who drives her chariot led by wild boars through the sky;   there are the Sea Goat, the Danish Elephant, the Long Blue Cloud-Eating Shark, and the White-Bone-Snake;   up there is Theodosius turned into a star and the head of John the Baptist turned into a star and Li Po's breath, a star his poems make brighter;   there are the Two Gates, one through which the souls descend when they are ready to enter human bodies, and the other through which they rise at death;   there a puma springs on its prey, and a Yellow Dragon climbs the Steps of Heaven;

up there is the Literary Woman, the Frigid Maiden, the Moist Daughters, and the Head of the Woman in Chains;

there is the Thirsty Camel, the Camel Striving to Get to Pasture, and the Camel Pasturing Freely;   there the Crown of Thorns or the crown that Bacchus gave Ariadne as a wedding gift;   look: the Horse's Navel, the Lion's Liver, the Balls of the Bear;   there is Rohni, the Red Deer, so beautiful that the moon, though he had twenty-seven wives, loved her alone;   up there the Announcer of Invasion on the Border, the Child of the Waters, the Pile of Bricks, the Exaltation of Piled-Up Corpses, the Excessively Minute, the Dry Lake, the Sacks of Coals, the Three Guardians of the Heir Apparent, the Tower of Wonders, the Overturned Chair;   up there is a cloud of dust kicked up by a buffalo, and the steamy breath of the elephant that lies in the waters that surround the earth, and the muddy water churned by a turtle swimming across the sky;   up there is the broken circle that is a chipped dish, or a boomerang, or the opening of the cave where the Great Bear sleeps; up there the two donkeys whose braying made such a racket they frightened away the giants and were rewarded with a place in the sky;   there is the Star of a Thousand Colors, the Hand of Justice, the Plain and Even Way; there is the Double Double;   there the Roadside Inn;   there the State Umbrella;   there the Shepherd's Hut   there the Vulture;   look: the Winnowing Fan; there the Growing Small;   there the Court of God; there the Quail's Fire;   there St. Peter's Ship and the Star of the Sea;   there: look: up there: the stars.

Joel Weishaus

Bamboo

Slim green, tough-rooted clumps
blossom amid dead yellow stumps

For homes, fences, booby traps,
blow guns, stretchers, so many
uses and makes a fine flute too.

Sung Chung-wen used red in painting bamboo,
Ch'eng T'ang used purple, Chieh Ch'u-Chung
painted bamboo in the snow.

This information may not be found in books.

Lesley Wheeler

The Petroglyphs at Puakō

The first time earth spoke to me it said,
Get out. The message began at the trailhead,
where indignant quail scattered. Scrubby trees,
thorns flexed, guarded the silence from tourists
and golfers by the beach. I walked over cold
lava, through a kiawe forest, its wet black
boughs tangled over the path, toward a field
of petroglyphs. Halfway down, I followed
a spur to the sagging mouth of a cave
and heard its warnings with my whole
body. At the base of one trunk, a waterfall
of bees muttered. I did not touch the glyph:
one man standing on broken rock,
his chest wide with drawn breath.

A cowboy imported long-thorned kiawe
To the islands just two hundred years ago.
I found it later on the federal noxious weed list.
I emerged from the trees onto a reddish plain,
Signs etched over older signs: women
giving birth, families grouped together.
Mainlanders trampled the marks, mused
on the dicey weather. As I read them reading,
the sudden rain washed down on us like years
of attention diffused into a single low verb.

Touch this page. The letters began in a brain's
ropy pāhoehoe, pecked into the stone's chance
flow, but their gorges erode through each iteration:
pen scraped on paper, scaly printer ink,
a book's smooth leaf. Some shapes are sacred,
some run messages, but all can vanish,
erased by eruption, rainstorm, footstep.

C. K. Williams

Tar

The first morning of Three Mile Island: those first disquieting, uncertain, mystifying hours.

All morning a crew of workmen have been tearing the old decrepit roof off our building,

and all morning, trying to distract myself, I've been wandering out to watch them

as they hack away the leaden layers of asbestos paper and disassemble the disintegrating drains.

After half a night of listening to the news, wondering how to know a hundred miles downwind

if and when to make a run for it and where, then a coming bolt awake at seven

when the roofers we've been waiting for since winter sent their ladders shrieking up our wall,

we still know less than nothing: the utility company continues making little of the accident,

the slick federal spokesmen still have their evasions in some semblance of order.

Surely we suspect now we're being lied to, but in the meantime, there are the roofers,

setting winch-frames, sledging rounds of tar apart, and there I am, on the curb across, gawking.

I never realized what brutal work it is, how matter-of-factly and harrowingly dangerous.

The ladders flex and quiver, things skid from the edge, the materials are bulky and recalcitrant.

When the rusty, antique nails are levered out, their heads pull off; the underroofing crumbles.

Even the battered little furnace, roaring along as patient as a donkey, chokes and clogs,

a dense, malignant smoke shoots up, and someone has to fiddle with a cock, then hammer it,

before the gush and stench will deintensify, the dark, Dantean broth
    wearily subside.
In its crucible, the stuff looks bland, like licorice, spill it, though, on
    your boots or coveralls,
it sears, and everything is permeated with it, the furnace gunked with
    burst and half-burst bubbles,
the men themselves so completely slashed and mucked they seem almost
    from another realm, like trolls.
When they take their break, they leave their brooms standing at attention
    in the asphalt pails,
work gloves clinging like Br'er Rabbit to the bitten shafts, and they slouch
    along the precipitous lip,
the enormous sky behind them, the heavy noontime air alive with shim-
    mers and mirages.

Sometime in the afternoon I had to go inside: the advent of our vigil was
    upon us.
However much we didn't want to, however little we would do about it,
    we'd understood:
we were going to perish of all this, if not now, then soon, if not soon,
    then someday.
Someday, some final generation, hysterically aswarm beneath an at-
    mosphere as unrelenting as rock,
would rue us all, anathematize our earthly comforts, curse our surfeits
    and submissions.
I think I know, though I might rather not, why my roofers stay so clear
    to me and why the rest,
the terror of that time, the reflexive disbelief and distancing, all we should
    hold on to, dims so.
I remember the president in his absurd protective booties, looking
    absolutely unafraid, the fool.
I remember a woman on the front page glaring across the misty Sus-
    quehanna at those looming stacks.
But, more vividly, the men, silvered with glitter from the shingles, cling-
    ing like starlings beneath the eaves.
Even the leftover carats of tar in the gutter, so black they seemed to suck
    the light out of the air.
By nightfall kids had come across them: every sidewalk on the block was
    scribbled with obscenities and hearts.

Blackbird

There was nothing I could have done—
a flurry of blackbirds burst
from the weeds at the edge of a field
and one veered out into my wheel
and went under. I had a moment
to hope he'd emerge as sometimes
they will from beneath the back
of the car and fly off,
but I saw him behind on the roadbed,
the shadowless sail of a wing
lifted vainly from the clumsy
bundle of matter he'd become.

There was nothing I could have done,
though perhaps I was distracted:
I'd been listening to news of the war,
hearing that what we'd suspected
were lies had proved to be lies,
that many were dying for those lies,
but as usual now, it wouldn't matter.
I'd been thinking of Lincoln's
" . . . You can't fool all of the people
all of the time . . . ," how I once
took comfort from the hope and trust
it implied, but no longer.

I had to slow down now,
a tractor hauling a load of hay
was approaching on the narrow lane.
The farmer and I gave way and waved:
the high-piled bales swayed
menacingly over my head but held.
Out in the harvested fields,
already disked and raw,
more blackbirds, uncountable
clouds of them, rose, held
for an instant, then broke,
scattered as though by a gale.

Canal

The almost deliciously ill, dank, dark algae on the stone of its sides,
the putrid richness of its flow which spontaneously brings forth refuse,
dead fish, crusts, condoms, all slowly surging in its muck of gruel,
under the tonnage of winter sky which darkens everything still more,
soils the trash, fruit, paper, dead leaves, water, impossibly still more.

Yet trudging, freezing, along beside it, I seem taken by it, to be of it,
its shape, its ooze; in the biting wind it and I make one single thing,
this murky, glass-hard lid with gulls fixed in it lifting and falling,
this dulled sheet, dense as darkness, winding by indifferent buildings,
we compose a single entity, a unity, not as fanciful speculation

but as though one actually might be the sentient mind of something,
as though only watching this indolent swell would bring into me
all that ever touched it, went across, perished and dissolved in it,
all caught lymph-like in this mortal trench, this ark, this cognizance;
a craving spirit flung across it, a tranquil stillness within it.

Not Soul

Not soul,
not that tired tale anyway about preliterate
people believing cameras would extract
their spiritual essence, nothing so obvious,

but what is it I feel has been stripped,
stolen, negated, when I look out across
this valley of old farms, mist, trees,
a narrow, steep-banked brook,

and have the thought take me that all this
is a kind of reservation, a museum,
of land, plants, houses, even people—
a woman now, crossing a field—

that it all endures only by the happenstance
of no one having decided to "develop" it,
bring in a highway from the turnpike,
construct subdivisions, parking lots, malls?

Not soul,
soul is what religions believed subsumes
experience and will, what philosophers
surmised compels us to beauty and virtue,

is what even the most skeptical still save
for any resolving description of inner life,
this intricately knotted compound
which resists any less ambiguous locution.

How imagine so purely human a term
applying to things, to the rushing brook
which follows the slant of soil beneath it,
the mist functioned by the warmth of air,

even the houses to be torn down or crowded
into anonymity according to patterns
which have no discernible logic, certainly
nothing one mind might consider sufficient?

Not soul,
but still, anthropomorphism or not,
the very shape and hue and texture of reality,
the sheen of surface, depth of shadow,

seem unfocused now, hollowed out,
as though the pact between ourselves and world
that lets the world stand for more than itself
were violated, so that everything I see,

the lowering clouds, the tempered light,
and even all I only bring to mind, is dulled,
despoiled, as though consciousness no longer
could distill such truths within itself,

as though a gel of sadness had been interposed
between me and so much loveliness
so much at risk, as though a tear
had ineradicably fixed upon the eye.

Susan Settlemyre Williams

Johnny Appleseed Contemplates Heaven

> Swedenborgian doctrine, which holds that everything here on
> Earth corresponds directly to something in the afterlife, might
> explain the strange and wonderful ways Chapman conducted
> himself in nature.
>
> —MICHAEL POLLAN, *THE BOTANY OF DESIRE*

The Angel Chapman with His sacks of seed. How like
to me? I sometimes wonder, feedsack
shirt? Cooking pot for headgear?
His feet are bare.

Who told thee that thou wast naked?

(For crushing a worm, I've made John's earthly sole to suffer
mortification of flesh, cast off its shoe leather.)

*I will put enmity between thee and the woman, and between thy seed and
her seed; it shall bruise thy head, and thou shalt bruise his heel.*

There is in Heaven one thing & on Earth
its counterpart,

And the Lord God planted a garden eastward in Eden

that we may know the Lord's Ways.

*and out of the ground made the Lord God to grow
every tree that is pleasant to the sight, and good for food.*

Thus, the Celestial orchards, their bees,

*And the Lord God took the man, and put him into the garden
of Eden to dress it and to keep it*

the Sower more Beautiful than Ohio John,

the tree of life also in the midst of the garden, and the tree
of knowledge of good and evil

as the fruit and the Heavenly worms are more, and the blossoms a Perfection
of Eternal transience. Seraphs like wasps cluster
the windfalls   *Of every tree in the garden thou mayest freely eat*

        already flowing with Honey of ferment. Desire

And when the woman saw that it was . . . a tree to be desired
to make one wise, she took of the fruit thereof, and did eat

which is There the yearning for God & drunkenness

I will make mine arrows drunk with blood, and my sword shall devour flesh.

the Knowledge. *I will hide my face from them.* For Paradise

Behold the man is become as one of us, to know
good and evil: and now, lest he put forth his hand and take
also of the tree of life, and eat, and live for ever

                    your
earthly Apple-John eats of the Fruit, seeking its Stars.

In the day that thou eatest thereof thou shalt surely die.

I scatter my sackfuls along the Ohio, for the Flood

and a river went out of Eden to water the Garden

of cider running out of Eden. For Revelation, Lord.

C. D. Wright

Song of the Gourd

In gardening I continued to sit on my side of the car: to drive whenever possible at the usual level of distraction: in gardening I shat nails glass contaminated dirt and threw up on the new shoots: in gardening I learned to praise things I had dreaded: I pushed the hair out of my face: I felt less responsible for one man's death one woman's long-term isolation: my bones softened: in gardening I lost nickels and ring settings I uncovered buttons and marbles: I lay half the worm aside and sought the rest: I sought myself in the bucket and wondered why I came into being in the first place: in gardening I turned away from the television and went around smelling of offal the inedible parts of the chicken: in gardening I said excelsior: in gardening I required no company I had to forgive my own failure to perceive how things were: I went out barelegged at dusk and dug and dug and dug: I hit rock my ovaries softened: in gardening I was protean as in no other realm before or since: I longed to torch my old belongings and belch a little flame of satisfaction: in gardening I longed to stroll farther into soundlessness: I could almost forget what happened many swift years ago in arkansas: I felt like a god from down under: chthonian: in gardening I thought this is it body and soul I am home at last: excelsior: praise the grass: in gardening I fled the fold that supported the war: only in gardening could I stop shrieking: stop: stop the slaughter: only in gardening could I press my ear to the ground to hear my soul let out an unyielding noise: my lines softened: I turned the water onto the joy-filled boychild: only in gardening did I feel fit to partake to go on trembling in the last light: I confess the abject urge to weed your beds while the bittersweet overwhelmed my daylilies: I summoned the courage to grin: I climbed the hill with my bucket and slept like a dipper in the cool of your body: besotted with growth: shot through by green

from Deepstep Come Shining

First visual memory; one of vagrant white splotches in a clearing, a fat, diapered baby in a field of timothy chasing another diapered bottom through the timothy. Last visual memory: one of vagrant white splotches in a clearing, a fat, diapered baby in a field of timothy chasing another diapered bottom through the timothy. When it's mowed, and the fodder's fresh. I remember. I was there. No other features vex the view: Not the barn, the Gold Bond Medicated Powder sign fading from its highway plane. The black dog tearing after us. (*Night*, the black lab, the family's ecstatic.) The specific lighting from the sky never impinged upon the eye. Not individualized rocks. Split-rail fencing edged with fleabane. The proximity of a neglected pitchfork. Never never never . . .

Early every evening she sits on the steps of her trailer. The dirt yard raked. Caterpillar fording the furrows. Mercy, Louise. If it wasn't hot hot hot. Cornlight. Eyes drink the color and are refreshed. Images seen but not interpreted. Thanks to her lovely twin trees the water she drew was cool. Cool the water she drank from the pump.

When the aim is to feel wholeness itself. She laid her hand on the deeply furrowed bark, groping for the area of darkest color. The trunks would be painted with a palette. Solids would develop from the center outward. Avoiding any kind of line. The body pressed against the trunk until she were certain of being extinguished by the darkness. One achieves a concealed drawing. Which is most like night.

First the light sinks to shadows. The shadows become flooded with broad washes of dark. Watch. As the dark comes entirely into its own. Watch. The light being eaten. Devoured. Sonorous certainty of the dark. What sets the hangers in a closet singing in unison. The light murdered, that the truth become apparent.

from One Big Self

My Dear Affluent Reader,

Welcome to the Pecanland Mall. Sadly, the pecan grove had to be dozed to build it. Home Depot razed another grove. There is just the one grove left and the creeper and the ivy have blunted its sun. The uglification of your landscape is all but concluded. We are driving around the shorn suburb of your intelligence, the photographer and her factotum. Later we'll walk in the shadows of South Grand. They say, in the heyday of natural gas, there were houses with hinges of gold. They say so. We are gaining on the cancerous alley of our death. Which, when all is said or unsaid, done or left undone, shriven or unforgiven, this business of dying, is our most commonly held goal.

Ready or not. 0 exceptions.

Don't ask.

.

Dear Dying Town,

The food is cheap; the squirrels are black; the box factories have all moved offshore; the light reproaches us, and our coffee is watered down, but we have an offer from the Feds to make nerve gas; the tribe is lobbying hard for another casino; the bids are out to attract a nuclear dump; and there's talk of a supermax—

In the descending order of your feelings

Please identify your concerns

P.S.: Remember Susanville, where Restore the Night Sky has become the town cry.

Charles Wright

Hardin County

CPW, 1904–1972

There are birds that are parts of speech, bones
That are suns in the quick earth.
There are ice floes that die of cold.
There are rivers with many doors, and names
That pull their thread from their own skins.
Your grief was something like this.

Or self-pity, I might add, as you did
When you were afraid to sleep,
And not sleep, afraid to touch your bare palm;
Afraid of the wooden dog, the rose
Bleating beside your nightstand; afraid
Of the slur in the May wind.

It wasn't always like that, not in those first years
When the moon went on without its waters,
When the cores blew out of their graves in Hardin County.
How useless it is to cry out, to try
And track that light, now
Reduced to a grain of salt in the salt snow.

I want the dirt to go loose, the east wind
To pivot and fold like a string.
I want the pencil to eat its words,
The star to be sucked through its black hole.
And everything stays the same,
Locks unpicked, shavings unswept on the stone floor.

The grass reissues its green music; the leaves
Of the sassafras tree take it and pass it on;
The sunlight scatters its small change.

The dew falls, the birds smudge on their limbs.
And, over Oak Hill, the clouds, those mansions of nothingness,
Keep to their own appointments, and hurry by.

Rural Route

The stars come out to graze, wild-eyed in the new dark.
The dead squeeze close together,
Strung out like a seam of coal through the raw earth.
I smell its fragrance, I touch its velvet walls.

The willow lets down her hooks.
On the holly leaves, the smears of light
Retrench and repeat their alphabet,
That slow code. The boxwood leans out to take it on,

Quicker, but still unbroken.
Inside the house, in one room, a twelve-year-old
Looks at his face on the windowpane, a face
Once mine, the same twitch to the eye.

The willow flashes her hooks.
I step closer. Azalea branches and box snags
Drag at my pants leg, twenty-six years gone by.
I enter the wedge of light.

And the face stays on the window, the eyes unchanged.
It still looks in, still unaware of the willow, the boxwood
Or any light on any leaf. Or me.
Somewhere a tire squeals, somewhere a door is shut twice.

And what it sees is what it has always seen:
Stuffed birds on a desk top, a deer head
On the wall, and all the small things we used once
To push the twelve rings of the night back.

How silly! And still they call us
Across the decades, fog horns,
Not destinations; outposts of things to avoid, reefs
To steer clear of, pockets of great abandon.

I back off, and the face stays.
I leave the back yard, and the front yard, and the face stays.
I am back on the West Coast, in my studio,
My wife and my son asleep, and the face stays.

Snow

If we, as we are, are dust, and dust, as it will, rises,
Then we will rise, and recongregate
In the wind, in the cloud, and be their issue,

Things in a fall in a world of fall, and slip
Through the spiked branches and snapped joints of the evergreens,
White ants, white ants and the little ribs.

After Reading Tu Fu, I Go Outside to the Dwarf Orchard

East of me, west of me, full summer.
How deeper than elsewhere the dusk is in your own yard.
Birds fly back and forth across the lawn
                                        looking for home

As night drifts up like a little boat.

Day after day, I become of less use to myself.
Like this mockingbird,
                        I flit from one thing to the next.
What do I have to look forward to at fifty-four?
Tomorrow is dark.
                Day-after-tomorrow is darker still.

The sky dogs are whimpering.
Fireflies are dragging the hush of evening
                                up from the damp grass.
Into the world's tumult, into the chaos of every day,
Go quietly, quietly.

William Wright

from Chernobyl Eclogue

DAY

Guards nod our white van toward Pripyat's yellow prairie, where
refusniks hunker in robin's-egg-blue sheds. Peat-smoke
coughs from chimneys. "That smoke makes
plutonium," I say, and Sasha answers
"*Da*," almost too soft to hear.

Sasha is contaminated. We ride to his district,
the tall grasses iridescent, swath of weak sun
peeling more than bark from birch. "It's the little
things," he says, though the forest
that's overtaken the carnival,

bleached of color, first catches my eyes. I know I won't
remember this: It's the sort of forgetfulness
the day demands: Sky's milky iris
dragging the afternoon, light
like a snapped bone.

Strontium roots deeper in his teeth when he speaks.
Licks his lips: "Old mother will say: 'We've survived
two bouts of starvation, and now
something invisible will kill us?
We'll stay here.'"

In the middle distance, her husband steps out from the fence,
his legs wrapped in pig hide below the knees.
He smiles, toothless, and as we close in,
I see the Holsteins, the harnesses.
The man's white eyes.

Inside, mushrooms. The couple has spent the day at harvest,
cooked these brown ribs cored with cesium,
wet with steam. They smell like rye but taste
of the autumn floor, rills spiced
with leaf-mold and rain.

At dusk, my head feels like a gourd in which the day
rattles. The sheds swarm and puddle with laughs,
and a little girl, her shaved head like a stubble
of gray corn, trails her soiled dress
through mud-slick grass.

Robert Wrigley

Ravens at Deer Creek

Something's dead in that stand of fir
one ridge over. Ravens circle and swoop
above the trees, while others
swirl up from below, like paper scraps
blackened in a fire. In the mountains
in winter, it's true: death is a joyful flame,
those caws and cartwheels pure celebration.
It is a long snowy mile I've come
to see this, thanks to dumb luck or grace.
I meant only a hard ski through powder,
my pulse in my ears, and sweat, the pace
like a mainspring, my breath louder and louder
until I stopped, body an engine
ticking to be cool. And now the birds.
I watch them and think, maybe I have seen
these very ones, speaking without words,
cleared-eyed and clerical, ironic, peering in at me
from the berm of snow outside my window,
where I sprinkled a few crumbs of bread. We
are neighbors in the neighborhood of silence.
They've accepted my crumbs, and when the fire was hot
and smokeless huddled in ranks against
the cold at the top of the chimney. And they're not
without gratitude. Though I'm clearly visible
to them now, they swirl on and sing,
and if, in the early dusk, I should fall
on my way back home and—injured, weeping—
rail against the stars and frigid night
and crawl a while on my hopeless way
then stop, numb, easing into the darkening white
like a candle, I know they'll stay

with me, keeping watch, moving limb to limb,
angels down Jacob's ladder, wise
to the moon, and waiting for me, simple as sin,
that they may know the delicacy of my eyes.

Anything the River Gives

Basalt, granite, tourmaline, the male wash
of off-white seed from an elderberry,
the fly's-eye, pincushion nubbins yellow
balsamroot extrudes from hot spring soil,
confetti of eggshell on a shelf of stone.
Here's a flotilla of beaver-peeled branches,
a cottonwood mile the shade of your skin.
Every day I bring some small offering
from my morning walk along the river:
something steel, blackened amber with rust,
an odd pin or bushing shed by the train
or torqued loose from the track, a mashed penny,
the muddy bulge of snowmelt current.
I lie headlong on a bed of rocks,
dip my cheek in the shallows,
and see the water mid-channel three feet
above my eyes. Overhead the swallows
loop for hornets, stinkbugs, black flies and bees,
gone grass shows a snakeskin shed last summer.
The year's first flowers are always yellow,
dogtooth violet dangling downcast and small.
Here is fennel, witches' broom, and bunchgrass,
an ancient horseshoe nailed to a cottonwood
and halfway swallowed in its punky flesh.
Here is an agate polished over years,
a few bones picked clean and gnawed by mice.
Here is every beautiful rock I've seen
in my life, here is my breath still singing
from a reedy flute, here the river
telling my blood your name without end.

Take the sky and wear it, take the moon's skid
over waves, that monthly jewel.
If there are wounds in this world no love heals,
then the things I haul up—feather and bone,
tonnage of stone and the pale green trumpets
of stump lichens—are ounce by ounce
a weight to counterbalance your doubts.
In another month there won't be room left
on the windowsills and cluttered shelves,
and still you'll see me, standing before you,
presenting some husk or rusty souvenir,
anything the river gives, and I believe
you will love.

Why Do the Crickets Sing?

Because it is not enough to open the door
or sit on the porch, I have to go inside
the clamor the crickets send up
after a morning's long rain. I have to climb down
from the birdsong heights, let the water
wick my clothes cold and let spit
salsify dabble my neck and eyelids with its kisses.

The nightcrawlers' earth musk makes me dizzy;
they lie spent and glistening in the light of the clouds.
Now the bells, the bells! The succulent hell boil
clamor of their wings, singing the hearts
of the one sun deep inside the seeds.
Let us open the mud book and pray.

Even the slug glister looms: perfect firmaments,
polestar and moon, only now
my eyes too focus on the blur of the bells,
fingertip whorls spin sudden into music.
It is like drowning, chorus and string,
a billion breath-moaned horns breaking like waves.

Taproot is thunder and moss is rain,
the drum of it what finally wakes me,
or brings me back from some brink,
some light that held me down to pull me up:
or else it is the kettledrum rumble of the field mouse—
a shriek of terror, soar of the hawk descending.

CONTRIBUTORS' NOTes

ANN FISHER-WIRTH (b. 1947) is the author of the poetry books *Blue Window* (2003), *Five Terraces* (2005), *Carta Marina* (2009), and *Dream Cabinet* (2012); the chapbook *Slide Shows* (2009); and *William Carlos Williams and Autobiography: The Woods of His Own Nature*. Her awards include the *Malahat Review* Long Poem Prize, the Rita Dove Poetry Award, two Mississippi Arts Commission Poetry fellowships, and the Mississippi Institute of Arts and Letters Poetry Prize. She teaches in the English Department at the University of Mississippi, where she also directs the minor in environmental studies.

LAURA-GRAY STREET (b. 1962) is the author of *Pigment and Fume* (2014), and her work has appeared in *Poet Lore*, *Hawk & Handsaw*, *Many Mountains Moving*, *Gargoyle*, *ISLE*, *Shenandoah*, *Blackbird*, the *Notre Dame Review*, and *Best New Poets 2005*. Her honors include four Pushcart Prize nominations, a poetry fellowship from the Virginia Commission for the Arts, Terrain.org's Poetry Prize, *Isotope's* Editors' Prize in Poetry, the Southern Women Writers Conference Emerging Writer in Poetry Award, the Dana Award in Poetry, and the *Greensboro Review's* Literary Award. Street is an assistant professor of English at Randolph College and president of the Greater Lynchburg Environmental Network.

ROBERT HASS's (b. 1941) recent books are *The Apple Trees at Olema: New and Selected Poems* (2010) and *What Light Can Do: Essays 1985–2010* (2012). *Time and Materials* won the 2007 National Book Award and the 2008 Pulitzer Prize. Hass has served as U.S. poet laureate and cofounded the environmental education program River of Words. He teaches at the University of California, Berkeley.

Born in Bethlehem, Pennsylvania, STEPHEN VINCENT BENÉT (1898–1943) published his first two collections, *Five Men and Pompey* (1915) and *The Drug-Shop* (1917), while attending Yale University. In 1921 he published his first novel, *The Beginning of Wisdom*. A celebrated poet, novelist, short story writer, playwright, and librettist, Benét received a Pulitzer Prize for the long narrative poem *John Brown's Body* (1928) and a second Pulitzer for *Western Star* (1943), an epic focused on American history.

ELIZABETH BISHOP (1911–1979) was born in Massachusetts and later moved to Brazil, which came to be a major influence on her poetry. Marianne Moore was an important early mentor. Bishop's distinct voice and revitalization of closed forms were esteemed by her peers. She served as U.S. poet laureate from 1949 to 1950. She won the 1956 Pulitzer Prize for *North and South* and the 1970 National Book Award for *Complete Poems*. She taught at Harvard University during her last years.

STERLING A. BROWN (1901–1989) was born in Washington, D.C., and attended Harvard University. He said his first education came from the African American culture of the South, where he taught writers including Toni Morrison and Amiri Baraka. Brown's interest in folklore was the focus of his first book of poems, *Southern Road* (1932). Many years later his poetry books *The Last Ride of Wild Bill and Eleven Narratives* (1975) and *The Collected Poems* (1985) were published. An essayist, sociologist, and historicist, he edited anthologies of African American writing, beginning with *The Negro Caravan* (1941).

HART CRANE's (1899–1933) poetry is perhaps best known for its intense lyricism combined with elements from American pop culture, a method he explored most fully in *The Bridge* (1930), an epic on modern America. His writing is characterized by a tone both hopeful and apocalyptic that focused on the potential for transformation inherent in all things, particularly in the image of the bridge. In his last year of life, he was awarded a Guggenheim fellowship. He committed suicide on his way back from the Yucatán, where he had been writing an epic on the conquest of Mexico.

E. E. CUMMINGS's (1894–1962) poetry is perhaps best known for its idiosyncratic punctuation, capitalization, and grammar, but beneath these techniques lie a beautiful lyricism and sharp wit. After attending Harvard University, he volunteered in an ambulance corps in France, where his pacifism landed him in a concentration camp. He documented the experience in *The Enormous Room* (1922). His first book of poems, *Tulips and Chimneys*, was published in 1923.

Born in Georgia, JAMES DICKEY (1923–1997) returned often to the South as an advertiser, professor, and writer. After receiving a Guggenheim fellowship to go to Italy, he published the poetry collections *Helmets* (1964) and *Buckdancer's Choice* (1965). His first novel, *Deliverance* (1970), later became a major film. He served as U.S. poet laureate from 1966 to 1968, read at Jimmy Carter's inauguration in 1977, and was writer-in-residence at the University of South Carolina from 1968 until his death.

EMILY DICKINSON (1830–1886) was born in Amherst, Massachusetts, where she lived her entire life among a small group of family and friends. *Poems by Emily Dickinson* (1890) was published four years after her death, when her fascicles, small hand-bound booklets, were discovered. Though the first collections of her works did not retain the brilliant stylistic eccentricities of Dickinson's handwritten poems, subsequent editions, such as *The Poems of Emily Dickinson* (1955), more accurately reflect the poet's intensely complex and imaginative writings.

The occult practices of ROBERT DUNCAN's (1919–1988) adoptive parents would greatly influence his mystical poetry. He worked with Charles Olson at Black Mountain College and later helped make San Francisco a literary hub with Kenneth Rexroth. His first mature work was *The Opening of the Field* (1960). *Ground Work: Before the War* (1984) and *Ground Work II: In the Dark* (1987) focused on Duncan's outrage over the Vietnam War.

A poet, editor, essayist, and playwright, T. S. ELIOT (1888–1965) was an internationally known leader of modernism. Born in St. Louis, he moved to London in 1914, where he met and was greatly influenced by Ezra Pound. Soon after *The Waste Land* (1922) was published, Eliot established the *Criterion*, an important literary journal. In 1927 he converted from Unitarianism to Anglicanism and became a British citizen. His last major works were *Ash Wednesday* (1930) and *Four Quartets* (1943). In 1948 he received the Nobel Prize for Literature.

WILLIAM EVERSON (Brother Antoninus) (1912–1994) has been categorized as a nature poet, an erotic poet, a confessional poet, and, having served eighteen years as a Dominican monk, a religious poet. His early collections—*These Are the Ravens* (1935), *San Joaquin* (1939), and *The Masculine Dead* (1940)—focused on the changing seasons on his farm in California. His later collected poems, *The Residual Years* (1948), focused on the violence of relationships during World War II. Known as a Beat poet when he joined Kenneth Rexroth in San Francisco, Everson would go on to write over fifty volumes of poetry.

The landscape of New England, where ROBERT FROST (1874–1963) moved with his family at the age of eleven, informed much of the poet's work. His first book, *A Boy's Will* (1913), was followed a year later by *North of Boston*. Frost became arguably the most popular American poet of his time, winning four Pulitzer Prizes, serving as U.S. poet laureate in 1958–59, and reading at the inauguration of John F. Kennedy in 1961.

BARBARA GUEST (1920–2006) was a member of the first generation of the New York School of poetry. She is known for her book *Herself Defined: The Poet H.D. and Her World* (1984) and her many collections of poetry, including *The Red Gaze* (2005), *Miniatures and Other Poems* (2002), and *Symbiosis* (1999). Among her many honors are the Frost Medal for Lifetime Achievement from the Poetry Society of America and the Lawrence Lipton Award for Literature.

H.D. (Hilda Doolittle) (1886–1961) was born in Pennsylvania and later moved to Europe, where she remained for the rest of her life. H.D. was close friends with Ezra Pound and William Carlos Williams, and her early work, *Sea Garden* (1916), became associated with the imagist movement, though she also wrote a three-part meditative work, *Trilogy* (1946), and the epic poem *Helen in Egypt* (1961). H.D.'s work is characterized by its unadorned imagery, economical language, and reimagining of Greek mythology.

Born in Detroit, ROBERT HAYDEN (1913–1980) left in 1936 to participate in the Federal Writers' Project. He enrolled at the University of Michigan, where he studied with W. H. Auden and published his first book, *Heart-Shape in the Dust* (1940). Though much of his writing focuses on the African American experience, Hayden used race to explore larger questions about language and art. He was elected to the American Academy of Poets in 1975 and served as the first African American U.S. poet laureate in 1976–78.

LANGSTON HUGHES (1902–1967), a central figure of the Harlem Renaissance, is known for his incorporation of jazz and blues rhythms in poetry. He looked to the black urban poor for his poetic subject and embraced the music and humor of their oral tradition in *The Weary Blues* (1926) and other books. He worked as a poet, novelist, dramatist, essayist, and translator, publishing his first novel, *Not Without Laughter*, in 1930.

ROBINSON JEFFERS (1887–1962) lived much of his life in Big Sur, California, in a house he built for his family by the sea. This location figures prominently in his work, which focuses on expressing the natural landscape's beauty and his doctrine of "Inhumanism." His first major book of narrative poems was *The Woman at Point Sur* (1927), followed by *Cawdor and Other Poems* (1928), *Thurso's Landing* (1932), and *Solstice and Other Poems* (1935), which secured his reputation as a master of book-length verse narratives.

Born in England, DENISE LEVERTOV (1923–1997) moved to the United States during World War II and later became involved in anti-war activism. An experimental poet, she was an important part of the Black Mountain School. *With Eyes at the Backs of Our Heads* (1959) established her as a major American poet, and *The Sorrow Dance* (1967) furthered her reputation as an antiwar activist. Her work in poetry, translation, and criticism received numerous honors, including the Shelley Memorial Award, the Robert Frost Medal, and the Lenore Marshall Prize.

MARIANNE MOORE's (1887–1972) poetry most often focuses on the natural world, combining scientific accuracy and colorful imagination in her syllabic verse. *Poems* (1921) was published in England and was quickly followed by *Observations* (1924). For three years she was editor at the *Dial*. Her contemporaries included Wallace Stevens, Ezra Pound, William Carlos Williams, T. S. Eliot, and H.D., and she was a key player in a leading group of modernists.

Influenced by imagism and objectivism, LORINE NIEDECKER's (1903–1970) work keeps the line short and the language concise, a method she called "condensery." She lived most of her life on Black Hawk Island, Wisconsin, with her parents, and her lengthy correspondence with Louis Zukofsky was an important tie to the literary world. She was not widely known during her lifetime. *New Goose* (1946) was followed by *My Friend Tree* (1962), and editions of her collected works and letters have been published posthumously.

Known as the leader of the Black Mountain School of poetics, CHARLES OLSON (1910–1970) urged writers to experiment with open forms, which he explored in his influential 1950 essay "Projective Verse." *The Maximus Poems* appeared in 1960, though he had begun working on his opus two decades earlier when he took his first teaching post. He served as rector at Black Mountain College from 1951 to 1956 and taught at several New York universities until his death.

Stripping poetry of sentimentality, GEORGE OPPEN's (1908–1984) objectivist work views the world with clarity. The poet was born in New York and worked much of his life doing odd jobs. He was awarded the Purple Heart for his service during World War II. After setting up the Objectivist Press with Louis Zukofsky, William Carlos Williams, and Charles Reznikoff in 1933 and publishing his first collection, *Discrete Series* (1934), Oppen turned to political activism. He lived in Mexico until 1958, when he returned to the United States and to writing poetry. *Of Being Numerous* won the 1968 Pulitzer Prize.

In 1909 EZRA POUND (1885–1972) visited England, where he met many leading writers of his day, including William Butler Yeats. Pound established his reputation with *Hugh Selwyn Mauberley* (1920). He was a proponent of the imagist movement and defined several major schools of modernism. The initial draft of *The Cantos*, a book he worked on for nearly fifty years, appeared in 1921. During his first self-exile in Italy, Pound became a supporter of Fascist ideals; when the Allies invaded Italy, he was imprisoned and nearly tried for treason. He was incarcerated instead at St. Elizabeth's psychiatric hospital for over twelve years before being released and returning to Italy, where he lived for the remainder of his life.

A prolific poet and translator, KENNETH REXROTH (1905–1982) helped open American poetry to Asian influences through his mystical and erotic work focused on nature. Though not a Beat poet, he encouraged antiestablishment writing and worked against what he saw as a strain of sentimentality in American writing. *In What Hour* (1940) was followed by *The Phoenix and the Tortoise* (1944), which expressed his views as a pacifist during World War II. During this time he began working toward what would later become the San Francisco Renaissance. *Selected Poems* (1984) and *Complete Poems* (2003) appeared posthumously.

THEODORE ROETHKE (1908–1963) often wrote in closed forms, using powerful rhetoric to describe nature's beauty and darkness. Born in Michigan, he taught at several universities, though his time at each was punctuated by breakdowns. He was an important mentor to young poets. His first book, *Open House*, appeared in 1941. He won the Pulitzer Prize for *The Waking* (1953), followed by the Bollingen Prize and National Book Award in 1959. *The Far Field* (1964) was published posthumously.

MURIEL RUKEYSER (1913–1980) was born in New York City. *Theory of Flight* (1935) was published in the Yale Series of Younger Poets. She is known for her extensive work translating the poems of Octavio Paz. She founded the left-wing *Student Review*, protested against the war in the 1960s, and became associated with the feminist movement. *U.S. 1* (1938) featured her long poem "The Book of the Dead."

JAMES SCHUYLER (1923–1991) was born in Chicago. He lived in Italy from 1947 to 1949, staying in Auden's house and working as his secretary. After returning to New York, he lived with Frank O'Hara and John Ashbery and became involved in the New York art scene and the New York School of poetry. He won the Pulitzer Prize for *The Morning of the Poem* (1980). In the 1980s his poor health caused him to turn to a life of seclusion.

Known for a lack of opulence, WILLIAM STAFFORD's (1914–1993) lucid and mystical poems on memory and nature have been widely read for many years. *Traveling Through the Dark* won the 1963 National Book Award and was the first of many collections. Stafford served as U.S. poet laureate in 1970–71 and as Oregon's poet laureate from 1975 until his death.

WALLACE STEVENS (1879–1955) was born in Reading, Pennsylvania, and eventually became the vice president of an insurance company in Hartford, Connecticut, where he worked for much of his life. He often wrote at night and during vacations in the Florida Keys. *Harmonium* (1923), along with his treatises on poetry's ability to take the place of religion, secured his reputation as a leading modernist. *Collected Poems* (1955) won the Pulitzer Prize.

JEAN TOOMER (1894–1967) was born in Washington, D.C., and attended five colleges before deciding on a literary career. In 1921 he moved to the South, where he was inspired to write *Cane* (1923), a hybrid work interweaving narrative and poetry. He later developed an interest in Unitism, a religion founded by Gurdjieff preaching unity, transcendence, and self-mastery through yoga, which he practiced for much of his life. Toomer was an important figure in the Harlem Renaissance.

WALT WHITMAN (1819–1892) called his poetry a "barbaric yawp" to describe an expansive voice that spoke for the people by focusing on individualism and democratic ideals through expressions of the body and nature. *Leaves of Grass*, made up of twelve poems, was published in 1855. By the second edition a year later, the book had more than doubled in size, and Whitman would go on to publish six more editions. When the Civil War broke out, he cared for and wrote about thousands of Union and Confederate soldiers, which he later turned into the collection *Drum Taps* (1865).

Born in Rutherford, New Jersey, WILLIAM CARLOS WILLIAMS (1883–1963) worked as an obstetrician, pediatrician, and general practitioner in Rutherford and Paterson. Though he was friends with Ezra Pound, Williams's wide-ranging work broke from European cultural traditions, focusing on the everyday as expressed through the American idiom and grounding poetry in the specific conditions of place. His forty books—poetry, short fiction, novels, improvisational prose poems, plays, and essays—include the seminal works *Spring and All* (1923) and *In the American Grain* (1925), as well as his epic poem *Paterson*, which won the first National Book Award for poetry in 1950.

• CONTEMPORARY

A. R. AMMONS's (1926–2001) nearly thirty poetry collections include *Collected Poems 1951–1971*, winner of the National Book Award; *Sphere*, winner of the Bollingen Prize; *A Coast of Trees* (1989), winner of the National Book Critics Circle Award; and *Garbage* (1993), winner of the National Book Award and the Rebekah Johnson Bobbitt National Prize for Poetry. His other honors include a Wallace Stevens Award, the Robert Frost Medal, the Ruth Lilly Poetry Prize, and fellowships from the Guggenheim Foundation, the MacArthur Fellows Program, and the American Academy of Arts and Letters.

KAREN LEONA ANDERSON (b. 1973) is the author of *Punish honey* (2009). Her work has appeared in *ecopoetics*, *jubilat*, *Verse*, the *Indiana Review*, *Fence*, and *Volt*. She is an assistant professor of English at St. Mary's College of Maryland.

CHRISTOPHER ARIGO (b. 1974) is the author of *Lit interim* (2003), which won the Transcontinental Poetry Prize, and *In the archives* (2007). He coedits the literary journal *Interim* with poet Claudia Keelan and is an assistant professor of English at Washington State University.

RAE ARMANTROUT (b. 1947) was raised in San Diego, where she has taught at the University of California for more than twenty years. Her eleventh poetry collection, *Versed*, won the 2009 National Book Critics Circle Award and the 2010 Pulitzer Prize. Her most recent collection is *Money Shot* (2012).

JOHN ASHBERY's (b. 1927) recent books are *Planisphere* (2009) and *Notes from the Air: Selected Later Poems* (2007). His awards include the Bollingen Prize, the Ruth Lilly Poetry Prize, the Griffin International Award, and a MacArthur fellowship. *Self-Portrait in a Convex Mirror* (1976) received the Pulitzer Prize, the National Book Award, and the National Book Critics Circle Award.

JIMMY SANTIAGO BACA (b. 1952) composed his first poems in prison, where he taught himself to read and write after being convicted for drug possession. He is the author of more than a dozen books, including *Martin and Meditations on the South Valley* (1987), which won the American Book Award. He leads workshops in schools, reservations, housing projects, and prisons and is the founder of the literary nonprofit Cedar Tree.

JULIANNA BAGGOTT (b. 1969) is the author of eighteen books, under her own name as well as the pen names N. E. Bode and Bridget Asher. Her most recent novel is *Pure* (2012), the first in a dystopian trilogy, and her recent poetry collections are *Lizzie Borden in Love* (2006) and *Compulsions of Silk Worms and Bees* (2007).

ELLEN BASS (b. 1947) is the author of the poetry collections *The Human Line* (2007) and *Mules of Love* (2002) and coeditor of *No More Masks!* (1973), the first major anthology of poetry by women. Her work has appeared in the *Atlantic*, the *American Poetry Review*, *New Republic*, *Kenyon Review*, and *Ploughshares*. She teaches in the MFA program at Pacific University.

DAN BEACHY-QUICK (b. 1973) is the author of five books of poems, most recently *Circle's Apprentice* (2011). His prose collections are *A Whaler's Dictionary* (2008) and *Wonderful Investigations* (2012). He teaches in the MFA program at Colorado State University and is poetry adviser for the literary journal *A Public Space*.

Ojibwa-Lacandon artist, writer, and teacher LOIS BEARDSLEE (b. 1954) is the author of *Lies to Live By* (2003), *Rachel's Children: Stories from a Contemporary Native American Woman* (2004), *Not Far Away: The Real-Life Adventures of Ima Pipiig* (2007), and *The Women's Warrior Society* (2008).

SANDRA BEASLEY (b. 1980) is the author of *I Was the Jukebox* (2010), winner of the Barnard Women Poets Prize, *Theories of Falling* (2008), and *Don't Kill the Birthday Girl: Tales from an Allergic Life* (2011). Her poetry appeared in *Best American Poetry 2010* and *Best New Poets 2005*.

MARVIN BELL (b. 1937) is the author of more than twenty books of poetry, most recently *Vertigo: The Living Dead Man Poems* (2011) and *Whiteout* (2011), with photographer Nathan Lyons. He has received National Endowment for the Arts and Guggenheim fellowships and two Fulbright appointments, and he was named Iowa's first poet laureate in 2000.

DAN BELLM (b. 1952) has published three books of poetry, most recently *Practice*, winner of the 2009 California Book Award. He translates poetry and fiction from Spanish and French and teaches literary translation at Antioch University–Los Angeles and New York University.

MARGO BERDESHEVSKY (b. 1945) is author of the poetry collections *Between Soul and Stone* (2011) and *But a Passage in Wilderness* (2007), as well as a book of illustrated stories, *Beautiful Soon Enough* (2009), which received the Ronald Sukenick American Book Review Innovative Fiction Prize. Other honors include the Robert H. Winner Memorial Award and seven Pushcart Prize nominations.

WENDELL BERRY (b. 1934) is a poet, essayist, and novelist, as well as a Kentucky farmer and activist. His forty books include *The Selected Poems of Wendell Berry* (2008), which won the Poets' Prize, *The Unsettling of America: Culture and Agriculture* (1996), and *Home Economics: Fourteen Essays* (1987). His honors include the T. S. Eliot Prize, the Thomas Merton Award, a National Humanities Medal, and fellowships from the Rockefeller Foundation, the Guggenheim Foundation, and the National Endowment for the Arts.

MEI-MEI BERSSENBRUGGE's (b. 1947) collections of poetry include *Love Artists: New and Selected Poems* (2006), *Four Year Old Girl* (1998), *Empathy* (1989), and *The Heat Bird* (1983). She is the recipient of two American Book Awards and two fellowships from the National Endowment for the Arts.

LINDA BIERDS (b. 1945) is the author of numerous books, including *Flight: New and Selected Poems* (2008), *First Hand* (2005), *The Seconds* (2001), and *The Ghost Trio* (1994). Among her honors are fellowships from the National Endowment for the Arts, the Guggenheim Foundation, the Poetry Society of America, and the MacArthur Fellows Program. She teaches at the University of Washington.

RALPH BLACK (b. 1960) is the author of *The Apple Psalms* (2008) and *Turning Over the Earth* (2000). He is the recipient of the Anne Halley Poetry Prize and the Chelsea Poetry Prize. He is codirector of the Brockport Writers Forum at the State University of New York at Brockport.

ROBERT BLY (b. 1926) is the author of more than thirty poetry collections, most recently *Reaching Out to the World: New and Selected Prose Poems* (2009), *My*

Sentence Was a Thousand Years of Joy (2006), and *The Night Abraham Called to the Stars* (2001). His honors include fellowships from the Guggenheim Foundation, the Rockefeller Foundation, and the National Endowment for the Arts.

MARIANNE BORUCH (b. 1950) is the author of eight poetry collections, including *Cadaver, Speak* (forthcoming), *Grace, Fallen from* (2008), and *Poems New and Selected* (2004), a finalist for the Lenore Marshall Poetry Prize. She has received fellowships from the Guggenheim Foundation and the National Endowment for the Arts, two Pushcart Prizes, and the Terrence Des Pres Prize. She teaches at Purdue University and Warren Wilson College.

ANNIE BOUTELLE (b. 1943) is the author of the poetry collections *Becoming Bone* (2005) and *Nest of Thistles* (2005). She was the Grace Hazard Conkling Poet in Residence at Smith College and is currently a senior lecturer. She is also the founder of the Smith College Poetry Center.

ELIZABETH BRADFIELD (b. 1971) is the author of *Approaching Ice* (2010) and *Interpretive Work* (2008). Her poems have appeared in the *Atlantic*, the *Believer*, and *Poetry*, and her honors include the Audre Lorde Prize and a Stegner fellowship. She is founder and editor-in-chief of Broadsided Press, and she works as a naturalist and teacher.

LAYNIE BROWNE (b. 1966) is the author of nine poetry collections and one novel. Her most recent books are *Roseate, Points of Gold* (2011), *The Desires of Letters* (2010), and *The Scented Fox* (2007), which received the National Poetry Series Award. She is the coeditor of *I'll Drown My Book: Conceptual Writing by Women* (2012).

DERICK BURLESON's (b. 1963) poetry collections are *Melt* (2012), *Never Night* (2007), and *Ejo: Poems, Rwanda, 1991–1994* (2000). His poems have appeared in the *Georgia Review*, the *Kenyon Review*, the *Paris Review*, the *Southern Review*, and *Poetry*. He teaches in the MFA program at the University of Alaska–Fairbanks.

CYRUS CASSELLS (b. 1957) is the author of *The Crossed-Out Swastika* (2012), *More Than Peace and Cypresses* (2004), *Soul Make a Path through Shouting* (1994), and *Beautiful Signor* (1997). The recipient of a Pushcart Prize, two National Endowment for the Arts grants, and a Lannan Literary Award, he teaches at Texas State University.

GRACE CAVALIERI (b. 1932) is the author of sixteen poetry books and chapbooks, most recently *Millie's Sunshine Tiki Villas: A Novella in Verse* (2011), and she has seen twenty-six of her plays produced on American stages. She founded and produces *The Poet and the Poem*, recorded at the Library of Congress and broadcast on public radio.

LORNA DEE CERVANTES (b. 1954) is the author of *Ciento: 100 100-Word Love Poems* (2011), *Drive: The First Quartet: New Poems, 1980–2005* (2006), *From the Cables of Genocide* (1991), and *Emplumada* (1982), winner of the American Book Award. She teaches at the University of Colorado–Boulder.

JENNIFER CHANG (b. 1976) is a Ph.D. candidate at the University of Virginia and co-chairs Kundiman, an organization dedicated to the support of Asian American poetry. *The History of Anonymity* (2008) was selected for the *Virginia Quarterly Review*'s Poetry Series.

PATRICIA CLARK (b. 1951) is poet-in-residence and a professor at Grand Valley State University. Her work has appeared in the *Atlantic*, the *Gettysburg Review*, and elsewhere. Her recent books are *Sunday Rising* (2013) and *She Walks into the Sea* (2009).

LUCILLE CLIFTON (1936–2010) is the author of more than ten poetry collections, several memoirs, and sixteen children's books. *Blessing the Boats* (2000) won the National Book Award, and *Two-Headed Woman* (1980) and *Good Woman* (1987) were Pulitzer Prize nominees. Clifton's numerous awards included the 2007 Ruth Lilly Poetry Prize, and she served for several years as poet laureate of Maryland.

HENRI COLE's (b. 1956) recent poetry collections are *Touch* (2011) and *Middle Earth* (2004), a finalist for the Pulitzer Prize. He has received the Kingsley Tufts Poetry Award, the Rome Prize, the Berlin Prize, a Guggenheim fellowship, and the Lenore Marshall Award. He teaches at Ohio State University and is the poetry editor of the *New Republic*.

JACK COLLOM (b. 1931) is the author of twenty-three books, including *Situations, Sings*, with Lyn Hejinian (2008), *Red Car Goes By* (2001), and *Dog Sonnets* (1998). He has taught for Poets-in-the-Schools and was a professor at Naropa University. His awards include a National Endowment for the Arts fellowship.

JULIA CONNOR (b. 1942) is the author of seven books and chapbooks, including *Oar* (2009), *X-ing the Acheron* (2002), *Gradual* Map (1999), and *A Canto for the Birds* (1995). She was poet laureate of Sacramento from 2005 to 2009.

MATTHEW COOPERMAN (b. 1964) is the author of *Still: Of the Earth as the Ark Which Does Not Move* (2011), *DaZE* (2006), *A Sacrificial Zinc* (2001), and three chapbooks. A founding editor of *Quarter After Eight* and poetry editor of the *Colorado Review*, he teaches in the MFA program at Colorado State University.

STEPHEN CUSHMAN (b. 1956) is the Robert C. Taylor Professor of English at the University of Virginia and general editor of the *Princeton Encyclopedia of Poetry and Poetics*, fourth edition. He is the author of the poetry collections *Riff-raff* (2011), *Heart Island* (2006), *Cussing Lesson* (2002), and *Blue Pajamas* (1998), as well as works of literary criticism and Civil War history.

KWAME DAWES (b. 1962) is the author of sixteen books of poetry, most recently *Duppy Conqueror* (2013). He is the Glenna Luschei Editor of *Prairie Schooner*, the Chancellor's Professor of English at the University of Nebraska–Lincoln, associate poetry editor at Peepal Tree Press, and program director of the Calabash International Literary Festival.

ALISON HAWTHORNE DEMING'S (b. 1946) four poetry collections include *Rope* (2009), *Genius Loci* (2005), and *Science and Other Poems* (1994), winner of the Walt Whitman Award. Among her nonfiction works is the forthcoming *Zoologies: On Animals and the Human Spirit*. She teaches at the University of Arizona.

DEBORAH DIGGES (1950–2009) is the author of four poetry collections and two memoirs. *Vesper Sparrows* (1986) won the Delmore Schwartz Memorial Prize, and *Rough Music* (1995) won the Kingsley Tufts Poetry Award. Digges received grants from the Guggenheim Foundation, the National Endowment for the Arts, and the Ingram Merrill Foundation and taught at several universities.

ELIZABETH DODD (b. 1962) teaches at Kansas State University. She is the author of six books, including *Horizon's Lens* (2012) and *Archetypal Light* (2001). *In the Mind's Eye: Essays Across the Animate World* won the 2009 Creative Book Prize from the Association for the Study of Literature and Environment.

SHARON DOLIN (b. 1956) is the author of five books of poetry, most recently *Whirlwind* (2012) and *Burn and Dodge* (2008), winner of the AWP Donald Hall Prize in Poetry. She teaches at the 92nd Street Y in New York City and directs the Center for Book Arts Annual Letterpress Poetry Chapbook Competition.

CAMILLE T. DUNGY (b. 1972) is the author of four poetry books, most recently *Smith Blue* (2011), and the editor of *Black Nature: Four Centuries of African American Nature Poetry* (2009). Recipient of an American Book Award, two Northern California Book Awards, a National Endowment for the Arts fellowship, and two NAACP Image Award nominations, she is a professor of creative writing at San Francisco State University.

RACHEL BLAU DuPLESSIS (b. 1941) is a poet, feminist literary critic, and professor emerita at Temple University. Her collections include *Pitch: Drafts 77–95* (2010), *Torques: Drafts 58–76* (2007), and *Drafts 1–38, Toll* (2001). Among her honors are a residency at Bellagio, the Roy Harvey Pearce/Archive for New Poetry Prize, and a Pew Fellowship in the Arts.

TIM EARLEY (b. 1972) is the author of the collections *The Spooking of Mavens* (2010) and *Boondoggle* (2005). He has received two fellowships from the Fine Arts Work Center in Provincetown, Massachusetts, and his poems have appeared in the *Chicago Review*, the *New Orleans Review*, *Hotel Amerika*, and the *Colorado Review*. He lives and teaches in Oxford, Mississippi.

LARRY EIGNER (1927–1996) is the author of more than forty books of poetry, including *From the Sustaining Air* (1953), published by Robert Creeley, and the four-volume *The Collected Poems of Larry Eigner* (2010). Eigner's work regularly appeared in *L=A=N=G=U=A=G=E* and many other journals.

LOUISE ERDRICH (b. 1954) is the author of novels, poetry, and children's fiction. Her awards include a Guggenheim fellowship and the National Book Critics Circle Award for her novel *Love Medicine* (1984). Her poetry collections include *Original Fire* (2003), *Baptism of Desire* (1989), and *Jacklight* (1984).

B. H. FAIRCHILD's (b. 1942) first major work was a critical study of William Blake. He has since published six chapbooks and collections, including *Early Occult Memory Systems of the Lower Midwest* (2003) and *The Art of the Lathe* (1998). His honors include the William Carlos Williams Award, the National Book Critics Circle Award, and the Kingsley Tufts Poetry Award.

PATRICIA FARGNOLI (b. 1937), the New Hampshire poet laureate from 2006 to 2009, is the author of six poetry collections. *Then, Something* (2009) won *ForeWord* magazine's Silver Book Award and was cowinner of the New England Poetry Club's Shelia Mooton Award. A retired clinical social worker, she has published work in *Ploughshares*, the *Alaska Quarterly*, and the *Harvard Review*.

ANNIE FINCH (b. 1956) has written or edited fifteen books of poetry, translation, and criticism, most recently *Spells: Selected Poetry, Translations, and Performance Work 1970–2010*. A fellow of the Black Earth Institute and the artist-in-residence at Cherry Hill Seminary, she directs the Stonecoast MFA in Creative Writing at the University of Southern Maine.

JESSICA FISHER (b. 1976) is the author of *Inmost* (2012), winner of the Nightboat Poetry Prize, and *Frail-Craft* (2007), which won the Yale Younger Poets award. Her other honors include a 2012–13 Rome Prize from the American Academy of Arts and Letters.

LISA FISHMAN's (b. 1966) poetry collections include *Current* (2010), *The Happiness Experiment* (2007), and *Dear, Read* (2002). She has taught at Beloit College and Columbia College and now runs a "poetry farm" in Wisconsin with her husband and the poet Richard Meier.

KATHLEEN FLENNIKEN (b. 1960) is the 2012–14 poet laureate of Washington. *Plume* (2012) is a book-length meditation on the Hanford nuclear site. *Famous* (2006) won the Prairie Schooner Book Prize in Poetry and was named a Notable Book by the American Library Association.

CAROLYN FORCHÉ (b. 1950) is the author of *Blue Hour* (2003), *The Angel of History* (1994), *The Country Between Us* (1981), and *Gathering the Tribes* (1976), winner of the Yale Younger Poets award. She has received fellowships from the

Lannan Foundation and the National Endowment for the Arts, and won the Edita and Ira Morris Hiroshima Foundation Award. She directs the Lannan Center for Poetry and Poetics and holds the Lannan Chair in Poetry at Georgetown University.

CAROL FROST's (b. 1948) poetry collections include *Honeycomb* (2010), *The Queen's Desertion* (2006), *I Will Say Beauty* (2003), and *Love and Scorn* (2000). The recipient of two National Endowment for the Arts fellowships and four Pushcart Prizes, she founded the Catskill Poetry Workshop at Hartwick College. She is the Theodore Bruce and Barbara Lawrence Alfond Chair of English at Rollins College.

JUAN CARLOS GALEANO (b. 1958) is the author of *Amazonia* (2003) and several other collections and has translated North American poets into Spanish. His poetry has appeared in *Casa de las Américas*, the *Atlantic Monthly*, *Ploughshares*, and other journals. He teaches at Florida State University.

BRENDAN GALVIN is the author of twenty-one poetry books and chapbooks, most recently *Habitat: New and Selected Poems, 1965–2005* (2005), a finalist for the National Book Award. Additional awards include the Iowa Poetry Prize and fellowships from the Guggenheim Foundation and the National Endowment for the Arts.

JAMES GALVIN (b. 1951) has published six collections of poetry, including *As Is* (2009), *X: Poems* (2003), and *God's Mistress* (1984), selected for the National Poetry Series. He divides his time between Wyoming, where he is a rancher, and Iowa City, where he is on the faculty at the Iowa Writers' Workshop.

FORREST GANDER's (b. 1956) recent books include *Redstart: An Ecological Poetics* (2012), with John Kinsella, and *Core Samples from the World* (2011). The recipient of fellowships from the Library of Congress and the Rockefeller, Guggenheim, Howard, and Whiting Foundations, Gander is the Adele Kellenberg Seaver Professor of Literary Arts and Comparative Literature at Brown University.

C. S. GISCOMBE (b. 1950) is the author of *Prairie Style* (2008), winner of the American Book Award; *Into and Out of Dislocation* (2001); *Giscome Road* (1998), winner of the Carl Sandburg Prize; and *Here* (1994). His recognitions include the Stephen Henderson Award. He teaches at the University of California–Berkeley.

PETER GIZZI's (b. 1959) books include *Threshold Songs* (2011) and *The Outernationale* (2007). He was poetry editor for the *Nation* and founding coeditor of *o·blēk: a journal of language arts*. His honors include the Peter I. B. Lavan Younger Poet Award and fellowships from the Howard, Rex, and Guggenheim Foundations and the Foundation for Contemporary Arts. He teaches at the University of Massachusetts–Amherst.

LOUISE GLÜCK (b. 1943) is the author of eleven books of poems and an essay collection. Her honors include the Pulitzer Prize for *The Wild Iris* (1993), the National Book Critics Circle Award, the Bollingen Prize, and the Wallace Stevens Award. She has served as U.S. special consultant in poetry, U.S. poet laureate, and judge of the Yale Series of Younger Poets. She is writer-in-residence at Yale University.

RAY GONZALEZ (b. 1952) is the editor of numerous anthologies and the author of ten poetry collections, most recently *Consideration of the Guitar: New and Selected Poems* (2005), *The Religion of Hands* (2005), and *Human Crying Daisies* (2003). He received the 1988 Governor's Award for Excellence in the Arts for his work as editor-in-chief of *La Voz*, Colorado's Latino newspaper, and as poetry editor for the *Bloomsbury Review*.

CHARLES GOODRICH (b. 1951) is the author of *Going to Seed: Dispatches from the Garden* (2010), *Insects of South Corvallis* (2007), and *The Practice of Home* (2004). His work has appeared in *Orion, Willow Springs*, the *Sun*, and *Best Essays Northwest*. He directs the Spring Creek Project at Oregon State University.

JORIE GRAHAM (b. 1950) is the author of twelve poetry collections, including *Sea Change* (2008), *Never* (2002), *Swarm* (2000), and the Pulitzer Prize–winning *The Dream of the Unified Field* (1996). She is the recipient of a MacArthur fellowship and the Morton Dauwen Zabel Award, and from 1997 to 2003, she served as chancellor of the Academy of American Poets. She is the Boylston Professor of Rhetoric and Oratory at Harvard University.

MICHAEL GREGORY's (b. 1940) books include *Mr America Drives His Car* (2013), *re: Play* (2008), *The Valley Floor* (1975), and *Hunger Weather 1959–1975* (1982). He is a founder of the Bisbee Poetry Festival and founding director of the Central School Project in Bisbee, Arizona. Before his retirement he was an internationally recognized toxics activist.

TAMI HAALAND's (b. 1960) poetry collections include *When We Wake in the Night* (2012) and *Breath in Every Room* (2001), which won the Nicholas Roerich Prize. She is the recipient of the Artist's Innovation Award from the Montana Arts Council, and her work has appeared in *High Desert Journal, Letters to the World*, and *Calyx*. She is an associate professor of English at Montana State University–Billings, and the editor of *Stone's Throw*, an online literary journal.

JOHN HAINES's (1924–2011) books include *For the Century's End: Poems 1990–1999* (2001), *At the End of This Summer: Poems 1948–1954* (1997), and *New Poems 1980–88* (1990), which received a Lenore Marshall Poetry Prize. Haines taught at Ohio University, George Washington University, and the University of Cincinnati. His awards include fellowships from the Guggenheim Foundation and the National Endowment for the Arts and a Lifetime Achievement Award from the Library of Congress.

DONALD HALL (b. 1928) is the author of *The Back Chamber* (2011) and dozens of other poetry collections, as well as essays, fiction, plays, and children's fiction. His honors include two Guggenheim fellowships, the Robert Frost Silver medal, a Lifetime Achievement Award from the New Hampshire Writers and Publisher Project, and the Ruth Lilly Poetry Prize. He has served as U.S. poet laureate and poet laureate of New Hampshire.

JOY HARJO's (b. 1951) eight books of poetry include *How We Became Human* (2002), *A Map to the Next World* (2000), and *The Woman Who Fell From the Sky* (1994), which received the Oklahoma Book Arts Award. Her honors include the American Indian Distinguished Achievement in the Arts Award, the Josephine Miles Poetry Award, and the William Carlos Williams Award.

LOLA HASKINS's (b. 1943) tenth book of poems is *The Grace to Leave* (2012). *Still, the Mountain* (2010) won the Florida Book Awards Silver Medal for Poetry. She has received two National Endowment for the Arts fellowships. She teaches in Pacific Lutheran University's low-residency MFA program and serves on the board of Florida Defenders of the Environment.

BROOKS HAXTON (b. 1950) is the author of eight collections of poetry, including *They Lift Their Wings to Cry* (2008), *Uproar* (2006), and *The Sun at Night* (2001). He is the recipient of fellowships from the National Endowment for the Arts, the National Endowment for the Humanities, and the Guggenheim Foundation. He teaches in the writing programs at Syracuse University and Warren Wilson College.

CHRIS HAYES (b. 1981), a Tennessee native, has published poems in the *Gettysburg Review*, *Beloit Poetry Journal*, and *Tar River Poetry*. He is at work on his first collection of poems and lives in Tallahassee with his wife and daughter.

ALLISON HEDGE COKE (b. 1958) is the author of *Dog Road Woman* (1997), winner of the American Book Award; *Off-Season City Pipe* (2005); a memoir, *Rock Ghost, Willow, Deer* (2004); and a verse play, *Blood Run* (2006). She is a professor at the University of Nebraska–Kearney and has taught at the Naropa Institute.

WILLIAM HEYEN's (b. 1940) poetry collections include *The Angel Voices* (2010); *Shoah Train* (2003), a finalist for the National Book Award; and *Pig Notes and Dumb Music: Prose on Poetry* (1998). His honors include fellowships from the National Endowment for the Arts, the Guggenheim Foundation, and the American Academy and Institute of Arts and Letters. He taught at the State University of New York–Brockport for over thirty years.

BRENDA HILLMAN (b. 1951) is the author of eight collections of poetry, most recently *Practical Water* (2011) and *Pieces of Air in the Epic* (2007), and coeditor of *The Grand Permission: New Writings on Poetics and Motherhood* (2003). The recipient of Pushcart Prizes and fellowships from the National Endowment for the Arts and the Guggenheim Foundation, she is the Olivia Fillippi Professor of Poetry at St. Mary's College in northern California.

JANE HIRSHFIELD (b. 1953) is the author of seven books of poetry, most recently *Come, Thief* (2011), and a book of essays, *Nine Gates: Entering the Mind of Poetry* (1997). She has edited and co-translated four books by world poets of the past. Her poems appear in the *New Yorker*, the *Atlantic, Poetry, Orion*, and *The Best American Poetry*. She is a chancellor of the Academy of American Poets.

H. L. HIX's (b. 1960) recent books include his ninth poetry collection, *First Fire, Then Birds: Obsessionals 1985–2010* (2010); a translation of Eugenijus Ališanka's *from unwritten histories*, with the author (2011); and an essay collection, *Lines of Inquiry* (2011). He teaches and directs the creative writing MFA program at the University of Wyoming.

TONY HOAGLAND's (b. 1953) recent books are *Unincorporated Persons in the Late Honda Dynasty* (2010) and *What Narcissism Means to Me* (2003). He has received fellowships from the National Endowment for the Arts, the Guggenheim Foundation, and the Provincetown Fine Arts Work Center. Winner of the Poetry Foundation's Mark Twain Award, he teaches at the University of Houston and Warren Wilson College.

RICHARD HOFFMAN (b. 1949) is the author of the poetry collections *Emblem* (2011); *Gold Star Road* (2007), which won the Barrow Street Press Prize and the New England Poetry Club's Sheila Motton Award; and *Without Paradise* (2002). His prose includes *Interference and Other Stories* (2009) and the memoir *Half the House* (2005). He teaches at Emerson College.

LINDA HOGAN (b. 1947) is a poet, essayist, environmentalist, and fiction writer whose recent collections are *Indios* (2012), *Rounding the Human Corners* (2008), and *People of the Whale* (2008). Her honors include a Lannan Literary Award, the Mountains and Plains Booksellers Spirit of the West Literary Achievement Award, and a Lifetime Achievement Award from the Native Writers Circle of the Americas.

CYNTHIA HOGUE (b. 1951) is the author of seven collections of poetry, most recently *Or Consequence* (2010), and the co-author of *When the Water Came: Evacuees of Hurricane Katrina* (2010). Her honors include a National Endowment for the Arts fellowship and the H.D. Fellowship at Yale University. She is the Maxine and Jonathan Chair in Modern and Contemporary Poetry at Arizona State University.

RICHARD HUGO's (1923–1982) works include *The Right Madness on Skye* (1980), *31 Letters and 13 Dreams* (1977), *What Thou Lovest Well, Remains American* (1975), *Death of the Kapowsin Tavern* (1965), and *A Run of Jacks* (1961). In 1977 he was named the editor of the Yale Younger Poets Series. He taught at the University of Montana.

LUISA A. IGLORIA (b. 1961) is the author of *Juan Luna's Revolver* (2009), winner of the Ernest Sandeen Prize; *Trill and Mordent* (2005); and eight other books. Her work since November 2010 is archived on her poem-a-day project at *Via Negativa*. She is director of the Old Dominion University's MFA program in creative writing.

RONALD JOHNSON (1935–1998) is the author of more than a dozen collections of poetry. *ARK*, an epic poem he worked on from 1970 to 1991, consisted of the books *The Foundations*, *The Spires*, and *The Ramparts*, each made up of thirty-three sections.

RODNEY JONES's (b. 1950) collections include *Imaginary Logic* (2011); *Salvation Blues*, winner of the 2007 Kingsley Tufts Poetry Award and shortlisted for the Griffin International Poetry Award; *Elegy for the Southern Drawl*, a 2000 Pulitzer Prize finalist; and *Transparent Gestures*, winner of the 1990 National Book Critics Circle Award. He is a professor of English at Southern Illinois University–Carbondale.

JUDY JORDAN (b. 1961) is the author of *Sixty Cent Coffee and a Quarter to Dance* (2008) and *Carolina Ghost Woods*, which won the 1999 Walt Whitman Award and the 2000 National Book Critics Circle Award. She teaches creative writing at Southern Illinois University–Carbondale.

BRIGIT PEGEEN KELLY's (b. 1951) collection *The Orchard* (2004) was a Pulitzer Prize finalist; *Song* (1995) was the Lamont Poetry Selection of the Academy of American Poets; and *To the Place of Trumpets* (1987) was chosen for the Yale Series of Younger Poets. Her honors include fellowships from the Academy of American Poets, the National Endowment for the Arts, and the Guggenheim Foundation. She is a professor at the University of Illinois–Urbana-Champaign.

GALWAY KINNELL's (b. 1927) collections include *Strong Is Your Hold* (2006) and *Selected Poems* (1982), which won the Pulitzer Prize and the National Book Award. His honors include the Wallace Stevens Award, a MacArthur fellowship, and a Rockefeller grant. He served as a chancellor of the Academy of American Poets from 2001 to 2007 and as poet-in-residence at the University of California–Irvine, Columbia University, Sarah Lawrence College, and Brandeis University.

YUSEF KOMUNYAKAA (b. 1947) is the author of fifteen books, including *Neon Vernacular: New and Selected Poems 1977–1989* (1994), which received the Pulitzer Prize and the Kingsley Tufts Poetry Award, and *Dien Cai Dau* (1988), which won the Dark Room Poetry Prize. He was elected a chancellor of the Academy of American Poets in 1999 and serves as Distinguished Senior Poet at New York University.

TED KOOSER's (b. 1939) ten collections of poetry include *Delights and Shadows* (2004); *Winter Morning Walks: One Hundred Postcards to Jim Harrison* (2000), which won the Nebraska Book Award; and *Weather Central* (1994). U.S. poet laureate from 2004 to 2006, he is the recipient of two National Endowment for the Arts fellowships, a Pushcart Prize, and the Stanley Kunitz Prize. He is a Presidential Professor at the University of Nebraska–Lincoln.

MAXINE KUMIN's (1925–2014) poetry collections include *Where I Live* (2010), *Still to Mow* (2009), and the Pulitzer Prize–winning *Up Country: Poems of New England* (1972). She was also the author of a memoir, novels, short stories, essays, and children's books. Her honors include the Aiken Taylor Award for Modern Poetry, an American Academy of Arts and Letters award, the Sarah Joseph Hale Award, and the Levinson Prize. She was poet laureate of New Hampshire and of the United States.

STANLEY KUNITZ's (1905–2006) poetry collections include *Selected Poems 1928–1958*, which won the 1959 Pulitzer Prize, and *Passing Through: The Later Poems* (1995), which won the National Book Award. His other honors include the Bollingen Prize, a Ford Foundation grant, Harvard University's Centennial Medal, the Levinson Prize, a National Endowment for the Arts senior fellowship, the National Medal of the Arts, and the Shelley Memorial Award. He was U.S. poet laureate in 1974–76 and 2000–2001.

DORIANNE LAUX (b. 1952) is the author of *The Book of Men* (2011), winner of the Paterson Poetry Prize, and *Facts about the Moon* (2005), winner of the Oregon Book Award. She teaches in the MFA program at North Carolina State University and is on the core faculty of Pacific University's low-residency MFA program.

PATRICK LAWLER (b. 1948) is the author of the poetry collections *Feeding the Fear of the Earth* (2006) and *reading a burning book* (1994). *Underground (Notes toward an Autobiography)* (2011) combines an interview, poetry, and memoir. *Rescuers of Skydivers Search among the Clouds* (2012) won the Ronald Sukenick American Book Review Innovative Fiction Prize.

JAY LEEMING (b. 1969) is the editor and founder of the magazine *Rowboat: Poetry in Translation* and the author of the poetry books *Miracle Atlas* (2011) and *Dynamite on a China Plate* (2006). His honors include a National Endowment for the Arts fellowship.

SHARA LESSLEY (b. 1975) is the author of *Two-Headed Nightingale* (2012) and her poems have appeared in *Ploughshares*, the *Kenyon Review*, the *Southern Review*, and *Threepenny Review*. She received a Discovery/The Nation Award as well as fellowships from Stanford, the Wisconsin Institute for Creative Writing, Colgate University, and The Gilman School.

PHILIP LEVINE's (b. 1928) collections include *News of the World* (2010), *Breath* (2004), *The Mercy* (1999), *The Simple Truth* (1994), which won the Pulitzer Prize, and *What Work Is* (1991), which won the National Book Award. His honors include the Ruth Lilly Poetry Prize, the Harriet Monroe Memorial Prize, the Frank O'Hara Prize, and two Guggenheim fellowships. Levine was U.S. poet laureate in 2011–12 and was elected a chancellor of the Academy of American Poets in 2000.

LARRY LEVIS's (1946–1996) work includes *The Widening Spell of the Leaves* (1991), *Elegy* (1997), *Wrecking Crew* (1972), and a book of essays, *The Seeker Within* (2000). He was the receipient of a YM-YWHA Discovery Award, a Fulbright scholarship, and fellowships from the Guggenheim Foundation and the National Endowment for the Arts. He was director of the University of Utah's creative writing program for twelve years and a professor of English at Virginia Commonwealth University from 1992 until his death.

AUDRE LORDE's (1934–1992) twelve collections of poetry include *From a Land Where Other People Live* (1972), *Cables to Rage* (1970), and *The First Cities* (1968). She was a professor at John Jay College of Criminal Justice and at Hunter College and was poet laureate of New York from 1991 to 1992. *The Cancer Journals* (1980), a prose piece, chronicles her struggle with breast cancer.

ANNE MARIE MACARI (b. 1955) is the author of *She Heads Into the Wilderness* (2008), *Gloryland* (2005), and *Ivory Cradle* (2000), which won the Honickman First Book Prize. Her honors include the James Dickey Award from *Five Points* magazine. Macari lives in New Jersey and teaches at Drew University and the Prague Summer Workshops.

KELLY MADIGAN (b. 1962) works as a licensed alcohol and drug counselor in Nebraska and is the author of *Getting Sober: A Practical Guide to Making It Through the First 30 Days* (2007). Her poetry has been published in *Prairie Schooner*, *Crazyhorse*, and *Barrow Street*. She is a recipient of a fellowship from the National Endowment for the Arts.

DAVIS McCOMBS (b. 1969) is the author of *Ultima Thule* (2000) and *Dismal Rock* (2007), winner of the Tupelo Press Dorset Prize. The recipient of fellowships from the Ruth Lilly Poetry Foundation, the Kentucky Arts Council, and the National Endowment for the Arts, he directs the creative writing program at the University of Arkansas.

JANE MEAD (b. 1958) is the author of *The Usable Field* (2008), *House of Poured-Out Waters* (2001), and *The Lord and the General Din of the World* (1996). Her honors include fellowships from the Lannan and Guggenheim Foundations and a Whiting Writers' Award. She teaches in Drew University's low-residency MFA program and co-owns Prairie Lights in Iowa City.

SANDRA MEEK's (b. 1962) poetry collections are *Road Scatter* (2012); *Biogeography* (2008), winner of the Tupelo Press Dorset Prize; *Burn* (2005); and *Nomadic Foundations* (2002), winner of the Peace Corps Writers Award. She received a National Endowment for the Arts fellowship and has twice been named Georgia Author of the Year. She is co-founding editor of Ninebark Press and the Dana Professor of English, Rhetoric, and Writing at Berry College.

W. S. MERWIN (b. 1927) is the author of more than twenty poetry collections. *A Mask for Janus* (1952) won the Yale Younger Poets award, and *The Carrier of Ladders* (1970) and *The Shadow of Sirius* (2008) both received Pulitzer Prizes. His honors include the Aiken Taylor Award for Modern American Poetry, the Bollingen Prize, a Ford Foundation grant, the Ruth Lilly Poetry Prize, the PEN Translation Prize, the Shelley Memorial Award, the Wallace Stevens Award, and a Lila Wallace-Reader's Digest Writers' Award. He has served as a U.S. special consultant in poetry and a U.S. poet laureate.

DEBORAH A. MIRANDA (b. 1961) is an enrolled member of the Ohlone Costanoan Esselen Nation of the Greater Monterey Bay Area and the author of *Bad Indians: A Tribal Memoir* (2013). She teaches creative writing, literature, and composition at Washington and Lee University.

THORPE MOECKEL (b. 1971) is the author of *Venison* (2010), *Making a Map of the River* (2008), *Odd Botany* (2002), and the chapbook *Meltlines* (2001). He teaches in the writing program at Hollins University.

PATRICIA MONAGHAN (b. 1946) is the author of four books of poems, including *Dancing with Chaos* (2002), and the chapbook *Grace of Ancient Land* (2003). She is a professor at DePaul University and a founding fellow of the Black Earth Institute, a progressive think tank for artists.

RICHARD O. MOORE (b. 1920) is a poet, documentary filmmaker, and public television executive. He founded KPFA, the first U.S. listener-supported public radio station, in 1949. He is the author of *Writing the Silences* (2010) and the documentaries *USA: Poetry* and *The Writer in America*.

LORI ANDERSON MOSEMAN's (b. 1958) poetry collections include *All Steel* (2012), *Temporary Bunk* (2009), *Persona* (2003), *Cultivating Excess* (1993), and *Walking the Dead* (1991). She founded the press Stockport Flats in the wake of Federal Disaster #1649, a flood along the Upper Delaware River. She edits and curates the bimonthly *High Watermark Salo[o]n* Chapbook Series, which pairs poets and visual artists.

HARRYETTE MULLEN's (b. 1953) books include *Muse and Drudge* (1995), *S*PeRM**K*T* (1992), *Trimmings* (1991), and *Tree Tall Woman* (1981). *Sleeping with the Dictionary* (2002) was nominated for a National Book Award. Mullen is a professor at the University of California–Los Angeles.

NAOMI SHIHAB NYE's (b. 1952) books include *You and Yours* (2005), which won the Isabella Gardner Poetry Award; *19 Varieties of Gazelle: Poems of the Middle East* (2002); and *Fuel* (1998). Among her honors are the Carity Randall Prize, four Pushcart Prizes, and the Academy of American Poets Lavan Award. She has also received fellowships from the Lannan, Guggenheim, and Witter Bynner Foundations.

DG NANOUK OKPIK (b. 1966) is the author of *Corpse Whale* (2012) and the chapbook *Effigies* (2009). Her work has appeared in *Washington Square, Many Mountains Moving*, and the American Poets Emerging Poets series. She is the recipient of the Truman Capote Award.

MARY OLIVER's (b. 1935) books include *American Primitive* (1984), which won the Pulitzer Prize; *Dream Work* (1986); and *New and Selected Poems* (1992), which won the National Book Award. She has received fellowships from the National Endowment for the Arts and the Guggenheim Foundation and she has won an American Academy of Arts and Letters Award, the Shelley Memorial Award, and the Alice Fay di Castagnola Award.

ALICIA SUSKIN OSTRIKER's (b. 1937) thirteenth poetry collection, *The Book of Seventy* (2009), received the National Jewish Book Award for Poetry, and she is a two-time finalist for the National Book Award. Her most recent collection is *The Book of Life: Selected Jewish Poems 1979–2011* (2012). She teaches in Drew University's low-residency MFA program in poetry and poetry in translation.

MICHAEL PALMER's (b. 1943) recent publications include *Thread* (2011), *Company of Moths* (2005), and *Codes Appearing: Poems 1979–1988* (2001). His honors include two National Endowment for the Arts grants, a Lila Wallace-Reader's Digest Writers' Award, a Guggenheim fellowship, the Shelley Memorial Award, and the Wallace Stevens Award. In 1999 he was elected a chancellor of the Academy of American Poets.

G. E. PATTERSON (b. 1939) is the author of *From* (2008) and *Tug* (1999), which won the Minnesota Book Award. His other honors include fellowships from the Bread Loaf Writers Conference, Cave Canem, the Djerassi Foundation, the MacDowell Colony, and the Minnesota State Arts Board. He teaches and lives in Minnesota.

LUCIA PERILLO's (b. 1958) books include *Dangerous Life* (1989), winner of the Norma Farber Award; *The Body Mutinies* (1996), winner of the Kate Tufts Prize; *Luck Is Luck* (2005), winner of the Kingsley Tufts Poetry Award; and *Inseminating the Elephant* (2009), a finalist for the Pulitzer Prize and winner of the Library of Congress Rebekah Johnson Bobbitt Prize. She has taught at Syracuse University, Southern Illinois University, and Warren Wilson College.

JIM PETERSON's (b. 1948) books include the poetry collections *The Bob and Weave* (2006) and *The Owning Stone* (2000), winner of the Red Hen Press Benjamin Saltman Award, and the novel *Paper Crown* (2005). His poems have appeared in *Poetry*, the *Georgia Review*, and *Shenandoah*. He teaches in the University of Nebraska's MFA program and is coordinator of creative writing and writer-in-residence at Randolph College.

D. A. POWELL's (b. 1963) books include *Chronic* (2012) and *Cocktails* (2004), both finalists for Publishing Triangle and National Book Critics Circle Awards, and *Useless Landscape, or A Guide for Boys* (2012). His honors include the Kingsley Tufts Poetry Award and a Guggenheim fellowship.

JOHN PURSLEY III (b. 1976) is the author of *If You Have Ghosts* (2010), an Editors' Poetry Prize Selection for Zone 3 Press, and the chapbooks *A Story Without Poverty* (2010), *Supposing, for Instance, Here in the Space-Time Continuum* (2009), *A Conventional Weather* (2007), and *When, by the Titanic* (2006). He teaches at Clemson University.

BERNARD QUETCHENBACH's (b. 1955) books include *The Hermit's Place* (2010) and *Back from the Far Field: American Nature Poetry in the Late Twentieth Century* (2000). He teaches at Montana State University–Billings.

JANISSE RAY (b. 1962) is the author of five books of literary nonfiction, including *The Seed Underground: A Growing Revolution to Save Food* (2012), and the poetry collection *A House of Branches* (2010). She is a Woodrow Wilson visiting fellow and is on the faculty of Chatham University's low-residency MFA program.

SRIKANTH REDDY (b. 1973) is the author of the collections *Voyager* (2011) and *Facts for Visitors* (2004). His awards include fellowships from the Whiting Foundation, the Wisconsin Institute for Creative Writing, and the Mellon Foundation. He is the literacy director for the Mahatma Gandhi Memorial Trust in Bhimavaram, Andhra Pradesh, India, and teaches at the University of Chicago.

CARTER REVARD's (b. 1931) poetry and essay collections include *How the Songs Come Down* (2005), *Winning the Dust Bowl* (2001), *Family Matters, Tribal Affairs* (1998), *Cowboys and Indians: An Eagle Nation* (1993), and *Ponca War Dancers* (1980). He was born and raised on the Osage Reservation in Oklahoma and taught at Amherst College and Washington University in St. Louis.

DONALD REVELL (b. 1954) is the author of more than a dozen books of poetry, translation, and essays, including *A Thief of Strings* (2007) and *From Abandoned Cities* (1983), a National Poetry Series winner. His awards include Pushcart Prizes,

Shestack Prizes, the Gertrude Stein Award in Innovative American Poetry, PEN Center USA Awards, and fellowships. He edits the *Colorado Review*.

ADRIENNE RICH (1929–2012) is the author of over thirty books of poems and essays, including *Diving into the Wreck* (1973), winner of the National Book Award, a prize she refused. She began her career with *A Change of World* (1951), which won the Yale Younger Poets award. Her other honors include the Ruth Lilly Poetry Prize, the Lannan Lifetime Achievement Award, the Bollingen Prize, Academy of American Poets and MacArthur fellowships, and the Wallace Stevens Award.

ALBERTO RÍOS's (b. 1952) poetry collections include *The Dangerous Shirt* (2009) and *The Theater of Night* (2006), winner of the PEN/Beyond Margins Award. A finalist for the National Book Award and recipient of the Western Literature Association Distinguished Achievement Award, Ríos has taught at Arizona State University for more than thirty years.

ED ROBERSON (b. 1948) is the Distinguished Artist in Residence at Northwestern University and a widely traveled limnologist. His books include *To See the Earth Before the End of the World* (2010), *City Eclogue* (2006), and *Atmosphere Conditions* (2000), winner of the National Poetry Award series. In 2008 he received the Shelley Memorial Award.

PATTIANN ROGERS (b. 1940) is the author of the essay collection *The Grand Array* (2010) and many books of poetry. *Firekeeper: New and Selected Poems* (1994) was a finalist for the Lenore Marshall Poetry Prize. Her awards include two National Endowment for the Arts grants, Guggenheim and Lannan fellowships, the Tietjens and Bess Hokin Prizes, the Roethke Prize, the Strousse Award, and four Pushcart Prizes. She teaches in the low-residency creative writing program at Pacific University.

WILLIAM PITT ROOT's (b. 1941) most recent books are *Trace Elements from a Recurring Kingdom* (2010), a Nation Notable Book, and *White Boots: New and Selected Poems of the West* (2006). *The Storm and Other Poems* (2005) was nominated for the Pulitzer and Lamont Prizes. He has received fellowships from the Rockefeller and Guggenheim Foundations, Stanford University, and the National Endowment for the Arts.

MICHAEL ROTHENBERG (b. 1951) is a poet, songwriter, editor, publisher of the online literary magazine *Big Bridge*, and co-founder of the global poetry movement 100 Thousand Poets for Change. His poetry books include *My Youth as a Train* (2010), *Choose* (2009), *Unhurried Vision* (2003), and *The Paris Journals* (2000).

IRA SADOFF (b. 1945) is the author of eight collections of poetry, most recently *True Faith* (2012), *Barter* (2007), and *Grazing* (1998); the novel *Uncoupling*

(1982); and *History Matters: Contemporary Poetry on the Margins of American Culture* (2009). He has received grants from the Guggenheim Foundation and the National Endowment for the Arts and teaches at Colby College and Drew University.

Poet, novelist, essayist, and children's book author BENJAMIN ALIRE SÁENZ (b. 1954) lives in the border region between Texas and New Mexico and teaches creative writing at the University of Texas–El Paso. His recent books include *The Book of What Remains* (2010), *Dreaming the End of War* (2006), and *Elegies in Blue* (2002).

CRAIG SANTOS PEREZ (b. 1980) is the cofounder of Ala Press and author of the poetry collections *from unincorporated territory* [hacha] (2008) and *from unincorporated territory* [saina] (2010), a finalist for the LA Times Book Prize for Poetry and winner of the PEN Center USA Literary Award for Poetry. He is an assistant professor at the University of Hawai'i Manoa.

TIM SEIBLES (b. 1955) is the author of five books of poetry, including *Fast Animal* (2012) and *Buffalo Head Solos* (2004). His honors include the Open Voice Award and fellowships from the National Endowment for the Arts and the Provincetown Fine Arts Work Center. He teaches at Old Dominion University and in the Stonecoast MFA program and runs workshops for Cave Canem.

ANTHONY SEIDMAN (b. 1973) is the author of *Where Thirsts Intersect* (2006) and *On Carbon-Dating Hunger* (2000). His poetry, essays, and translations have appeared in *Nimrod, Poetry International, Cider Press Review,* and *Borderlands: Texas Poetry Review,* and in journals, magazines, and newspapers in Mexico.

MARTHA SERPAS (b. 1965) is the author of *The Dirty Side of the Storm* (2006) and *Côte Blanche* (2002). Her work has appeared in the *New Yorker,* the *Nation,* and elsewhere. She co-produced *Veins in the Gulf,* a documentary about Louisiana's disappearing wetlands. She is a hospital trauma chaplain and teaches at the University of Houston.

ERIC PAUL SHAFFER (b. 1955) is the author of the poetry collections *Lāhaina Noon* (2005), *Living at the Monastery, Working in the Kitchen* (2001), and *Portable Planet* (2000), and the novel *Burn and Learn* (2009). He received Hawai'i's Elliot Cades Award for Literature, a Ka Palapala Po'okela Book Award, and the James M. Vaughan Award for Poetry. He teaches at Honolulu Community College.

DEREK SHEFFIELD (b. 1968) is the author of *Through the Second Skin* (2013) and *A Revised Account of the West* (2008), winner of the Hazel Lipa Environmental Chapbook Award. His poems have appeared in *Poetry, Orion,* the *Southern Review, Ecotone,* the *Georgia Review,* and *Wilderness.* He teaches at Wenatchee Valley College in Washington.

REGINALD SHEPHERD's (1963–2008) five poetry collections include *Some Are Drowning* (1994), which won the AWP Award in Poetry; *Otherhood* (2003), a finalist for the Lenore Marshall Poetry Prize; and *Fata Morgana* (2007). His honors include grants from the National Endowment for the Arts, the Illinois Arts Council, the Florida Arts Council, and the Guggenheim Foundation.

EVIE SHOCKLEY (b. 1965) is the author of *the new black* (2011), *a half-red sea* (2006), and *Renegade Poetics: Black Aesthetics and Formal Innovation in African American Poetry* (2011). She is an associate professor at Rutgers University.

GARY SHORT (b. 1953) is the author of three poetry collections, including *10 Moons and 13 Horses* (2004) and *Flying over Sonny Liston* (1996), and three chapbooks. He has received the Western States Book Award, a Pushcart Prize, and fellowships from Stanford and the National Endowment for the Arts.

KEVIN SIMMONDS (b. 1972) is the author of the poetry collections *Mad for Meat* (2012) and *Ota Benga Under My Mother's Roof* (2012) and editor of *Collective Brightness: LGBTIQ Poets on Faith, Religion and Spirituality* (2011). He wrote the music for *Hope: Living and Loving with HIV in Jamaica* and for *Voices of Haiti: A Post-Quake Odyssey in Verse*. His films, which include *feti(sh)ame* and *Singing Whitman*, have shown internationally.

GIOVANNI SINGLETON's (b. 1969) collection *Ascension* (2012) received the California Book Award. She is the founding editor of *nocturnes (re)view of the literary arts* and has taught at Saint Mary's College and Naropa University.

JONATHAN SKINNER (b. 1967) is the founder and editor of the journal *ecopoetics*. His poetry collections include *Birds of Tifft* (2011) and *Political Cactus Poems* (2005), and his essays have appeared in *Qui Parle* and *The Ecolanguage Reader*. A 2011–12 fellow at the Cornell Society for the Humanities, Skinner teaches at the University of Warwick.

CHARLIE SMITH's (b. 1947) work includes novels and poetry collections, five of which have been named Notable Books by *New York Times*. *Red Roads* (1987) was chosen for the National Poetry Series. His other honors include the Great Lakes New Poets award and grants from the Guggenheim Foundation, the National Endowment for the Arts, and the New York Foundation for the Arts.

PATRICIA SMITH's (b. 1955) six books include *Shoulda Been Jimi Savannah* (2012); *Blood Dazzler* (2008), a National Book Award finalist; and *Teahouse of the Almighty* (2006), winner of the National Poetry Series Award and the Hurston/Wright Legacy Award. She is a professor at the City University of New York and is on the faculty of Cave Canem and the low-residency MFA program at Sierra Nevada College.

GARY SNYDER's (b. 1930) works include *No Nature* (1993), a finalist for the National Book Award; *Axe Handles* (1983), which won an American Book Award; and *Turtle Island* (1974), which won the Pulitzer Prize. He has also received an American Academy of Arts and Letters award, the Bollingen Prize, a Guggenheim fellowship, the Bess Hokin Prize, the Levinson Prize, the Robert Kirsch Lifetime Achievement Award, and the Shelley Memorial Award.

JULIANA SPAHR's (b. 1966) poetry collections include *Well Then There Now* (2011), *This Connection of Everyone with Lungs* (2005), *Fuck You—Aloha—I Love You* (2001), and *Response* (1996), which won the National Poetry Series Award. Her honors include the Folger Shakespeare Library's Hardison Poetry Prize. An editor for the book series Chain Links and the collective Subpress, Spahr teaches at Mills College.

GERALD STERN (b. 1925) is the author of eighteen poetry collections, most recently *Early Collected Poems 1965–1992* (2010) and *Save the Last Dance* (2008), and the essay collections *Stealing History* (2012) and *What I Can't Bear Losing* (2009). His honors include the Bess Hokin Prize, the Ruth Lilly Poetry Prize, the Wallace Stevens Award, and four National Endowment for the Arts grants. Stern is a chancellor of the Academy of American Poets and Distinguished Poet-in-Residence at Drew University.

SUSAN STEWART's (b. 1952) poetry collections include *Red Rover* (2008); *Columbarium* (2003), which won the National Book Critics Circle Award; and *The Forest* (1995). She has received fellowships from the Pew Charitable Trusts, the Guggenheim Foundation, and the MacArthur Foundation and grants from the National Endowment for the Arts. She is a professor of English at Princeton University.

SHERYL ST. GERMAIN's (b. 1954) books include *Let It Be a Dark Roux: New and Selected Poems* (2007), *How Heavy the Breath of God* (1994), *Making Bread at Midnight* (1992), the memoir *Swamp Songs: The Making of an Unruly Woman* (2003), and *Between Song and Story: Essays for the Twenty-First Century* (2011), which she co-edited. She directs the MFA program at Chatham University.

ARTHUR SZE's (b. 1950) poetry collections include *The Ginkgo Light* (2009), *Quipu* (2005), *The Redshifting Web* (1998), and *Archipelago* (1995). He has received a Lila Wallace–Reader's Digest Writers' Award, an American Book Award, and a Lannan Literary Award, and fellowships from the Guggenheim Foundation and the National Endowment for the Arts. Sze is the first poet laureate of Santa Fe and a professor emeritus at the Institute of American Indian Arts.

NATHANIEL TARN (b. 1928) is the author of ten poetry collections, including *Ins and Outs of the Forest Rivers* (2008), *Avia: A Poem of International Air Combat, 1939–1945* (2008), and *Selected Poems 1950–2000* (2002). He lives near Santa Fe, New Mexico.

SUSAN TERRIS (b. 1937) is the author of numerous children's books and five collections of poetry, most recently *The Homelessness of Self* (2011), *Double-Edged* (2009), and *Contrariwise* (2007). She is editor of *Spillway Magazine* and a poetry editor for *Pedestal Magazine* and *In Posse Review*.

JEFFREY THOMSON's (b. 1967) poetry collections include *Birdwatching in Wartime* (2009), winner of the Maine Book Award and the ASLE Award in Environmental Creative Writing, and *Renovation* (2005). He was the 2012 Fulbright Distinguished Scholar in Creative Writing at the Seamus Heaney Poetry Centre at Queen's University Belfast and is an associate professor at the University of Maine in Farmington.

MELISSA TUCKEY (b. 1966) is a poet, translator, activist, and teacher. She is a cofounder of Split This Rock and author of the chapbook *Rope as Witness* (2007). Her poems have appeared in the *Beloit Poetry Journal*, the *Cincinnati Poetry Review*, *Painted Bride Quarterly*, and elsewhere.

CHASE TWICHELL (b. 1950) is the author of *Horses Where the Answers Should Have Been* (2010), *Dog Language* (2005), *The Snow Watcher* (1998), and several other collections. Her honors include fellowships from the National Endowment for the Arts and the Guggenheim Foundation and awards from the New Jersey State Council on the Arts and the American Academy of Arts and Letters.

PAMELA USCHUK (b. 1948) is the author of six books of poems, including *Crazy Love* (2009), winner of a 2010 American Book Award, and *Wild in the Plaza of Memory* (2012). She lives in the Rocky Mountains and is an associate professor at Fort Lewis College in Durango.

JEAN VALENTINE's (b. 1934) collections include *Little Boat* (2007), *Door in the Mountain: New and Collected Poems 1965–2003* (2004), which won the National Book Award, and *The River at Wolf* (1992). She has received Bunting Institute and Guggenheim fellowships and a Shelley Memorial Award. She has taught at Columbia University, Sarah Lawrence College, and the 92nd Street Y in New York.

ELLEN BRYANT VOIGT's (b. 1943) poetry collections include *Messenger: New and Selected Poems 1976–2006* (2007) and *Shadow of Heaven* (2002). She has received fellowships from the Academy of American Poets, the Guggenheim Foundation, and the National Endowment for the Arts, as well as the 2002 O. B. Hardison Jr. Poetry Prize, a Lila Wallace-Reader's Digest Writers' Award, and a Pushcart Prize. She founded the country's first low-residency MFA program, originally at Goddard College and now at Warren Wilson College.

GYORGYI VOROS (b. 1943) is the author of the poetry collection *Unwavering* (2007) and *Notations of the Wild: Ecology in the Poetry of Wallace Stevens* (1997). She teaches creative writing at Virginia Tech University.

FRANK X. WALKER's (b. 1961) books include *When Winter Come: The Ascension of York* (2008), *Black Box* (2005), and *Buffalo Dance: The Journey of York* (2003). Recipient of the Thomas D. Clark Literary Award for Excellence and a Lannan Literary Fellowship in Poetry, he is a professor at the University of Kentucky and publishes *Pluck! Journal of Affrilachian Art and Culture.*

EMILY WARN (b. 1953) is the author of *Shadow Architect* (2008), *The Novice Insomniac* (1996), and *The Leaf Path* (1982). She was a Stegner fellow, has worked for Microsoft, and most recently served as Webby Award–winning founding editor of the Poetry Foundation website.

ROSANNA WARREN's (b. 1953) five poetry collections include *Ghost in a Red Hat* (2011), *Departure* (2003), and *Stained Glass* (1993), a Lamont Poetry Selection. She has received a Pushcart Prize, the Witter Bynner Prize, a Lila Wallace-Reader's Digest Writers' Award, a Discovery/the Nation Prize, and fellowships from the Guggenheim Foundation and the American Council of Learned Societies. She is a professor at the University of Chicago.

ELIOT WEINBERGER (b. 1949) is the primary translator of Octavio Paz into English. His honors include the 1992 PEN Gregory Kolovakos Award for his promotion of Hispanic literature and the first Order of the Aztec Eagle award to an American literary writer in 2000. He has written twelve books of poetry in translation, most recently *Unlock* (2000), and four books of essays.

JOEL WEISHAUS (b. 1939) is the artist-in-residence at Pacifica Graduate Institute and a visiting scholar at the University of California–Santa Barbara. His archives are at Virginia Polytechnic University's Center for Digital Discourse and Culture and at the University of New Mexico's Zimmerman Library.

LESLEY WHEELER (b. 1967) is the author of *The Receptionist and Other Tales* (2012); *Heterotopia* (2010), winner of the Barrow Street Press Poetry Prize; *Heathen* (2009); and the critical study *Voicing American Poetry* (2008). She blogs on poetry at *The Cave, the Hive* and is the Henry S. Fox Professor of English at Washington and Lee University.

C. K. WILLIAMS (b. 1936) is the author of more than two dozen poetry collections, essays, a memoir, and works in translation. His collections include *Wait: Poems* (2010); *Collected Poems* (2007); *The Singing* (2003), which won the National Book Award; and *Repair* (1999), which won a Pulitzer Prize. Among his honors are an American Academy of Arts and Letters Award, a Guggenheim fellowship, the Lila Wallace-Reader's Digest Writers' Award, the PEN/Voelcker Award for Poetry, and a Pushcart Prize. He teaches in the creative writing program at Princeton University.

SUSAN SETTLEMYRE WILLIAMS (b. 1946) is the author of *Ashes in Midair* (2008) and the chapbook *Possession* (2007). Her poetry has appeared in *Prairie*

Schooner, Mississippi Review, diode, Shenandoah, and *Best New Poets 2006*. She is a book review editor and literary editor for the online journal *Blackbird*.

C. D. WRIGHT (b. 1949) is the author of more than a dozen collections of poetry and prose, including *Rising Falling Hovering* (2008), which won the Griffin Poetry Prize. Her most recent book is *One With Others: a little book of her days* (2010), winner of the National Book Critics Circle Award. The recipient of Guggenheim and MacArthur fellowships, she teaches at Brown University.

Among CHARLES WRIGHT's (b. 1935) collections are *Country Music* (1983), which won a National Book Award; *Chickamauga* (1995), which won the Lenore Marshall Poetry Prize; and *Black Zodiac* (1997), which won the Pulitzer Prize and the *Los Angeles Times* Book Prize. His honors include the American Academy of Arts and Letters Award of Merit and the Ruth Lilly Poetry Prize. He is the Souder Family Professor of English at the University of Virginia.

WILLIAM WRIGHT (b. 1979) is the author of the poetry collections *Night Field Anecdote* (2011), *Bledsoe* (2011), and *Dark Orchard* (2005), winner of the Breakthrough Poetry Prize; and two chapbooks. His work has appeared in *Shenandoah*, the *North American Review, AGNI,* and the *Colorado Review*. He is series editor of the *Southern Poetry Anthology*.

ROBERT WRIGLEY (b. 1951) is the author of eight poetry collections, most recently *Beautiful Country* (2010). His honors include fellowships from the National Endowment for the Arts, the Idaho State Commission on the Arts, and the Guggenheim Foundation. He teaches in the graduate writing program at the University of Idaho.

ACKNOWLEDGMENTS AND CREDITS

It has been a labor of love to coedit *The Ecopoetry Anthology*. Over the years many people helped bring this project to fruition, and I am pleased to acknowledge them here. Most of all I thank my dear friend and coeditor Laura-Gray Street; Barbara Ras, director of Trinity University Press; and the team at Trinity, especially Sarah Nawrocki and Tom Payton, for a work experience that was challenging, instructive, and fruitful, and for their dedication to excellence every step of the way.

I am grateful to the College of Liberal Arts and the English Department at the University of Mississippi, my past chair Patrick Quinn, and my current chair Ivo Kamps for their generous support in the form of faculty development grants and funding for assistants. The cheerful help of graduate assistants Travis Blankenship, Jessica Comola, James Everett, Chris Hayes, Taylor Ivy, and Corinna McClanahan Schroeder with various aspects of the manuscript saved me countless hours of work. I have happy memories of working with them and also with Caleb Fisher-Wirth, whom I thank not only for help with typing but also for his keen editorial judgment in the early stages of the project. Allan Hance's reading and critique of the editors' introduction was also helpful toward the end.

I am grateful as well to every poet whose work is included in *The Ecopoetry Anthology* and to every poet who sent us work we could not ultimately include. We had many difficult decisions to make.

Bob Hass, who suggested that the book begin with a historical section and who wrote the book's beautiful introduction, has been part of the book at every step of the way. Brenda Hillman's unflagging enthusiasm for the project was a constant source of encouragement. I think of Bob and Brenda as *The Ecopoetry Anthology*'s godparents and extend my deepest thanks to them both.

My husband, Peter Wirth, is my toughest reader. He challenges my ideas and examines my words. I do not always agree with him, but I treasure his brilliant scrutiny and his passionate devotion to clear and accurate writing. To him; to our five children, Pascale, Jessica, Lucas, Rebecca, and Caleb; and to our five grandchildren, Sylvie, Benjamin, Eve, Dylan, and Rowan, I offer my thanks and my love.

—*Ann Fisher-Wirth*

The Ecopoetry Anthology has been a journey of discovery from start to finish, one of many joys, one of hard decisions. And I couldn't have asked for a better person to make that journey with than Ann Fisher-Wirth. She has been a dear friend, a role model, and an advocate. I am also grateful to Barbara Ras, the director at Trinity University Press, and to Sarah Nawrocki, Tom Payton, Haley Mathis, Burgin Streetman, and everyone at the press for their excellent work.

I am indebted to the Summer Research Program at Randolph College and to Peter Sheldon, program chair, for funding my work on the anthology for two summers and for giving me the opportunity to work with such conscientious and inspiring students as Ashley Hale and Anneka Freeman. The help of these two student researchers was invaluable, and I am delighted to finally acknowledge their work in the book. The Faculty Development Committee and the Office of the Dean of the College, including former deans Bill Coulter and Dennis Stevens, are owed thanks for the support they provided through grants and travel funds. Thank you to my colleagues in the English Department, particularly Jim Peterson, director of creative writing, and in the Environmental Studies Department. Thanks also go out to former colleague Camille Dungy, who has long been a friend, an adviser, and an inspiration. And to friend and uber-mentor Ira Sadoff, thank you, always.

Finally, my gratitude to my family: My father was a lifelong buttress, stanchion, and joist, and my mother continues to be. Because of them, I spent my early years talking to cows and digging in sand. I thank my brother, Bill Street, for his inspiring and untiring efforts for the Chesapeake Bay and now the James River. Many thanks go to my partner, Jay

Kardan, for his intelligence, his patience, his critical and proofreading skills, and his capacity to have his nose in a book and his hands in the dirt. And I especially thank my children—Sydna Mundy, who is spending her summer encountering elk, moose, and grizzlies at Yellowstone, and Kyle Mundy, who is out to sea on his first deployment as I write this. They are the foundational motivators and muses for my work on this and every project.

—*Laura-Gray Street*

A. R. Ammons, "Corsons Inlet" and "Gravelly Run" from *Collected Poems 1951–1971*. Copyright © 1972 by A. R. Ammons. "Garbage" (Section 12) from *Garbage*. Copyright © 1993 by A. R. Ammons. All used by permission of W. W. Norton & Company, Inc.

Karen Leona Anderson, "Snowshoe Hare" from *Punish honey* (Durham, North Carolina: Carolina Wren Press, 2009). Copyright © 2009 by Karen Leona Anderson. Reprinted with the permission of the author.

Christopher Arigo, "Gone feral: minor gestures." Reprinted with the permission of the author.

Rae Armentrout, "Thing" from *Next Life*. Copyright © 2007 by Rae Armentrout. "Natural History" and "Dusk" from *Veil*. Copyright © 2001 by Rae Armentrout. All reprinted by permission of Wesleyan University Press.

John Ashbery, "Into the Dusk-Charged Air" from *Rivers and Mountains*. Copyright © 1966, 1977 by John Ashbery. "For John Clare" from *The Double Dream of Spring*. Copyright © 1970, 1976 by John Ashbery. Both reprinted by permission of Georges Borchardt, Inc., on behalf of the author, and Carcanet Press, Ltd. "Alcove" and "River of the Canoefish" from *Planisphere: New Poems*. Copyright © 2009 by John Ashbery. Reprinted by permission of HarperCollins Publishers and Carcanet Press, Ltd.

Jimmy Santiago Baca, "As Children Know" from *Black Mesa Poems*. Copyright © 1989 by Jimmy Santiago Baca. Reprinted by permission of New Directions Publishing Corp.

Julianna Baggott, "The Place Poem: Sparrow's Point" from *Compulsions of Silkworms and Bees* (Warrensburg, Missouri: Pleiades Press, 2007). Copyright © 2007 by Julianna Baggott. Reprinted with the permission of the author. "Living Where They Raised Me" from *This Country of Mothers*. Copyright © 2001 by